POLITICS AGAINST DOMINATION

POLITICS · AGAINST
DOMINATION

· IAN SHAPIRO ·

·

THE BELKNAP PRESS
OF HARVARD UNIVERSITY PRESS

Cambridge, Massachusetts
London, England
2016

First printing

Library of Congress Cataloging-in-Publication Data

Shapiro, Ian, author.
Politics against domination / Ian Shapiro.
    pages cm
    "This book is a companion to Democratic Justice, which appeared
in 1999."—Preface.
    Includes bibliographical references and index.
    ISBN 978-0-674-74384-7 (alk. paper)
1. Equality before the law.   2. Associations, institutions, etc.—Political
aspects.   3. Power (Social sciences)   4. Justice.   5. Political science.
6. Intergroup relations.   I. Title.
    JC578.S44 2016
    323.42—dc23

                                                              2015031485

In Memoriam Brian Barry

CONTENTS

PREFACE

This book is a companion to *Democratic Justice*, which appeared in 1999. There I developed an account of justice rooted in the impulse to resist domination, and I applied it to the analysis of major civil institutions. A separate volume was promised on public institutions. This is not exactly the book I had in mind, but Chapters 2 through 4 come close enough to delivering on the pledge that they render another book from me on the subject unnecessary. Chapters 5 and 6 deal with global challenges to an antidomination ethic that I had not envisaged writing about at the time. But these challenges have become so intimately connected with national politics in recent decades that it seems impossible to think about the exercise of public power without attending to them. Not that my discussion of these matters is comprehensive. In particular, it only scratches the surface of distributive justice considerations that I will address more fully in a book on democracy and distribution that is currently in preparation.

The term *nondomination* carries a lot of freight in this book. Its distinctive appeal for me is that it anchors philosophical reflection in real politics. Specifically, it captures the reactive character of the human condition in ways that ideals like freedom, equality, and impartiality do not. Political philosophers pay too little attention to the reality that people know a lot more about what they are against than what they favor, and that one of the central things they resist is domination or the prospect of it. My work takes this fact about the human condition seriously, and builds on it.

A number of other writers have also found nondomination fruitful, though for varying reasons. Michel Foucault brought the idea of resisting domination to my generation's consciousness with a series of brilliant histories of the dark side of Western cultural and intellectual history. Jürgen Habermas developed the idea of an ideal speech situation as the antithesis

of domination. Iris Marion Young held that John Rawls and his successors missed important features of injustice by focusing on distribution
rather than on resisting domination. Michael Walzer distinguishes benign
inequalities from malevolent ones based on whether they facilitate domination. Quentin Skinner and Phillip Pettit focus on nondomination due
to their interest in republicanism, Skinner as part of his venture to rescue
the idea of negative freedom from Hobbes and his successors and Pettit
to develop an account of freedom that sustains his republican political
theory.

I have written elsewhere about why nondomination provides a better
normative basis for thinking about politics than do alternative ideals, and
about the differences between my account of it and those of the other nondomination theorists just mentioned. I have elected not to rehearse these
various debates here, partly but not wholly in the interest of saving trees.
This book is centrally about political action and institutions in the contemporary world. These concerns are not severable from historical and
philosophical considerations, but, as we say to graduate students, all things
are connected to all things yet it is nonetheless important to write about
one thing at a time. I have focused on my arguments about politics and
institutions in that spirit, referring to other theorists only where our disagreements bear on my political arguments or where it was necessary to
craft a book that can stand on its own even though it is part of a larger
conversation. Some readers might still want to chase me down what others
will regard as philosophical rabbit holes, for which purpose they should
look to these other writings.[1]

I should say a word about Brian Barry, to whom this book is dedicated,
partly because its seed was the Inaugural Brian Barry Lecture that I delivered at the London School of Economics in May 2010 and partly because
I have never appropriately recorded my large debt to him. Writing in *Mind*
in 1992, Jonathan Wolff declared that political theory is "what Brian Barry
does." That resonated with me instantly; as did Wolff's elaboration that
Barry's distinctive method involved "trampling over conventional disci-
plinary boundaries" while displaying an "unmatched command of an im-
mense range of political topics, from the concrete study of conflict resolution in modern states, to the most abstract questions of justice and social
choice theory."[2] I would add that Barry's work was never contrived. There
was always something substantive at stake in his writing, even when he
was at his most abstract.

Barry's approach to the subject is a model of what political theory at
its best can be. Some, including Wolff, took him to task for spending so
much time and energy criticizing others and comparatively little devel-

oping his own theories. Barry was aware of the criticism and to some extent stung by it. I believe it missed the mark and I urged him to ignore it. Pricking balloons that gave ballast to specious theories was important to him when he thought they sustained bad social science or unjust political arrangements.

And theory building was not Barry's thing. His most self-consciously constructive work, volume 2 of his *Treatise on Social Justice* (1995), was also his least successful.[3] I was pleased by his decision to abandon that venture and return, in *Culture and Equality* (2001) and *Why Social Justice Matters* (2005), to what he did best. Barry had the finest critical mind of his generation. No one held a candle to him when he was at the height of his powers, which he was for many decades. *Political Argument* (1965) and *Sociologists, Economists and Democracy* (1970) are both works of unsurpassed quality that still repay careful reading, yet his last books also exhibit the devastating critical acumen that had made him famous half a century earlier.

Barry's irreverence reflected his astonishing wit. It was an inescapably humbling capacity that basked in a wickedly funny sense of humor that could be quite brutal. Yet he was neither cynical nor mean-spirited. Barry always took on people his own size, and he was generous to a fault with the younger generation of political theorists—including me. When he socked people on the nose, more often than not this reflected his conviction that, as Wolff put it, "political theory can be much easier than most people make it, provided that one keeps things clear, puts down one's ideological axe, and resists the temptation to seek novelty or paradox for its own sake." We agreed about a lot and disagreed about a lot, which he never minded, as there was nothing Brian liked better than a good argument. He was an irreplaceable friend, and I miss him. This would have been a better book had he been around to criticize it.

Others have helped me a great deal. In addition to the LSE, where I have presented several chapters at the political theory and comparative politics workshops, I have tried out drafts on various groups at University College London, Oxford University, Sciences Po, the University of Pennsylvania, Texas A&M University, Griffith University, the University of Melbourne, the University of Toronto, Brown University, Columbia University, City University in New York, the Institute for Advanced Study in Vienna, the Juan March Institute in Madrid, the University of Oslo, and annual meetings of the American Political Science Association in 2012, 2013, and 2015. Most of the manuscript has been put through the mill at the Yale workshops on political theory and international relations and the Conference for the Study of Political Thought that Yale hosts. It would be impossible to list all the colleagues who have made helpful comments and suggestions in these settings. You know who you are and I am grateful. It would be remiss of me, however, not to single out Bruce Ackerman, John Kane, David Mayhew, Doug Rae, and Rogers Smith, who read much of the manuscript closely and constructively, saving me from myself in more ways than it is comfortable to think about, and Frances Rosenbluth, with whom all the arguments were debated at inordinate length on morning runs with the dogs.

People sometimes ask me why I have never left Yale, where I have been in one guise or another since the 1970s. High on the list of reasons I find myself giving is the students, both graduate and undergraduate. Some remarkable students have contributed to this book. I developed some of the main arguments in the seminar "Nondomination as a Political Ideal" that I taught in the spring and fall of 2011, where the level of discussion was as good as it gets. In addition I have been the beneficiary of some astonishingly able research assistants: Ezra Husney, Adira Levine, Geng Ngarmboonanant, Korinayao Thompson, and Rachel Silberman. It would hard to exaggerate the value these individuals have added to this venture.

Finally I must thank Yale University for research funding, my agent Wendy Strothman for her invariably sound advice, two anonymous readers for Harvard University Press, and Ian Malcolm, an exemplary specimen of the vanishing breed of university press editors who actually read and edit manuscripts. The help of all these people is gratefully acknowledged. The usual caveats apply.

Some arguments developed here grew out of discussions advanced in my earlier articles: "On Non-domination," which appeared in the *University of Toronto Law Journal* (vol. 62, 2012, pp. 293–335); "Democracy and Inequality," a chapter that I wrote for a second edition of Robert Dahl's *On Democracy* (Yale University Press, 2015); "Cosmopolitanism and Containment," which was published in my collection of essays, *The Real World of Democratic Theory* (Princeton University Press, 2011); and "Against Impartiality," *Journal of Politics* 78, no. 2 (April 2016). I thank their publishers for providing venues that turned out to be stepping-stones.

POLITICS AGAINST DOMINATION

I indeed affirm it anew to be very true, according to what is seen through all the histories, that men can second fortune but not oppose it, that they can weave its warp but not break it. They should indeed never give up for, since they do not know its end and it proceeds by oblique and unknown ways, they have always to hope and, since they hope, not to give up in whatever fortune and whatever travail they may find themselves.

—Niccolò Machiavelli, *Discourses on Livy*

CHAPTER ONE

ADAPTING AGAINST DOMINATION

Human beings live in flux. For millennia we have been adapting to an environment that changes partly as a result of what we do. In some ways we are more fragile than many other species; in other ways we are more resilient. Crocodiles have persisted in more or less their present form for hundreds of millions of years and through countless calamities. *Homo sapiens* emerged in Africa about 200,000 years ago and reached full behavioral modernity only about 50,000 years ago—a blink of an eye from a crocodilian point of view. On their time scale, we have scarcely been tested. Yet humans could render crocodiles extinct in a few generations by destroying their habitats. Indeed, we might do so inadvertently unless we take active conservationist measures. Cockroaches have been around for at least as long as crocodiles, but so far we have been unable to stamp them out—not for want of trying. Cockroaches beat just about everything on the resilience front.

Even if we wiped out crocodiles and cockroaches, this would not mean that we were better survivors. One would have to be pretty sanguine to bet that we humans could have a 200-million-year run in anything like our present form, given our vulnerability to fairly moderate changes in the environment and our capacity for self-destructive behavior. A large meteorite or some comparable catastrophe could wipe us out. Or we might do it to ourselves, if not as the result of some monumental Armageddon that we contrive, then as a by-product of activities that we find ourselves unable to curb in a timely way. We might turn out to be lethal mutations of nature.

But we might not. And how we turn out is to some extent in our hands, a fact that differentiates us from crocodiles and cockroaches. Their survival depends wholly on whether their blind instincts continue working in their favor, given changes that they can neither comprehend nor control.

We can contemplate our circumstances, understand them to some extent at least, and think imaginatively about alternative courses of action that might improve our lot. Our social, economic, and political arrangements live in the shadow of untested possibilities that we envision with varying degrees of clarity and enthusiasm.

How realistic these alternatives are, and how pressing—if urgent at all—is the imperative to experiment with them, is congenitally controversial among humans, if only because we are so differently situated from one another. No system of human organization has yet been devised that operates to the mutual benefit of all, and even when there are shared gains from cooperation, these can be distributed in many different ways. As a result, people's relative fortunes vary. They often strive to create circumstances in which they think things would be better for themselves, for groups with which they identify, or for everyone. But no recipe for improvement has ever commanded universal assent.

Demands for change frequently emanate from the disadvantaged, but not always. Greed and the desire for glory can also put pressure on existing practices, as can people with fervent religious or ideological commitments. People who are determined to achieve change can shake the world up radically—whether they succeed or fail. Nor does the possibility of doing things differently arise only in connection with seeking improvements. Sometimes it arises from losses that must be coped with and apportioned, most obviously as the result of economic depressions, environmental catastrophes, and military defeats.

Those who benefit from the status quo will usually resist the pressure for change, sometimes violently. But repressing all opposition is almost never entirely successful—whether those who try to do so claim divine authority, hereditary power, the will of the people, or any other basis for their authority. Even that most notable defender of absolute power Thomas Hobbes recognized that no political system can endure if it rests exclusively on repression and fear. Rather, it must claim the legitimacy that comes from governing in the interests of its subjects.[1]

There is invariably a gap between prevailing political arrangements and better ones that might displace them. How consequential the gap is depends on how many in the population are dissatisfied with existing practices and believe some particular alternative would be better, how intensely they believe it, and whether—given the risks—they have the inclination and resources to try to replace the status quo with the alternative. The aspiration to create a More Perfect Union, as the preamble to the United States Constitution has it, reflects the understanding by its authors that the health—and perhaps even the survival—of any political order depends on narrowing the gap or at least keeping it manageable.

Those who aspire to bridge the gap are constrained by the reality that our reach often, perhaps even characteristically, exceeds our grasp. It is easy to misdiagnose the sources of present dissatisfaction, given the meager condition of causal understanding in the human sciences. Moreover, critics often underestimate the disadvantages of untried possibilities, comparing flawed existing arrangements with idealized versions of proffered alternatives. And even when objectives have been well thought out and would be workable in principle, we often lack viable means of reaching them. Much that passes for political philosophy calls to mind the joke about the traveler who approached a farmer in Donegal asking for directions to Dublin and elicited the response, "Well, sonny, I wouldn't start out from here." People who are confident of the desirability of change often overestimate their ability to bring it about. If they are political philosophers, this condemns them to irrelevance. If they are energetic political agents, they can do great harm.

But if reckless reform is perilous, mindless resistance to change scarcely makes sense either. Burke recommended "infinite caution" before rejecting established ways of doing things.[2] Interpreting that admonition literally would blind people to genuine opportunities for improvement, enabling bad institutions to persist unnecessarily. And as circumstances change, ways of doing things that worked in the past can become dysfunctional. In the early 1920s the British Liberal Party effectively committed suicide when H. H. Asquith misread the emerging dynamics of working-class politics and ceded the anti-Tory role to Ramsay MacDonald's ascending Labour Party rather than adapt to the new reality. In 1979, by contrast, at the height of apartheid, Afrikaner leader P. W. Botha recognized that his people had to "adapt or die"—though many of them were then unwilling to hear it.[3] But his successor, F. W. de Klerk, convinced them to accept the imperative and embrace terrifying change. Although it would cost their National Party its existence, it was a wise decision because more than a political party was at stake. Their choice avoided civil war and gave the Afrikaners a viable place in a new democratic order.[4]

The South African example underscores how much can be at stake in assessing claims about the need for change. The world's population, which grew from under a billion to more than six times that number over the past two centuries, will likely close in on ten billion by the middle of our own.[5] Countries with populations in the hundreds of millions, and even billions, confront new challenges of political accountability. Snowballing industrialization has altered the planet and its atmosphere, perhaps irreversibly.

This has produced transnational ecological threats that were unimagined only a few decades ago. The proliferation of weapons of mass destruction creates security dilemmas that have been transposed into a new key by the end of the Cold War, as does the widely unanticipated resurgence of ethnic, national, and religious political affiliations across the world.[6] The political institutions of the modern West might be tried and tested, but their capacity to cope with present and future challenges is debatable. Designing viable alternatives, and devising incentives to move people toward them, are tasks to which we might not prove equal. We might feel constrained to try, but we are stuck with the limitations of our actual minds and the possible worlds we can conjure up.[7] The imperative to adapt and reinvent inherited practices and institutions is seldom accompanied by workable blueprints.

People often know more about what is inadequate than what would be adequate. During the 1980s, many who lived in Soviet bloc countries could detail the fine contours of their oppression, as could victims of apartheid in South Africa. Yet they could supply only haziest accounts of what their worlds would be like without communism or apartheid, and why they would be better. Comparable stories could be told about those who have opposed fascism and other forms of subjugation. The inability to depict the details of a viable alternative was not a failing on their part. It reflected the reactive character of the human condition. People reject what is painful and oppressive in the hope that something better can be created, even though the destination and path forward are often, perhaps congenitally, shrouded in fog. My goal in this book is to develop an account of political action and institutions that takes these reactive features of the human condition seriously, and builds on them.

I begin by exploring of how best to think about untested possibilities, given our critical and imaginative limitations. Starting from Immanuel Kant's dictum that "ought entails can," I argue in sections 1.1 and 1.2 for a pragmatic and experimental attitude to the limits of possibility that involves ruling out what is plainly impossible and developing, and constantly recalibrating, strategies to move away from oppressive circumstances in the direction of something better. This leads to a discussion of the role of counterfactual thinking in political argument, where I contend that we should agree with the elder John Rawls that there is no reason to require more agreement in politics than is needed to sustain the goals we seek to achieve. However, Rawls is implausible in claiming that this can support one ideal theory of political arrangements as superior to other pretenders. Moreover, his tabula rasa focus on what he describes as the "basic structure" of political institutions belies our reality. Humans inevitably make political choices at the margin, redesigning inherited institutions as they reproduce them into the future. We rebuild our ships at sea.

People who resist domination hope to create something better, even though it is often impossible for them to determine the odds of success. Human cognitive capacities are easily overwhelmed by the social world's complexity, and the behavior of others—on which success often depends—can defy prediction. But this does not make hope irrational. In section 1.3 I note that hope helps motivate people to act in the face of daunting challenges, and it can be integral to securing cooperation from others to escape domination. Drawing on Robert Axelrod's research on cooperation in the face of uncertainty, I argue in section 1.4 that adopting hopeful strategies, geared to discovering and securing cooperation from others, can be vital for combating domination. Hopeful strategies are not mindlessly cooperative or forgiving, but they lead people to test the cooperative waters and to open themselves to reciprocation and comparable probing from others. Cooperative solutions are not always available, but when they are, hopeful strategies help us converge on and build upon them.

But what are people avoiding when they avoid domination? Defining domination is difficult because it is what Ludwig Wittgenstein referred to as a family resemblance concept. Each instance of domination shares features with others, but there is no single defining element common to them all.[8] This should caution us not to search overly hard for watertight definitions, or to expect too much of any account that we can supply. There will be exceptions and borderline cases to almost everything we say about domination, but this need not render our observations about it wrongheaded or useless. Instead, it suggests that we calibrate our expectations to take account of the kind of subject at hand. With these cautions in mind, I characterize domination in section 1.5 as involving the avoidable and illegitimate exercise of power that compromises people's basic interests, and I argue that attempts to escape it are rooted in the particular—in ways that appeals to ideals like freedom, equality, and impartiality are not. Rather than try to escape domination as such, people try to escape instances of domination that they experience or by which they feel threatened.

The flipside of uncertainty over whether domination can be undermined is uncertainty over whether it can be sustained. This works in nondomination's favor, generating a rationale for resisting domination that stretches at least from primitive hunter-gatherer societies through George Kennan's defense of containment in the 1940s. It cleaves to the idea that if you cannot be confident of your ability to dominate others, the next best thing is to create a world that no one can dominate. I explore the foundations and some implications of this logic in section 1.6, noting its elective affinities with democratic politics understood as institutionalized uncertainty of outcomes. This is a logic that arises in different ways throughout the book, captured in Machiavelli's defense of democracy on the grounds that it allocates power to those who want not to be dominated rather than those who seek to dominate others. It is a logic that, once established, can become durable, though it is by no means immune to invasion by less sanguine political agendas and dynamics. As I note in section 1.7, history promises us nothing.

1.1 Utopian Thinking and the Limits of Possibility

Responding to present dissatisfactions by positing a future in which they will melt away is as old as the human condition. Sometimes these portrayals combine past and future utopias as endpoints in a teleological sequence, as with the Judeo-Christian narrative in which an innocent world has been lost but in which redemption is available to adherents who follow a prescribed course. Utopias are often connected to—even defined against—dystopias, which might be eternal hell or reincarnation as a lower form of life. Dystopias figure in utopian thinking partly to incorporate and emphasize the human capacity for choice; they speak to our proclivity to believe that our fate is in our hands. Choosing well is defined against the possibility of choosing poorly, both for an individual, where damnation or salvation is at stake, and for peoples who risk catastrophe if gods are displeased or vital actions are not taken to stave off an apocalypse.

Secular utopias might carry less metaphysical freight, though they sometimes echo religious teleologies: an innocent, if not entirely agreeable, world has been lost, but something hinted at by its virtues can be recreated if our dehumanizing institutions and practices are appropriately transformed. Rousseau's noble savage and Marx's primitive man were alienated from their true selves by the advent of private property and the division of labor, producing orders warped by oppression and exploitation. We can be liberated, on such accounts, only by replacing our enslaving institutions with new arrangements that will end exploitative conflict and usher in governance in the general interest.[9]

How should we evaluate such utopian claims? John Rawls once declared that "political philosophy is realistically utopian when it extends what are ordinarily thought of as the limits of practical possibility."[10] But how are we to know what those limits are and how far they might be extended? And how should we think about the relations between those possibilities and imperatives for action? Perhaps we should start from what we believe morality requires and then push the world in that direction, as some believe Kant had in mind when he insisted that "ought entails can."[11] That approach strains credulity, however. Why assume that reality—including the reality comprised by human action—can be made to conform to the moral nostrums that people devise?

A more plausible reading of Kant's maxim would be to begin with "can" rather than "ought," insisting that no one is required to attempt what is clearly impossible. This approach courts an opposite danger in which we miss opportunities for change by naturalizing current practices—as in Rousseau's contention that Hobbes treated as immutable the behavior characteristic of his society.[12] Surely it is important to be realistic in politics, especially when the stakes are high, but so-called realism can blind people to feasible alternatives. Had there been orthodox neoclassical economists around at the turn of the nineteenth century, they would have insisted that any effort to abolish the slave trade must fail. Yet as I discuss in section 5.4.1, the Atlantic slave trade was outlawed in Britain and the United States in 1807 and 1808, slavery was abolished in most of the British Empire in 1833, and the bulk of the remaining Atlantic slave trade (by Spain, Portugal, Brazil, and Cuba) was suppressed by the late 1860s. Rousseau was right that "the bounds of the possible in moral matters are less narrow than we think."[13] But how can we know what they are?

An intermediate reading of the Kantian dictum suggested by Casiano Hacker-Cordón is that "ought entails must try!"[14] Appealing as this might be, it leaves open two vital matters: how to determine what we ought to do, and how to set about doing it. On the first question it seems unlikely that an adaptive approach to politics will be much advanced by the hunt for categorical imperatives. Something only rises to the level of a categorical imperative, on Kant's account, if we can will it from every conceivable standpoint. Our limited knowledge and capacities rule that out. The political choices people face are typically too complex, and too dependent on such contingencies as the unpredictable actions of others, to be evaluated by that test. Politics depends on hypothetical imperatives all the way down. It forces us to experiment with, and sometimes bet on, imponderables.

Consider the choice whether to fight, submit, or seek some intermediate strategy such as nonviolent resistance or negotiation in the face of political domination. It would be hard to come away from the study of the debates surrounding these issues in an actual political movement such as the African National Congress (ANC) over the course of its history believing that categorical judgments about such dilemmas are possible.[15] They depend on too many nuances of context, and they require too many fine judgments in the face of uncertainty. The search for universally valid judgments about politics that rise above the banal seems chimerical. Even if there were some, Raymond Guess usefully reminds us that there is no reason to suppose that they would generally be recognized.[16] Kant was well aware of this, insisting that "welfare does not have any ruling principle" because it depends "on the will's material aspect, which is empirical and thus incapable of becoming a universal rule."[17]

Something approaching categorical confidence makes better sense in considering what we should rule out in politics rather than in the search for maxims to guide political action. Consider the Marxist account of a communist world in which distributive conflict is transcended. Karl Marx and Friedrich Engels took great pains to contrast their "scientific" argument with the "utopian" socialism of Pierre-Joseph Proudhon and others whom they dismissed as fanciful, but their own account is frankly utopian in one major respect: it assumes that there can be a world devoid of the conflicts that arise from scarcity.

Marx defined communism as a world governed by the principle "From each according to his ability to each according to his needs."[18] It was his transposition of Hegel's end of history, made possible by the existence of a superabundance of wealth that capitalism would by then have created. Part of what Marx meant was that this would be a world in which there would no longer be conflicting rights claims. It would, famously if somewhat vaguely, be a world in which "the free development of each is the condition for the free development of all."[19]

Marx thought that capitalism generates imperatives to induce demand for unnecessary goods, buttressing the conflation of needs with wants and hence the idea of limitless desires. His followers have been less sure than Marx was that we can ever reach a stage of literal superabundance, but some continue to embrace the idea that we can plausibly envisage what G. A Cohen describes as a world of "lesser abundance which enables resolutions of conflicts of interests without coercion."[20] Capitalism "brings society to the threshold of abundance and locks the door," but once we no longer live in a system driven by "febrile product innovation, huge investments in sales and advertising, and contrived obsolescence," then the prospect of "a balanced human existence" becomes feasible.[21]

Any such project must fail. Even on the most rudimentary definition of human needs by reference to the wherewithal for survival, needs will always outstrip available resources. Mere mention of dialysis machines and artificial hearts, or the possibility of research on AIDS, cancer, or other fatal diseases, makes it obvious that the resources to save lives are inherently scarce. Deploying them in one way rather than another will always involve opportunity costs. This means, in turn, that adjudicating competing claims is inescapable, and so, therefore, is what Marx would have described as a regime of rights. No matter what the level of abundance, managing scarcity is endemic to collective human life.

To assume the contrary is to embrace a static and unchanging—not to say notably un-Marxist—view of the human condition that would have to include a need to die after some allotted time. Three score years and ten? Whatever it was, we would also need an account of how people would be brought to accept it. Anyone who doubts that trying to manufacture that result would produce a dystopia should read Anthony Trollope's *The Fixed Period,* which depicts the political breakdown of an imaginary society in which a law has been enacted to euthanize people at the of age sixty-eight.[22] We will never be able to abolish scarcity or distributive conflict, and any guide to political action that assumes that we can is unlikely to lead us in a profitable direction. This is not to deny that it is possible, perhaps even likely, that technological advances will produce opportunities for increased abundance and greater longevity than we can scarcely imagine today. These will, in turn, generate novel conflicts and dilemmas, and perhaps possibilities for dealing with them. But they will never go away.

1.2 Counterfactual Ideals

We can agree with Kant not to be distracted by utopian impossibility, and we can share his skepticism at the prospect that reasoning about politics will yield categorical imperatives. But that still leaves open quite a bit of territory for those tempted by the quest for counterfactual theories that carry some kind of superobligatory force. In particular, it leaves open the search for what Rawls once described as "procedural expressions" of the categorical imperative.[23] Rawls thought that people could be persuaded to converge on a shared vision of a just society that takes account of endemic scarcity and differences in people's values.

Actual political systems are shaped by wars and by the rough-and-tumble interactions of countless people leading ordinary lives over centuries, but we can still consider what arrangements people would choose if they had the chance to build a society anew. And we can eradicate bias from those considerations, Rawls thought, by focusing on what people would choose if ignorant of specific knowledge of themselves and their circumstances. It was an exercise in ideal theory: behind this veil of ignorance, he argued, people would embrace guarantees of basic rights and liberties, equality of opportunity, and distributive arrangements that work to the benefit of the least advantaged members of society. This scheme would be chosen over the going alternatives, providing an Archimedean standard that we can deploy in our actual "second best" world to see how it measures up and where it needs improvement.

If Rawls were right, his conjecture could give impetus and direction to an adaptive political theory venture, but things are tougher than that. The difficulty is a cousin of the one that Rousseau attributed to Hobbes, to wit: Most of the heavy lifting in Rawls's argument is done by contentious assumptions about how the world works and what motivates people. His veil of ignorance ruled out knowledge of "particular facts" about people and their circumstances, which could be used to bias things in their favor, but not the "laws of psychology and economics" and "general facts" about society.[24] This is a hard distinction to make, however, because general facts and uncontroversial laws are few and far between, and decisions about which ones to employ have different implications for differently situated groups. For instance, Rawls insists that behind the veil of ignorance no one would countenance the "grave risks" involved in embracing inequalities that do not redound to the advantage of the least advantaged, on the grounds that even in affluent societies the poor can face dire straits. But if we were to attribute greater tolerance for risk to people than did Rawls, as John Harsanyi—among others—suggested that we should, then we would get a different result.[25] Rawls's original position was self-consciously crafted to yield the conclusions he sought, a tactic I have discussed elsewhere.[26] Here I simply note that it is unlikely to move anyone who stands in need of persuasion.[27]

In later work Rawls abandoned his claim that people would agree on why to endorse his principles, noting that it was sufficient that there would be an "overlapping consensus" on them behind the veil of ignorance.[28] This "political not metaphysical" stance is congenial to the adaptive enterprise in political theory because there is no reason to make political decisions more metaphysically demanding than necessary. Cass Sunstein calls it "incompletely theorized agreement," observing that collectivities often agree on outcomes even though they could never agree on why.[29] Democracies implicitly adopt a similar stance with the secret ballot, which shields people from having to justify their choices to others.

Appealing as this economical approach to metaphysics might be, Amartya Sen (who endorses a version of it by appealing to "plural reasons" for desired outcomes) has noted that Rawls never in fact shows that there would be an overlapping consensus on one set of principles, let alone on his.[30]

The Rawlsian approach is unhelpful to an adaptive political project also because his defining focus is on the "basic structure" of political institutions, but most of the time we must make choices and decisions on the margin.[31] True, in the final stages of his thought experiment Rawls asks us to reason from the standpoint of legislators and judges—once the principles of justice and constitutional commitments have been chosen. Yet it is far from clear what this would yield in the world of real politics. In a rare venture into that world, Rawls once declared in a footnote that his theory supports a woman's right to abortion, at least in the first trimester.[32] He soon backtracked, however, when critics asked why.[33] Elsewhere Rawls has said that mandates for publicly funded elections, less inequality than currently exists in the United States, and universal medical insurance can all be derived from his theory.[34] But these claims are easily challenged. Rawls might be right that preserving the "fair value" of equal political liberties requires public election funding.[35] Yet he never explains why that goal should trump the right to free speech, also protected by his first principle.[36] Those who are more convinced by trickle-down theories than Rawls's neo-Keynesian view of the multiplier effects of helping people at the bottom will be unmoved by his objection to current American levels of inequality.[37] His conjecture that justice requires "normal" medical treatment for all leaves unaddressed the huge difficulty, already noted, of deciding what counts as normal or how it should be traded off against other values also protected by his scheme.[38] As the South African Constitutional Court discovered in 1997, when it sought to delineate the limits of a constitutional right to medical treatment for someone dying of renal failure, there is no theoretically compelling solution to these trade-offs.[39] Certainly Rawls's theory offers no help.

Even when issues about basic structure are up for grabs, they seldom arise in ways that are illuminated by the kinds of principles Rawls defends. Should the United States Constitution have been rammed through in violation of the Articles of Confederation? Was the three-fifths rule a defensible price to pay in order to get it? Did the Missouri Compromise of 1820 to regulate slavery in the West merit support as part of what would turn out to be a vain attempt to hold the Union together without civil war? In 1992 the South African government and ANC leadership negotiated a secret pact and then unveiled it as a fait accompli to potential spoilers. Should they have done that? The pact guaranteed protections for minorities and power sharing in an interim constitution. But de Klerk dissembled to his followers about the fact that he had no guarantee that these protections would make it into the final constitution, a move that he judged necessary to achieve a settlement without civil war.[40] Was this the right move? That is how questions about basic structure come up in real politics. They combine issues of principle with those of tactics and strategy in messy ways to which ideal theory, as Rawls advocates it, is irrelevant.

1.3 Hope versus Optimism

Political action is often motivated by the hope that we can improve the world by our own efforts. But what is the basis for that hope, given how little we understand and how much of what we think we know turns out on inspection to be debatable? Hope, as Christopher Lasch has said, "is a temperamental predisposition rather than an estimate of the direction of historical change."[41] Hope is not the same thing as optimism, which is rooted—however imperfectly—in probability. We can hope that a favored candidate will win an election even when we are not optimistic that she will win. This can be because she has less money than her opponent, the polls reveal that she is behind, or we know for some other reason that the odds are stacked against her. Indeed, we can have hope even when there is scant reason for optimism—as when we hope that our team, which has been badly beaten the first three games, will win the playoffs. Being hopeful is also different from being happy. One can be unhappy in an unrewarding job or a bad marriage, yet hopeful that these circumstances might improve. Whereas the antithesis of optimism is pessimism and the antithesis of happiness is unhappiness, the antithesis of hope is despair. These distinctions help us make sense of Martin Luther King's sober observation to his Atlanta congregation near the end of his life that, while he was no longer an optimist, he still had hope.[42]

Losing hope means giving up on life. It hovers as the dispiriting possibility Gerard Manley Hopkins captured in his terrible sonnets, as he battled the dark night of his soul. Lamenting that "no worst, there is none," and unable to fathom God's purpose in the suffering he saw around him, Hopkins could do little more than howl into the void: "Comforter, where, where is your comforting?"[43] Less dramatically, but no less starkly, Thomas Hardy conjured up the bleakness of life without hope when he wrote to a grieving father that "the death of a child is never really to be regretted when one reflects on what he has escaped."[44] The remark is shocking because it belies the hope we routinely embrace.[45] As King put it, "Even in the inevitable moments when all seems hopeless, men know that without hope they cannot really live, and in agonizing desperation they cry for the bread of hope."[46] George Bernard Shaw was right to remind us that "he who has never hoped can never despair," but he might have added that despair displaces hope permanently only in people who truly are broken.[47]

We all face a tunnel at the end of the light, but the common aphorism reverses the order of the two nouns with good reason. Hope is integral to living. Often we cannot measure the distance of the approaching darkness with much precision, though we know that this can be affected by our choices—as can the quality of the lives we live along the way. Nor does death's predictable finality extinguish hope. We might not be "traveling eternity road" as the Moody Blues' song has it, but the band was right that people are buoyed by knowing that their children's children's children might experience and achieve wonderful things.[48] Granted, suffering and the prospect of it can darken anyone's outlook. We can all imagine circumstances in which someone might reasonably choose death—most obviously to escape a debilitating terminal illness. But giving up on life as such to avoid—even predictable—human suffering is scarcely thinkable, as R. N. Smart famously noted by pointing out that it would generate an imperative to destroy the entire human race if this could be painlessly achieved.[49]

The defeatist sentiment that marks Hardy as depressed seems plainly mad when contemplated as a guide for collective human choice. It flies in the face of our reluctance to allow anyone to give up on life on behalf of others, regardless of his beliefs. When it happens—as with the mass "revolutionary suicide" by cyanide poisoning in Jonestown, Guyana, in 1978—we attribute it to cultish manipulation. Contemplating Smart's observation is appalling also because it invites us to sidestep our knowledge of human fallibility, which reasonably breeds skepticism of all final solutions. Moreover, it ignores the human propensity to value life—even cling to it—regardless of cost-benefit calculations, and it is innocent of the premium people place on the mere possibility of improvement. The knowledge that their efforts might enhance things is often enough to motivate people to try, even if they cannot know what difference, if any, their efforts will ultimately make. We cannot be sure that *fortuna audax iuvat*, but nor do we know that it does not, and there are reasons to load the dice in its favor.[50]

1.4 Hope and Adaptive Rationality

Acting out of hope is central to adaptive political theory because of its role in human interaction. Just because hopeful action takes place in the face of uncertainty about its beneficial effects, this gives people reasons to trust the commitment of those who engage in it. When directed at others whose cooperation is needed for success, this makes hopeful action a variant of what game theorists describe as costly signaling. People who act out of hope show that they can be counted on to bear a cost even though its instrumental benefits are uncertain. If putting my shoulder to the wheel or taking a risk makes it obvious that I am not strategic or self-interested all the way down, perhaps you will also feel less constrained to be utterly selfish than otherwise you might be.

Sometimes this has a performative dimension, whereby costly action actually transforms the situation in a beneficial way. When F. W. de Klerk called the 1992 referendum and invested all his political capital in campaigning for a yes vote in support of his negotiations with the ANC, he took on the Afrikaner hard right in a loser-lose-all fight in which there would be no second round. The danger was great because his government had been defeated in a series of by-elections by opponents of his negotiations, and he acted without seeking support from his cabinet or the NP leadership.[51] By courting the political oblivion that would surely have followed a lost referendum or failed subsequent negotiations, he also gave Nelson Mandela what he needed to convince ANC skeptics to work with him. The government and the ANC had been through decades of bitter conflict in which countless people had been uprooted, imprisoned, tortured, and killed. There was scant basis for trust between their leaders. Yet de Klerk waded into the middle of the Rubicon, even though he lacked the wherewithal to make it all the way across or to wade back if it turned out that Mandela was not there with a rope to help him. By manifestly acting on the basis of hope, de Klerk made it easier for Mandela to negotiate with him. Thus he increased the chances that the negotiations could succeed even though there was no way that he could have known by how much.

Costly signaling can be helpful in many less dramatic situations. If a critical number of supporters is needed for joint action to be effective, the fact that someone steps forward makes it correspondingly less likely that the next person's effort will be wasted.[52] When the numbers are small, the reduction in those odds can be significant.[53] Getting countries to sign up to environmental agreements and international human rights accords sometimes follows that pattern. A threshold of about a third seems to be the tipping point, after which support for a new norm starts diffusing through the system.[54] This logic is more elusive with large numbers, but Susanne Lohmann has suggested that moderate opponents of authoritarian regimes can be emboldened to act on their disaffection if intense opponents—the costly signalers—act first and the regime turns out to be unwilling or unable to crush them. Its paper-tiger quality becomes evident. Previously timid opponents begin expressing their dissatisfaction, leading them to discover that it is widely shared. The resulting "information cascade" enables them to sweep the regime away, as happened, she argues, in East Germany in October 1989.[55] Comparable dynamics might have operated elsewhere in Eastern Europe in 1989, in Russia two years later, and in Tunisia and Egypt in 2011.

Lohmann's story, while suggestive, exhibits the limits of accounts of political action rooted exclusively in rational calculations. Even if the regime appears weak, its moderate opponents face enormous collective action hurdles. Risky effort is needed in the early stages of the information cascade; afterward it is unnecessary. Why not stay at home until the dust settles, or at most cheer others on from the sidelines as a "timid rebel" who can stand up and be noticed if things go well but melt away into the crowd if they do not?[56] This is to say nothing of the intense early movers, who must be motivated by something other than strategic rationality. As we saw in Iran following the disputed 2009 presidential election and in the protracted 2011 struggles in Libya and Syria, there is always the chance that a regime has been misjudged: the apparent paper tiger opens its jaws to reveal deadly teeth.

These examples suggest that something besides self-interested calculation is needed, be it a desire to express outrage, to do the right thing, to be the one who inspired others, to be a part of history, to be respected by one's children, or some other more-than-purely-self-interested impulse. Indeed, even when comparatively small groups are involved in negotiating over whether to sign up to multilateral accords, Martha Finnemore and Kathryn Sikkink note, shaming and other forms of peer pressure are often needed to move people past the tipping point that ushers in a durable a new norm.[57] We will see in sections 3.1.2 and 5.4 that because political coalitions based exclusively on interests are inherently unstable, moral arguments are often essential to keep them together in the face of efforts to splinter them or dismantle their achievements.

Hopeful adaptation occupies the territory somewhere between hapless suckerdom and myopic rationality. People might often try to be rational, as Axelrod has noted, but "they can rarely meet the requirements of information or foresight that rational models impose."[58] Axelrod deployed the notion of adaptive behavior to capture the reality that we strive fallibly in environments that are usually too complex and opaque to game out much into the future. His famous prisoner's dilemma simulation tournaments revealed that "nice" strategies, in which people cooperate provided that others do likewise, are generally preferred over time. Nice strategies resist invasion by "nasty" strategies geared to exploiting cooperation.[59] Tit-for-tat, in which you first cooperate and then mimic what your opponent does indefinitely, is the winning nice strategy. It beats every nasty strategy ever devised.

Axelrod also found that when tit-for-tat breaks down into mutually reinforcing defection, players look for ways to restore cooperation. They test the waters with "generous tit-for-tat" (cooperating in the face of an opponent's defection) and "contrite tit-for-tat" (cooperating when the opponent has defected in response to their earlier defection).[60] Restorative strategies must be tentative to be effective; they fall well short of the biblical injunction to turn the other cheek. Tit-for-two-tats is too forgiving; nasty strategies quickly invade it. For generous and contrite tit-for-tat to succeed in restoring virtuous cycles, they can be tried only about 10 percent of the time.[61]

Axelrod thinks restorative strategies reflect our grasp of the possibility of error. People know that they might defect by mistake or be unnecessarily punitive; restorative strategies provide a measure of insurance against that danger. But restorative strategies might also reflect the human propensity for hope. People might turn to them in the midst of vicious cycles to try to restore virtuous ones. Indeed, tit-for-tat itself reflects a hopeful disposition inasmuch as it opens with a cooperative move. This belies what we know from the social psychology literature: that from a very young age people are distrustful of strangers.[62] Hopeful strategies embody calculated risks to overcome that impulse.

There are, to be sure, limits to what can be inferred from Axelrod's tournaments. They do not tell us what real people would do in actual situations, particularly when the stakes are high.[63] The tournaments cannot involve life-or-death situations, by definition, or there could be no presumption of iteration. Yet there are many circumstances short of life or death where greed or fear can overwhelm people's hopeful impulses, leading them to defect and then refuse to risk restorative strategies.[64] Indeed, I will argue later that among democracy's advantages is its promise to reduce stakes in ways that are friendly to cooperative and restorative strategies.

Another difficulty is that in the real world there are limits to iteration, whereas the logic behind tit-for-tat and other hopeful strategies depends on openness to an indefinite future—or at least to an uncertain one. Notice, however, that the value of open-ended iteration is that it builds considerations about possible future choices into calculations about present conduct. In a one-shot prisoner's dilemma, or in what is known by both sides to be the final round of a finite sequence, there is no reason for people to consider the future. And if everyone knows which will be the last round, then the dominant strategy is to defect in the penultimate round. But then everyone knows which is the penultimate round, making defection on the round before that the dominant strategy—and so on. By backward induction defection becomes the dominant strategy from the start. Forestalling this dynamic depends on no one knowing which round will be last. Here, too, I will argue that democracy can offer advantages. The fact that politics involves many more players than Axelrod's tournaments can enhance desirable forms of unpredictability, so long as there are propitious cleavages of interest in the population and the right institutions are adopted. Hope, as J. Glen Gray says, is "directed toward the future in trust rather than in confidence."[65] But there must be some basis for that trust. People need grounds to believe that they will be better protected over time by democracy than by the going alternatives, even though there is no certainty about this. Appropriately structured, democracy gives people reasons to emulate supporters of the losing team in the World Series who trail out of the stadium muttering "wait 'til next year."

This does not divorce hope from considerations of probability. It makes little sense to hope for something that is vanishingly unlikely, though this has to be discounted by the stakes. Buying lottery tickets with spare change can be a fun thrill or diversion, but spending the rent money in that way is self-destructive. The higher the stakes, the more important it is to have a compelling basis for acting in trust toward the future. Participants in the 1989 uprisings across Eastern Europe and in Beijing, or in those that spread from Tunisia to Egypt, Bahrain, Libya, and Syria in 2010–2011, all took enormous risks when they had no real way to gauge the odds of their success—as the divergent subsequent trajectories of those conflicts has underscored.

This is why Locke was wise to counsel revolution only in response to "a long train of abuses, prevarications, and artifices, all tending the same way."[66] These are settings in which people judge the status quo to be intolerably bad and unlikely to improve. In that sense, even though the stakes are high, there may not be much to lose. They are also settings in which it is plausible to think that one's discontent might be widely shared. This, in turn, supplies reason to hope that others will at least be receptive to resistance if it can gain traction—even if that speculation is fraught with imponderables, as we have seen. Locke discounted the imponderables, confident in the belief that resisting tyranny in good faith will be rewarded in the next life even if it fails in this one.[67] In a secular world, hope has to do the work of faith.

But to be adaptively useful, hope must be embedded in the search for authentic knowledge about politics. Political choices are often hampered by misconceptions about what is feasible—as when people are ignorant of preconditions for viable democracy or the effects of different electoral systems on the distribution of income and wealth. We often have to choose in the face of imponderables, but we have an interest in limiting the extent to which this is so. Hopeful adaptation will do best when it takes account of what is known in the human sciences. Fallible and partial as this might be, there is no better basis to inform efforts to sort the realistic from the unrealistic when assessing the causes of present maladies and the bets we should make on proffered alternatives. True, prevailing opinion can be wrong, and in politics there can always be surprises. Indeed, political creativity may involve seeing possibilities that others miss or dismiss. Yet it is important to distinguish tilting at windmills from having achievable goals and plausible means of pursuing them. Particular outcomes often depend partly, but seldom wholly, on unpredictable contingencies. Some courses of action and some institutional setups make some outcomes more likely than others. When there is expert knowledge about such things, people have an interest in taking it into account, even though, as I argue in sections 2.1 and 4.2.3, they should never abdicate to it.

People must often make decisions while lacking relevant information about the future—including the future behavior of others. It is inherent in the human condition that much about the future is unknown and perhaps unknowable. The behavior of others in many circumstances will be difficult to predict, though there might be ways to structure human interaction that make it less unpredictable. Diminishing stakes and institutionalizing uncertainty are cases in point. Notice, also, that people have good reasons to believe that the others with whom they must deal are similarly lacking in knowledge about the future. This turns out to be consequential for evaluating vanguardist arguments, as we will see.

A related difficulty with models that assume people to be strategically rational is that the information people do have is in any case often too complex for them to process. Soon it will be possible to create computer software programs that can defeat every possible strategy in chess, but this will not render competitive chess obsolete.[68] Economists and psychologists have responded to the realities of human cognitive limitation in divergent ways. Economists often reach for the Bayesian impulse to think of humans as emerging *Homo economicus:* we might not start out behaving as their models predict, but we update our beliefs and expectations over time so as to evolve in that direction.[69] There is even literature suggesting that selfish behavior increases with the number of economics courses people take.[70]

Setting aside the obvious questions about the direction of causation here, there is another interpretation of such associations suggested by the psychology literature on framing effects.[71] Perhaps someone whose economics courses were followed by anthropology and sociology courses would end up being deprogrammed of selfishness and then reprogrammed as a traditionalist. Our cognitive limitations might well make us susceptible to people around us and the ways in which choices are framed. The scholarship on priming and push-polling suggests that people's attitudes are flexible, if variably and in ways that are not well understood.[72] But it would be hard to come away from that literature with the sense that attitudes evolve in any particular direction—let alone cumulatively.

The framing-effects literature offers a useful corrective to the rational teleology built into the Bayesian story, but it goes too far by portraying people as passive responders to choices that are framed for them by others. Axelrod's alternative is more realistic in that it incorporates the purposive human capacity to strive for improvement. Often, perhaps typically in politics, people want to act so as to advance their interests. But this turns out to be enormously difficult in view of our cognitive limitations, our limited grasp of how the world works, and our inability to predict much about the future—including the future behavior of others. Hence the plausibility of Axelrod's picture in which people explore cooperation where they think this might be beneficial and reciprocated. But they do it tentatively. They test the waters, they see how others respond, and they adapt. They recognize that although it is foolhardy to ignore strategic considerations, being mechanically strategic can often be self-defeating. They factor in the reality that people make mistakes, and that they overreact in ways that they sometimes come to regret.

Apart from being alive to the possibility of error, people know that being too strategic breeds distrust. They understand that convincing others that you are sincere about seeking a positive path forward gives them reason to trust you. They develop greater confidence in you as you continue to forego opportunities to abuse their trust. Being hopeful in your dealings with others gives them reasons to be hopeful in dealing with you. We can never know that hopeful strategies will work, but it is reasonable to think that they might. When they do, they allow people to spend less time looking over their shoulders, and more time grappling with life's other challenges.

1.5 Domination and Nondomination

What is the domination that people have an interest in avoiding? This question is more easily asked than answered. Domination is related to freedom and the lack of it, but freedom can be compromised in ways that do not amount to domination. Domination often results from the maldistribution of resources, but many distributive inequalities do not breed domination. Domination obviously involves power relations, but not every exercise of power is domination. Indeed, power is frequently needed to combat domination. People often know domination when they see it or experience it, but it is hard to define partly because it is a family resemblance idea, as I have noted. Yet is possible to identify five characteristic features.

First, domination always compromises someone's freedom, but for a loss of freedom to count as domination it must be rooted in human action. A natural chasm or a medical condition might limit someone's freedom, but we would not identify either as a source of domination. People experience domination when their freedom is curtailed because they are in the power of others—be they slaveholders, torturers, spouses, or employers. This human element differentiates domination from other kinds of unfreedom, and it means that appeals to eliminate sources of domination are always in some sense—however attenuated—directed at changing things that human beings do.

Domination is a distinctive kind of unfreedom, second, in that it is generally taken to be alterable by those who are responsible for it—at least in principle. A crying infant curtails a parent's freedom, but this is not domination because the infant is powerless to do anything about it. Complaining about domination triggers the presumption that relevant people could behave differently in ways that would alleviate the domination—at least in principle. People can, of course, be wrong about what will work. They might attribute their powerlessness to the vindictiveness of an angry god who can be appeased only by making a human sacrifice. Or they might correctly identify ethnic hatred as a source of their oppression and be right that in principle it could be eliminated, yet no one may know how to accomplish this. Describing unfreedom as domination alludes to the possibility of reducing or eliminating it by changing human action. Realizing that possibility is another matter.

Max Weber said that domination requires "the actual presence of one person successfully issuing orders to others."[73] That is too narrow. Domination can, and often does, occur without explicit orders emanating from identifiable agents. Inadvertent and unconscious actions can foster domination. Domination can also be a by-product of the distribution of resources and can be embedded in structural relationships. We should not, however, go as far as Philip Pettit, who insists that merely having the capacity to interfere in the lives of others at will constitutes domination of them.[74] This is to confuse the potential for something with its occurrence. That might sound like a semantic quibble, but suppose a playground bully is able to beat up any of the smaller children but is widely known only to beat up black children. Does he dominate the children who are not black?[75] Senator Joseph McCarthy had the capacity to interfere in the lives of many Americans, but those on the political left plausibly lived in fear of him in ways that others did not. To say that he dominated all those with whom he could have interfered trivializes the plight of those who had good reasons to fear him. Today the United States has the capacity for arbitrary interference in Cuba, Mexico, Canada, and Lesotho, but it stands in very different relations to them from the standpoint of domination. Cuba has endured explicit coercive interference for decades; Mexico periodically feels the pressure of American "soft power"; Canada is subject to the influence of a stronger but largely like-minded ally; and Lesotho is unaffected by American power in the ways that are relevant to the other three. Pettit's account is insensitive to such distinctions, and it diverts attention from the ways in which interference can mitigate domination. The strongest child in the playground might be a bully, but she might also be the person who protects the weaker children from bullies.

Third, some kinds of domination matter more than others. Michel Foucault was too quick to find domination lurking behind every tree.[76] He might have been right that throwing off one domineering yoke often creates new possibilities for domination, but it is an open question whether this is always so. Even when it is, some kinds of domination are more severe than others and some kinds are borne by people who are more vulnerable to its deleterious effects than are others. Limiting the power of investment bankers involves enhancing that of government regulators. This then raises questions about whether the regulators are more or less prone than the bankers to engage in domination, what the effects of such domination will be, and who will be vulnerable to it. Some of these questions are empirical, but there are underlying normative issues at stake in deciding which kinds of domination should concern us most. It is best to think about them by reference to the importance of the interests at stake.

People's most important, or basic, interests concern what is essential for successful survival in the environments in which they will live. One common approach to this, traceable at least to Aristotle's distinction between instrumental and final goods, is to focus on the resources and capacities that people generally need regardless of their goals and aspirations.[77] Knowing that people often disagree over the number and nature of final goods, we can still try to identify what meeting their basic interests will require.[78] Indeed, many theorists have followed Rawls's lead in arguing that, just because we disagree about final goods and even value the freedom to choose them for ourselves, we should chiefly be concerned with the most important instrumental goods—which he identified as primary goods.[79] They are, as Philip Pettit puts it, things that "a person has instrumental reasons to want."[80] In a like spirit Ronald Dworkin maintained that the emphasis should be on the resources that are valuable to people regardless of their tastes and ambitions, and Amartya Sen and Martha Nussbaum focused on people's basic capabilities as the relevant metric for thinking about justice, while leaving them free to identify the uses to which those capabilities will be put.[81] Part of the appeal of these views is that they make it possible to identify and reason about people's basic interests without second-guessing their freedom to choose and pursue their own final goods.

There is an additional, power-based, reason to embrace resourcism. People are at their most vulnerable when their basic interests can be threatened. If I control resources that you need to vindicate your basic interests, that gives me power over you—whether or not I decide to exercise it. John Locke put it dramatically: "A man can no more justly make use of another's necessity, to force him to become his vassal . . . than he that has more strength can seize upon a weaker, master him to his obedience, and with a dagger at his throat offer him death or slavery."[82] Locke's example involves withholding what people need to escape "extreme want"—surely an easy case. But any situation in which people can "make use of another's necessity" brings with it the possibility of domination. We should therefore include access to the sources of security, nutrition, health, and education required to become effective adults in the prevailing economic system and to participate fully in a democratic political order.[83] If people are, or can be, excluded from access to these resources, they become vulnerable to domination. The more important these resources are to them, the more intense is their "necessity," and the more vulnerable they are to the possibility of domination as a result.[84]

Domination is, fourth, a kind of unfreedom that carries the whiff of illicitness. Our freedom is often curtailed when we are in the power of others, but this is not domination unless that power is somehow abused or pressed into the service of an illegitimate purpose. Children are in the power of parents, students of teachers, workers of employers; in all these cases their freedom is limited. But we think of it as domination only if those in positions of authority abuse their power in some way, as when an employer or teacher demands sexual favors as a condition for a promotion or a good grade or parental authority is abused for the parent's gratification. When people accuse one another of domination, they do it in order to question the legitimacy of a power relationship. Even domination fantasies underscore this; they involve fetishizing dungeons, slavery, or other illicit forms of control. When we say someone is domineering, we express disdain; calling them powerful connotes no necessary negative valence. Wars of domination are not seen as just, whereas wars to escape its yoke are defensible. There are exceptions, to be sure. Sports teams can be said to dominate one another without prejudice to the dominator, and game theorists talk neutrally of dominant strategies, as we have seen, but these really are exceptions. Even Friedrich Nietzsche, whose views are taken up in section 1.6, argued less for the domination of others than for acting with indifference to them.

This raises the question: Who determines illicitness, and how? The idea of basic interests helps here as well. There are good reasons to defer to participants concerning an activity's legitimate purposes, particularly in civil institutions like families, churches, universities, and firms. They understand their activities from the inside and have the relevant street-level knowledge or insiders' wisdom. But deferring to insiders' wisdom is less defensible in power-laden contexts when people's basic interests are at stake. We have good reasons to defer to insiders in deciding what constitutes legitimate religious authority, but not if it leads Christian Scientists to deny a blood transfusion to a child who will otherwise die. We have good reasons to defer to insiders in how to run firms, but the reasons become weaker when employees can easily be fired and they have few protections against the costs of unemployment. The greater the risk of domination, the less we should defer to insiders' wisdom.[85] In politics, I argue in section 2.1, no one should defer to it.

Finally, when people speak of domination and nondomination, a distinctive kind of particularism is invoked that need not be present when people refer to freedom or the lack of it more generally. Perhaps people are unfree in some existential sense if determinism is true, if we are "being towards death" as Heidegger said, or for some other reason unrelated to human social relations.[86] But we need not hold the case for nondomination hostage to these metaphysical issues. Domination's particularism flows from its rootedness in human collective arrangements. If domination depends on the actions or practices of others, then any charge about domination naturally leads to pointed questions about those actions or practices. Whose actions? With what results? How do these actions control others, and why is it illicit? Arguments about domination invariably come down to specifics. Domination is rooted in the particular.[87]

1.6 Why Not Domination?

Do people really have an interest in avoiding domination, thus conceived? Especially from an evolutionary standpoint, why not anticipate that politics will simply be about brute force in which the strongest prevail? Political theorists have sometimes puzzled over why this is not true more often than it is. For instance, in 1741 David Hume remarked that in politics there is no greater surprise than "the easiness with which the many are governed by the few." That the masses submit to their rulers amazed him in view of the stark reality that "force is always on the side of the governed." This puzzled Hume most with respect to popular governments, but he noted that even despots and tyrants must rely on "mamalukes" and "praetorian bands" to subdue their subject peoples. These henchmen could easily turn on their masters, yet most of the time they do not. Getting people to accept subservient political roles that they manifestly have the power to reject stood, he thought, in obvious need of an explanation.[88]

The standard answers, already alluded to in my discussion of rebellion, have to do with the perils of opposition. People must trust one another to take dangerous risks when they cannot know that others will do likewise. These collective action dilemmas compound the difficulties inherent in gauging the prospects for success. If institutions can be created to reduce these risks, it becomes more likely that people can hold their rulers to account. Indeed, such partisans of evolutionary thinking about politics as Nietzsche objected to democracy for exactly that reason. By solving the collective action problem, democratic institutions enable the weak to control the strong. For Nietzsche, this buttressed a "democratic idiosyncrasy" that fostered widespread hatred of rulers.[89]

This misarchy, as Nietzsche called it, shocked him all the more because it flew in the face of emerging orthodoxy about evolution. Three decades earlier Charles Darwin had set forth his theory of the survival of the fittest, yet at every turn Nietzsche saw the powerful abandoning their power—complicit in their emasculation by the masses. It looked to him as though Darwin had it backward as far as humans are concerned. The mediocre and the weak had subdued the excellent and the strong, and were replicating themselves into the future. It is not entirely clear whether Nietzsche believed that the pathetic mediocrities he thought human beings were becoming could ultimately endure, but he was convinced that they had achieved a perverse supremacy in his day.[90]

Hume's and Nietzsche's competing assessments partly reflected differing points of view, but consider how much of the political landscape that Hume took for granted had changed by the late 1880s when Nietzsche was writing. The French and American Revolutions had reordered assumptions about the relations between rulers and ruled. Revolutionary tides had again swept Europe in 1830 and in 1848, placing democracy unambiguously on the table for the long run. Even in Britain, where outright rebellion was avoided, Chartism had produced irresistible pressure to expand the franchise. Parliament's decision to increase the electorate by half in 1832 had seemed radical at the time,[91] yet they doubled it again in 1867 and then tripled in 1884–1885—giving a majority of adult males the vote for the first time and bringing Britain into line with much of Europe. In Nietzsche's own Germany, universal male franchise had been granted in the Reichstag in 1871—the same year that the Communards seized power in Paris. The few were having a lot more trouble governing the many than they had in David Hume's world.

This is not to say that the masses had triumphed as irreversibly as Nietzsche postulated. Like the French Revolution, the revolutions of 1830 and 1848 soon collapsed and monarchies were restored. When Nietzsche died in 1900, a truly universal franchise still remained a long way off—even in the most democratic countries. Nor did the growing political power of the masses successfully translate into social and economic advantage. Many besides Nietzsche had made apocalyptic predictions in this regard. Rather more soberly than Hume, Adam Smith had said in *The Wealth of Nations* that the rich are always surrounded by "unknown enemies" from whom they "can be protected only by the powerful arm of the civil magistrate."[92] Anxieties about what newly empowered masses might do worried even liberal figures like John Stuart Mill and Alexis de Tocqueville. But for the most part these fears were unfounded. One of the most enduring puzzles of modern political economy is that the poor have not done through the ballot box what they failed to achieve at the barricades. Democracies remain highly inegalitarian; indeed, expanding the franchise provides no guarantee that inequality will not increase with it.[93]

Still, Nietzsche had a point. The elites might not have lost control, yet in an important sense the battle had been joined. The twentieth century would bring major setbacks for democracy in the garbs of fascism and communism, but in the longer run it would survive them both. To be sure, democracy's progress has been neither linear nor guaranteed. Its prospects would have been bleak had the Axis powers prevailed in World War II.[94] Democracies failed across much of Africa, Asia, and Latin America in the 1950s and 1960s.[95] Democracy had a pretty good—if patchy—run after the 1970s, and especially after 1989.[96] But democracies can still fall apart, as has happened in countries as different as Algeria, Pakistan, Fiji, and Egypt and could well happen in Russia.[97] Some political theorists have even wondered how long the United States will continue to qualify as a democracy, given the corruption of its politics by money and the erosion of its civil liberties by the war on terror.[98] Today there are more democracies in the world than ever before, and the majority of the world's regimes qualify as democratic by standard definitions, yet most people are still governed by nondemocracies. New challenges have arisen from authoritarian populists and Eurasian despots governing in the name of democracy, not to mention resurgent fundamentalisms that a previous generation of political scientists had expected would disappear in the wake of modernization. But the fact that even religious theocracies like Iran claim the mantle of democracy, as did the "People's Republics" before them, underscores just how much political legitimation has become tied to democracy.[99] Historically contingent and fragile as democracies might often be, Nietzsche seems to have been right that it is the antidemocrats who are on the defensive.

Less plausible is Nietzsche's claim that democracy subverts evolutionary logic. Long before Nietzsche wrote, Hobbes had noted that "the weakest has strength enough to kill the strongest, either by secret machination or by confederacy with others that are in the same danger with himself."[100] Hobbes's reasoning here dovetails with the findings of modern social anthropologists, who trace the earliest democratic political practices not to any egalitarian impulse or instinct, nor to the resentment Nietzsche postulates, but rather to the inherent instability of any human individual's quest for dominance. Whereas apes instinctively create hierarchies in which the alpha rises to the top and subordinates arrange themselves according to their relative strength, humans differ because of their inventive, critical, and communicative capacities. Inventiveness led to the early creation of weapons, rendering alphas perpetually vulnerable to attack. As a result, human power hierarchies have always been potentially unstable, but critical, communicative, and organizational skills are needed to dislodge them. Critical abilities are required to imagine counterfactual possibilities, and communicative and organizational skills are needed to implement them.

Christopher Boehm, among others, has detailed what is known about how these dynamics played out in hunter-gatherer societies—which were often surprisingly hostile to domination. People seem to have converged on norms of resisting domination and enforced them through various strategies, the most important being the separation of functions between warriors and political leaders and slapping down upstarts through shunning, ostracism, physical punishment, and sometimes even execution. This seems to have resulted not from an affinity for egalitarian mores, but instead from the realization that if the chances of becoming and remaining dominant are low, then even those with a taste for dominance will realize that the next best thing is a political order in which no one can dominate. It is this that accounts for the creation of "upside-down hierarchies" in hunter-gatherer societies, through which ambitious individuals and self-aggrandizing warriors were kept in check. The inherent uncertainties of power meant that the best strategy was to form and maintain coalitions to resist domination.[101]

The evidence suggests that, while quite resilient, these upside-down hierarchies were also vulnerable. Outsiders could hijack them or they could fail for lack of ongoing tending. Power is alluring and its exercise often enjoyable, rendering the need to flex collective muscles and to discipline potential usurpers a continuing endeavor. If this vigilance flagged, power could solidify in the hands of an ambitious individual—at least for a while.[102] In any event, the transition to sedentary agriculture displaced the upside-down hierarchies characteristic of hunter-gatherer societies. This was partly because it led to more settled divisions of labor and accumulations of wealth that people would then want to protect and transmit to progeny. The same factors would render upside-down hierarchies vulnerable to divide-and-rule strategies and to the creation of subordinate hierarchies in which rewards would depend on maintaining an autocrat in power. This is to say nothing of the challenges of scale. Once small bands of hunter-gatherers were displaced by larger groups, the potential for collective action problems to undermine Boehm's upside-down hierarchies inevitably grew. As we have seen, large groups might not be able implement strategies to remove highly unpopular autocrats.

Yet the logic Boehm identifies has enduring significance. The notion that a world in which no one can dominate beats the going alternatives is a durable one that lies at the core of the institutional arrangements defended in this book. In the Western tradition it stands as the main alternative to Hobbes's answer: that the perpetual threat of domination by others makes it rational for everyone to submit to an absolute ruler. Hobbes's solution is less stable than he believed. Authoritarian systems cannot generate reliable information, because they lack both meaningful competition over ideas and deliberation that is not tainted by the imperative to kiss up. This makes them chronically vulnerable to imprudent decisions and poor at adaptation and renewal.[103] But the Hobbesian solution is in any case fatally flawed, as I argue in Chapter 4, because it fails to protect the people from the autocrat. Hobbes's myopic focus on the chaotic effects of anarchy led him to discount the challenges inherent in wielding power. Taking these into account, the attractiveness of an order in which no one can dominate becomes manifest. Nondomination becomes the dominant strategy, as does the search for mechanisms to sustain it.

Nondomination strategies will always have to compete with other logics, making resistance to domination a perpetual project. Institutions designed to prevent domination can be subverted, co-opted, or fail for other reasons. They also have the potential to become Maginot lines, partly because of our limited grasp of how they will operate in untested settings and partly because of human inventiveness. Constitutional separations of powers, ballot initiatives, limitations on regulating speech, protections for minorities, proportional representation, and grassroots control of political parties all exemplify these hazards, as we will see. Life often has more imagination than us, so that reifying any particular scheme as best is misguided.

Partisans of nondomination can be agnostic about who seeks to dominate, or why. Perhaps Machiavelli was right that only elites seek to dominate while others simply desire not to be dominated.[104] Alternatively, it might be, as Nietzsche insisted, that the many envy and despise the few, and seek for that reason to emasculate and subdue them.[105] On both these views different people are taken to be hardwired to have different personalities—"humors" as Machiavelli labeled them. Boehm's account of hunter-gatherers assumes that anyone might aspire to become dominant, whether from a deep psychological drive, opportunism, or the addictive enjoyment of power once tasted. Worrying about that last possibility motivated the American founders and informs the liberal fear of power captured in Acton's famous dictum: "Power tends to corrupt, and absolute power corrupts absolutely."[106] The antidomination ethic does not require us to choose among these views of human motivation.

1.7 Adapting against Domination

Adaptive and evolutionary arguments are sometimes linked to assumptions that better displaces worse over time; that we are progressing. To the extent that this is suggested by biological evolution, it rests on a misinterpretation. The conditions that favored organisms that have been "selected for" might change. Any life form can be destroyed by exogenous shocks or other contingencies, as were the dinosaurs. And any species that appears to us to be surviving might in fact be dying out; it might be in the process of being "selected against" but not wiped out yet.

The same is true of social and political arrangements. Perhaps they can improve, and perhaps our understanding of them will help us take a constructive hand in bringing about improvements. That possibility motivates this book. But it is always only a possibility. History is littered with the prognostications of people who wrongly predicted its course or heralded some imminent definitive ending.[107] We can never be sure that improvements will endure. The coalition that achieved a particular improvement might dissipate. More powerful groups whose leaders harbor different agendas might displace them. On some theories of politics all regimes decay.[108] That might not be universally true, and part of this adaptive political enterprise pursued here is to find ways to try to protect advances when they occur. But it is always possible that a once-viable regime will atrophy or fall casualty to an unexpected threat. History promises us nothing.

In the chapters that follow I develop the political implications of the view sketched here, both within countries and beyond their borders. In Chapters 2–4, I defend democratic institutions based on majority rule as best suited to combatting domination in national politics. I explain democracy's advantages over various republican, constitutionalist, and vanguardist alternatives, and I spell out its implications for pressing debates about representation and the control of political power. Then I turn to global politics. In Chapter 5 I argue that although nondomination is a cosmopolitan ideal, this does not support a commitment to world government. Even if we could replace the nation-state system with one consisting of unified global governance, this would be unlikely to combat the worst forms of domination that plague the current world system. The better course is to devise principles and strategies to combat the kinds of domination that are perpetrated across, or shielded by, national borders. Taking the abolition of the slave trade as an exemplary case study, I explore the elements of successful international campaigns to reduce domination, with an eye to the how these might inform the campaign for a global minimum wage. In Chapter 6 I turn to violent domination that either crosses borders or can be resisted only by transgressing them. I pay particular attention to the conditions under which humanitarian intervention and toppling oppressive regimes make sense from the standpoint of a nondomination ethic. In Chapter 7 I take stock and draw out some larger lessons for partisans of nondomination going forward.

CHAPTER TWO

POWER AND MAJORITY RULE

POLITICAL INSTITUTIONS ARE centrally concerned with power. This differentiates them from civil institutions, which, though invariably suffused by power dynamics, are ultimately geared to the pursuit of other goals. The challenge for partisans of nondomination in civil institutions is to domesticate the power dimensions of human interaction while minimizing interference with those other goals. Governments should stay out unless people's basic interests are at stake, and even when they are, it is best to seek the least intrusive available means to protect them.[1]

But political institutions are different because politics is about power through and through. The political regimes that emerge to manage it will either be public goods or public evils, depending on whether they prevent or foster domination. Democratic institutions are the best bet to push things in the public goods direction over time, but democracies come in various kinds and we will see that the differences matter. In Chapter 4 I argue for competitive democracy as superior to the main alternative that has been defended by proponents of nondomination: a divided-authority regime built on the separation-of-powers doctrine spelled out by the American founders, championed by republican theorists like Philip Pettit, and exemplified most fully in the contemporary world by the United States.[2] As a prelude to that, in this chapter and in Chapter 3 I make the underlying case for a democratic commitment, rooted in majority rule, against those who would limit democracy by appeal to contractual understandings of politics, constitutional constraints, and supermajoritarian requirements of various sorts.

2.1 Public versus Civil Institutions

Democracy is valuable, but it is not the only valuable thing. Nor is it the most important thing. It is, however, the most important political thing. By describing democracy as a foundational good I mean to call attention to that fact. We should be free to be liberals or conservatives; ascetics or hedonists; traditionalists, libertarians, or communitarians; conformists, heretics, agnostics, or atheists; but when push comes to shove, democracy should trump them all. A good part of my enterprise is aimed at finding ways to prevent push from coming to shove. But sometimes the clash is inescapable, and then democracy should win. That is the view I mean to render plausible and attractive here.

In *Democratic Justice* I dealt with the tensions between democracy and other goods by defending democracy as a subordinate or conditioning good. In my view, Foucault was right to claim that power permeates all collective human activities, but that does not mean that those activities can be reduced to the power relations that suffuse them.[3] Moreover, exercising power is vital to the pursuit of many human goods, and it does not always result in domination. Even when domination does occur, it can be more or less serious. The challenge is to democratize the power dimensions of human interaction while fettering the rest as little as possible, and to do it in ways that forestall the worst forms of domination. Those who care most about an activity and understand it from the inside—those with insiders' wisdom, as I dubbed it in section 1.5—are usually best placed to think creatively about the relevant trade-offs. It makes sense to defer to them unless the risk of domination becomes too great.

My earlier account focused on civil institutions. I characterized them as organized to pursue goods other than the power relations that suffuse them. Power is wielded in classrooms, families, and firms, but deploying power in such settings is not the object of the exercise. The superordinate good, as I called it—enlightening students, nurturing children, or creating goods and services—is the object. Democratic control is best geared to structuring the power dimensions of civil institutions by giving those with basic interests at stake a say in their governance, and by institutionalizing forums for opposition within them. What shape these arrangements should take varies with the good in question and is best left to insiders as much as possible. Beyond ensuring that people's basic interests can be vindicated, instruments of democratic control should remain—from the point of view of outsiders—in a subordinate role. If insiders want to beef them up for their own reasons, that should be up to them. This means that there is no one-size-fits-all decision rule for governing civil institutions. Modes of governance should be contextually designed and redesigned, with a strong presumption of deference to insiders.

Public institutions differ because there is no superordinate good. Power goes all the way to the top. In families, classrooms, and firms there is often disagreement about how to raise children and educate them, or about how best to produce goods and services. But debates about the activity in question are tied to the existence of a superordinate good; it gives disagreements their focus and point. This is the element of truth in Aristotle's otherwise overblown claim that human beings do not deliberate about ends, only about the means of achieving them.[4] Politics differs in that it is concerned in the last instance, as well as in the first, with managing power relations. People often think the state should have additional objectives: to promote equality, to produce virtuous citizens or national glory, to convert the infidels; the list is long. But politics is controversial in a deeper sense than are arguments about goods in civil institutions, because no conception of political purpose emanates from the nature of the beast, and some people—including political philosophers at least from Thomas Hobbes to Robert Nozick—reject all superordinate conceptions of politics. What makes government unavoidable and supplies its raison d'être is the need to manage power relations. Political theorists often link this reality to the additional claim that the power to coerce is, as Nozick put it, a natural monopoly—identifying government as its inevitable repository, as Max Weber did when he defined the state by reference to the capacity to monopolize legitimate coercive force in a given territory.[5]

Even if there is no overarching political good, is there insiders' wisdom in politics? Is there political expertise? Some political philosophers, most famously Plato, have embraced the notion that there are people whose wisdom qualifies them to rule—but this is rare. Even in Plato's case, the quality that marked someone as suitable was unrelated to expertise as such. It was the love of truth he attributed to philosophers which he believed would make them reluctant rulers and therefore uniquely immune to the corrosive effects of office.[6] Whether philosophers are less corruptible than others is debatable, but most invocations of political expertise differ from Plato's by appealing to the vanguardist assumption that there are right political answers that are knowable to a political elect. This is the view I resisted in sections 1.3 and 1.4. The fallibilism I defended there militates against any suggestion that there is political insiders' wisdom that merits deference from the rest of us, and it gives us good reasons to be wary of anyone who claims access to esoteric political knowledge. Even when technical knowledge is relevant to politics, that knowledge will not generate impartial solutions to political conflicts. Different decisions benefit and harm different groups differently, and there may be no commanding answer to the question who should prevail, or by how much. Those realities of politics will not go away.

This is not to deny the relevance of claims to expertise or knowledge of truth in democratic politics, but they should occupy a distinctive place in public institutions. In civil institutions, deference is owed to insiders about the nature of the superordinate good in question and how best to pursue it. In public institutions, by contrast, claims to knowledge and expertise should always be subordinate to democratic control. I will have more to say in section 4.2.3 about what this means for the relations between elected officials and scholars, lobbyists, generals, activists, policy experts, and others who seek standing to influence political outcomes. The general point is that we should devise ways to take advantage of their expertise while subordinating them to democratic control. We call on expert testimony from psychiatrists in legal proceedings to determine whether someone meets the criteria for an insanity defense to a criminal charge, but we do not cede them the authority to decide the question. That remains the province of the jury after hearing experts testify on both sides of the question. Those with claims to expertise inform a lay decision, but it remains a lay decision. That is a suggestive model, I will argue, for the appropriate place of expertise in democratic political institutions. First we must attend to the institutions themselves.

2.2 The Majoritarian Presumption

Political orders are either public goods or public evils.[7] They are public in that no one within a state's purview can be excluded from the order that it creates, if it creates an order at all. Whether that order is good or evil depends on how people experience it. Nozick noted long ago that for coercive force to be exercised as a public good, it must be supplied as a monopoly.[8] But he was acutely aware that some people might be unconvinced of the benefits of the prevailing order—preferring to take their chances without it. "Nonrivalrous consumption," as economists call it, would feel to them more like force-feeding: unilateral interference with their freedom. Whatever their motives, such "independents" would experience the prevailing political order as a public evil. For them, the state would be no better than institutionalized pollution. Nozick did backflips to describe conditions under which the independents' objections might fairly be ignored, so that a state, provided its functions remain minimal, can be construed as a public good rather than a public evil. The backflips failed, but the reasons why are instructive: they open the way to seeing why majority rule is the font of legitimate politics.

Nozick's defense of his minimal state turned on the potential threat posed by those who refuse to acknowledge the state's legitimacy. Perhaps they are whimsical anarchists who just want to mind their own business, but people have to live with the possibility that they are not. This might seem like the worst sort of contrived philosopher's example, but the 1995 Oklahoma City bombing and the 9/11 terrorist attacks six years later make it clear that Nozick had put his finger on something real. He was right to insist that no polity will likely tolerate for very long the danger posed by such independents. It might not be worth a government's resources to pursue harmless anarchists living in withdrawing communities, or to track down people whom they have no reason to fear in distant lands, but anyone who poses a genuine threat will forcibly be incorporated or otherwise rendered harmless. The philosophical burden Nozick had to shoulder was to identify the conditions under which this could be defensible. Because, for Nozick, the consent of every affected individual is the sole basis for political legitimacy, he had to show that the forcible incorporation of independents did not violate that consent. A tall order.

Nozick tried to square his circle by combining a claim about necessity with an argument about compensation. He conjectured that if the society could in principle compensate the independents for violating their rights (by forcing them to join it), without the cost of the compensation making society's members worse off than had they left the independents alone and continued living in fear of a possible attack, then the forcible incorporation could be deemed legitimate. No compensation would be actually paid; the fact that it could be paid, he thought, was sufficient.[9] This might sound disconcertingly like utilitarian cost-benefit analysis for a card-carrying Kantian like Nozick, but he was a Kantian who believed not only that individual freedom is a good—indeed he thought it the only good—but one who also embraced the Kantian dictum that ought entails can; hence his appeal to necessity. Power will inevitably be exercised as a monopoly on his account. This importantly renders moot the mirror-image question whether the independents might in principle be able to remain independent, compensate society's members for their fears, and still be better off. Given that they are bound to be incorporated willy-nilly, his question was: What could make this legitimate? He turned to the welfare economics literature on compensation for an answer.

The inevitability argument is a good one. That is why Nozick's conjecture is a useful point of departure for us. But it is fatally flawed as a defense of the minimal state and as a unique solution to the problem of legitimacy as Nozick construed it. For one thing, if it proves anything then it proves too much. One could easily deploy his logic to say that if most people were afraid of losing their jobs and insisted on an unemployment insurance scheme financed by a universal tax, this would be legitimate so long as they could in principle compensate those who opposed it yet still be better off than they would living in fear of destitution. So much for the idea of the minimal state as a unique solution: fear plus hypothetical compensation can easily be deployed to scale up the state to something more extensive.

Apart from failing as a unique solution, the minimal state is not, in any case, a solution. Critics have noted that it fails to serve Nozick's purpose because the welfare economists to whom he appealed were unable to avoid paternalistic judgments in defending their accounts of compensation. Some metric is needed along which to compare the relative gains and losses, a metric that the independents would surely abjure. We often see this in disputes over eminent domain when a recalcitrant property owner values her home differently from its assessed or market value—and that is when compensation is actually paid.[10] If we think of independents as preferring to die rather than succumb, as some of the most frightening terrorists do, then it is plain that the amount of compensation that would have to be paid them is infinite—rubbishing Nozick's conjecture. So much for his claim that the minimal state meets his standards for legitimacy.[11]

Nozick's argument is really a reductio ad absurdum that defeats his own account of political legitimacy. Establishing that coercive force is a natural monopoly undermines the social contract metaphor he deploys because it underscores the reality that collective life without government is impossible. This, in turn, reveals why it was misleading for Nozick to declare the fundamental question of political theory to be "whether or not there should be any state at all."[12] That is about as illuminating as declaring the fundamental question of dental theory to be whether or not people should have any teeth at all. It obscures exactly what we should focus on: that the basic question is not "Whether government?" but "What sort?" That is the right place to start thinking about legitimacy.

Nozick's formulation directs attention away from a vital reality: that governments came along before efforts to render them accountable. Indeed, demands for accountability were prompted not by musing about the conditions under which people would agree to collective arrangements *de novo*, but rather by the presence of unaccountable power. People did not worry about domesticating the commanding heights of the state until there were commanding heights that stood in need of domestication. Modern nation-states are the progeny of wars and the centralizing agendas of absolutist monarchs and nationalist politicians. Whatever the ostensible motivations of those who created them, the fact that anything less than a power monopoly will be unstable surely supplied energy to their enterprises.

John Locke was one of the first to see why these facts about power give impetus to a default commitment to majority rule.[13] In chapter 8 of the *Second Treatise,* he contended that for a political community to act as a single body, it must be subservient to the will of the majority. At first blush Locke seems just to be talking about brute force, in ways that are not obviously compatible with the standard picture of him as a social contract theorist committed to individual consent. Locke insists that if a community is to have the "power to act as one body," it must be governed "by the will and determination of the majority." The reason is that "it is necessary the body should move that way whither the greater force carries it, which is the consent of the majority." Otherwise "it is impossible it should act or continue one body, one community." Yet in the same paragraph Locke also contends that a default presumption in favor of majority rule embodies "the consent of every individual" whose actions have "made that community one body." Moreover, he insists that "the act of the majority" embodies "the law of nature and reason."[14]

Locke's argument here is partly bound up with his knotty discussion of the differences between tacit and express consent that I take up in section 2.3 below. We can set them aside for now by assuming that he is discussing people for whom leaving the polity is not a relevant option. Either they want to stay, or leaving is prohibited or prohibitively costly. Such people, Locke insists, are "under an obligation, to every one of that society, to submit to the determination of the majority, and to be concluded by it." Resisting the will of the majority would be tantamount to declaring the social compact null and void. "For what appearance would there be of any compact? What new engagement if he were no farther tied by any decrees of the society, than he himself thought fit, and did actually consent to?" Someone who resists a majority decision whenever he "thinks fit" in effect insists that he remains "free, and under no other ties than he was in before in the state of nature."[15]

These comments might seem to conflict with Locke's defense of the right to resist that I discussed in section 1.4, but that conclusion conflates the right to revolution with a putative right to resist particular government decisions. Locke is unequivocal that the right to resist is indefeasible, but that is a right to overthrow the government, not a right to engage in selective compliance with its decisions. Indeed, it is because the costs and risks of revolution are so great that Locke admonishes people not to try it "upon every little mismanagement of public affairs," but only in the face of enduring and serious abuse by government of its fiduciary authority.[16] Short of deciding to overthrow the regime, people are bound to accept "the consent of the majority" as "the act of the whole." In politics this is embodied in the supremacy of the legislature, which can delegate power to an executive and "federative" power (responsible for foreign affairs). But these agents always remain subordinate to the legislature, ensuring that "the community perpetually retains a supreme power of saving themselves from any body" who might "carry on designs against the liberties and properties of the subject."[17]

We are obliged to obey the majority even though everyone's consent is "next to impossible ever to be had," given the variety of "opinions, and contrariety of interests, which unavoidably happen in all collections of men." People who continue to get the benefits of society must live within the confines of majority rule. Otherwise no government could function. The life of even "a mighty Leviathan" would be "of a shorter duration, than the feeblest creatures, and not let it outlast the day it was born in."[18] It is this public goods rationale that led Locke to deploy the idioms of reason and obligation as well as that of power here: people are obliged to obey because of the continuing benefits they receive; if they were not thus obligated, there would be no possibility of "any lawful government in the world."[19] In short, majority rule prevents politics from descending into civil war.

But not always. Abraham Lincoln would expose the unforgiving bedrock of majoritarian politics when the Southern states began seceding in response to the Republican victory in the 1860 election in the United States. No doubt the fact that Lincoln won with less than 40 percent of the popular vote (the lowest percentage since 1824) fed his opponents' perceptions of his lack of legitimacy.[20] A strict majority is always better than a plurality, but not due to any magical link between majorities and what Jean-Jacques Rousseau would later describe as the "general will."[21] On the Lockean view, elections are, as Adam Przeworski says, about "flexing muscles"; they are a "reading of the chances in the eventual war."[22] Lincoln's confidence about those chances might have been bolstered because his opponents were divided among themselves and perhaps by a judgment that disenfranchised Southern populations would take his side if push came to shove as it eventually did. Someone had to win, and Lincoln's claim was in any case the strongest.

On the merits, things would have been more complex for Lincoln had abolition of Southern slavery been at issue from the start, but that became a war aim only later.[23] What split the Union was the Southern rejection

of the platform on which Lincoln had prevailed: that slavery would not
be extended to the new territories. As James Read has noted, allowing the
Southern states to go in peace was therefore scarcely an option—either in
Lincoln's mind or in reality.[24] Had they seceded in order to preempt the
exclusion of slavery from the western territories, the Southern states
would not, as a new nation, peacefully have abandoned its claims to those
territories. As John Quincy Adams had predicted four decades earlier, "A
dissolution of the Union for the cause of slavery would be followed by a
servile war in the slave-holding States, combined with a war between the
two severed portions of the Union."[25] The latter conflict would be a war
rather than a civil war, with its center of gravity shifted west, but Lincoln
was clear that it would nonetheless be a case of a minority resorting to
force to achieve what it had lost at the ballot box. He was quick to note
that if minorities could secede in such circumstances, it would make government infeasible, "for a minority of their own will secede from them,
whenever a majority refuses to be controlled by such a minority."[26] As
Read notes, this logic of iterated dissolution played itself out in Yugoslavia in the 1990s, prompting the famous bleak joke: "Why should I be
a minority in your country, when you can be a minority in mine?"[27]

But why is the default presumption majority rule? Why is it, in Locke's
words, that "barely by agreeing to unite into one political society," people
must be understood to have given up "all the power, necessary to the ends
for which they unite into society, to the majority of the community, unless
they expressly agreed in any number greater than the majority?"[28] As my
earlier discussion of Nozick revealed, contemporary thinkers who deploy
Locke's approach typically differ from him by starting with unanimity as
the default presumption. James Buchanan and Gordon Tullock provide
another illuminating example. Larger groups take longer to agree than
smaller ones, they note, and people reasonably want to minimize not only
the risk of having to live with an adverse decision but also the time they
have to spend forestalling that possibility. The moral they draw from
Oscar Wilde's worry that democracy takes up too many evenings is that
the number of people needed for a decision should vary with its importance to them.[29] This makes it rational to embrace a hierarchy of decision
rules starting with unanimity for the most important matters, and then
descending to supermajorities, majority rule, and perhaps even fewer, as
outcomes diminish in importance and the demands on people's time loom
correspondingly larger.[30]

Locke was also worried about the obstacles to reaching agreement in
heterogeneous populations, as we have just seen. But the reason he endorsed a different benchmark presumption was, ironically, that he saw the
limitations of the contractarian metaphor more clearly than did Buchanan

and Tullock or Nozick. Locke believed that humans have inalienable natural rights, to be sure, but he would have had no time for the libertarian conceit that a minimal state compromises those rights less than the going alternatives. Any set of laws, including one that protects the rights libertarians cherish, is a collective action regime imposed on those who would prefer alternatives. Those who dispute this conflate the impossible notion of unanimity qua state of affairs in the world in which everyone actually agrees with unanimity qua decision rule—which is really rule by a dissenting minority of one. Whether unanimity rule is attractive depends on how well disposed one is toward the inherited system of prevailing laws. Lincoln made the same point more sharply in his first inaugural. "Unanimity is impossible; the rule by a minority, as a permanent arrangement, is wholly inadmissible; so that, rejecting the majority principle, anarchy, or despotism in some form, is all that is left."[31]

Brian Barry and Douglas Rae, among others, have noted—*pace* Buchanan and Tullock—that if we assume uncertainty about our future preferences, there is no good reason to bias things in favor of the status quo. If we are as likely to be against the status quo as to favor it, then the logical default decision rule is majority rule or something very close to it.[32] Any number of things, ranging from changed political circumstances to demographic or environmental developments, to evolving technologies of destruction, might lead to what Rae has called "utility drift" in our attitude toward the status quo—whereby outcomes that once were welfare improving no longer are.[33] In *Political Bubbles,* Nolan McCarthy, Keith Poole, and Howard Rosenthal illustrate how the institutional bias toward the status quo makes the U.S. political system insufficiently nimble to achieve effective financial regulation either to ward off financial crises or to respond to them.[34] Locke understood the deleterious features of a bias toward the status quo implicitly. This is why his defense of majority rule went beyond observations about the "greater force." He insisted that reason, no less than power, requires everyone to embrace an obligation to obey the will of the majority.[35] To be sure, he thought different institutional arrangements made sense in different circumstances—including the British monarchy of his own day. But in the final analysis they were all subordinate to majority rule.

2.3 Constitutional Constraints

Many people have dismissed as too minimal the idea that majority rule is enough to render political orders public goods rather than public evils.

At least since Plato's vivid depiction of the gullible masses being easily manipulated by unscrupulous usurpers, it has been standard to argue that constraints are needed to limit the excesses of "pure democracy"—Madison's phrase in *Federalist* #10.[36] In the grip of this fear, commentators often call for constitutional constraints to tame democracy's "wild instincts," as Tocqueville labeled them.[37] Constitutionalists like to describe this as "the countermajoritarian problem," arguing for constraints on majority rule to protect minority rights. This constraining view of the purpose and import of constitutions has proved hardy. Written constitutions and accompanying bills of rights, with independent courts charged to enforce them, are near-universal features of the new democracies that have swept the world since the 1970s. Even in older democracies like Britain, the power of courts to constrain Parliament in the name of constitutional mandates has grown dramatically since the 1980s.[38]

If constitutions constrain majority rule, questions must arise about where they get their legitimacy. At different times natural law, higher law, tradition, the rule of law, or some religious or quasi-religious imperative has been invoked, but as Robert Dahl pointed out long ago and Jeremy Waldron has since reiterated, any such appeal in turn requires a procedure of some sort to determine the constitutional charter's content and to settle disagreements about its meaning.[39] So it is not surprising that constitutions are often said to be the progeny of some founding event—a convention, a referendum, or some other consecrating covenant—even if it has since been "lost in the mists of time."[40] The obvious chicken-and-egg challenge to such legitimation is typically avoided by invoking unanimity at the moment of creation.

But unanimity is as misleading in thinking about founding moments as when it is invoked in ongoing politics; it is either a deceptive metaphor or a flat-out lie. When Buchanan and Tullock describe their imaginary constitutional convention as "roughly similar to the United States of 1787," or Rawls describes his original position as "suggested by the United States constitution and its history," they ignore that history.[41] The Constitution was never endorsed unanimously; it was rammed through in violation of the Articles of Confederation.[42] And when they, Rawls, Nozick, and others plump for original-agreement metaphors, their make-believe preconstitutional benchmarks obscure the reality that unanimity rule is really minority tyranny. Perhaps the state sovereignty codified in the Articles of Confederation should have trumped the Constitution as secessionists in the Southern states began arguing after the 1860 election, or perhaps—as President Lincoln insisted—the Declaration of Independence trumped both.[43] Then again, Native Americans have plenty to say about what should have trumped the Declaration of Independence. What trumps the Native Americans? In the Middle East, Palestinians and Jews play this game from 1973 to 1967, to 1948, all the way back to the Hebrew bible. The truth is that it's turtles all the way down. Unanimity rule sounds consensual, but it is really the veto power of a single dissenter at some arbitrary point in time.[44]

Even if a constitution could be traced to an unambiguous authorizing event, why should its writ continue running into the future? There has never been a meeting of the minds among people living today and those who converged on the Unites States Constitution. Some, famously Antonin Scalia in the United States, are unperturbed by this, insisting that we are bound not only by the Constitution but also by the Constitution as its framers understood it. So he has no truck, for instance, with those who object to the death penalty as cruel and unusual punishment today because it was not thought to be such when that proscription was adopted as part of the Eighth Amendment in 1791.[45] Unless we can muster the two-thirds majorities in Congress and three-quarters of the states to change it, we are just stuck. Few go all the way with Scalia.[46] Most who want to grant the framers continuing authority over us say that we should reinterpret their views in light of changing circumstances, or that we should reconstruct what they would think in our contemporary circumstances.[47] Views of that kind require the designated updaters (typically judges sitting on constitutional courts) to engage in inherently contestable exercises of imaginative reconstruction informed by their take on how the relevant circumstances have changed. Scalia plausibly observes that no one has the tools or the expertise to do that. Judges who try are easily lambasted as self-appointed aristocrats who cherry-pick arguments and public opinion data to suit their own predilections. Scalia's view exhibits a certain obdurate consistency, but it leaves unexplained why anyone should be bound by constitutions that were adopted hundreds of years ago.[48]

One standard move to square this circle is to invoke a variant of Locke's account of tacit consent, the notion that anyone who has "possessions, or enjoyment of any part of the dominions of any government," is thereby obliged to obey "the laws of that government" unless they choose to leave.[49] In fairness to Locke, he contrasted this with express consent on the grounds that only the latter is irrevocable—a radically permissive view for his day.[50] As late as the War of 1812, the British government was still insisting that Americans born on British soil were the king's subjects and could be seized from American merchant ships and impressed into the Royal Navy.[51] Locke would have denied the British government that

authority on the grounds that those Americans had never expressly consented to be subjects of the Crown. But Locke's account of tacit consent
is nonetheless vulnerable to the objection that it is captive to the availability of an option to leave.[52] In reality, the costs of leaving will typically
be insuperably high for many, if not most, people. This makes the possibility of withholding tacit consent available only to the unusually rich or
to those for whom the status quo is so intolerable that they are willing to
pay dearly to escape—as with German Jews in the 1930s who abandoned
vast assets to the Nazi regime in order to secure exit visas to Palestine.[53]
This undermines tacit consent as a basis for constitutional legitimacy. As
Nozick quipped: "It isn't worth the paper it's not written on."[54]

That is a good line, even if it is directed at a straw opponent. Locke's
main concern, after all, was with the conditions under which consent can
be withdrawn. He viewed living in a community as entailing mutual obligations because everyone derives benefits from its existence. My giving
up the freedom to enforce my rights has value only if I can assume that
everyone else does likewise. But it is more than a reliance argument,
because there has also been what lawyers call mutual consideration.
Everyone gets something of value from the conduct of others: the higher
quality of life that results when physical security can be taken for granted
and the productivity gains of enclosure that all are presumed to enjoy.
This is why anyone "that hath any possessions, or enjoyment of any part
of the dominions of any government, doth thereby give his tacit consent,
during such enjoyment, as any one under it."[55] It also explains why people
cannot take selective advantage of the system: either they must accept the
rules, which means subordinating themselves to majority rule, or they
must pay the costs of trying to change the system if they are unwilling or
unable to leave.[56]

Constitutionalists like Bruce Ackerman inject a democratic additive
into the project of constitutional authorization, claiming that we are
bound by inherited constitutional mandates only until a new "constitutional moment" comes along to sweep fundamental change through all the
branches of government and replace the inherited order with something
else. On Ackerman's "dualist" theory of democracy, constitutional moments set the terms of the "normal politics" that prevail the rest of the
time.[57] Contemplating why those who dislike the dead hand of the past
should have to rely on the possibility of the fortuitous tsunami of a favorable constitutional moment is reminiscent of Locke's admonitions
concerning long trains of abuses, discussed in section 1.4. But warning
people of the risks of rebellion if they are disinclined to wait for vindica-
tion in the next life is one thing; establishing the legitimacy of political

institutions is another. If a constitution's legitimacy is rooted in the authorizing consent of the governed, it is hard to see why the burden should ever shift to the disaffected or those who have withheld their consent. Shouldn't the shoe be on the other foot?

Thomas Jefferson posed that question in a letter to Madison in 1789, answering it with a decisive yes. Insisting that "the earth always belongs to the living generation" and that "the dead have neither powers nor rights over it," Jefferson argued that no one is free—individually or collectively—to bind future generations. Jefferson was in the first instance concerned with public debts, which he thought should not be contracted for more than nineteen years—the duration of a living adult majority as he calculated it based on the actuarial tables of his day. But Jefferson extended his logic to all other legislation, including constitutions, which he thought should sunset every generation. The right of repeal was not enough. The power of incumbents to protect the status quo, when combined with the collective action problems associated with undoing it, "prove to every practical man that a law of limited duration is much more manageable than one which needs repeal."[58]

Jefferson's view does not exactly ooze with practicality either. Personal interests that lead politicians to stray from what he described as "the general interests of their constituents" and the "other impediments" to collective action would surely hamper the reauthorization of legislation, not to mention constitutional arrangements, every nineteen years as readily as they would permit stonewalling attempts at repeal. It is in any case unclear why, on Jefferson's reasoning, majorities should be free to bind others irrevocably even for the lifetime of the average adult. It is one thing to disallow reneging on individual contracts on a whim—the parties received gains from counterparties who depended, in turn, on the agreement.[59] But the composition of majorities in politics is endlessly changing. We can agree with Jefferson and Locke that the majority should be taken as authoritative for the community, yet still recognize that it does not express anything like a social welfare function or Rousseau's general will. This means that there is no reason to make a fetish of any particular majority's endurance.

The case for majority rule is that it minimizes the chances of domination when compared to the going alternatives, but this in no way precludes a majority from undoing what a different majority has done—whether in the recent or distant past. Indeed, the possibility that new majorities might upset the status quo is part of what contributes to democratic stability, as is discussed more fully in section 3.1. Note, for now, that if we take the backward-looking search for "the right" authorizing moment for collective action as seriously as Jefferson thought we should, it is hard to see where to stop. Why not go even further than the Leveller and Anti-Federalist demands for annual elections? James Burgh declared: "Where annual elections end, slavery begins." But maybe it begins after a month, a week, or even a day or an hour . . . Perhaps we should embrace and extend the Progressive penchant for recall elections as well, or postulate that anyone can demand a new constitutional convention at will.[60] The more we search for unassailable defining moments of historical authorization, the more the whole enterprise calls to mind Amartya Sen's line about hunting in a dark room for a nonexistent black cat.[61]

CHAPTER THREE

THE STAKES OF POLITICAL CONFLICT

OUR CONCERN WITH where we come from should be tempered, as Paul Gauguin might have said, by attention to where we are and where we hope to go.[1] Why would it be otherwise? It is an odd feature of much constitutional theorizing that unless past enactments are pronounced fully controlling or utterly irrelevant, many commentators feel the need to construct elaborate theoretical barricades around some intermediate point of view. But it is the wrong preoccupation. Stephen Sedley reminds us that there is nothing perplexing about the notion that Magna Carta, while still seminal, lacks the significance it held in 1215.[2] A good part of the reason, I think, is that the legitimacy of any political order depends on the problems it solves, and promises to solve, for people who are subject to it—far more than on when, how, and by whom it was created. This does not render authorization moot; far from it. But the politics of authorization depends much more on what the regime delivers for those who live under it than on its history. When millions of Egyptians took to the streets in July 2013 to force Mohammed Morsi from power, it was not because they no longer thought he had been legitimately elected a year earlier. Rather, he had failed to supply them the basis for a viable existence. With unemployment, poverty, and food insecurity all accelerating as tourism, infrastructure, and even basic electrical power were all falling apart, the millions who took to the streets—many of the most vulnerable of whom did not qualify for government-funded ration cards—were demanding new elections to get a government that would address their desperate plight.[3]

The central challenges for thinking about democracy's institutional architecture flow from its raison d'être to combat domination. Hobbes was right up to a point in arguing that people's allegiance to a political order depends on its capacity to protect them from one another.[4] But the flip side of this myopic focus was his blindness to the need also to protect them from agents of the state. As Madison said, "You must first enable the government to control the governed; and in the next place oblige it to control itself."[5] The institutional capacities of government are vital to minimizing the prospects for domination in any society, but we have to take seriously the possibility Hobbes ignored: that they can themselves atrophy into systems of domination. Some form of democratic control of the state has long been understood as an essential component for minimizing that possibility. But at least since the American Revolution, even democracy's advocates have worried that there is no guarantee that democracies will not themselves become instruments of domination.

Madison had two different fears about democracy. One was the standard worry about majority tyranny mentioned in section 2.3. The other fear, just noted, concerns tyranny by the government itself. Madison and his contemporaries sometimes conflated the two threats because they were convinced that the legislature would be the most dangerous branch of government. Even if it remained faithful to its representative obligations, it would still push majority interests. And if it got out of control, its representatives would abuse the legitimacy they derived from being closer than other officials to "the people" to usurp authority and morph into a tyrannous state. Hemming in the legislature could thus limit the powers of the most dangerous officials, who were, in any case, agents of the most dangerous societal interests. Understandable as this conflation might have been in Madison's mind, we should not embrace it. The reasons to worry about institutional encroachment differ from those motivating fear of majority tyranny, and the remedies do not, in any case, overlap. Accordingly, I defer attention to the dangers of government domination to Chapter 4 and focus here on the first responsibility Madison mentions—control of the governed. But I describe it in the more pointed Hobbesian way as a responsibility to prevent people from controlling one another.

Thanks to Tocqueville and Mill this is usually construed as the problem of majority tyranny, though, as the line of thinking from Locke to Lincoln, Barry, Rae, and Read explored in section 2.2 reminds us, vigilance against minority tyranny is no less consequential. My point of departure is Madison's claim that if factions are inevitable, it is best to have lots of them. This produces crosscutting divisions or cleavages of interest, he thought, reducing the odds that political competition will foster domination. Madison's motivating intuition was sound and he was on the right track, but I argue in section 3.1 that he conflated the role of crosscutting cleavages with that of divisible goods—goods that can be can be divided and distributed in many different ways. Crosscutting cleavages do their best benign work when divisible goods underpin them. This is not to say that indivisible goods—typically those rooted in religion, race, and ethnic identities—should be banished from politics by constitutional fiat. Nothing should be banished by constitutional fiat. It does mean, however, that it is best to avoid reifying indivisible goods by catering to them in politics, just as it is wise to avoid deferring to intense preferences. There are good reasons why democracies count how many people want something rather than how much they want it. Institutional designers who ignore those reasons will likely construct self-defeating political arrangements from the standpoint of nondomination, as I argue in section 3.2. Theorists like Arend Lijphart illustrate this failing by pushing for consociational arrangements that defer to intense preferences but have the effect of entrenching them. Defending these claims sets the stage for my discussion of institutional rules and electoral arrangements in Chapter 4.

3.1 Factions and Majority Tyranny

Madison's antipathy for the "dangerous vice" of popular government boils down to the anxiety that factions militate against the common good. Whether they represent minorities or majorities, factions are "united and actuated by some common impulse of passion" that sets them at odds with both other citizens and the "permanent and aggregate interests of the community."[6] But eliminating factions would involve either unacceptable levels of coercion or a degree of conformism that would itself be subversive of good government. "Liberty is to faction," he said, "what air is to fire."[7] Accordingly, the only viable option is to recognize the causes of factions as "sown in the nature of man" and devise ways to mitigate and manage their effects. His intuitions about how to do this provide a useful point of departure.

3.1.1 Using Factions

Factions would not develop in a homogeneous population whose members had the same interests, beliefs, and values. Madison mentions this possibility only to dismiss it, but it merits our attention as a benchmark. The Athenian model of democracy that he rejected took for granted a basic identity of interests among the citizenry, even if this was achieved by excluding women and slaves—along with barbarians—from consideration. Even so, it was an idealized image from Madison's point of view. He believed that disagreement over religion, politics, and "many other points" is endemic to the human condition, making "mutual animosity" ineradicable, and he thought conflicts of material interest inescapable. Those owning and lacking property have "distinct" interests, as do creditors and debtors, landowners and manufacturers, mercantile and moneyed interests, not to mention the numerous lesser allegiances that divide people "into different classes, actuated by different sentiments and views." Madison's account parallels my discussion of enduring conflicts of interest in section 1.1; and his impulse to domesticate and take advantage of them by lowering the stakes of political conflict, in order to reduce the likelihood of loser-lose-all politics, mirrors my agenda set out in section 1.4. "The regulation of these various and interfering interests forms the principal task of modern legislation," he says. It involves bringing "the spirit of party and faction" into "the necessary and ordinary operations of the government."[8]

How can this be done? What will cause the spirit of party and faction to sustain democratic politics when the "zeal for different opinions concerning religion, concerning government, and many other points" leads to "mutual animosity" that disposes people "to vex and oppress each other" rather than "co-operate for their common good"? Madison thought oppression most likely when one major cleavage divides the population, or, what amounts to the same thing, when cleavages of race, class, language, religion, and other salient differences follow the same fault lines so that they become mutually reinforcing. Then members of the majority know they will always win and those in the minority know they will lose—a recipe for tyranny because those in the majority have no reason to pull their punches. The risk can be mitigated by expansion. "Extend the sphere," says Madison, "and you take in a greater variety of parties and interests." This reduces the odds that a majority "will have a common motive to invade the rights of other citizens." Even if they want to, they will find it harder "to discover their own strength, and to act in unison with each other." In contrast to the classical ideal of democratic republics as small and homogeneous, Madison ties the prospects for viable democracy to large, diverse societies.[9]

Twentieth-century pluralists built on this Madisonian insight to develop the theory that democracy thrives on institutionalized instability. They saw that it is not just those in the majority who will be less inclined to be tyrannical when future alliances are unpredictable; minorities will also discern constructive democratic incentives. Indeed, as critics of majority rule since Kenneth Arrow have noted, there are many potential majorities—and hence many potential minorities—in any even modestly pluralistic population. Viewed from this vantage point, just who is a majority and who a minority is an artifact of the issues that are pitted against one another at any given time. Arrow's followers saw this as an indictment of majority rule for failing to deliver a "rational" ordering of society's preferences; it reveals no general will.[10] But that complaint reflects extravagant expectations about the properties of collective decisions that we have no reason to endorse. The case for majority rule that I traced back to Locke in section 2.2 in no way depends on the existence of a general will. The vital point is that those who lose in a given contest need not be alienated by the prospect of continued participation and tempted either to abandon politics or to reach for their guns, whether as criminals or as revolutionaries. As with the open-ended iterated prisoner's dilemmas discussed in section 1.4, there's always next year.

3.1.2 The Politics of Divisible Goods

The ultimate sources of political attachments are hard to fathom, but we know that their form and intensity are shaped by how they are mobilized. Every schoolyard bully knows that demonizing people as misfits or outsiders can generate support from others who fear similar ostracism; that it can bind people together with a sense shared purpose—however malevolent. And most successful activists and politicians know in their bones that William Golding was not just writing about children in *Lord of the Flies*. Having a convenient Piggy to pillory can be a sure path to power, especially if this is tied to protecting the community from insidiously threatening beasts. Not everyone succumbs to this McCarthyist temptation, but few are likely to be effective in politics without being vigilant about the possibility that their adversaries might do so. People often indulge in milder versions of demonization—white working-class voters "cling to guns or religion"; 47 percent of American voters are "takers, not makers"—to hold together alliances of convenience.[11] But there is always the possibility that this will escalate. In the real world there is no analogue of the British rescue ship that saved the heroic Ralph on the final page of Golding's novel.[12] If we want to minimize the temptations of dehumanizing politics, we need incentives to nudge things in benevolent directions. The question is: How to do that?

Madison was right that enduring factions would not emerge within a perfectly homogeneous population whose members had the same interests, beliefs, and values, but it is worth pausing to note that, even in that limiting case, majority rule would render prevailing arrangements potentially unstable. Game theorists have long been aware that any allocation of a divisible good—say a dollar—can be upended by majority rule so long as there is the kind of open-ended iteration discussed in section 1.4. If Anna and Beth agree to split the dollar equally, giving Cleo nothing, Cleo can respond in a future round by proposing a different split—perhaps sixty/forty—to Anna or Beth, either one of who can then find a majority partner to upend the new status quo. And so on ad infinitum. Even if all three agreed on an equal split, any two might form a majority coalition to change this—dividing the dollar among themselves at the expense of the third. The divide-a-dollar majority rule logic assumes nothing about motivation. People might upset the status quo to get more for themselves, but they could also do it to advance their conception of justice or fairness. The result is general and carries the implication that every conceivable distribution of a divisible good is potentially unstable under majority rule.[13]

Moreover, there is no need for a second politicized dimension, such as race or religion, to create the possibility of instability. The American founders understood this implicitly. Madison noted in *Federalist* #10 that different economic interests were enough to produce factional conflict.[14] And Jefferson predicted what in fact came to pass in the 1820s: that if the Federalist opposition collapsed so completely as to render the Republicans hegemonic, Republicans would soon "schismatize among themselves." In 1826 they split into the Jacksonian Democratic Republicans and the National Republicans, who would become the Whigs by the mid-1830s.[15]

A single political dimension can generate the requisite political competition for instability, provided that it is composed of divisible goods. We see this the great majority of the time in the United States, where, as Nolan McCarty, Keith Poole, and Howard Rosenthal note, over 90 percent of legislators' votes can be predicted from their positions on a left/right continuum along which differences can be represented as matters of degree.[16] The same result can sometimes be achieved by the crosscutting cleavages flowing from different dimensions. If race, religion, and gender divide people along different fault lines, then in principle people will form different coalitions on different issues. Some standard formulations of pluralism appeal to that logic. It plays out most unambiguously when sui generis coalitions (sometimes of strange bedfellows) form to push for particular measures—such as abolishing the slave trade, enacting civil rights legislation, or repealing an unpopular tax. But in elections, voters face the bundles of policies endorsed by the competing candidates. Voters must choose based on which, for them, matter most.

The danger derives from the presence of indivisible goods, like ethnicity, race, or religion, in the politicized mix. If they become dominant sources of political mobilization, overwhelming the divisible goods, then politics is more likely to be experienced as—and to become—winner-take-all. In the former Yugoslavia, relatively high levels of ethnic intermarriage and concomitant social integration did not prevent destructive ethnic conflict once the country split into states in which citizenship was defined by reference to the majority national group in each former republic.[17] Indeed, the highest levels of violence occurred in what had previously been the most integrated areas, as people found that they were either noncitizens or second-class citizens in lands they had inhabited all their lives.[18] Israel's Jewish public identity has had comparable consequences for Palestinians and Israeli Arabs, who are for all practical purposes second-class citizens. Their low rates of political participation reflect alienation from what, for them, must be the oxymoronic identity of a "Jewish democracy."[19] The lesson of the seventeenth-century wars of religion is that it is best to take indivisible goods off the political table. If the church is disestablished, it is less likely that there will be religious battles over the commanding heights of the state.

3.1.3 The Rules and the Game

For democracy to work, the government of the day must be vulnerable to replacement while the regime survives. Samuel Huntington and others have argued that there must, therefore, be acceptance of the basic rules of the game before political competition, and hence alternation in government, can take place. Order comes first.[20] Plausible as that might sound, it is too simple because everyday politics and the rules of the game bleed into one another. Aside from the difficulties, already noted in section 2.3, of identifying constitutional stages or moments, the rules of the game are never entirely fixed. Conflicts about minor issues—a tax on tea, say— can escalate into conflicts over fundamentals.[21] Effective demands to enforce the rule of law sometimes result from democratization rather than precede it, as happened after the decades-long hegemony of Mexico's Partido Revolucionario Institucional ended in 2000.[22] As Giovanni Carbone and Vincenzo Memoli have shown, there is considerable evidence that democratization can help states consolidate the rule of law. Running elections and having to respond to constituents creates incentives to build the institutional capacities of government.[23] On the other hand, population shifts can erode the extent to which electoral rules reflect salient interests until things reach a tipping point, as happened in Japan in the early 1990s, prompting irresistible pressure for major electoral reform.[24] Developments of that kind carry the whiff of punctuated equilibrium, but change in the rules can also occur piecemeal—as with the gradual expansion of the franchise in the nineteenth century in many European countries or with what has been happening to the British constitution due mainly to Britain's changing relations with Europe since the early 1990s.[25] Harrington argued long ago that for political institutions to endure, they must reflect the distribution of power in the society.[26] Adam Przeworski puts the point crisply with respect to democracy, noting that, "because there are no third parties to enforce it," democracy will not survive unless those with the power to overthrow it "prefer it to the feasible alternatives."[27]

Sometimes it is unclear whether the rules are at stake. In the 1800 election in the United States, many Federalists claimed—wrongly, as it turned out—that the new republic was too fragile to withstand a turnover of government to Jefferson's Republicans.[28] Indeed, depending on what the actors do, a conflict can go in one direction or the other. The British might have defused the tax rebellion in the American colonies before it escalated into a revolution.[29] Had the Federalists not accepted the result, turning over power in the critical early months of 1801, the fledgling American republic might have fallen apart. Examples of this sort suggest that whether alternation of governments in power becomes and remains established depends partly on contingencies of leadership and luck. That is true up to a point, but enlightened statesmen will not always be at the helm, as Madison said. Putting the imponderables to one side, the question is: What makes alternation more rather than less likely?

Modernization theorists used to see economic development as a harbinger of democracy, though they disagreed about why.[30] More recently scholars have observed that economic development does not make democracy inevitable, but that it is important for democracy's survival if it can get a foothold.[31] These debates are taken up more fully in section 6.4. Here I simply note that the reasons democracy survives in rich countries are not well understood. Some suggest that in wealthy countries both the rich and the poor have reasons to maintain democracy—if it exists—over supporting a coup. As Seymour Martin Lipset said over half a century ago: "If there is enough wealth in the country so that it does not make too much difference whether redistribution takes place, it is easier to accept the idea that it does not matter too much which side is in power. But if loss of office means serious losses for major groups, they will seek to retain office by any means available."[32] Jess Benhabib and Adam Przeworski put it more starkly: If we assume the diminishing marginal utility of income and that people also value the freedom that comes with democracy, the rich will accept a degree of redistribution in favor of the poor rather than give up their freedom (since it is relatively good bargain). Conversely, the poor will prefer the substantial utility gains they can achieve as beneficiaries of redistribution over attempting coups—which might fail and will, in any case, cost them their freedom as well.[33]

These arguments appeal to the plausible intuition that people will be more willing to accept losses when the stakes of doing so go down, but they ignore the reality that I have investigated at length elsewhere: that, despite predictions to the contrary by proponents of the median voter theorem, there is no systematic tendency toward downward redistribution in capitalist democracies.[34] The Benhabib and Przeworski reasoning also ignores obvious collective action problems among "the rich" and "the poor" that are underscored by the divide-a-dollar logic discussed in section 3.1.2. That logic militates against class affiliation as being sufficient to destroy a political order; this is one reason Marx was wrong to think that the working class would become a cohesive agent of enduring revolutionary change. When divisible goods like income and wealth are at stake, members of any class can in principle be bribed by some potential majority to abandon their class allegiance. Hitler exploited economic grievances to disaffiliate Germans from the Weimar order, but in order to mobilize them in support of his takeover, he needed an exclusionary ideology as well—one that would not lend itself to their turning against him.

People are unlikely to risk trying to overthrow a democracy unless they have a lot at stake. In principle, this could be a lot to gain or a lot to lose; in practice, only leaders are likely to be motivated by the possibility of gain. Hitler could be drawn to take huge risks by the glorious prospect of ushering in a Thousand Year Reich. Potential coup plotters might salivate at the thought of fleecing the nation's coffers to fill up their offshore bank accounts. But such motives are unlikely to animate the population at large, among whom material benefits would have to be widely shared, and in any case most people have conventional appetites for risk. Machiavelli's remark that elites want to dominate while the masses want to avoid being dominated captures this asymmetry.[35] Vulnerability gets the people into the streets, and, as Locke said, this takes long trains of abuses. Desperate people do desperate things. The way to protect democracy from mass rebellion is to forestall that desperation by reducing what they have at stake.

This is why, though democracy is compatible with exceedingly high levels of inequality, economic policies that protect the people at the bottom matter. Observers as different as Averell Harriman and Ralph Miliband have noted that welfare states are social democracy's best friend; they stop people from reaching the point where they have nothing to lose but their chains.[36] Similar considerations might explain why democracy has recently fared pretty well in countries like Mexico, Brazil, Indonesia, and Poland, where effective efforts were made to reduce inherited poverty and to insulate the most vulnerable from the shocks of structural reform.[37] In Thailand, Nigeria, and Egypt, by contrast, the failure to protect the vulnerable left large sectors of the population primed for mobilization against the democratic order.[38]

As for political leaders, democracy depends minimally, but vitally, on their willingness to leave office when they lose an election. This, too, is influenced by the economic context, which shapes the options available to former politicians. Leaders will be more inclined to walk away from power if there is somewhere reasonably appealing for them to go. When George Herbert Walker Bush lost the presidency in 1992, he could go onto corporate boards, create foundations, and become wealthier than he could ever have done by remaining in office. Sending the tanks down Pennsylvania Avenue is scarcely worth contemplating in such circumstances. In a winner-take-all economy, losing political office means losing access to lucrative rents that will not likely be replicable once you are out of power.

By the time Bush left office, the practice of alternation was so deeply entrenched in American politics that it would have been hard to imagine a losing candidate even considering trying a coup, even when—as with Al Gore and the Democrats in 2000—the losers believe that the election had been stolen.[39] Przeworski has noted that the best predictor of alternation is, indeed, alternation: if it can get started, the odds of its continuing quickly increase.[40] This raises the question: How does alternation get started? Far-sighted acts of statesmanship no doubt play their part. The fact that Nelson Mandela had stepped down in 1999, when he could have stayed on as president, made it easier for opponents to shoot down Thabo Mbeki's flirtation with changing the South African Constitution to permit himself a third term in 2007.[41] No doubt it helped that Mbeki faced a future of corporate boards, institutes, foundations, and elder statesman awards rather than exile or prison.[42] It is difficult to read Susan Dunn's account of turnover in America's first several elections without concluding that the prospects for alternation were substantially enhanced by the low appeal that politics held for Washington, Jefferson, Adams, Burr, and Madison, particularly in light of the more lucrative and appealing ways they could spend their time.[43] It probably helped with several of them that in those days Washington, D.C., was in a mosquito-infested swamp in which malaria ran rampant.[44] Even at that early stage, the American polity and economy offered elites opportunities that dampened the costs of losing office or the benefits of winning it. Indeed, they often viewed political failure as liberating.[45]

This reasoning suggests an explanation for why democracy often struggles to survive in single-commodity export economies (the "oil curse"), where access to the levers of political power is often vital to the continuing well-being of economic elites. In such settings, even if per capita income (PCI) reaches levels that should be expected to sustain democracy, it might nonetheless be vulnerable to a coup by elites who fear losing power or who find themselves in a position to grab it.[46] On this account, the diversification of the economy is just as likely to matter as PCI or relative inequality, because diversification offers multiple paths to economic well-being and social status.[47] If all the eggs are in one basket, then the incentive to fight over who holds the basket is high. In effect, the conflict-dampening advantages of divisible goods are lost. Politics is more likely to become a life-or-death struggle for control when the government has a lock on access to the means of prosperity.

3.2 Intensity and Organized Interests

There is invariably a gap between what voters in a democracy want and what legislators do. Part of this derives from the policy bundling forced on candidates, mentioned in section 3.1.2. Much of it, however, flows from the fact that voters focus on the few issues that matter most intensely to them and that they can easily understand. Technical issues, or issues that seem fleeting to most voters, do not command their attention—or not for long enough to shape much of what happens. If a crisis is big enough to keep voters' attention until it is dealt with, decisive action can occur. Amartya Sen notes that democracies respond comparatively well to famines.[48] But that is the exception. Even when voters become exercised, their attention often atrophies before the issue has been dealt with. Responding to intense voter outrage at huge bonuses that had been paid to American Insurance Group executives following hard on the heels of government bailouts, in March 2009 the U.S. House of Representatives passed a 90 percent tax on the bonuses. By the time the bill died in the Senate, voter attention had moved on.[49] As E. E. Schattschneider said, if an issue is not salient to voters, the moneyed interests rule. "The flaw in the pluralist heaven," he concluded, "is that the heavenly chorus sings with a strongly upper class accent."[50]

Some will say that if voters don't care that much, why does it matter? Indeed, theorists have occasionally noted that allowing vote trading and even vote buying would have its advantages. If there were markets in votes just as with other commodities, then people who cared a great deal about something could pay off those who cared less or were indifferent— leaving everyone better off.[51] Robert Dahl flirted with the notion that attending to intensity might be desirable from the standpoint of political stability, though he was skeptical that it could be measured.[52] In fact, vote buying and vote trading provide a market solution that makes measurement unnecessary. But netting out the balance of intensities misses what is at sake when basic interests or values clash. Vilfredo Pareto put it well, if rhetorically, when he asked: "Should we compare the painful sentiments of the robbed with the agreeable sentiments of the robbers, and look for those with the greater intensity?"[53]

This myopic utilitarianism grates against democratic sensibilities, but it is worth pausing to reflect on why. The U.S. government abandoned Reconstruction in the mid-1870s because Southern whites were more intensely committed to maintaining racial supremacy than Northern whites were to abolishing it.[54] Jim Crow legislation survived until the 1960s partly for the same reason.[55] Maybe the toll was worth paying, but scarcely on the grounds that intensity of preference merits respect in democratic politics. As Ira Katznelson notes, it was an agonizing choice for many Northern Democrats, ambivalently justified by their strategic bet that extending New Deal benefits to blacks would be achievable later. The Vietnam War provides another vivid instance of triumphant intensity. In the early 1960s an intense minority of Americans favored escalating the Vietnam War while the majority was indifferent—at least as a voting matter.[56] Democratic accounting exhibits a leveling quality that militates against the notion that this made escalation the best policy.

Even when the purpose is benign, taking account of intensity is a tough sell in a democratic idiom. Lani Guinier discovered this in June 1993, when President Clinton withdrew her nomination for assistant attorney general for civil rights after she had been pilloried during Senate confirmation hearings for an article she had written advocating schemes to allow people to register intense preferences for minority candidates by casting more than one vote for them.[57] It was impossible for her to overcome the idea that democracy is about counting how many people want something rather than how much they want it.

Democracy's hostility to intense preferences runs deeper, however. Reflecting on the post-Reconstruction American South and the escalation in Vietnam illuminates the reality that, at its core, politics is about managing power relations, not utility maximization. The amount of passion with which Southern whites wanted to preserve Jim Crow, or how much utility they derived from its existence, is beside the point; it was an oppressive racial order. The decision to escalate in Vietnam required Americans to finance—and many to risk their lives fighting for—a cause that jeopardized the lives of millions.[58] The idea that intense supporters of escalation should have exercised disproportionate influence on the decision to subject others to those dangers runs counter to democracy's underlying rationale: to manage power relations so as to mitigate domination that cannot be avoided. That some people want a war a great deal is not a good reason to make other people fight or endure it.

A related reason to be wary of intensity is that in politics it is expressed preferences that count, and expression of preferences is always subject to a budget constraint. People who are in a position to organize themselves or others to insinuate their preferences into the political process are more likely to have them acted on than those who are not. No doubt this accounts for a large part of why the National Rifle Association can get the U.S. Senate to reject gun reform measures that are favored by 90 percent of the electorate.[59] Members of United for a Fair Economy and Citizens for Tax Justice might well have favored retaining the federal estate tax paid by America's richest 2 percent just as intensely as members of the Family Business Estate Tax Coalition favored its repeal, but the repeal coalition was bankrolled by some of America's wealthiest families while their opponents operated on shoestrings. This was a major factor in the successful phase-out of the estate tax signed into law by George W. Bush in 2001.[60] There were many differences between Occupy Wall Street and the Tea Party, but a major one that shaped their relative political impact was the huge financial clout behind the Tea Party.[61] The hundreds of millions of dollars spent by the financial industry lobbying to defang the Dodd-Frank Act regulating financial markets in the wake of the global financial crisis dwarfed anything that was spent by the other side.[62] In short, the political market responds to intensely expressed preferences, not intensely experienced ones.

These considerations prompt the additional worry that catering to intense preferences might augment their intensity. When like-minded people deliberate, not only do they become more susceptible to groupthink, their views also become more extreme.[63] Extremism is not the same thing as intensity, but they are often connected. We know from Daniel Kahneman that the more people participate in group efforts, the more deeply invested they become in them—even in the face of evidence that their chances of success are vanishingly slim.[64] This suggests that if the political system rewards those who organize to get their shared preferences implemented, the activity of organizing will likely augment the intensity of their commitments as they participate in meetings and strategize to achieve their goals. The Family Business Estate Tax Coalition exhibited just that quality, to the point that many of its members came to support positions that contravened their own interests. The Democrats tried repeatedly to split the coalition by offering farmers and small businesses exemptions that would immediately have freed most of them permanently from the tax. Yet they stayed on board to fight for a comprehensive repeal that had to be phased in over a decade, would sunset after a year, and whose subsequent fate was impossible to predict.[65] According to their own accounts, the coalition meetings were vital for building and sustaining their commitments to this wider antitax cause, of which they saw themselves as vital parts.[66] In effect, they became so intensely committed that a divisible good came to seem indivisible to them, obviating the possibility of reducing the stakes of the conflict in which they were engaged.

Intensely organized activists might be unrepresentative of voters, but that need not limit their political power. In fact this is what we have seen in the United States in recent decades. Though the media often talk about an increasingly polarized electorate, political scientists note that activists are much more polarized than the public.[67] Politicians have also become more polarized in ways that make them less representative of voters who elect them.[68] This seems partly due to the sorting of voters into red and blue constituencies; partly to the rise of primaries, which increase the leverage of extremists over politicians in their constituencies; and partly because, on many issues, U.S. politicians face incentives to respond more to organized interests and less to voters than do their counterparts at Westminster. This subject is taken up more fully in section 4.2.2. Here the relevant conclusion is that creating incentives to reward intense preferences is a bad idea from the standpoint of nondomination. Intense preferences pull toward, rather than away from, winner-take-all politics, reducing the prospects for cooperation and increasing the stakes of conflict.

A final concern is that catering to intensity can entrench it. A classic illustration is the overrepresentation of slave states in the U.S. constitutional settlement of 1787. Daniel Walker Howe notes that Southern support for slavery strengthened substantially in the decades that followed.[69] This was partly because burgeoning cotton production replaced the less profitable and in any case declining tobacco industry, stimulating demand for slaves. But Southern attachment to slavery also intensified for other reasons. Overrepresentation of Southern states in the Senate and the three-fifths rule, which augmented their seats in the House and the Electoral College by a third, became more consequential for preserving Southern advantages after the Missouri Compromise ushered in an agreement by which free states could enter the Union only in tandem with slave states. Breeding slaves for western export also became a lucrative protected industry after importing foreign slaves was outlawed in 1808.[70] Slave owners wanted markets for their surplus slaves, partly to make money but also due to distaste for the growth of nonwhite populations in their own states.[71] These sentiments were buttressed by the prospect of exporting some of the burden of paying compensation when emancipation eventually came, which led Jefferson, among others, to embrace an oxymoronic defense of extending slavery to the territories on the grounds that it would enhance the long-term prospects for emancipation.[72]

Catering to intense preferences is especially worrying in light of my discussion of divisible and indivisible goods, because indivisible goods often underlie intense political attachments. This is what leads theorists like Arend Lijphart to run scared of them. Lijphart has long maintained that if divisions over religion, race, or ethnicity are intense enough to produce deep divisions, then competitive elections just pour gasoline on the embers of conflict. The better course, he thinks, is to give the intense politicized groups veto rights and then mandate power-sharing rules to force deals among their leaders—so-called "consociational democracy."[73] During the South African transition, Lijphart backed constitutionally mandated power-sharing proposals aimed at bridging the racial divide, even though by then most of the violent conflict was between the ANC and the Inkatha Freedom Party, who were competing for Zulu support in the eastern part of the country.[74] Lijphart's advice was not followed, yet violent ethnic and racial conflicts among citizens have not turned out to be prominent among South Africa's political challenges in the decades since the transition. Indeed, in 2007 the Zulu Jacob Zuma displaced the Xhosa Thabo Mbeki as leader of the ANC and then the nation, without violence, an outcome that those who viewed South Africa through Lijphart's spectacles would have deemed impossible.[75]

Consociational plans are obviously vulnerable to Przeworski's observation mentioned in section 3.1.3 that, lacking third-party enforcement, there is no reason to expect antagonists to abide by them when divisions are so intense that they really are needed. After all, the consociational elements in the U.S. Constitution did not prevent the Civil War. It is not surprising, therefore, that critics like Donald Horowitz and Brian Barry point out that consociational arrangements have no demonstrable track record of preventing sectarian conflict. It seems more likely, as Horowitz says, that Lijphart has his causation backward; that the "moderation and fluidity" he attributes to older European consociational arrangements were in fact what made them possible.[76]

But it is worse than that, because consociational arrangements can perpetuate and entrench the very divisions they seek to heal.[77] The Lijphartian impulse calls to mind a novice skier who is too fearful to lean away from the mountain, even though this would give him greater control, and instead leans in—making him more vulnerable to a fall. Group memberships might be more or less fixed, depending on whether they rest on ascriptive traits like skin color or acquired ones like religion. But how and why group memberships are politicized is another matter. Racial differences are benign in some circumstances; in others they can be used to mobilize people for war. Religious cleavages can be hugely consequential or wholly unimportant in politics, and, when they do matter, sometimes differences within religions produce more conflict than differences between them; heretics can be more hated than heathens.

Groups have to be mobilized for politics. Madison was right that the latent causes of faction are endemic to the human condition, but for the latent causes to manifest themselves in one way rather than another, people must be mobilized in the service of an agenda. If aspiring leaders respond to incentives to mobilize people along inherited sectarian lines, this will tend to ensconce them in their balkanized constituencies.[78] This will make politics less likely to evolve away from winner-take-all conflict and toward disputes over divisible goods, where stakes are lower and less likely to render people vulnerable to domination. Which institutions are best from that point of view is the subject I take up next.

CHAPTER FOUR

DEMOCRACY AGAINST REPUBLICANISM

STATES ARE DOUBLE-EDGED. By monopolizing coercive force, they develop vital capabilities to prevent domination. These capabilities are essential to outlaw such obvious threats to people's basic interests as slavery and indentured servitude, and to forestall private violence. Anyone who doubts the importance of the state's police powers would be well advised to spend some time wandering around Somalia, Afghanistan, or Iraq. But states are also potential sources of domination. The histories of fascism, communism, and more recent military and theocratic despotisms make it clear that Madison was right to worry that getting governments to regulate themselves is at least as challenging as enabling them to prevent domination. Some form of democratic accountability has to be the answer, but which?

In one respect that is the wrong question. The adaptive political theory venture sketched in Chapter 1 tells us to start where we are, not with a blueprint of where we want to end up. As John Dewey noted in *The Public and Its Problems,* democratic revolutions are usually undertaken less to implement abstract ideals than "to remedy evils experienced in consequence of prior political institutions."[1] There is no perfectly democratic order, and even if there were one, it might be impossible to create in any actual situation. There might be no road to Dublin. Institutions are in any case more often redesigned than designed, and this is usually reactive, as Dewey says; to some extent we are congenitally inclined to fight the last war. Institutions are also subject to erosion, decay, and cooptation; those that worked well for a time can become dysfunctional, hijacked by illicit interests, or otherwise lose legitimacy—making once valuable institutions ripe for reform or replacement. All this suggests that, rather than focus on the best democratic institutions, it might make better sense to address defects of inherited institutions from the standpoint of nondomination and then figure out how best to respond.

This Deweyan outlook is defensible with two caveats. One is that our situation differs from that of democracy's early architects because we have the advantage of more than two centuries of experience. Wise as the framers were, they had no familiarity with large-scale democratic government.[2] Indeed, as I discuss in section 4.2.4, Madison's political experience in the first years of the new republic led him to abandon his famous hostility to majority rule. It looked decidedly less troubling once he found himself at odds with the financial interests of powerful minorities championed by Alexander Hamilton.[3] This evolution in the thinking of the Constitution's most influential craftsman led Robert Dahl to conclude that had the Philadelphia convention been held in 1820, a very different constitution would have been adopted—even if we cannot know what would have resulted.[4] This is another reason, beyond those adduced in section 2.3, to avoid fetishizing the institutional arrangements agreed upon in 1787.

We have also learned quite a bit about democratic electoral politics and institutions since the eighteenth century from experience around the world. We know that presidential systems are generally less stable than parliamentary ones, though this instability can be offset in various ways.[5] We know—thanks to Maurice Duverger—that single-member districts with plurality rule (SMPs) tend to produce two large parties, whereas parties proliferate under proportional representation (PR).[6] We know that PR is more responsive than SMP systems to sectoral interests such as unions and organized business.[7] We have learned a lot about the relations between democracy and distribution. In particular, we now know that majority rule lacks the leveling redistributive impetus that many attributed to it—whether fearfully or hopefully—for much of the nineteenth and twentieth centuries.[8] And, as I explore in this chapter, we know more about the dynamics of legislatures, courts, executive power, public opinion, and the role of organized interests in democratic politics than the American founders did or could possibly have done.

This kind of knowledge does not dictate institutional choices, but it alerts us to relevant factors in evaluating them. Consider the differences fostered by electoral systems. Party proliferation under PR makes parties more representative of voters during elections: green-party supporters and ultranationalists can get their favorite representatives elected. But this comes at a cost. The need to govern with coalitions in PR systems can enable tiny parties to extract disproportionate premiums to sustain governments, as often happens with Israel's ultrareligious parties. In that sense PR is less representative than SMP systems are. Governing by coalition often also means sacrificing the advantages of a well-defined "loyal" opposition in the legislature—a government-in-waiting that offers voters clear alternatives to prevailing policies. These matters are taken up in section 4.2.4, where I make the case that the costs are not generally worth paying from the standpoint of nondomination.

The other caveat derives from the fact that the U.S. system, often euphemistically dubbed "the world's oldest democracy," is something of an attractive nuisance.[9] Several of its most widely trumpeted features—the separation of powers, judicial review, and its treatment of political speech—are often obstacles to combatting domination. Some of these were pragmatic compromises, needed to build enough support to establish the new regime, that serve no good purpose today. Others are the progeny of faulty logic and insufficient attention to the empirical record. But their venerated status creates barriers to appropriate reforms at home and problems abroad, where architects of new democracies are too often persuaded or pressed to emulate them. It is therefore worthwhile to identify their deficiencies in light of what we know today about democratic politics and institutions.

An inescapable truth shapes the terms of the problem: Monopolies are bad in politics just as they are in the economy, yet we are stuck with the reality that political power is a natural monopoly. The basic choice is between trying to divide it up institutionally, as republicans have being arguing we should at least since the time of Montesquieu, and subjecting it to alternating control over time. I defend this latter course, originally sketched by Joseph Schumpeter in *Capitalism, Socialism, and Democracy* in 1942, as superior. Schumpeter's model eventually breaks down, but its enduring insights are more serviceable that the separation-of-powers thinking that so many republican commentators seem to believe is joined at the hip to the nondomination ideal. I make this case in section 4.2, arguing that competitive alternation is desirable on three counts: it institutionalizes the presumption in favor of majority rule defended in section 2.2; it embodies Mill's emphasis on competition over ideas as the best antidote to human fallibility; and it suitably constrains political elites while also giving them incentives to respond to voters' interests.

In section 4.3 I turn to economic inequality's impact on democratic politics. Substantial inequalities always pose significant threats, but I make the case that they are greater in separation-of-powers systems than in majoritarian ones. The inertia fostered by multiple veto players is less of a challenge to the well-heeled than it is to the rest of us, making it comparatively easy for them to bend separation-of-powers systems to their wills when it suits them. Institutional complexity also works to their advantage. It lets them hide in the weeds of principal-agent problems that are characteristic of separation-of-powers systems, capturing players who are vital to their agendas more easily than is true in majoritarian systems. In the United States, big money's power has been amplified by the Supreme Court's ill-advised identification of money with constitutionally protected speech since 1976, an additional and, unfortunately, influential cost of the American penchant for separation of powers and judicial review. It would be better to think of political speech in and around electoral politics as part of the organized contest for public power, I argue, than as libertarian self-expression. Failure to see this produces damaging political market failures that might be impossibly hard to rectify in the U.S. constitutional system and should not be emulated elsewhere.

There is some irony to the fact that Madison is so widely associated in the American mind with the need for institutional checks on the legislature. When he pressed this case in the articles that would become *The Federalist Papers,* he was a young man of thirty-six and the bulk of his political experience lay ahead of him. Perhaps this is why much of what he wrote there about institutional design reads like the work of someone who is trying to learn how to swim by walking up and down next to a lake while contemplating the theory of swimming. What is less well known is that the mature Madison rejected the republican thinking routinely attributed to him and to which Philip Pettit and other contemporary republicans make ritualistic appeal. Almost a quarter-century in the rough and tumble of politics in Congress (1789–1797), as secretary of state (1801–1809), and as the fourth president of the United States (1809–1817) convinced Madison that democratic competition is the best available guarantor of the values that republicans seek to protect. In 1833, three years before his death, he was unequivocal that those who attack majoritarian politics "must either join the avowed disciples of aristocracy, oligarchy or monarchy, or look for a Utopia exhibiting a perfect homogeneousness of interests, opinions and feelings nowhere yet found in civilized communities."[10] The gravamen of my claim here is that the mature Madison was right.

4.1 Power in Public Institutions

I noted at the start of Chapter 2 that public institutions are distinctive in lacking the superordinate goods around which civil institutions are organized. States are sui generis in another way: the prospects for reducing domination within them are not much helped by the possibility of leaving. In *Democratic Justice* I drew on Albert Hirschman's reasoning to argue that nondomination is best served by giving people incentives to treat one another well while pursuing their shared objectives.[11] If the most vulnerable people have the wherewithal to walk away, their collective endeavors are less likely to atrophy into systems of domination. Insiders have good reasons not to abuse them and outsiders concerned for their welfare have comparatively few grounds for concern when apparently vulnerable people choose to remain. Hence my defense of a robust social wage: the less people depend on employers, spouses, children, charities, and parents to vindicate their basic interests, the less reason there is for government to concern itself with what goes on inside firms, families, hospitals, and old-age homes.

Focusing on exit costs offers less leverage for reducing the prospects for state domination, though it highlights what is at issue. Jews who could escape Nazi Germany only by selling their assets to Germans at exploitative prices were obvious victims of domination, as were Soviet and East European dissidents who found leaving the Soviet bloc prohibitively costly during the Cold War. Ronald Reagan's admonition to Mikhail Gorbachev at the Brandenburg Gate in June 1987—"Tear down this wall!"—was not mere rhetoric; that became undeniable when the wall came down two-and-a-half years later and tens of thousands streamed westward. But most of the time there is not much that outsiders can do to help victims of state domination escape, not least because of hostility to immigration within their own countries. Even in the Nazi era, FDR faced an uphill battle in Congress over admitting European refugees to the United States.[12]

A different difficulty is that often it is the least vulnerable people, not the most vulnerable, who have the wherewithal to leave their country. That Gérard Depardieu can evade France's progressive tax system by moving his domicile to Russia does nothing to protect people whose basic interests might be threatened by the French state.[13] Indeed, because the mobility of capital has outstripped that of labor in recent decades, the wealthy are more insulated and the vulnerable less so.[14] This is not to deny that the threat of exit by the well-endowed can help diminish state domination. Indeed, according to one theory it is when that threat becomes plausible that authoritarian regimes start to democratize.[15] But in established democracies the threat of capital flight all too often hamstrings legitimate governments.[16] It reduces their efficacy and can force them to kowtow to powerful private interests that might themselves be engaging in domination. When exit fails, Hirschman advises us to turn instead to voice. This is imperfect too, but it is where we are bound to go.

Hirschman's notion of voice is best institutionalized by ensuring that those who wield state power can be checked and challenged by those over whom it is wielded. But arguments that invoke checks differ notably from those involving challenges. The first exemplify the republican proclivity for "checks and balances" embodied in the American separation-of-powers system. Joseph Schumpeter famously depicted the second—epitomized in principle, at least, at Westminster—as depending on a competitive struggle for the people's vote. Divisions of authority within the regime animate the republican democratic ideal, whereas the Schumpeterian vision depends on alternation: governments enjoy temporary power monopolies but they replace one another over time.

The actual regimes in Washington and Westminster contain elements of both models. In the United States, elections regularly replace presidents (who have been limited to two terms since 1951), and there is some turnover in the legislature—though this is muddied by two-year terms in the House, staggered six-year terms in the Senate, and gerrymandered incumbency advantages that rival those of the old Soviet Union. The UK has adopted elements of divided authority, as I noted in section 3.1.3, particularly with respect to the judiciary and the European Union, and there are forces in British politics pressing to move further in that direction by adopting an elected, and therefore inevitably de-emasculated, House of Lords, which I take up in section 4.2.3. But the centers of gravity in the two systems differ in ways that matter here, so it will be useful to keep them separate.

4.2 Democracy versus Republicanism

The republican institutional scheme is a kludgy setup to render power-holders accountable to those over whom power is wielded. Incumbents in the other branches do the checking in "checks and balances"; protection of the people is meant to be a kind of invisible-hand by-product. In the long history of republican theory there were representational elements, to be sure, inasmuch as the different components of government were taken to embody the interests of the one, the few, and the many. And the framers were at least partly motivated by a "country" perception that rotten boroughs and other usurpations had contributed to the political corruption in eighteenth-century England that they were determined to avoid in their new republic.[17] But just as republican writers tended to ignore conflicts of interest within the ranks of the few and the many, they also paid scant attention to matters of agency. By declaring power to be "of an encroaching nature" and laying down the corresponding dictum that "ambition must be made to counteract ambition,"[18] Madison was motivated less by a nascent idea of accountability to voters than by the classical liberal fear of power that Lord Acton would later memorialize.[19]

Part of the reason the framers paid relatively little attention to questions of agency was that they assumed that the legislature would embody the interests of the common people. It was, after all, because the House of Representatives was thought to be too close to the people that it threatened to become the engine of majority tyranny. This is why the framers judged it the most dangerous branch of government, in need of hemming in by the others.[20] The people must be shielded from the vices of bad government, but this would be an externality of the competition among departments—at most an early version of whistle blowing. That observation is not, by itself, an impeachment of the republican theory. Indeed, it will become plain in section 4.2.4 that the Schumpeterian alternative faces principal-agent problems of its own, though it deals with them differently. First we should evaluate the republican account on its own terms.

4.2.1 Counteracting Ambition?

Madison was careful to note that, for his theory to work, it had to be based on incentives, not the mere "exterior provisions" of the Constitution. Experience in Virginia, Pennsylvania, and elsewhere had confirmed what should, he thought, have been learned from the example of Venetian republic: "Parchment barriers" are not enough to quench the voracious appetite of the legislative department that is "everywhere extending the sphere of its activity, and drawing all power into its impetuous vortex." Just as much as aristocrats or monarchs, elected politicians are motivated— and corrupted—by the desire for power. Preventing them from ushering in an "elective despotism" requires the presence of equally ambitious figures in the other branches to stop them.[21]

Madison's recognition that constitutional provisions are not enough was valuable, but his proffered solution failed his own test. Robert Dahl noted long ago that Madison's call for incentives to structure the exercise of power was long on rhetoric and short on mechanisms to make it work.[22] Dividing politicians among legislative, executive, and judicial branches, and declaring that mutual jealousy will keep all the aggrandizing occupants of different departments at bay, sounds good. But what is the Federalists' institutional scheme other than a list of exterior provisions, scribbled on a parchment? Why should we expect it to have been any more effective at actually dividing up power than was Lincoln's insistence to leaders of the rebel states in the spring of 1861 that they could not secede because the Constitution contains no provision for secession?[23]

Occupants of the different branches might protect them against encroachment by others, but they might not. As Keith Whittington has shown, in periods when the U.S. Supreme Court has increased its power, this was often not because the Justices seized it. Rather, presidents often found it to be useful to cede the Justices power—sometimes with congressional complicity.[24] At times Congress has given away vast authority to presidents. Ira Katznelson notes that the War Powers Acts of 1941 and 1942, granting FDR powers that extended "well beyond those claimed in wars by Abraham Lincoln and Woodrow Wilson," sailed through Congress virtually unopposed.[25] The second of these greatly empowered J. Edgar Hoover's FBI, with almost no oversight, to investigate "subversive" groups and individuals. It also facilitated the internment of 112,000 people of Japanese ancestry (79,000 of whom were U.S. citizens).[26] Congress did nothing to limit this, and the Supreme Court blessed it in 1944.[27]

This dynamic accelerated after the war. The National Security Act of 1947 created a Central Intelligence Agency whose activities and budget were secret from Congress, and a National Security Council that ceded to the executive any ongoing congressional role in national security policy. Katznelson notes that although these measures shifted power from Congress to the executive branch, it was not wrested from the legislature. Rather, "members of Congress actively consented to a reduction of its exercise of traditional, democratic controls."[28] The longer-run corrosive effects of all this on rights and freedoms has been substantial. It is scarcely ballast for the proposition that the people will be protected from state domination as the invisible-hand by-product of the jealous conflict among occupants of the branches.

If we bracket these difficulties and think of each branch as composed of players with an interest in guarding their turf vis-à-vis the other two, John Ferejohn and Rick Hills have noted that they are quite differently situated to pull it off. Whereas the president's personal interest in this tussle typically dovetails neatly with guarding the presidency, 100 senators and 435 House members must grapple with potentially formidable collective action challenges to act as corporate agents of their institution vis-à-vis the others.[29] Moreover, they have their own constituency interests, many of which might live in considerable tension with thwarting or even snarling at a president. If the president's agenda is more popular in a congressional district or a state than it is with the congressional leadership, the legislator might need to buck the leadership and instead follow the bumper sticker advice to "Bark less! Wag more!" at the president. And when legislators do confront a president, as when most southern Democrats abandoned large parts of FDR's domestic agenda after 1936, this might have more to do with partisan interests—in this case, regional partisan interests—than institutional jealousy.[30] This is to say nothing of pecking-order struggles within the branches and individual prerogatives such as the Senate filibuster, which might matter more to members than keeping a president in check. Ambition might counteract ambition. Then again, it might not.

Collective action difficulties might be less severe for nine Justices, many of whom care more deeply about the Supreme Court as an institution than do members of a fractious legislature. But Justices are also often invested in individual legacies, conflicts with one another, and political agendas that can limit the extent to which they man the Court's barricades. Chief Justice Taney's flagrant collusion with President-Elect James Buchanan in 1856 over the imminent *Dred Scott* decision denying U.S. citizenship to blacks is one legendary instance.[31] *Bush v. Gore,* where the five conservative members of the Rehnquist Court upheld George W. Bush's challenge of the recount of disputed ballots ordered by Florida's supreme court, is another. The cost of that brazenly political move to the Court's legitimacy was substantial, yet the majority did it anyway to help an ideological soul mate.[32] Sometimes Justices are moved to protect the Court more than by partisan agendas or other considerations, such as safeguarding their individual legacies. But sometimes they are not, and it is far from clear that the founders were right to believe that the protective institutional incentives predominate.

Whether for the reasons adduced by Ferejohn and Hills or for others, Congress has turned out to be notably less potent than the founders feared. The Supreme Court has enjoyed more authority than they envisaged, and no one doubts that the presidency is vastly more powerful than they anticipated—even if commentators differ on the significance they attach to this reality.[33] It is clear, however, that no convincing case has yet been made that interbranch competition leaves the population at large, or those whose basic interests are most likely to be threatened, less vulnerable to state domination than they otherwise would be. This leaves open the possibility that it is not interbranch competition as such, but instead the particular role of an independent judiciary charged to safeguard the Constitution and Bill of Rights, that on balance protects the vulnerable from the more rapacious institutions of the Leviathan.

4.2.2 Constitutional Courts

American-inspired judicial review has spread. Many of the U.S. Supreme Court's defining features are rare by global standards: lifetime judicial appointments, the ban on advisory opinions, and the strict Article III limits on standing have not been widely copied. But the basic idea of an independent court whose job it is to interpret a constitution, including or supplemented by a bill of rights, is a standard American export. It is a near-universal institutional feature of the third wave of democratization that started in 1974, and is often declared indispensable to democratic consolidation by political consultants and international agencies.[34] An independent judiciary is sold as the best bet to protect the rule of law and minority rights from the double jeopardy posed by majoritarian sentiment and the politicians and bureaucrats who control the machinery of government. The "least dangerous branch"—as Alexander Bickel's 1962 book put it, echoing another Alexander Hamilton in *Federalist* #78, put it— offers vital insurance against the more dangerous ones. And it offers the best response to what he dubbed the "countermajoritarian difficulty."[35]

The merits of judicial review have been greatly oversold. Its main champions were born between the wars and hit their intellectual strides during the Warren Court era (Earl Warren was appointed Chief Justice in 1953 by Dwight Eisenhower, and he served until 1969). People like Ronald Dworkin, John Hart Ely, and Laurence Tribe championed that Court, and many in their generation expressed mounting distress as much of its work was undone by the Burger (1969–1986), Rehnquist (1986–2005), and Roberts (2005–) courts. They saw the Warren Court's achievements as vital for protecting individual rights and for the health of American democracy; its eclipse, they thought, put both in serious jeopardy.[36] More attention to the longer sweep of American history, and especially the Taney (1836–1864), Waite (1874–1888), Fuller (1888–1910), White (1910–1921), and Taft (1921–1930) Courts, might have alerted them to expect such developments. Given decisions like *Dred Scott* or *Plessy v. Ferguson,* the Court's complicity in undermining Reconstruction and limiting the Civil War Amendments in the *Slaughterhouse* and *Civil Rights Cases,* or its evisceration of much New Deal and other reform legislation during the *Lochner* era, there was plenty of evidence at the time that the Warren Court was an outlier.[37] Certainly Eisenhower got more than he bargained for in appointing Warren ("the biggest damn fool mistake I ever made"), a former Republican governor who, as California's attorney general, had been the moving force behind the internment of U.S. citizens of Japanese descent during the war, who was confirmed 96–0 by the U.S. Senate, and whose subsequent trajectory was predicted by no one.[38]

Most judges are conventional establishment figures, and most presidents succeed in appointing justices who reflect their own values. If they do stray, it is more likely to be in the direction of public opinion as expressed through elected branches than away from it.[39] Lord Devlin might have overstated things when he declared that judges reflect the views of the man on the Clapham omnibus, but not by much.[40] When the U.S. Supreme Court refused to strike down Georgia's proscription of homosexual conduct in 1986, homosexuality was still illegal in half of the states. By the time the Justices reversed themselves, seventeen years later, thirty-six states had repealed the ban.[41] When public opinion is seriously divided, the Court tends to duck. *Roe v. Wade* is the exception that proves that rule. The Court aggressively rewrote the law of abortion in the face of a divided public, acting in an imperialistic way that failed to settle the question and harmed the Court's legitimacy—even in the estimation of many who favored the outcome.[42] More typical is the story of school desegregation. Despite extravagant claims often made for the Court's 1954 decision in *Brown v. Board of Education* reversing *Plessy v. Ferguson* and declaring "separate but equal" to be unconstitutional, it seems clear that the advances that have occurred in desegregating schools were achieved through legislative action, not courts.[43]

It is in fact exceedingly difficult to show that judicial review matters for the prevention of domination. Authoritarian governments routinely flout courts when they are intent on oppression, as anyone who lived through fascism, communism, the era of Latin American "disappearances," or South African apartheid will attest. Democracies do vastly better from the perspective of nondomination, but there is no compelling evidence that judicial review has much—if anything—to do with this. Rather, it seems clear that democracy does the heavy lifting. Countries like Britain, Sweden, Norway, and until recently the Netherlands, which have shown little appetite for judicial review, have not done demonstrably less well at protecting human rights than has the United States.

As early as 1956 Dahl registered skepticism that democracies with constitutional courts could be shown to have a positive effect on the degree to which individual freedoms are respected when compared to democracies without them, a view he developed more fully in a definitive article the following year.[44] Subsequent scholarship has shown that Dahl's skepticism was well founded.[45] Indeed, it is plausible to wonder whether the popularity of independent courts in democracies has more in common with the recent popularity of independent banks than with the protection of individual freedoms. These "independent" institutions signal to foreign investors and gatekeepers at international economic institutions that the capacity of elected officials to engage in redistributive policies or interfere with property rights will be limited. That is, they might be devices by which governments can signal their willingness to limit domestic political opposition to unpopular policies by taking them off the political table.[46]

4.2.3 Deliberation versus Obstruction

The U.S. Senate is the most potent upper house in the democratic world, a stark contrast to the House of Lords in the UK, which was stripped of the power to reject legislation by the Parliament Act of 1911.[47] Various rationales were put forward for the Sherman Compromise on Senate representation eventually agreed to in 1787, but Gordon Wood notes that the most frequently repeated was "the need to distribute and separate mistrusted governmental power."[48] As Madison said in *Federalist* #63, the risk that legislators might betray the people's interest was "evidently greater where the whole legislative trust is lodged in the hands of one body of men, than where the concurrence of separate and dissimilar bodies is required in every public act."[49] The dissimilarity was guaranteed by different bases of representation: House constituencies reflect population, but, in the only feature of the Constitution that is practically immune from amendment, each state is guaranteed two senators regardless of population.[50] Add to this the Senate's filibuster rules, which were rarely deployed until the early twentieth century but have become standard fare in recent decades (even if modestly curtailed for appointing inferior court judges and cabinet appointees in 2013), and the Senate must be seen as a formidable institutional brake on the House.[51]

Some of America's founders saw the Senate as home to the "aristocracy of virtue and talent" that, Jefferson said, "nature has wisely provided for the direction of the interests of society."[52] At least some observers agreed. In 1835 Alexis de Tocqueville opined that the Senate was peopled by America's "ablest citizens"; men moved by "lofty thoughts and generous instincts." House members, by contrast, were "village lawyers, tradesmen, or even men of the lowest class." Many were men of "vulgar demeanor," animated by "vices" and "petty passions."[53] Tocqueville put the difference down to the indirect election of senators by state legislatures (abolished in 1913 by the Seventeenth Amendment). Whether or not he was right about that, versions of his happy narrative have enjoyed staying power. The idea that the Senate is the world's greatest deliberative body, which first gained currency with Daniel Webster's three-hour soliloquy in defense of the Union in 1850, is now repeated to the point of banality.[54] But it scarcely squares with the role the Senate has played in American politics since the 1930s.

Again, the southern role in the New Deal is instructive. Southern senators scarred the New Deal by insisting on the exclusion of predominantly black farm laborers and domestic workers from Social Security and other social protections. Those at greatest risk for domination in the South were thus least protected, a path-dependent infirmity whose effects persist to this day. Nor was this a case of protecting "the people" from an out-of-control legislature of the sort feared by Madison in *Federalist* #63. Southern senators repeatedly blocked anti-lynching legislation and attempts to insist on federal supervision of voting in national elections. As a result, blacks were routinely terrorized and stripped of the de facto right to vote or hold office—and sometimes even of de jure rights as well.[55] This had nothing to do with aristocracies of virtue and talent, lofty thoughts, or generous instincts. It was the raw assertion of power by those who controlled institutional rules and prerogatives. They were veto players and everyone knew it—including FDR, who was explicit that throwing his weight behind anti-lynching legislation would jeopardize too much of his legislative agenda to be worth trying.[56]

We should not be surprised that the Senate comes up short as a deliberative body. The main way to institutionalize deliberation is via rules requiring agreement. The goal is to get people to talk things out, either in the hope that they will converge on the truth (insisting that juries reach unanimous verdicts) or, if truth is not at issue, getting adversaries to seek out common ground. But there is no way to make people deliberate. A jury might talk until everyone is persuaded, but fatigued jurors might throw in the towel at the behest of a recalcitrant crank. Likewise, people might deliberate in politics, but they might just as easily use their institutional leverage to veto disfavored outcomes, or to bargain. As a result, the concerns I raised in connection with catering to intense preferences in section 3.2 also come into play here: rules to institutionalize deliberation reward extremists and strategically pivotal players. This is what happened in the U.S. Senate over Jim Crow, and it has become more common since—now that the costs of filibustering have diminished and the use of individual senatorial "holds" has proliferated.[57] These rules are instruments for legislative minorities to throw sand in the wheels of government.

The British House of Lords has also sometimes been praised as a deliberative body, though Bagehot famously said that the best cure for admiring the Lords was to go and look at it.[58] Interestingly, after 1911 the Lords became less partisan and more deliberative once they lost the power to do anything except delay most legislation. Lords who showed up were more likely to be those interested in improving the quality of legislation, given that there was no longer any partisan advantage to be had. The Lords became more of a repository of expertise. And because they could no longer force the Commons to listen to them, they had incentives to give cogent reasons for their views—to try to persuade.[59] But they have become more partisan and assertive since the 1999 reforms restored some of their legitimacy as a somewhat democratic institution, albeit one at a considerable distance from the ballot box.[60] Meg Russell notes that the remaining peers believe that the House of Lords has gained legitimacy from reform, and this "has increased their confidence to challenge government policy."[61] The ironic conclusion is that the odds that a second chamber will be home to a dispassionate natural aristocracy moved by lofty thoughts and generous instincts might vary inversely with its power and democratic authority. Its members can be expected to show most interest in reasoned persuasion when there is no other way for them to prevail—the one way for Habermas to triumph in real politics. The British public seems to want some version of this. Polls reveal substantial support for the experts and non-party-aligned members in the Lords and little appetite for their replacement by party representatives.[62]

Seen in this light, the move to reform the Lords into an elected body that has been gathering steam for some years in the UK is misguided.[63] The American example should stand as a warning of the dangers. Members of an elected second chamber would inevitably undermine the supremacy of the Commons, which lies at the heart of the Westminster system's desirability as an institutionalized system of political competition. Heredity is, to be sure, no legitimate basis for enfranchisement, and the 1999 reforms have all but abolished it.[64] Yet two competing universal franchise chambers serve no purpose other than to multiply veto players— enhancing institutional sclerosis. Rather than augment the Lords' democratic legitimacy, it would be better to deemphasize it so that the second chamber can continue as a repository of experts who inform the competitive democratic process in the Commons while remaining subordinate to it. Russell notes that the Lords' reputation "for careful scrutiny of government policy" is widely appreciated, but that it would soon be damaged if it became "an oppositionist chamber, dominated by party politicking."[65]

The best way to think about this and other kinds of expertise is by analogy to expert opinion in criminal trials. I argued in section 2.1 that although we should never endorse the notion that there is political expertise as such, this does not render expert knowledge irrelevant to politics. We all have an interest in our decisions being informed by the best available knowledge, but we should not succumb to the illusion that has tempted so many Enlightenment thinkers: that technical expertise can displace politics or render it redundant. This is not so much because experts usually know less than they claim or believe, though this is often true. The more important reason is that technical knowledge is never neutral in its applications. Choosing one course of action over another invariably creates winners and losers, or different relative gains even when everyone benefits. This, in turn, means that there are always people with an interest in getting policies that suit them endorsed as technically the best choice. Even when it is technically the best choice, the costs and trade-offs for others are all too easily obscured when economic, public health, military, and other experts are not held to account in public forums where their claims are contested and their arguments must be defended. What form the forum should take will vary with the issue at hand and the type of expertise involved. It might be a committee hearing, a commission of inquiry, or some other forum for public comment, appeal, or debate. No matter what form it takes, the goal should be to take advantage of expert opinion without being held hostage to it.

Some, like Frank Vilbert and Bruce Ackerman, argue that experts should occupy new branches in expanded or reinvented separation-of-powers systems. Vilbert contends that the unelected experts who run independent central banks, risk-management bodies, and economics and ethics regulatory bodies should be recognized as an additional branch of government, along the lines of an independent judiciary.[66] Ackerman prefers parliamentary systems over American-style separation of powers, but he believes that professionalism in government and administration would be enhanced by an independent "integrity branch" to scrutinize government for "corruption and similar abuses" and a "regulatory branch" whose job is to make the bureaucracy "explain how its supplemental rule-making will actually improve upon the results generated by the invisible hand." He would also like to see a "democracy branch" that would function as an independent electoral commission geared to safeguarding to "each citizen's participatory rights"; a "distributive justice branch" that would concern itself with "minimum economic provision" for the most vulnerable; and a constitutional court "dedicated to the protection of fundamental human rights for all."[67]

Proposals of this sort conjure up the image of treating a paraplegic who is in need of spinal therapy by transplanting additional limbs onto his atrophying torso. Ackerman believes his proposed new separation of powers would fare better than the American-style version inspired by Montesquieu, because it is based on "functional specialization," with members of each branch sticking to their areas of expertise. But there is no reason to think that it would produce any less institutional sclerosis than the current American variant when members of the different branches interpret their specialized mandates in mutually conflicting ways. It does not take great leaps of imagination to foresee the distributive justice division insisting on redistributive transfers that the constitutional court decides to regard as unconstitutional takings, or the democracy branch fighting with it over the regulation of money in politics just as Congress has done with the U.S. Supreme Court. More important, Ackerman says nothing about why parliamentary democracy needs all these constraints in the first place, other than to repeat the standard mantra that "a constitution ought to constrain the exercise of democratic self-rule by protecting fundamental individual rights," and to assert that a constitutional court is needed to do the job.[68] As we have seen, commonplace as this claim might be among constitutional lawyers, there is scant evidence to render it plausible.

There are better ways to inform political decisions with expertise. British parliaments have encountered no difficulty in creating boundary commissions to manage redistricting without ceding parliamentary supremacy in this field. First established as permanent bodies in 1944 and significantly revised in 1986 and 2011, boundary commissions make periodic adjustments within numerical and territorial limits specified by Parliament. Following periods for public comment, the Commission makes a recommendation that Parliament can accept or reject, but not amend.[69] As with military base-closing commissions in the United States, Parliament recognized the endemic problem of partisan and constituency temptation in this area and created a limited Ulysses-and-the-Sirens solution.[70] But there is nothing to prevent Parliament from altering the enabling legislation, as it periodically does. Indeed, it might be a lot harder if the independent status of boundary commissions were constitutionalized, freezing what people think they know about the possibilities of representation into the indefinite future. As will become plain in section 4.2.5, that is a bad idea.

Independent central banks (ICBs) are the flavor of the moment, or at least the flavor of the past few decades, and the Blair government in the UK followed the global trend by granting "operational" independence for monetary policy to the Bank of England in 1998.[71] Whether ICBs have been as vital to fighting inflation as is often claimed can be debated.[72] Even if they have, a time might come when voters conclude that the price is not worth paying beyond a certain point, given the partiality of IC bankers to policies that operate to the disproportionate benefit of the ultrarich.[73] If that happened, moves to rein in ICBs would face even tougher sledding than they would anyhow if ICBs had been constitutionalized in the meantime. Just as the periodic and, fortunately, thus-far failed attempts to pass balanced-budget constitutional amendments in the United States would trap future governments in the straitjacket of a dubious macroeconomic theory, constitutionalizing central bank independence would ossify a status quo that might turn out to be an albatross.[74] After all, the trendiness of ICBs was propelled by what we now know to have been vastly overblown self-confidence of IC bankers in the 1990s and early 2000s. There will always be technocrats impressed by their own abilities who seek to displace or rein in politicians, and it will often be tempting for politicians to shirk responsibility by colluding with them.[75] But the better bet is to retain or create institutions that take human fallibility for granted, facilitating the adoption of public policies that are informed by adaptive rationality. Expert bodies, like deliberative chambers, should remain subordinate to competitively elected parliaments.

4.2.4 Competition or Representation?

Joseph Schumpeter offered a helpful perspective on political competition by pressing analogies from economics.[76] He understood implicitly what Nozick would later make explicit: that state power is a natural monopoly. But Schumpeter also knew that monopolies are problematic in politics no less than they are in the economy, because those who control them lack what competition normally supplies: information about what people want and the incentive to try to do better at providing it than anyone else. In politics, he argued, the best response to this state of affairs is for political parties to compete for temporary control over the monopoly. Schumpeter thought of the votes that parties seek as political analogues of the profits that motivate firms, and he likened the policies they advocate to the goods and services that firms try to sell to consumers. Democratic accountability is the analogue of consumer sovereignty in this stylized picture: the party that convinces most voters that it will provide the policies they want wins power and a mandate to implement them for a limited time.

This admittedly spare account is often faulted as too minimalist, especially by those who advocate more full-blooded participation as the hallmark of democratic politics.[77] But minimal is not negligible. For one thing, as Adam Przeworski notes, people will be less likely to press this objection if they have lived in countries that lack a minimalist democracy.[78] For another, the Schumpeterian view of accountability is more robust than both the classical liberal and the republican accounts mentioned in connection with Acton and Madison in section 4.2. For all their differences, partisans of those views share a preoccupation with insulating people from the predations of corrupt and power-hungry politicians. Limited government is the main instrument for classical liberals; for republicans it is slicing and dicing institutional authority. Schumpeter shared their joint apprehension at unchecked political power, but his solution, to subject politicians to a "competitive struggle for the people's vote," does a different and double duty.[79] Politicians are perpetually constrained by others who seek to replace them, but they must achieve power by propounding alternative visions of national policy and proffering them to voters for approval. Majority rule thus has a dual purpose: competition constrains elites, but the party that prevails is also the one that best figures out what most people want the government to do. This dual account fails to measure up in a multitude of ways in practice, but its distinctive center of gravity is accountability of governments to voters.

Proportional representation undermines this advantage of Schumpeterianism. Parties garner votes by campaigning on their preferred platforms, but the need for coalitions to form governments muddies the waters when it comes to competition over the policies governments actually implement. Britain's Liberal Democrats, longtime advocates of "more representative" electoral reform, got a taste of this after 2010 when the rare circumstance of a hung parliament enabled them to join David Cameron's Tories as junior partners. The subsequent collapse in their grassroots support reflected disillusionment at the inability of the party leader and deputy prime minister, Nick Clegg, to have a discernible impact on many of his government's policies.[80] This experience of coalition government seems to have immunized the British electorate against the temptations of electoral reforms that would strengthen small parties. Their decisive rejection of the Alternative Vote (AV) system by referendum in May 2011 suggests as much.[81] If so, they will have dodged the bullet of fixing something that was not broken. Coalition governments diffuse accountability, allowing party leaders to finger-point and blame one another for unpopular outcomes. Electoral politics operates best when efficacious governments must face off against strong oppositions, institutionalizing competition over what governments actually do.

SMP systems are appealing because they facilitate this accountability, not because there is anything desirable about geography as a basis for the franchise. Territory, just like heredity, is an anachronistic hangover; what matters is who is in a position to wield power over whom. Nor is "constituency service," which can all too easily degenerate into clientelism, an unmixed blessing. The best case for SMP systems is that, provided certain conditions spelled out below are met, they lend themselves to political competition between two large parties, as Duverger showed. This comes as close as possible to institutionalizing Locke's injunction, discussed in section 2.2, that the majority should guide the collective's direction. Something inevitably must, and this will likely lead to less domination than the going alternatives. The goal is to select politicians who compete over the direction of national policy, not people who logroll with one another to bring home the proverbial bacon. This is not to deny that large parties engage in implicit logrolling; this is a condition for their existence. But it takes place before the elections, so voters have a clearer sense of what they will be getting from government if their party wins. To the extent that single-member districts yield clientelist impulses, these are best thought of as a cost we pay for their other benefits—to be minimized by maintaining strong party leaderships in the legislature. This is one reason parliamentary systems are preferable to presidential ones.

Dualistic competition also incorporates and builds on the fallibilist outlook embraced in section 1.4. It institutionalizes John Stuart Mill's call for competition over ideas as the surest path to truth in a world in which knowledge claims are always corrigible, and usually only partly correct when they are correct at all.[82] On Mill's account, the best course is to subject arguments to the discipline of the marketplace of ideas: require their advocates continually to defend them against the going alternatives. It is an invisible-hand argument, but one rather different from that embraced by republican theorists of the separation of powers. The claim for institutionalizing Mill is that the truth is more likely to be the ongoing by-product of vigorous contestation than of any other process people have been able to devise. The adversary legal system again comes to mind as suggestive: each side makes the most powerful possible case for its position and the jury decides who carries their burden of persuasion. In competitive democratic politics, the parties make their conflicting cases and the voters decide.

This competitive vision differs notably from a deliberative one. Setting aside the difficulties, discussed in section 4.2.3, of institutionalizing deliberation, competition has a different motivating purpose. Deliberation is about reaching agreement; argument is about winning. Protagonists in a Schumpeterian political arena prevail not by convincing their adversaries, but by convincing those who are listening that they have better arguments than do their adversaries. This is what links their role of disciplining one another to their accountability to voters. It also means that, for the competitive model to do its double duty, protagonists must argue for conflicting visions of the policy alternatives confronting the country. Squabbling over institutional prerogatives might serve the Madisonian goal of counteracting ambition if the collective action and other difficulties identified in section 4.2.1 could be managed. But that does nothing to institutionalize the Millian imperative to have contenders for office debate alternative courses of public action. The Schumpeterian alternative does, at least in aspiration.

Some will object that this does not go far enough. For instance, Andrew Rehfeld proposes severing all links with geography through random assignment of voters, for their voting lifetimes, to identically sized SMP constituencies—say, 435 in the U.S. House.[83] This might sound like a good idea in light of what has just been said. For one thing, it would eliminate clientelist incentives, because there would be no homes to which representatives would feel impelled to bring bacon. It would be a world without logrolling, pork barrel projects, or bridges to nowhere. For another, it would reinforce the focus on national policy. Part of the reason the American founders favored territorial constituencies was to provide local information to legislators. But as Rehfeld notes, that begs the question of what information one wants legislators to have.[84] If constituencies were random samples of the national population rather than geographic neighbors, deliberation and campaigning (much of which he imagines being done via Internet chat rooms and the like) would focus on national issues.

Any prima facie appeal of this proposal dissolves on closer inspection. Setting practical difficulties aside, Rehfeld admits that the heterogeneity that random assignment creates in constituencies would find no expression in the legislature. If the constituencies truly were random samples of the population, as his model requires, whichever party was slightly more popular with the median voter would win every seat in Congress. Rehfeld speculates that, over time, candidates would learn to become less partisan so as to avoid the high risk of total electoral wipeout. Eventually everyone would turn into "a kind of non-partisan, professional legislator."[85] Appealing as this might be to Rehfeld, it will not do here. Legislators would start out as unopposed partisans on his account, and then turn into—or be replaced by—unopposed technocrats. Rehfeld seems unfazed by this, perhaps because he endorses a deliberative ideal of what should go on in legislatures. But as I noted in section 3.2, we know that deliberation among like-minded people makes them more extreme. If Rehfeld's speculation were right, we would end up with Congress filled with hyperconfident like-minded technocrats who could never be shaken by discordant evidence.[86] The typical legislator would be Larry Summers on crack.[87]

This disquieting specter casts the defects of Rehfeld's model into sharp relief. Whether the opposition party was vanquished from Congress by losing every seat or it just dissolved into Rehfeld's technocratic dystopia, ruling majorities would be isolated in their ideological bubbles. There would be no government-in-waiting; no shadow leadership with access to civil service support or classified information; no one to ask probing questions across the aisle. There would be no contrarian voices on committees. Any whistle-blowing benefits of a loyal opposition would be lost. Nor is it easy to see how alternation in government would easily occur, because the factors just mentioned would increase incumbency advantages by orders of magnitude over anything that currently exists. Presumably there would not even be much intraparty backbench opposition if every elected legislator had their seat in Congress because she or he had found the national median voter's sweet spot.

Rehfeld ends up in this untenable spot because of his focus on the agency relationship between voters and elected legislators. On this admittedly conventional view of representation, the voter is the principal and the legislator is the agent making decisions in the voter's stead. The challenge is to keep legislators on a sufficiently tight leash. Rehfeld worries greatly, for instance, that legislators will not be accountable enough to voters unless voters' constituency memberships are permanent.[88] But the conventional view is wrongheaded. From my Schumpeterian standpoint, by contrast, politicians and political parties are not agents of voters any more than firms are agents of consumers. Firms have incentives to respond to consumers. They succeed to the extent that they are better at that than is the competition. It is the felt imperative to increase profits, or perhaps market share, that generates their incentives to keep trying. Likewise, the success of political parties at winning votes and seats depends on doing better than the competition at supplying what voters want. They are interested in their own success, but the way to achieve it is to be more responsive to voters than is the opponent.[89] This is what ties their disciplining of one another to serving the interests of voters.

Pursuing the analogy to the point where it starts to become strained, notice that if firms are accountable to anyone, it is their shareholders, not consumers. But there is no obvious analogue of shareholders for political parties. Some might suggest that party activists, or maybe primary voters, are the political equivalent of shareholders. This is illuminating up to a point. After all, such groups try to control platforms and get candidates to pursue strategies and policies that they believe to be in their interests—that will bring them "a return" of sorts. Parties are also vulnerable to takeover attempts, which can be more or less hostile. Think of the Democratic Leadership Council's refashioning of the Democrats in the 1980s and the Tea Party's efforts among Republicans since 2008, not to mention the British Labour Party's 2015 leadership contest in which thousands of new members paid £3 apiece to ensure the election of Jeremy

Corbyn. Ceding a shareholder-like status to such groups inevitably means giving vent to intense preferences. In view of the associated difficulties discussed in section 3.2, it scarcely seems like a viable anchor for the agency relationship implicit in Rehfeld's account.

A different possibility would be to regard "the people" as the relevant principal, which writers like Pettit often like to do, and which could be taken as suggested by Rehfeld's myopic focus on the national median voter.[90] But that is a metaphysical conceit. Candidates for office often claim to speak for "the people" because they are trying to get as much support as they can; this is why Mitt Romney's candid admission in 2013 that his political agenda was a nonstarter with at least 47 percent of voters was so damaging.[91] But we are analyzing, not campaigning, which means recognizing that if there is a general interest of the "people," it is not represented by any political party.

Romney was right, of course. Political parties are invariably pressed into the service of particular economic and social agendas. This is why the Madison of *Federalist* #10 objected to them as instruments of factional conflict that would be feed division, undermining the union.[92] But he changed his mind as soon as it became obvious that resisting Hamilton's agenda would be hopeless without one, and indeed he and Jefferson minted America's first partisan split in the early 1790s in pursuit of that goal.[93] But Madison never quite got beyond seeing parties as necessary evils rather than dynamic instruments to foster political stability over time while minimizing the likelihood of domination. Indeed, he even flirted with the illusion that once Hamilton's mischievous Federalists were successfully vanquished, his new Republicans would become the natural party of government, obviating the need for an opposition.[94]

Parties do not cause conflicts of interest; they embody them. When they operate well, they give domesticating institutional expression to the resulting struggles, forestalling assaults on the regime's foundations. When they fail, we get the kind of conflict that erupted in Egypt in July 2013. To be sure, many factors contributed to that failure, among them the country's economic free fall and the fact that the military had never ceded ultimate control of the country to civilian leadership.[95] But the fact that those who opposed the Muslim Brotherhood lacked an effective party to resist its revamping of the constitution and country in its own image put them on what looked, increasingly, to be the permanent losing end of a winner-take-all conflict. In such circumstances, taking to the streets to overthrow the regime all too easily starts to seem like the only viable option—provoking a downward spiral that erodes the possibility of democratic politics.

4.2.5 Concentrated versus Diffuse Competition

The British system comes closer than most to the Schumpeterian ideal. Animated by competition over power rather than dividing it up, its center of gravity is a single chamber in which argument tends to be driven by the competing policy visions of the parties. The majority party controls the government temporarily, while the loyal opposition is a government-in-waiting with the interim job of whistle-blower and magnet for dissatisfaction with the government of the day. This system was not, of course, a product of institutional design inspired by Schumpeter. For the most part it was not a product of democratic institutional design at all. Dueling political parties emerged in the late seventeenth century as by-products of conflict over the appropriate institutional power of the crown.[96] The notion of loyal opposition arose, at least partly, to solve a monitoring problem: His Majesty's opposition kept tabs on His Majesty's ministers.[97] House of Commons supremacy arrived in stages, as monarchy, and then all forms of heredity, lost political legitimacy. Yet Westminster has evolved into a fairly effective regime to manage power along the lines suggested by the Schumpeterian model.[98]

The SMP electoral system in the United States also produces a two-party system, but republican institutions vitiate many of its advantages. The combined effects of presidentialism, bicameralism, federalism, and localized gerrymandering on the electoral system aggravate regional differences as we will see, promoting clientelism and veto-player obstructionism more than loyal opposition. Republican institutions also weaken congressional party leaderships, rendering backbenchers ripe for capture by intense and powerful interests. Republican institutions also undermine government accountability in ways that parallel the blurred responsibility fostered by PR and other coalition-prone systems discussed in section 4.2.4. The net effect is that political competition, while often intense, is also highly diffuse. This undermines the focused debate over ruling ideas that give Schumpeterianism its raison d'être.

An independently elected president enjoys a national mandate that congressional leaders lack. Presidents can be from a different party than the majority in one or both houses, can sometimes peel backbenchers away from the congressional leadership, and can create executive agencies that compete with the bureaucracies that legislators oversee. Even when the same party controls both branches, the president is not subject to votes of no-confidence by the majority, need not—and typically does not—select cabinet members from the legislature, and does not have to defend policy, like a prime minister, as the first among equals.

In a parliamentary system the majority party in parliament is the prime minister's most important constituency. That the American president does not depend on legislators in any analogous way diminishes their importance.

Two different houses, both of whose members have territorially based electoral mandates, can be in the hands of different parties. Even when they are not, members face different electoral incentives stemming from their differing constituencies. Majorities in both houses can also find themselves at mutual loggerheads because of their different rules and procedures, making it easier to blame one another for unpopular outcomes. The multidirectional finger-pointing that occurs when sword-of-Damocles mechanisms fail, as with expiring tax cuts, sunsets on legislation, or gimmicks like the Budget Control Act of 2011 ("the sequester") obscures authorship in ways that do not arise in unicameral systems where the majority party is manifestly responsible for what happens or fails to happen.

Federalism undermines national parties because the governing party often does not control state governments. This is especially pernicious in "dual" federal systems of enumerated powers like the American one, which entrenches jurisdictional conflicts between state and national governments.[99] The dual system was eclipsed by the nationalization of politics in the New Deal, but never fully, as Katznelson has recently emphasized.[100] It remains true that legislation enacted in Washington can be frustrated in the implementation, as with the refusal of many Republican governors to implement the Patient Protection and Affordable Care Act passed by Congress in 2010, contributing to its tortured debut in the fall of 2013. The fact that different units of government can raise their own taxes gives states additional wherewithal to defy national policies; this power grows in eras when the Supreme Court adopts expansive definitions of states' rights. As Charles Black has noted, supremacy clause issues are notably more common than the classic "countermajoritarian problem" that attracts so much scholarly attention in the United States.[101] In a unitary system, power might be devolved to lower units of government—but it can be reclaimed. Ultimate authority remains with the party in control of the national legislature.

For SMP systems to produce two strong parties that compete over national policy, constituencies have to be heterogeneous and fairly similar. We saw in section 4.2.4 that in principle this can go too far: identically heterogeneous constituencies as proposed by Rehfeld would produce single-party monopoly in the legislature. The real world tends to be beset by the opposite problem. Where there is substantial geographical variation in preferences and agendas, as in India, regional parties proliferate. In the United States, regional variation made southern Democrats virtually a separate party during the New Deal. Had southern blacks not been so effectively disenfranchised, this might have mattered less. As it was, white southern Democrats, sometimes voting in lockstep with northern Republicans, defanged the early New Deal legislation during the later 1930s and 1940s by resisting national planning, demanding regional variation to keep minimum wages low in the South, and cutting back on the Wagner Act's protections for organized labor.[102] These outcomes had more to do with intraparty Democratic competition than with conflicts between Democrats and Republicans.

Homogeneous districts produce comparable anomalies: balkanized representatives and "wasted" votes, when parties can win by large majorities in constituencies they dominate, as the Tories do in the Home Counties in the UK, as American Democrats do in urban areas where their votes tend to be concentrated, and as happens increasingly in the United States more generally due to the "sorting" that is making Red states redder and Blue states bluer.[103] This gives national parties few incentives to compete in the large number of safe seats. It also means that nominating processes effectively decide elections—and where this is by primaries, as has increasingly been the case in the United States since the 1970s, this cedes control over who gets elected to party extremists who vote disproportionately in primaries. It also reinforces the phenomenon that has been detailed by Nolan McCarty, Keith Poole, and Howard Rosenthal: that Congress has become more polarized even though the voting public generally has not.[104] Sorting into homogeneous constituencies also helps generate the kind of anomaly that occurred in the 2012 U.S. House elections, where Republicans won a majority of the seats while losing the popular vote.[105] Yet once in Washington, many members, hostage to Tea Party organizations in their districts, would routinely buck the House Republican leadership. In such circumstances it becomes virtually impossible for party leaders to count on backbenchers to support national party platforms.[106] The danger in the United States is thus that continued geographic sorting will further balkanize elections, exacerbating the deleterious effects of federalism and republican institutions on national political competition.[107]

The best antidote to this is to think about congressional districts themselves in Schumpeterian terms. Instead of designing districts for partisan benefit, to protect incumbents, to carve up spheres of influence for parties, or to enhance the descriptive representation of specified groups, the goal should be to design them to be competitive. Samuel Issacharoff has made this case most powerfully in discussing the criteria American courts should deploy when they become involved in redistricting disputes. He notes that the Supreme Court has been complicit in the gerrymandering geared to reducing competition in cases like *Gaffney v. Cummings,* the 1973 decision in which the Justices saw no reason to object to an agreement between Connecticut Democrats and Republicans to divide up the state in ways that roughly reflected their share of the vote.[108] The Court is also friendly to gerrymandering that locks in partisan advantage.[109] Gerrymandered districts often create safe seats that are contested, if at all, only in primaries. This denies voters a competitive airing of the issues at stake in national politics.[110] It undermines Schumpeterian competition, by, as Issacharoff puts it, letting parties "squeeze the competitive juices out of the process."[111] This amounts to collusion in restraint of democracy.

What about gerrymandering for those who are vulnerable to domination? Advocates of majority minority districts (MMDs) will declare it invidious to proscribe gerrymandering for dominated minorities, given how much of it is already going on for others. Indeed, as Desmond King and Rogers Smith note, much of the impetus to create MMDs in the first place came from the thinly disguised efforts to dilute black votes in the South that was a recalcitrant reaction to the Voting Rights Act (VRA) of 1965. Boundaries were redrawn to include more whites in predominantly black areas; at-large constituencies were minted for local elections; runoffs were mandated between the top two candidates for various positions; elective offices were made appointive to stop blacks from winning them; among other measures.[112] Moreover, because race is a "suspect classification" in American constitutional law, the Court has made it especially hard to gerrymander in favor of racial minorities. This is true even though Congress amended Section 2 of the Voting Rights act in 1982 to require districts that would prevent vote dilution for minorities and protect their ability to "participate in the political process and elect representatives of their choice."[113] But after a brief respite, perhaps because of the overwhelming congressional majorities that supported the 1982 reforms,[114] the Court has continued to limit MMDs, insisting that they pass its most demanding "strict scrutiny" test, which rules out drawing boundaries for the sole, or perhaps even explicit, purpose of achieving an MMD.[115] In such a world it would be unseemly, at a minimum, to endorse denunciations by some Justices of MMDs as racial balkanization when the Court also underwrites partisan, collusive, and territorial gerrymandering— which often operate to the lopsided benefit of incumbents and well-resourced extremists.[116]

A better path out of this tortured condition would be to read the 1982 revisions of the VRA to require consideration of race when designing districts along the lines proposed by Issacharoff. This would be compatible with the Court's viewing of the 1982 revisions through a "strict scrutiny" lens that permits self-conscious attention to race only when pursuing a legitimate goal of district design other than securing the election of minority candidates. That goal would be competitiveness. Districts that fell below a designated competitiveness threshold, measured by the winning candidate's share of the vote in several successive elections, would be redrawn so as to meet the threshold. But this could not be done in ways that dilute votes of protected minorities or compromise their ability to participate in the electoral process and elect representatives of their choice.

Self-conscious attention to race would thus pass constitutional muster as a constraint in the design and operation of competitive constituencies. One way to cash this out would be to select from proposed redistricting plans, all of which met the competitiveness threshold, the one that did best by the criteria enacted in the 1982 revisions to Section 2 of the VRA. This would provide a way around the double standard that results from the Court's perverse reading of the Fourteenth Amendment's prohibition of racial discrimination, which transforms a measure that was intended to help emancipate blacks into an instrument that subjects remedies designed for that purpose to stricter scrutiny than measures that benefit others.[117] What the competitiveness threshold should be, how many noncompliant elections would be needed to trigger boundary redrawing, who would have to carry the burden of showing that the 1982 Section 2 VRA revisions had been met, by what quantum of proof, and a host of related matters would have to be hammered out over time and as experience with competitive district design accrued. But the basic framework opens up the prospect of responding to disadvantaged minorities in redistricting while not subverting Duverger as MMDs obviously do.[118]

Redistricting plans come up in the courts in the United States, because that is where existing plans are challenged, but Issacharoff's proposal is severable from that institutional mooring. Rather than the patchwork of state-governed—still predominantly partisan—redistricting practices in the United States, it would be better, as he has argued in a different context, to entrust redistricting to quasi-independent bodies as recommended in 2002 by the Venice Commission in Europe, or to UK-style boundary commissions of the kind I discuss in section 4.2.3.[119] No matter who does the job, their charge should be to keep districts competitive.[120] This antitrust logic would militate against the forces that undermine Schumpeterian competition. In the United States this would mitigate the anomaly whereby national elections are contested only in a small number of constituencies.

4.3 Inequality's Impact

Though Madison insisted in *Federalist* #10 that the first object of government is to safeguard inequalities of property that result from "different and unequal faculties," even then he worried that inequality might aggravate factional divisions. In *Federalist* #62 he warned against giving "unreasonable advantage" to the "moneyed few over the industrious and uninformed mass of the people."[121] Within five years he would be notably less equivocal.[122] By that time he and Jefferson had become convinced that the new financial class posed an existential threat to their ideal of an agrarian republic, and they were in a series of pitched battles with Hamilton over the explosion of moneyed wealth generated by speculation in the new government's public debt.[123] In a series of articles on property, inequality, and political parties published in Philip Freneau's *National Gazette* (created in 1791 for the purpose of opposing Hamilton), Madison emphasized the importance, for political stability, of protecting employment, guaranteeing "a dignified sense of social rights," and reducing material inequalities. The evils of parties could be mitigated, he said, by denying "unnecessary opportunities" to the few to "increase the inequality of property, by an immoderate, and especially an unmerited, accumulation of riches." To be sure, property rights should be protected but steps should also be taken to "reduce extreme wealth towards a state of mediocrity, and raise extreme indigence towards a state of comfort."[124]

Madison was right to worry that extreme inequalities subvert democratic politics to the point of facilitating domination. This happens in three mutually reinforcing ways. Great inequalities produce a particular kind of political polarization that operates to the systematic disadvantage of those most vulnerable to domination. It also enables the well-endowed to take disproportionate advantage of the institutional complexities of the political system, utilizing them for private benefit in ways that exacerbate the vulnerability of those at the bottom. And severe inequality shapes ideology. It structures the range of possible futures that are seen as politically feasible. The first of these applies to all democracies, but the second and third gain particular purchase in republican institutions.

4.3.1 Weighted Polarization

A degree of polarization is not inherently bad, depending on the reasons for it. When strong parties offer clear alternatives, this is surely better than parties offering the same policies so that candidates have to compete by contrived disagreements and character assassination. However, the polarization generated by increased inequality has more malevolent implications. As McCarty, Keith Poole, and Rosenthal have shown in the United States, concentration of income and wealth at the top and the growth of a low-paid class at the bottom skews the incentives of politicians in both parties away from the interests of the poor. This becomes especially pronounced, they argue, when the ranks of the poor grow due to permissive immigration policies. Poor people vote in comparatively low numbers anyway and immigrants do not vote at all, so politicians have few incentives to attend to them. The rich, on the other hand, participate both directly by voting and indirectly by giving money.

The net effect is that as inequality increases, politics shifts to the right at the same time as it becomes more polarized for the reasons discussed in section 4.2.5. This happened during the Gilded Age, it declined steadily as inequality fell in the middle part of the century, and then returned with the resurgence of inequality driven by increased immigration and lopsided income growth at the top since the 1960s.[125] It is scarcely, surprising, in light of McCarty, Poole, and Rosenthal's account, that the New Democrats in the United States and New Labour in the UK adopted strongly pro-business and "neoliberal" economic policies in the 1990s that had been anathema to their predecessors as recently as the 1970s and 1980s.[126] The median resident, and perhaps even the median citizen, might not have moved much—or even at all—to the right. But the median voter had. There is invariably pressure from financial and other business interests to move in this direction, and it is always tempting for leaders of left-of-center parties to cater to those interests to the extent that they can without alienating their electoral base. By the 1990s the electoral base had changed enough for them to find that, in catering to those interests, they were paying a diminishing electoral price. This is the element of truth in claims by groups like Occupy Wall Street that both political parties speak for the rich.

4.3.2 Inertia and Complexity

Inequality also has an asymmetrical impact on status-quo bias. I noted in section 2.2 that hard-to-change systems are unresponsive to changing preferences and external shocks. By itself this need not operate to the disadvantage of those who are vulnerable to domination. In principle, unions and their political agents can use their organized power to block change just as organized business can. In the 1980s this was a significant factor in slowing welfare state retrenchment on both sides of the Atlantic.[127] Some protections for the vulnerable—famously the Social Security system in the United States—have proved especially hardy. But American Social Security is bulletproof for exceptional reasons.[128] Moreover, unions are imperfect instruments for protecting the most vulnerable. Their defense of members' jobs and wages often comes at the expense of the unemployed, an especially serious problem in emerging economies with high levels of structural unemployment.[129] Unions' characteristic embrace of seniority systems also disadvantages women.[130] These issues aside, organized labor's power has for the most part been declining in most capitalist democracies in recent decades, reflecting greater worldwide capital mobility and vast pools of cheap labor in China, India, and elsewhere in the developing world. In the United States, unions have been unable to block the erosion of the New Deal protections written into the Wagner Act in 1935—starting with the Taft-Hartley Act of 1947.[131]

If a system is hard to change, changing it is nonetheless easier for those with more resources—a systematic advantage for the well-heeled. In the United States, the minimum wage has steadily been eroded by inflation in recent decades, yet Democrats have found it increasingly difficult to enact minimum wage increases, and they have never managed to override the blocking power of their adversaries to get it indexed to inflation, which would solve the problem.[132] By contrast, the alternative minimum tax, which limits the deductions available to higher-income taxpayers, has been amended eleven times since 1986 to avoid bracket creep and in 2013 it was indexed for inflation.[133] The threshold for paying estate taxes has also seen significant increases in recent years. It, too, was indexed for inflation in 2013.[134] In short, status-quo bias is not neutral; it works to the systematic advantage of those who are best placed to move the elephant.[135]

Institutional complexity also works to the disproportionate advantage of powerful interests by fostering opacity. This allows those who understand the system to exploit principal-agent problems in the bureaucracy and between bureaucrats and politicians. Opacity is especially important on issues that matter intensely to voters, making capture of politicians correspondingly harder. This was well illustrated during the 2009–2010 battle over U.S. financial regulation in the two areas in which public opinion was strong enough to counter the unprecedented lobbying campaign against regulation: the ban on proprietary trading (the "Volcker rule") and the creation of a Consumer Financial Protection Bureau (CFPB) to police predatory lending.[136] Once it became obvious that some version of the Volcker rule would survive in the final bill, financial lobbyists pushed for strings of exceptions that would make it all but unenforceable.[137] They also pressed for much of the detail to be worked out by regulators, who were then deluged with tens of thousands of comments and objections that made meaningful rule-writing all but impossible.[138] On consumer protection, Alan Blinder likens what was eventually created to a Rube Goldberg machine.[139] The demoralization and mass exodus of staff from the new agency that was under way by mid-2013 reflected the extent to which the CFPB seems to have been designed to fail.[140]

Institutional complexity might matter less when voter preferences are not intense, because the legislators themselves are more easily captured by Schattschneider's moneyed interests discussed in section 3.2. This happens more easily with PR than in SMP systems because smaller parties are more easily captured than large ones,[141] though it can happen in the United States, as we saw with the 2001 repeal of the estate tax.[142] Institutional complexity might itself, however, be implicated in preventing voter preferences from intensifying. It is doubtful that many American voters realize how much legislation is written by lobbyists, often in conjunction with members of the bureaucracy. The bulk of the Dodd-Frank bill, for instance, was crafted in the Treasury under strong industry pressure, and on most important questions the Treasury's initial formulation eventually became law.[143] The secretary of the Treasury is answerable to the president, not Congress; this is one more way in which the complexity built into the separation-of-powers system makes it hard for legislators to keep control of the legislative process. In a crisis, they can issue subpoenas and mount investigations, but in the normal course of things they are often presented with bills to enact that neither they nor their subordinates have read—much less written.

McCarty, Poole, and Rosenthal contend that two related factors have made financial regulation susceptible to capture since the nineteenth century: politicians and regulators depend on the industry for relevant information, and major industry players have more resources, intellectual and financial, than anyone else with an interest in the outcome.[144] They are therefore best placed to pay the transaction costs of getting things done in a complex regulatory environment, and—as the Volcker comment-period story underscores—by shaping the content and flow of relevant information, they can increase the transaction costs of regulators and potential adversaries who oppose them. The Dodd-Frank experience is far from sui generis, however. Comparable stories can be told about industries as different as housing and meatpacking, in which powerful producer groups routinely forestall regulation or shape it to their own ends.[145] In this light it is notable that one of the most influential theories of regulation in the United States treats major industry players as regulation's principal beneficiaries. According to George Stigler, large firms are disproportionately able to coordinate among themselves, and they use their muscle to extract beneficial regulations from government. Politicians have to be somewhat responsive to consumers and voters, but the more powerful organized interests prevail much of the time.[146]

Nor is this just a matter of industry muscle. The intimacy between regulators and regulees facilitates what Citigroup economist Willem Buiter describes as cognitive capture. This occurs when regulators internalize the "objectives, interests, and perception of reality of the vested interest they are meant to regulate."[147] Cognitive capture was well illustrated in 2004 when then Goldman Sachs head Henry Paulson Jr. led a delegation that persuaded SEC regulators to exempt the largest banks from capital reserve requirements on the grounds that, with assets in excess of $5 billion, they could protect investors on their own. To believe this, the regulators had to enter a wonderland in which they could ignore the well-known fact that reserve requirements matter more for large banks, which pose systemic risk, than for smaller ones that do not; they had to believe that the larger banks were actually safer.[148] Alan Greenspan all but conceded after the bubble burst that he had been taken for a ride: "Those of us who have looked to the self-interest of lending institutions to protect shareholders' equity, myself included, are in a state of shocked disbelief."[149] But it is not really so surprising in light of the literature on framing effects discussed in section 1.4: regulators are overwhelmingly likely to identify with those who hold their hands through the maze. There is less need to twist arms when minds twist themselves.[150]

4.3.3 Money and Speech

Attending to capture raises the subject of money's role in politics. I noted in section 4.2.2 that constitutional courts have not plausibly been shown to offer security from domination over and above what democracy provides without them. But there is at least is one way in which the U.S. Supreme Court has seriously undermined democracy's capacity to guard against domination: by outlawing any meaningful constraints on the use of private money in politics. In its 1976 decision in *Buckley v. Valeo* the Court agreed that Congress could regulate contributions to political campaigns. But the Justices also equated money with speech that is protected by the First Amendment, a fateful decision that they deployed to justify prohibiting regulation of political "expenditures." Dismissing concerns that expenditures promote corruption (on the grounds that there is no quid pro quo relationship if the funds are not given to a campaign), the Court declared that any expenditure limitation "heavily burdens core First Amendment expression." Regulations of expenditures impose "direct and substantial restraints on the quantity of political speech." The constitutional imperative discerned by the Justices to outlaw all such restraints trumps any interest that the state might have in "equalizing the relative ability of individuals and groups to influence the outcome of elections."[151] Even when wealthy individuals finance their campaigns out of personal assets, the First Amendment "simply cannot tolerate" any limits on a candidate's freedom "to speak without legislative limit on behalf of his own candidacy."[152] *Buckley* opened the floodgates to unlimited spending in electoral politics, sanctified by the fig leaf that allows campaign commercials to be copied verbatim by groups and individuals engaged in "expenditures."

For a time the Court allowed some exceptions to the blanket prohibition on regulating political expenditures, but in 2010 the Justices extended *Buckley* to corporations in *Citizens United v. Federal Election Commission.*[153] And in the predictable subsequent mission creep, shortly thereafter the D.C. Court of Appeals extended its proscription to cover contributions to advocacy groups in *SpeechNow.org v. Federal Election Commission.*[154] Provided the money is not given to the candidates themselves, the Court saw no risk of corruption. This led to the birth and rapid growth of a new creature, the "independent expenditure only" political action committee or Super PAC.[155] One of the few remaining limits to contributions fell four years later, when the Court struck down limits on aggregate contributions, which had stood at $117,200 per election cycle, with the implication that a single donor can now give some $3.5 million per election cycle, divided among candidates, PACs, and parties.[156]

Moreover, although *Citizens United* allows Congress to require disclosure of corporate political expenditures, prior Court decisions and rulings by the Federal Election Commission have made this all but unenforceable.[157] The net effect, first seen in the 2012 election, is that unlimited amounts can be spent, much of it anonymously, by corporations as well as individuals to shape election results. The Court has also recently reaffirmed *Buckley's* insistence that there is no compelling interest in a level playing field in elections. Writing for the majority in *Davis v. Federal Election Commission* in 2008, Justice Samuel Alito struck down the bipartisan McCain-Feingold bill's "Millionaire's Amendment," which had allowed candidates facing self-funded opponents to raise political contributions above the federal maximum. Inter alia, Alito said that self-funded candidates are at less risk for corruption than those who must raise money from others.[158] They might indeed be at less risk for quid pro quo corruption, but they run afoul of the strictures against giving political vent to intense preferences that I discussed in section 3.2. They are also symptoms of structural corruption of the democratic process, as I explain below.

Citizens United has drawn plenty of well-merited criticism, but the underlying problem is the Burger Court's original insistence in *Buckley* that money is speech. This carried the implication that any regulation of money's role in the democratic process is tantamount to government interference with political speech, the protection of which lies at the core of the First Amendment. The answer to this, as Justice Byron White said in his dissent at the time, is that money is not speech. Money is money. And it is a vital resource for competing in elections. Congress was trying to regulate elections, not speech, by passing the Federal Election Campaign Acts of 1971 and 1974 struck down by *Buckley.* Limits on expenditures, White noted, do not "directly or indirectly purport to control the content of political speech by candidates or by their supporters or detractors. What the Act regulates is giving and spending money." The limits reflect "a considered judgment of Congress that elections are to be decided among candidates none of whom has overpowering advantage by reason of a huge campaign war chest." For the same reason, White would have upheld the Act's proscription of privately financed campaigns to "discourage any notion that the outcome of elections is primarily a function of money."[159] Interestingly, Thurgood Marshall and Warren Burger both agreed, even though this led them to divergent conclusions. For Marshall, personal financing gave wealthy candidates a "head start" and should be prohibited.[160] For Burger, because a personally financed candidate enjoys a "clear advantage" over one who must raise contributions from others, the Court should have struck down limits on contributions as well as on expenditures.[161] He had no objection to a tilted playing field, only to one tilted by the government.

But it is the tilting itself that is the problem. It is just not true, as the *Buckley* majority alleged, that limiting how much money a person or a group can spend on political communication during a campaign "necessarily" restricts "the number of issues discussed" or "the depth of their exploration."[162] Far from being a necessary truth, this dubious claim ignores what happens when many millions of dollars are spent to support (or attack) a candidate or policy, saturating the relevant media markets and drowning out competing views. The Court has recognized this danger in other contexts. Eight years before *Buckley,* a unanimous Court upheld the Federal Communications Commission's fairness doctrine, adopted by the Truman administration in 1949, which required holders of broadcast licenses to present conflicting sides of controversial issues. The limited number of channels meant that there was no other way to protect the public's "crucial" right "to receive suitable access to social, political, esthetic, moral, and other ideas and experiences."[163] The Reagan administration eventually abandoned the fairness doctrine on the grounds that the advent of cable channels had rendered the scarcity logic obsolete. We need not debate the wisdom of that decision to note that unlimited expenditures during political campaigns fosters scarcity by generating arms races in which the wealthy can perpetually outspend their opponents.

Saturation spending might actually reduce the number of issues discussed or the depth of their exploration. This follows from the reality that people have only finite capacities to listen. In his dissent in *Citizens United,* Justice Stevens heaped scorn on the majority opinion's assertion that "there is no such thing as too much speech." In the real world, he noted, "corporate domination of the airwaves prior to an election may decrease the average listener's exposure to relevant viewpoints, and it may diminish citizens' willingness and capacity to participate in the democratic process."[164] We should think of this as structural corruption, because rather than enhance discussion, the power of money is used to forestall it—a political market failure. Those with massive war chests can decide unilaterally whether they will be deployed to add issues to the agenda and promote in-depth discussion, or to drown out opposing views or engage in attack-ad character assassination.

Perhaps sensing that their reasoning was less than compelling, the *Buckley* majority declared in a sarcastic footnote that "being free to engage in unlimited political expression subject to a ceiling on expenditures is like being free to drive an automobile as far and as often as one desires on a single tank of gasoline."[165] But this non sequitur elides the truth that political expression during campaigns is not a consumption good like driving on the open road. People spend money during elections in order to achieve or forestall particular outcomes. In an era when corporate consolidation of media markets raises ancillary concerns about which voices can be heard in politics, this conflation of money with political speech is all the more damaging from the perspective of nondomination. Unfortunately, the European Court of Human Rights has begun following the U.S. example.[166] Taking this path sacrifices the integrity of elections as organized contests for power in favor of some version of a *Buckley*-style identification of money spent on political speech as expression that may be fettered, if at all, only in the narrow class of cases when it fosters demonstrable quid pro quo corruption.

The spillover effects of opening these floodgates in the United States should stand as a warning to others. Public financing of campaigns has fallen by the wayside as candidates, trapped in the arms-race logic of fund-raising, find that they cannot bind themselves to the voluntary limits that come with accepting public funds. The billion-dollar threshold crossed by Barack Obama and Mitt Romney in the 2012 campaign is a likely harbinger of the future, as are Senate campaigns in the tens of millions and the need for House members, facing reelection every two years, to run permanent fund-raising machines.[167] Even if some version of compulsory public funding could pass constitutional muster, it would not address the limitless expenditures that *Buckley* authorizes and *Citizens United* and *SpeechNow* amplifies. It would take either a constitutional amendment or a radical transformation of the Supreme Court to undo the damage that the justices have wrought in this area over the past four decades. Though many politicians would benefit from such a change, the collective action obstacles to their getting behind it are colossal. This is to say nothing of the moneyed interests that would throw their weight behind maintaining a new status quo that so substantially increases their political clout.

The story is no less gloomy when we turn to money's role in shaping the broader ideological landscape. McCarty, Poole, and Rosenthal call for a new public philosophy to undo the polarizing political effects the of growth of inequality since the 1970s.[168] The evidence suggests this will be hard to come by. There were two major changes in American public philosophy in the twentieth century. The first was the rise of the New Deal consensus after the Depression, a response to the devastating insecurity of mass unemployment helped along by elite fear of a communist alternative that might vie for the hearts and minds of American workers.[169] The spectacle of millionaires reduced to destitution in the 1929 crash fostered "there-but-for-fortune" prudence that pushed in the same direction.[170] The financial crisis of 2008–2009, though the worst since the Depression, was not comparable. Unemployment, cushioned by insurance, barely reached double digits. Financial elites were bailed out by the federal government. The communist threat was gone and, whatever the fear of Islamic fundamentalism, it was not a competitive threat to democratic capitalism. Moreover, McCarty, Poole, and Rosenthal make a compelling case that the New Deal consensus rested on the low levels of inequality that prevailed in the middle years of the century.[171] Today gated communities reinforce what Douglas Rae describes as America's segmented democracy.[172] The wealthy and, increasingly, the middle class separate themselves from the poor, who are easily demonized or ignored: out of sight is out of mind. In this setting, it is hard to see how a public philosophy that champions their interests will get much traction.

This conclusion is reinforced by reflecting on the other main change in public philosophy of the last century: the advent of the antitax conservatism since the 1970s, the most recent incarnation of which is the Tea Party movement. Partly the child of the increased polarization described by McCarty, Poole, and Rosenthal, it was magnified by the growth of activist think tanks with a mission to demolish the New Deal consensus. After the Nixon administration collapsed, a number of billionaires who were dedicated to reviving American conservatism began pouring money into institutions like the Heritage Foundation, the Cato Institute, and the American Enterprise Institute. They believed, correctly, that this would pay dividends in reshaping the ideological terrain. As Michael Graetz and I detail in *Death by a Thousand Cuts,* they massively outspent their liberal counterparts, by the 1980s opening up a major think tank gap that was vital to the Republicans' regaining control of Capitol Hill for the first time in a generation in 1994 and the tax-cutting agenda that came to fruition at the start of the new century.[173]

It is testimony to changed attitudes toward money in politics since *Buckley* that activist think tanks now routinely engage in political advocacy of the sort that almost cost the American Enterprise Institute its nonprofit status for supporting Barry Goldwater's campaign in 1964.[174] The law still requires them to refrain from political advocacy, but the standards have shifted so much as to erode this proscription almost completely.[175] This was well illuminated by the 2013 fiasco over IRS scrutiny of requests by conservative political groups for 501(c)(4) status, which allows donor lists to remain secret. A flood of applications from conservative groups garnered heightened scrutiny, prompting a storm of accusations, never substantiated, about whether the White House was in cahoots with the mid-level IRS employee who singled out the applications for attention.[176] Yet no one raised questions about the existence, in the first place, of a regulation that grants "dark money" status to groups so long as they spend less than 49 percent of their resources on political activity.[177] To the extent that this is enforceable, it means that the only limit on political spending from secret—individual or corporate—sources is a 51 percent tax. This is the logical outgrowth of an outlook in which any regulation of money spent to influence politics is seen as inherently suspect government interference with speech protected by the First Amendment. It means that the inequalities in the economy can be telescoped into the political system. It is difficult to imagine a more effective block to the emergence of a new public philosophy geared to protecting the interests of those most vulnerable to domination.

4.4 Conclusion

The American institutional system was created partly because there was no other way to get enough agreement to replace the existing confederation, and partly out of what turned out to be the mistaken conviction that it would prevent a civil war over slavery. But the founders were also motivated, wisely as it turned out, by fears about the double-edged character of government: that it can foster domination as well as prevent it. This follows inevitably from the fact that political power is a natural monopoly that some person or people inevitably will control. Hobbes might have been sufficiently traumatized by living through the English civil war to stick his head in the sand about the risks of state tyranny, but the American revolutionaries had experienced British oppression and were determined to minimize its likelihood in their own institutions. The subsequent history of state repression from the French Revolution through communist, fascist, and more recent military and religious dictatorships makes it incontrovertible that they were right to conclude that some sort of democratic control of public institutions is vital from the standpoint of preventing domination. The question is: What kind of democratic control? Here the American system falls illuminatingly short. The founders' obsession with hemming government in by trying to institutionalize interbranch warfare failed to achieve its own goals while compromising the state's capacity to limit nongovernmental forms of domination.

Schumpeter was no less distrustful of political elites than were the American founders, and he certainly wanted to limit their potential to engage in abusive behavior. But the genius of his system is that it requires neither the "parchment barriers" of traditional constitutionalist notions of limited government nor the conceit that a government locked in perpetual internal strife will benefit the rest of us. Rather, it links the ways in which political elites challenge one another to their ability to deliver policies that most voters will prefer over time. Schumpeterian democracy is often decried as minimalist because it gives up on traditional notions of representation and the general will. The latter, we saw in Chapter 2, has led to centuries of muddled distractions and is best abandoned in favor of the tradition that stretches from Locke to Lincoln and modern power-centered theorists of majority rule. People also attack competitive democracy for insufficient attention to deliberation, but we saw in section 4.2.3 that the benefits of deliberation are most likely to be achieved if deliberative political institutions are defanged. Once we abandon the fantasy that there is a general will on which deliberation converges, it becomes plain that deliberative chambers, like expert bodies, should be subordinate to competitive legislatures that are geared to institutionalizing Mill's ideal of public argument.

The idea of democratic representation is no less burdened than that of the general will. Democratic theorists have struggled to comprehend it as some kind of principal-agent relation ever since the advent of large diverse societies took the classical Athenian notion of "ruling and being ruled in turn" off the table. The conceptual knots people have tied themselves into by trying to figure out who is the right principal, who is the right agent, and how the agency relationship should work, are major—terminal, in fact, as we saw in section 4.2.4. "Peoples" are morally arbitrary to begin with. We will see in section 5.1 that the notion of "We, the People" all too easily makes implicit reference to "You, the Barbarians." There I argue that the division of the world into nation-states is justifiable, but only on the pragmatic grounds that doing away with national governments would be worse than keeping them from the standpoint of nondomination. Within nation-states, territory and locality might be less problematic than heredity as a basis for democratic representation, but not much less. When we link it, as we should, to the basic interests of those who are vulnerable to domination, we see that constituencies are best designed so as to produce two strong parties that can be expected to alternate in government and loyal opposition.

The principal-agent lens on representation has come at an especially high cost in the United States. We are stuck forever with massive overrepresentation of tiny populations in the Senate. The combination of primaries and regional and urban/rural sorting sends delegations to both chambers, many of whose members are hostage to small bands of extremists in their constituencies, if they face any political competition at all. Partisan and collusive gerrymandering, sanctified by the Supreme Court, creates additional obstacles to competition in the House. And as we saw in section 4.2.5, this operates to the systematic hindrance of America's most vulnerable minority, who have, for decades, been put at a disadvantage in redistricting by the Court's perverse reading of the Fourteenth Amendment, which was enacted in order to help them.[178] My proposal to sidestep this problem by making race a required consideration in the design of competitive constituencies would address that anomaly. Some will object that this is thin gruel, but at least it presses in the right direction.

A commitment to nondomination is not intrinsically hostile to inequality, but we saw in section 4.3 that inequalities of the scope that existed during the Gilded Age have been building in the United States since the 1970s, to the point where they undermine democracy's capacity to prevent legitimate power from atrophying into domination. Many have commented on the recent polarization of U.S. electoral politics, but the more consequential change, we saw, is the one documented by McCarty, Poole, and Rosenthal: the shift of both parties to the right even as the gap between them has grown. Some of its causes remain elusive, but McCarty, Poole, and Rosenthal are surely right that the wealthy participate with votes and money at higher rates than the poor, and that the immigrant poor seldom participate at all. Politicians in search of power behave accordingly in and around elections, but we saw that economic inequality has deleterious political consequences beyond the electoral cycle. The well-resourced take huge advantage of the inertia and complexity built into America's republican institutional scheme, using its opacity to insulate themselves from majoritarian sentiment when it is strong and working their way under the radar when it is not.

The diffuse competition that is characteristic of the U.S. system is not much of an antidote to any of this, as we saw. This is another reason to prefer the clearer lines and comparative transparency that characterize majoritarian democratic national politics. And if the sober assessment of judicial review offered until now in this book is insufficient to disabuse the reader of its often-touted benefits, my discussion in section 4.3.3 of the U.S. Supreme Court's free speech jurisprudence since 1976 surely provides the lay-down hand. The Court's corrosive identification of money with speech protected by the First Amendment locks into the political system wealth-based advantages that are impossible to counter over time, despite the arms races that they provoke—indeed, ultimately, because of them. The idea that elections are vehicles for people to express their individuality and work their unfettered wills as best they can, like driving on the open road, finds its tragicomic apotheosis in the Court's attacks on every meaningful effort by Congress to regulate elections as organized contests for power. If they achieve nothing else, hopefully these decisions will persuade others who are flirting with the American model to think twice.

CHAPTER FIVE

AGAINST WORLD GOVERNMENT

ANY DEFENSE OF democracy as geared to resisting domination must eventually confront the subject of national boundaries. Perhaps this is so for every account of democracy, but surely one centered on those most vulnerable to domination cannot long escape the reality that much of the power affecting their lives straddles national borders. This is always true to some extent, but it is especially so in eras of increased global integration like our own. More powerful governments dictate outcomes to less powerful ones, and all governments are to varying degrees price-takers in the global economy. The 1992 sterling crisis, when George Soros made over a billion pounds in a day by speculating against sterling, dramatized this vulnerability. The resulting run on the pound forced the UK out of the European Exchange Rate Mechanism, a staggering display of national political impotence by a major Western government.[1] Such episodes add ballast to the proposition that national governments are of decreasing efficacy in today's world—feeding calls for enhanced transnational and even global political institutions. The rolling Eurozone crisis since 2009, marked by the inability of governments either to act effectively on their own or to coordinate a collective response, is often cited as additional evidence for this view. If political institutions are to have any hope of taming power relations, it seems that they must go global.

Calls for world government can be traced at least from Francisco de Vitoria, who wrote of *res publica totius orbis* in the sixteenth century, to Pope Benedict XVI's appeal for a world community "with a corresponding authority" as recently as 2012.[2] Partisans of nondomination arguably belong in their camp. The case for resisting domination is not, after all, contingent on people's locations, national boundaries, or the artifacts of citizenship. These are morally arbitrary if anything is. This is why I have argued that the structure of decision rules should follow the contours of power relations, not citizenships, at least when basic interests are at stake.[3] In an era when access to the necessities of employment and even survival are increasingly influenced by transnational forces, the case for global institutions might seem both obvious and compelling. Proponents of nondomination are committed to democratizing power relations. How could this not involve global institutions? After all, if there is no global governance, how can there be global democratic governance?

Maybe world government is coming whether we like it or not. If power increasingly is being exercised globally, and if I was right in Chapter 2 that power is a natural monopoly, then perhaps world government is inescapable. Commentators have debated that possibility at least since Bertrand Russell mooted it in 1947 following the advent of nuclear weapons. Much of the anxiety during the Cold War flowed from a sense that deterrence was bound to be unstable because it sought to defy power's natural monopoly character. Alexander Wendt defends a version of this claim today in the service of an argument that a world state is inevitable. I take up these contentions in section 5.1, arguing that their proponents conflate the natural monopoly character of power with the institutional capacity to harness it. Taking that into account makes short work of arguments about inevitability, but it leaves open the subject I take up in section 5.2: whether a world state might in any case be feasible, as William Scheuerman among others has contended. But Scheuerman's argument fails, and his attempt to shift the burden of persuasion to the skeptic of world government's feasibility is unconvincing. I also take up a more plausible proposal to subject existing international institutions to constitutional constraints, but I argue that global constitutionalism is overrated for reasons that parallel the overrating of national constitutionalism.

If world government is neither inevitable nor likely, would it nonetheless be desirable to facilitate global democracy? My answer in section 5.3 is negative. Against received wisdom I note that centralized national power was neither necessary nor sufficient for national democracy, but that national analogies are beside the point because world democracy is impossible. Instead I endorse the line of commentary running from Immanuel Kant to Robert Dahl, which holds that effective global institutions would likely be tyrannical. A world state would therefore be a bad bet for partisans of nondomination, assuming it could be created. This is not to deny that the current system facilitates domination. Often it does, but there is no good reason to think that a world state, whether or not democratic, would ameliorate it. A better course, I maintain, is to pursue other forms of accountability across borders. These include pushing for greater civil and criminal culpability to redress harms and deter future perpetrators, and building coalitions to advance proximate goals that have some prospect of reducing the worst form of domination.

Some will object that civil litigation, criminal enforcement, and the proximate goals I describe miss the heart of the matter. The current order sustains systemic injustice, and terms like *national self-determination* and *respect for national sovereignty* obscure what is really apartheid on a world scale. There is truth to this charge, but I argue in section 5.3 that it, too, falls short as a reason to work toward world government. Debilitating global economic inequalities and the corrosive maldistribution of other incidents of national citizenship might well not be reduced by a world state. Indeed, they might increase. It is, in any case, a cosmopolitan conceit to suppose that widespread attachment to national citizenships will dissipate, not least because of the strong incentives that national politicians have to sustain them.

And it is wrong to deny that pursuing proximate goals can have an impact on systemic injustice. Indeed, the project of adaptive political theory suggests that this is likely the best path to take. I elaborate this case in section 5.4 with a look at the campaign to rid the world of slavery. This proceeded in stages from the assault on the transatlantic slave trade that started in the late eighteenth century to the abolition of slavery in most of the British Empire in 1833, through the American Civil War and the antislavery conventions adopted by the League of Nations and the International Labour Organization (ILO) in the 1920s and 1930s. The successful antislavery campaign provides a useful template, I argue, to address some of the worst forms of economic domination in the world today through the campaign for a global minimum wage. This opens the way for the discussion of political and military domination that crosses borders, my subject in Chapter 6.

5.1 Inevitability Arguments

If world government were inevitable, questions about its desirability would be moot. At most, the question would need reframing as an inquiry into how world government might best be geared to preventing domination. But why might anyone suppose world government to be inevitable? The answer lies in the argument, endorsed in section 2.2, that power is a natural monopoly. Assuming Nozick's allegorical account of the origins of the state is on the mark about that, the question arises: Why is there no world government already? After all, nation-states are the global analogues of his competing protection associations within a given territory;

they are protection rackets writ large. The Nozickian global expectation should therefore be that one nation must eventually co-opt, defeat, or otherwise edge out the others. But it has not happened.

Nozick's answer would presumably be: Wait up; it depends on the available technologies of force. World government is not here yet, but, on this telling, we will move steadily toward it as weapons too powerful to ignore can be delivered anywhere in the world. At some point, everyone will have to knuckle under to one power. Alexander Wendt elaborates on a variant of this claim, arguing that the availability of ever more destructive technologies makes states increasingly vulnerable to devastating attack. Eventually, he thinks, the resulting fear will induce them to submit to a common power. They will embrace a universal collective security system and a binding world authority to resolve conflicts peacefully; a kind of global Weberian state.[4]

Wendt was not the first to push this idea. Bertrand Russell thought the triggering moment had arrived with the bombing of Hiroshima and Nagasaki in August 1945. He was sufficiently traumatized by this that he set aside both his pacifism and his antipathy for things American, declaring that the United States should pronounce itself a world government and then develop the most powerful nuclear arsenal possible to back up its authority.[5] Realizing that the U.S. nuclear monopoly was bound to be temporary, he thought time was of the essence. "It is obvious," Russell insisted, "that the only way in which war can be permanently prevented is the creation of a single government for the whole world, possessed of all the more powerful weapons of war." In order to do its job, the world government would have to be irresistible. "Even the greatest of separate powers should be incapable of fighting against it with any hope of success." Limiting the development of terrible weapons should therefore not be part of the agenda. "The more deadly are the weapons monopolized by the international authority, the more obvious will be its capacity to enforce its will, and the less will be the likelihood of resistance to its decrees."[6]

Russell's plan would never have worked, even if the United States had followed his advice before the Soviets and others developed nuclear weapons. For one thing, only someone entirely innocent of the dynamics of electoral politics could believe that any U.S. government could engage in gratuitous threats of nuclear attack to bring the entire world to heel. More important, Russell conflated the valid argument that coercive force is a natural monopoly with the fallacious view that overwhelming military power is sufficient to sustain this monopoly in practice. The Vietnam War made it plain that there is a vast difference between overpowering military superiority and the capacity to win wars in the real world. Having the technological capability to destroy a country's military is something quite different from being able to marshal the resources to do it on the ground. Russell's argument ignores the need to retain domestic political support in the face of the costs, measured in blood and treasure, of doing what is needed to prevail over a recalcitrant population. These can be so high that even an authoritarian government, not subject to the ballot box, has to give up—as the Soviets discovered in Afghanistan in the 1980s. And even if a military victory can be won, this says nothing about being able to control populations on a day-to-day basis, as the British learned after the Boer War and the United States has painfully been reminded in Afghanistan and Iraq.

Russell's argument ignores many economies of smallness in enforcement. Perhaps some combination of increases in surveillance and coercive technology will eventually create a worldwide *Nineteen Eighty-Four* regime, but this remains a long way off. We know from the literature on community policing that effective enforcement often depends vitally on local information and relationships.[7] They generate essential street-level knowledge, but they also matter for the perceived legitimacy that effective enforcement requires. Not for nothing did Max Weber did define the state as aspiring to monopolize the *legitimate* use of force.[8] Fernand Braudel, James Scott, and others have observed that often the state's coercive capacities are incomplete and its legitimacy questioned by significant sectors of the population—who can make enforcement costly by turning to crime or such weapons of the weak as terrorism even if they are not strong enough to overthrow the government.[9] Even Hobbes saw that sheer coercive power is not enough to get people to obey over time. It will be an uphill battle for the state to maintain its coercive monopoly if the population does not perceive the state as serving its interests.[10] The hill becomes markedly steeper when a foreign population is involved. The issue then becomes how long the occupying power can maintain domestic political support for the foreign venture as the costs grow. At some point it usually gives up.[11]

Rather than taking Russell's Nozickian logic global, Wendt argues that nations will evolve toward a single global state as a by-product of the fear induced by nuclear proliferation. This would be a tall order for many reasons. For one thing, as Gregory Kavka has emphasized and the logic of deterrence theory assumes, states have to be suicidal to engage in a nuclear attack in a nuclear era.[12] This rather dampens the Hobbesian postulation of fear of death as an impetus toward consolidating coercive power beyond the national level; all a country really needs is a second-strike capability to deter others from attack. And who, in any case, would submit to a government that they truly thought to be suicidal? Try imagining the people who really do believe that Iran might launch a nuclear attack against Israel deciding to submit to Iran as part of the nucleus of a world government. Moreover, even if it would be in the interest of today's governments to submit to a world state if one happened to exist, giant collective active challenges stymie the possibility of ever bringing one into existence. As Wendt concedes, "it is only after a state is created that it becomes rational to sign the social contract, since only then can they trust it to be enforced."[13]

Wendt tries to pull the rabbit out of his hat by arguing that powerful states will become increasingly insecure due to proliferating destructive technologies. This will make it harder for them to sustain a system "in which their power and privileges are not tied to an enforceable rule of law." Maintaining their dominant position by force will become increasingly costly. Eventually, he thinks, living ever more insecure lives in their gilded cages will prompt the leaders of powerful countries to forswear violence in favor of benign forms of interaction. They will see the virtues of a world government as the best means to institutionalize this, and sign up more or less as European leaders clambered aboard the European project in the last decades of the twentieth century.

Wendt believes that this process will be helped along by the human desire for recognition. But not any old recognition. He has in mind Hegel's account of the instability of asymmetrical forms of recognition, and in particular his discussion of the master-slave dialectic in the *Phenomenology*.[14] Hegel famously insisted that the master-slave relationship is unstable, not just because the slave will rebel, but also because it will not satisfy the master, who needs recognition from an equal. The slave's fearful fawning will not do. It's a nice thought, but Hegel never cites any evidence in support of it and neither does Wendt. The actual abolition of slavery followed a rather different dynamic, as I discuss in section 5.4 below. And just as Hegel was wrong to think that history had reached its teleological terminus with the nineteenth-century Prussian state, Wendt is unconvincing that his posited human need for recognition will morph into a desire for symmetrical relations among governments and then their universal embrace of the permanent authority of a world state.

Skepticism is in order for many reasons, perhaps the most obvious being that one of the surest paths to power within states involves endorsing national identities that are tied to territorial claims. I argued in section 3.2.1 that the best way to undermine demonizing logics in politics is to replace indivisible goods with divisible ones that foster compromise when it is feasible and reduce the stakes of conflict when it is not.

But the cards are stacked against this in international politics, where politicians face strong incentives to sustain exclusive identities as cement for domestic coalitions, and to externalize costs onto outsiders on whom they do not depend. Think of how Hitler built up political support in the 1930s by exploiting Germany's claims against France over the Rhineland, or against the Czechs over the Sudetenland. Consider how Vladimir Putin enhanced his popularity in 2014 by milking Russia's conflicts with Ukraine over Crimea. Similar stories can be told about the India-Pakistan standoff over Kashmir, the Sino-Japanese dispute over the Senkaku Islands, the Israeli-Palestinian conflict . . . the list goes on. Political entrepreneurs have lived off all of them for generations, stoking their versions of Manifest Destiny for seductive political gains. Wendt believes that the antagonistic logic that such practices generate will disappear, but he never explains how this might happen—let alone why it must happen. The occasional Nelson Mandela or Václav Havel might resist the temptation to build coalitions by demonizing others, but that is a good part of the reason we regard them as outliers.

Wendt's appeal to history is no more convincing than is his theory. He believes that nations are steadily consolidating into larger units, but he relies on cherry-picked examples to make this case. The repeated efforts to create collective security systems after major conflicts in 1815, 1918, and 1945 feed his optimism, but the first two of these fell apart catastrophically and Mark Mazower makes a convincing case that post–World War II internationalism has been on the wane for decades, accelerating since the end of the Cold War.[15] Wendt also mentions colonialism as a force for consolidation, and sometimes it is.[16] But empires don't only consolidate; they also fall apart. The dozens of nations in contemporary Africa were spawned by decolonization after World War II, just as the collapse of the Austro-Hungarian empire half a century earlier had led to the proliferation of new nation-states in Central and Eastern Europe. Thirty-four countries have been manufactured since the Soviet Union and its satellites began collapsing in 1989.[17] By 2014 the number of countries in the world had more than doubled since World War II—scarcely evidence of consolidation.[18]

Wendt is also impressed by the European Union, but whether the EU is currently consolidating or deconsolidating is an open question. Tony Judt predicted in 2005 that it would face grave difficulties once it hit a real crisis, because unification has always been an elite project lacking in popular support.[19] The 2008 financial crisis revealed his caution to be well founded. Despite the technocratic pressure for more integration to manage the fallout, centrifugal political forces have prevented this. Three out of six national referendums have opposed greater integration, ten more have been canceled by political leaders fearful of the result, and anti-European parties outperform the major national parties in countries as different as Britain, France, and Holland in elections to the European Parliament.[20] The refugee crisis that erupted in 2015 intensified the centrifugal pressure. In short, neither the empirical record nor Wendt's theorizing provides a convincing basis for the claim that a world state is inevitable.

5.2 Feasible if not Inevitable?

If not inevitable, is world government at least feasible? William Scheuerman makes a case for this from what, he argues, are realist premises. His point of departure is to contend that such mid-twentieth-century realist scholars of international relations as Hans Morgenthau, E. H. Carr, Reinhold Niebuhr, and others were "progressive realists" who believed some form of global government to be desirable.[22] How persuasive his readings of these figures are need not detain us, however, because he does not claim that any of them set out a plausible path to world government; in fact, they were all avowed skeptics of that possibility.[21] Rather, his claim is that they were convincing that some form of world state would be both desirable and consistent with a realist reading of national states' interests—provided it exhibited certain criteria.

For one thing, it really must be a state. Some commentators believe that global governance is possible without a global government, but Scheuerman is not among them. His world state need not enjoy a perfect monopoly of global force, but it must be able to enforce a "system of binding law" on a global basis. The world state he envisages would nonetheless be benign. It would be federal in character, embody the kind of subsidiarity principles that prevail in the EU, and embody "core liberal democratic political ideals." Moreover, it would need to be underpinned by a global community that would be strong enough to support its institutions. By this he means, among other things, that populations governed by it would identify with the world state in ways that are comparable to their current identification with national states.

How could this be? Scheuerman concedes that under contemporary conditions a world state could be established only violently and that "if somehow set up would be plagued by civil wars" and other less than desirable features, particularly if there were not other supportive global social institutions. Yet he insists that "the long term possibility of a robust supranational society adequate to supporting world government" should not be "dismissed out of hand."[23] In this vein he takes commentators

from Hannah Arendt to Jean Cohen to task for worrying about the tyrannical possibilities inherent in a world state, insisting that they depend
on caricatures and mantras in the skeptical literature.[24] A world government "would only be worth having," he insists, "if its liberal democratic
ideals were sound."[25] Such a world state would render the tyranny objections moot.

Scheuerman's contention that his world state would not be beset by civil
wars depends on the claim that the impulse to fight them "could be contained by building on a stringent ethic of responsibility."[26] But he says
nothing about where that would come from. The worry that a world state
would not likely be democratic elicits the response that this would be
offset partly by federalism and subsidiarity and partly by advances in
communications technology. But his main claim is that "we should avoid
rigidly excluding the possibility of dramatic shifts in how we experience
and interact with government." Here he has in mind that "if worldwide
political authorities acted effectively to secure basic rights and secure the
peace, citizens would likely come to identify with them."[27] But why should
anyone believe political authorities would do that? Scheuerman seems to
think that pointing out that something is not utterly impossible shifts the
burden of proof to the skeptic. But social science does not work that way
any more than politics does. The social science question is: What evidence
supports the claim that posited developments are likely or even plausible? A credible political argument would include specifying changes that
could move the world toward the new order, identifying coalitions that could
be formed to achieve the those changes, and supplying an account of how
they could be held together in light of the likely opposition. Scheuerman
never attempts either.

Rejecting Scheuerman's far-fetched cosmopolitan project, Jean Cohen
proposes tackling the legitimacy deficit of existing international institutions by subjecting them to enhanced constitutional constraints. She
notes, and seeks to build on, the fact that the global political landscape is
shifting toward a dualistic world order in which power operates at two
levels: the enduring sovereign authority of conventional states and the
growing legal authority of international institutions—of which the UN is
the most important. She wants to find ways to enhance the legitimacy of
international institutions by subjecting them to constitutional constraints
in ways that will make them more appealing to national governments.
The best result would be a pluralist international order in which sovereign states, cooperating regionally in federal arrangements, exist along-
side constitutionally constrained international institutions.

Cohen thinks that the recent proliferation of global institutions and
agencies makes the imperative to rein them in all the more pressing. She

describes a number of reforms that would move things in the right direction. Central among them is reworking the UN Charter system to diminish, if not get rid of, the lawmaking and executive powers of the Security Council, elimination of the veto power of the permanent members on many major matters at least, strengthening the General Assembly, creating global courts "with jurisdiction to review rights violating resolutions that are legislative in character and directly and adversely affect individuals," and a policing mechanism to manage the relations between the reformed UN system and national political systems.[28]

Appealing as Cohen's proposals might be, her global constitutionalist agenda confronts overwhelming challenges. One concerns the motivation for change. She calls for the creation of formal legal rules to regulate the activities of global institutions and agencies, but never says where the impetus for the reforms that she advocates will come from. For instance, she offers searing indictments of the role of the Security Council in undermining constitutional behavior since the advent of the War on Terror as well as its increased willingness to authorize humanitarian intervention at the behest of major powers.[29] But it is difficult to imagine what would induce the veto players to change their behavior or what would induce their governments to change the Charter. Second, even if formal rules of the kind Cohen advocates were adopted, it is hard to see what difference this would this make in the absence of any system to enforce them. Both China and the United States refuse to submit to the authority of the International Criminal Court, a factor that undermines its legitimacy. What would make them change? Making a convincing political case for a new international rule or norm includes showing why embracing it would be in the interest of those who are in a position to flout it—or so I argue in Chapter 6. Third, the global constitutionalism movement derives much of its appeal from assumptions about the importance of constitutional rules in national politics. But this is greatly overrated, as we saw in sections 4.2.1 and 4.2.2. Constitutional orders endure when the underlying politics supports them, not the other way around. Why should we expect parchment barriers to fare any better in global politics than they do in national politics?

5.3 Democracy's Handmaiden?

But perhaps we should not give up the idea of world government too quickly. If democratic institutions are the best bet to institutionalize resistance to domination, as I have argued, and if many of the power relations that we should be trying to democratize are going global, it might seem obvious that global democratic institutions are required to do the job. The history of democracy's national triumph might be cited in support of this logic. Perry Anderson established long ago that what we now think of as the first wave of democracies in Europe did not evolve directly out of feudalism. Absolutism displaced feudalism; democracy came later.[30] David Held has explored how the centralization of power within Europe's absolutist monarchies facilitated this process.[31] There had to be commanding heights for democrats to seize. For analogous reasons, Held argues that advancing toward global democracy will require, at a minimum, creating an international *rechtsstaat:* a rule-of-law regime geared to advancing the cause of justice.[32] It is hard to see how that can happen in the absence of a world state.

In Chapter 6 I argue that there are good reasons to promote the rule of law internationally, but that is quite different from supposing that a Weberian coercive monopoly is either necessary or sufficient to create democracy on a world scale. With respect to the latter, Weberian states can persist for long periods of time—perhaps indefinitely, for all we know—without democratizing. China is one notable instance, but North Korea, Saudi Arabia, and Myanmar are among the many examples that could be given. Moreover, Weberian states that do democratize can revert to authoritarianism, as happened last century in Japan, Germany, and Italy—not to mention much of Africa and Latin America.[33] There is no more reason to think that democracies cannot unravel than to think that all states must evolve into democracies. Democracies are contingent, vulnerable achievements.

Nor is a Weberian state necessary for democracy. It has been conventional for political scientists from Hobbes to Huntington to insist that order comes first: that unless people accept the state's monopoly of coercive power, politics will disintegrate into anarchical chaos. But we saw in section 3.1.3 that reality can be more fluid. The United States is perhaps the preeminent instance in which democratization preceded, and was indeed instrumental in, national state building. The Constitutional Convention in 1787 and subsequent ratification campaign was an unprecedented, if flawed, democratic process. The decentralized confederation had almost lost the Revolutionary War because of its inability to marshal an effective army. The Convention replaced it with a centralized state capable, for the first time, of exercising a legitimate monopoly over instruments of coercive power.[34] Switzerland is another, albeit more gradual and less dramatic, instance in which democratization and state building proceeded in tandem.[35]

There are, however, good reasons to regard comparisons with national democracy as beside the point on the grounds that achieving world democracy is impossible. Trying to imagine democratic revolutionary forces storming the barricades of a world state is, to put it mildly, a challenge. The other main historical triggers of democratization—interstate war and external imposition—are clearly irrelevant in the present context.[36] This makes the proposal to displace the existing democracies with a world state on spec a pretty high-risk bet from a democratic point of view. And then there is the worry that it is far from obvious that a global democracy could work, even if it could somehow be instituted. Democracy champion Robert Dahl was persuasively skeptical. He noted that despite the many efficacies of scale, there is an inverse relationship between size and democratic accountability. For Dahl this meant that effective international institutions could not be democratic.[37] In this he echoed Immanuel Kant, who argued that, desirable as a benign world government would be, any actual world government would either be ineffective or tyrannical.[38] Accordingly, Kant favored working toward a federation of cooperative republics instead.

The major transnational institutions that do exist buttress the Kant-Dahl skepticism of world government. Typically these institutions are creatures of treaties. As such, they are even more tenuously accountable to the underlying populations than are national governments. Indeed, many regimes that are parties to the treaties, and active participants in the institutions they create, are not democracies at all. The EU is a partial exception in that members must be democracies and it directly elects a European Parliament that has gained some authority over European institutions and finances in recent years.[39] But the term *democratic deficit* is not routinely applied to the EU for nothing.[40] Perhaps this deficit will eventually be addressed, but efforts to date are less than encouraging. Other consequential pan-European institutions such as the European Central Bank and NATO are dominated by small numbers of powerful players; no one would invoke them as promising templates to scale up democracy. International institutions are, after all, as Mazower says, "chiefly executive bureaucracies, and mostly their most powerful members like them that way."[41]

Additional arguments for world democracy seem to flow naturally from the principle of affected interest. Democratic legitimacy rests on the notion that the people whose interests are at stake in a decision should have a say in making it. One reason national decision making can be troubling is that so often it operates at variance with this principle: in an increasingly global economy, decisions about trade, employment, and fiscal and monetary policy in one country have ramifications for people who live elsewhere. This is not to mention the spillover effects of environmental degradation, natural resource depletion, and military adventures. As power increasingly is exercised globally, the need to tether it to global institutions becomes stronger. If the principle of affected interest is the wellspring of democratic legitimacy, how can we justify regarding national governments as the presumptive repositories of decision making?

Yet these valid observations do not add up to a case for world government. For one thing, while everyone on earth might in some sense be affected by a decision, its importance will vary for different individuals. If people trivially affected by an outcome have the same say as those with basic interests at stake, perverse outcomes are likely to follow.[42] We see this when people who do not use publicly funded medical insurance have the same say in determining what it covers as those who must rely on it, or when those whose children do not attend public schools have the same say in their funding as those whose children do attend.[43] The same is true internationally. We would not want people in landlocked countries to have a say equal to that of waterfront states in a proposed global tax on harbors. The key is to find mechanisms of accountability that better protect those whose basic interests are vulnerable. Global institutions might well be counterproductive from this point of view, particularly if the most powerful players control them. The examples set by the International Monetary Fund and the World Trade Organization are not encouraging.

Moreover, if the goal is for decisions better to reflect the preferences of people whose basic interests are at stake, sometimes this will involve delegation to subnational units rather than scaling up. Arguments for devolution from Westminster to Scottish and Welsh assemblies appeal to this logic. And even when scaling up is called for, it might be to a regional body rather than a world legislature. The principle of subsidiarity embraced—if not always honored—by the EU recognizes this implicitly. Subsidiarity starts by presuming deference to local decision making, and then moving up the ladder if and when protecting relevant affected interests requires this. No doubt there will be disagreements about where particular decisions should be located, requiring, in turn, procedures to resolve those disagreements. But the essential point is that rather than dictating any particular unit of government as best, the principle of affected interest suggests disaggregating the demos decision by decision. Indeed, some decisions—such as whether to abandon life support for the terminally ill—should be devolved to even smaller decision-making units like families and perhaps (by living wills and durable powers of attorney) even to single individuals.[44]

Waiting for world government to combat cross-border domination carries, at best, a whiff of waiting for Godot. Arguably, it makes better sense to focus on more tractable possibilities. Coercive political and military threats are taken up in Chapter 6. In the economic realm there are ways to combat the possibility of cross-border domination that do not depend on international institutions. Multinational corporations can be sued, sometimes in their country of origin, for torts committed abroad when they put local populations at risk. A dramatic example was Union Carbide in Bhopal, India, in 1984, when half a million people were exposed to methyl isocyanate gas from which close to 20,000 people would eventually die.[45] The Alien Tort Claims Act allows prosecutions in U.S. courts of such "specific, universal, and obligatory" crimes as torture, genocide, war crimes, crimes against humanity, extrajudicial killing, slavery, and piracy committed outside the United States.[46] This eighteenth-century law was revived in 1980 as a helpful vehicle for international human rights litigation, though unfortunately in 2013 the U.S. Supreme Court cut back on its extraterritorial application.[47] It remains an open question whether corporations can be sued under this law.[48] Legislation like the Foreign Corrupt Practices Act in the United States and the OECD Convention on Combatting Foreign Bribery create other avenues for enforcing laws against corporate corruption and malfeasance in developing countries without the need for global institutions.[49]

5.4 Systemic Injustice and Moral Arbitrariness

Some will object that criminal enforcement and civil litigation ignore systemic injustices sustained by the world system. They will insist that the real problem is with the underlying architecture of the global system.[50] After all, the current division of the world has been forged by wars and imperial ventures, bequeathing an order in which most of the world's population is excluded from the lion's share of its wealth and power. Moreover, the nation-state system that we take for granted is young. Its roots can be traced to the Treaty of Westphalia that ended the Thirty Years War in 1648, but as Michael Doyle and Mark Mazower have noted, the sacrosanct character of national sovereignty is considerably younger. Our strong presumption against external interference made its debut in the Kellogg-Briand Pact of 1928, but it was not widely embraced until after World War II, when the UN Charter affirmed the right to national self-determination, extending it to the dozens of new nations that took shape as the European empires were dismantled in the 1960s and 1970s.[51] Since then, it has been eroded around the edges by developments like the creation of the International Criminal Court in 1998 and the UN's endorsement of the "Responsibility to Protect" in 2005.[52] But on economic and other distributive matters the system remains supreme, even as the power of national governments to manage it has atrophied.[53]

Moreover, none of the going conceptions of political legitimacy lend themselves to plausible defenses of nation-states. Various fictions about social contracts are just that, since no nation has actually come into being by agreement. We saw in sections 2.2 and 2.3 that the contractarian test is incoherent, and that in any case even the United States fails it, despite the fact that it was fashioned in an unusually self-conscious way. Such commentators as Shelly Kagan and Peter Singer have observed that the main liberal alternative to the social contract, utilitarianism, is at odds with the nation-state-based distribution of resources.[54] It concentrates them in the hands of those least likely to benefit most, if for no other reason than diminishing marginal utility. The main alternative contender to utilitarianism and the social contract is democracy, but it, too, comes up short as a source of legitimation for the nation-state. Democratic theory is notoriously impotent when confronted with questions about its own scope. It affirms majority rule as the basis for decision making, but by its terms this assumes that the question "Majority of whom?" has already been settled. We saw in section 2.2 that once that question is put into play, the results can be as politically explosive as they are philosophically intractable.[55] In short, the standard theories of political legitimacy do little for nation-states individually or, by extension, for the nation-state system.

This valid conclusion scarcely amounts to a case for world government. Economic inequalities should be redressed when they foster domination, regardless of whether national boundaries stand in the way. But abolishing nation-states hardly seems like a plausible path to that goal. Whatever the explanation for global inequalities, there is no convincing reason to suppose that a world government would redress them, even if it were democratic. Massive, and sometimes increasing, inequalities persist in democracies. Why this happens is a continuing puzzle for political economists, but it is hard to see why anyone would believe that scaling up to world government would help.[56] On the contrary, enforcement difficulties and collective action obstacles to change in such a large entity might well multiply them. An undemocratic global system would run afoul of nondomination for the reasons adduced against vanguardism in section 2.1, but there is in any case no good reason to think that it would reduce global inequalities either. Authoritarian systems seem to be egalitarian only when they are poor. Communist states defied this for a while, but as James Galbraith reminds us, they have proved unviable.[57]

Sometimes the arbitrariness objection is not about access to economic resources so much as access to the distribution of citizenship itself. Why should the accidents of birth privilege some to live in countries with benign regimes while others must survive where life is nasty, brutish, and short? Why should the former garner the windfalls associated with one country's citizenship while the latter suffer the costs of another? These are good questions, but what is at issue with them is really the maldistribution of freedoms and life chances associated with different citizenships, not national citizenships as such. As a result, considerations like those just adduced about economic resources apply: there is no better reason to expect a world government to reduce the maldistribution of noneconomic factors that shape freedoms and life chances than it would the maldistribution of economic resources.

There is, in any case, a non sequitur involved in arguing for the abolition of national citizenship on the grounds that some citizenships are more valuable than others. It's a bit like saying that because some people have better eyesight than others, the world would be improved if everyone were rendered blind. Perhaps pointing to the differing values of various citizenships might support an argument for the most liberal sustainable immigration policies, or one that held that those with more desirable citizenships should compensate those with less desirable ones if some relevant causal relationship between the two could be established. But none of this amounts to a case for the abolition of national citizenship as such. To establish the desirability of that, one would have to shoulder an additional burden: show that people would be better served by being global citizens only. This seems an obvious nonstarter in view of the exceedingly strong attachments that most people have to their national political identities and their abiding reluctance to transfer them even to institutions like the EU.

There is nothing inherently objectionable about exclusion. Denying this would mean embracing the idea that people are entitled to inclusion in any association that they choose. Why assume that? Unrequited love involves exclusion, yet we routinely expect people to accept it.[58] Any plausible case that exclusion from national citizenship is different would soon lapse into instrumental considerations already discussed: that it distributes resources and opportunities in unjustifiable ways. That might be true, but we have seen these considerations do not support the conclusion that national citizenship should be abolished in favor of universal membership of a world state. Anyone who embraces that conclusion nonetheless is really expressing cosmopolitan disdain for parochialism. But that is just snobbery; most people are content to be parochial.

Sometimes antipathy for national citizenship has to do less with those who are excluded from it and more with allegiances and practices that it fosters. Nationalism certainly has its ugly and xenophobic sides. It can underwrite imperialist and other expansionist agendas that breed domination. But xenophobia and imperialism are a lot older than territorial nation-states, so it is hard to see that they imply anything distinctively objectionable about nation-states. Indeed, Steven Pinker has made a convincing case that the period during which the nation-state system developed was also one of declining violence and cruelty in most countries and in the world taken as a whole. To be sure, romantic variants of nationalism combined with the revolution in military technology to produce increasingly lethal forms of military conflict, but this was more than offset by the pacifying effects of nation-states as monopolies of coercive force within their borders.[59] And Benedict Anderson has reminded us that while some variants of national affiliation are malevolent, patriotism can also take benign forms. It is not national affiliation itself that is troublesome, but the ways in which it is often politicized.[60]

We saw in section 3.1.2 that politics is more likely to be benign when conflict is over divisible goods rather than indivisible ones. That is hard to achieve in international politics, as I have just noted, because of the incentives that tempt national leaders to mobilize political support by demonizing outsiders in ways that often involve asserting exclusive claims against them, not to mention resisting exclusive claims advanced by others. Palestinians and Israelis would surely be better off if they could agree on a one-state solution that guaranteed access to religious sites for all, but this does not mean political leaders advocating that outcome will ever become successful in Palestinian or Israeli politics. Advocates of world government from Russell to Wendt achieve what surface plausibility they do by focusing on alleged functional imperatives to the exclusion of these political dynamics that are not going to go away. What to do about that is taken up in Chapter 6. The essential conclusion here is that there is no good reason to think that national bases of affiliation are worse than other kinds of group identification history has thrown up or is likely to, or that replacing nation-states with world government, *per impossible,* would have a felicitous effect on systemic injustice.

5.5 Proximate Goals and Systemic Change

This, in turn, suggests that we should not be too quick to dismiss more focused and reactive responses to injustice. Some of these strategies go beyond the legal remedies mentioned at the end of section 5.2, though they are similar in not depending on the existence of transnational institutions. Often they are all there is, and sometimes they deliver more than we expect. The campaign to abolish slavery that took off in the late eighteenth century is suggestive.

5.5.1 The Campaign against Slavery

I noted in section 1.1 that had there been neoclassical economists around before the fact, they would have scoffed at the possibility of abolishing the slave trade. Arguments about free riding and the race to the bottom would have been wheeled out to buttress the proposition that no abolition regime would be sustainable. The outcome seems all the more remarkable in view of recent scholarship that has debunked older conventional wisdom that held that slavery was comparatively inefficient and that its abolition was primarily due to changing international norms. We now know that abolition involved imposing huge losses on industries that deployed slave labor and that it also required the British government to internalize the massive costs of a six-decades-long enforcement effort. These included the direct costs to the British Treasury of the enforcement regime, as well as the indirect but very substantial costs to the economies that benefited from the products of slave labor.[61] Yet it was done.

Essential to the abolitionists' success was that they pursued well-defined proximate goals around which effective coalitions could be built, and they managed to coopt or marginalize enough of the opposition for long enough to get the job done. The initial aim was to eliminate the transatlantic slave trade. A small group of Dissenting MPs engineered a vote in Parliament to forbid it in 1807.[62] They knew that the United States would likely outlaw the slave trade when this became constitutionally permissible the following year, if for dubious reasons: there was growing American sentiment to limit America's nonwhite populations, and many Southerners wanted to protect the—by then robust—American domestic slave trade.[63] Politics can make strange bedfellows.

The initial parliamentary votes led to a series of bilateral treaties, but meaningful enforcement had to wait until Dissenting MPs came to hold the balance of power in Parliament in the 1830s. This enabled them to auction their support to governments that were willing to advance the abolitionist cause.[64] The British outlawed slavery in most of the empire by 1833.[65] Enforcement was ramped up outside the empire by aggressive diplomacy and unilateral military action, which escalated to an undeclared war against Brazil in 1850 to end the slave trade there. The United States finally agreed to searches of its ships in 1862, and five years later Cuba was pressured into ending its slave imports.

It was, by any measure, a creative political achievement. Success depended on a combination of persistence by entrepreneurs for the cause, creative coalition building at home and abroad, and aggressive deployment of diplomacy and force. Slave owners in the empire were bought off with some £20 million in reparations (£16.5 billion in today's terms).[66] American acquiescence was secured by focusing initially on the transatlantic trade only. This also blunted opposition from Britain's domestic commercial interests. Ending the slave trade posed no immediate threat to the flow of cheap materials, notably cotton and sugar, produced by slave labor abroad. Most Tories opposed abolition, but they felt more immediately threatened by other mounting demands: to emancipate Catholics, expand the franchise, abolish rotten boroughs, reduce royal prerogatives, and enact social legislation on behalf of the growing industrial workforce. Moderate Whigs who wanted tactical concessions to stanch these more radical demands had earlier convinced pragmatists like William Pitt to go along on the slavery question.[67] The slave traders in the West Indies stood to lose plenty, but they had no political clout at Westminster. Most workers lacked the vote, but to the extent their views mattered they had every reason to oppose the threat slavery posed to their wages and employment, which they did in churches and public meetings.[68]

Parliamentary arithmetic helped. Chaim Kaufmann and Robert Pape point out that in each of the six elections between 1835 through 1857, the Dissenters' share of the vote exceeded the difference between the Tories and other Whigs—giving them the balance of power at Westminster, which they used to force successive governments into proactive action on slavery. They scotched any possible doubts about their seriousness by toppling Viscount Melbourne's Whig administration in 1841, even though this meant the return of Sir Robert Peel's Tories to office and therefore major losses (at least for the moment) on free trade and the other Whig causes they supported.[69] The Dissenters' success underscores the great advantages of single-issue politics. It is hard for opponents to buy people off if there is nothing to buy them off with.[70] Indeed, it was the fact that their adversaries were more exercised about other matters that gave the Dissenters the upper hand. They made themselves the wedge issue.

An implication of this is it that systemic injustice might be better addressed obliquely than directly. This is true for strategic reasons, but not only for strategic reasons. It also embodies the "political, not metaphysical" stance I embraced in section 1.2 as well suited to adaptive resistance to domination. Pursuing proximate goals can appeal to diverse coalitions whose members could never agree on many aspects of a theory of systemic injustice or even on why they favor the proximate goal in question. And a proximate goal is helpful in mobilizing governments and others to commit effort and resources, because it means that there is a destination in sight where one can declare victory, however provisional. This has the potential to create a new reality on the ground, one that structures the possibilities going forward. Abolition of the slave trade became a way station in the longer battle to abolish slavery. It reduced the dependence of major economies on slave labor, decreasing the number and power of slavery's defenders while energizing abolitionists. It was a realistically utopian venture.[71]

This is not to say that the moral case against slavery was irrelevant. Moral arguments against slavery were vital in motivating the Dissenters in Parliament to stick together. They united behind William Wilberforce in his twenty-six-year battle that culminated in the Slave Trade Act of 1807, and then in the multidecade enforcement effort that he led within Parliament until 1826, and outside it until his death shortly after the Slavery Abolition Act passed in 1833. Indeed, it was the intensity of the Dissenters' moral commitment that led them to subordinate their other goals to it.

And it was not just their own commitment that mattered. Part of what sustained them was the moral crusade outside Westminster that was fostered in antislavery societies, churches, Quaker gatherings, and other public meetings. The resulting petition drives made it obvious that opposition to slavery was intense and widespread. Sixty thousand signatures were delivered to Parliament after a three-month petition drive in 1787–1778. After Wilberforce's first antislavery bill failed in 1791, abolitionists flooded Parliament with almost 390,000 signatures in over 500 petitions in less than a year. This was at a time when England's population was under 9 million and its electorate fewer than 400,000.[72] The external pressure empowered abolitionists at Westminster and made it more likely that their opponents would give way, as they eventually did.

That moral arguments were important does not mean that there was a single winning one, either for the political elites who fought the battle at Westminster or among those who organized and took part in public meetings, petition drives, and other forms of orchestrated pressure like writing and disseminating pamphlet literature. The Quaker and other Christian arguments were always powerful motivators, but they were never undisputed. Just as David Goldfield notes that every Christian denomination in America split over slavery in the decades leading up to the Civil War,

David Brion Davis reminds us that slavery was hotly contested among Christians, and between them and deists, during late-eighteenth-century mobilization in England.[73]

Secular critics of slavery also made various, sometimes incompatible, arguments. As Dorina Outram has noted, Enlightenment thinkers did not speak against slavery in a single unambivalent voice any more than the religious thinkers did. Francis Hutcheson made egalitarian appeal to the universal human capacity for suffering. But Adam Smith favored abolition because of the superiority of free labor, and David Hume was a more ambivalent abolitionist who affirmed the existence of racial hierarchies.[74] What mattered more than abolitionists agreeing on a single moral argument, religious or secular, was that they found some moral argument compelling.

The slavery precedent should not be oversold. Even if abolishing the slave trade in regions controlled by European empires weakened slavery's defenders, it still took a civil war to end American slavery. Southern whites stood to lose too much to give up without a fight, or to concede the inevitable when they lost the Civil War. They fought Reconstruction to a standstill and defanged the Civil War amendments as much as they could, even though this left them clinging to a vanishing way of life supported by a marginalizing sharecropper economy that would sideline the South from full participation in America's explosive economic growth in the coming decades.[75] But their eventual acquiescence would doubtless have been harder to secure had they not increasingly been isolated by the successful abolition of the slave trade—and of slavery itself—in almost all of the British Empire and much of Latin America by the 1860s. As David Brion Davis puts it, "The fall of New World slavery could not have occurred if there had been no abolitionist movements."[76] In retrospect, it is hard to second-guess their campaigns.

Some might object that the slavery example can be oversold in another way. Hard fought as the battle against slavery was, it was a system on the way out that would have few defenders, at least in the West, by the turn of the twentieth century. Perhaps, but the campaign is instructive nonetheless. It suggests a way to think through some of the most challenging features of globalization today from the standpoint of justice: outsourcing, social dumping, sweatshops, and other global practices that drive poverty and inequality to levels that render many of the world's poorest populations vulnerable to acute forms of domination. The successful battle against slavery suggests that a viable path forward is to build and sustain coalitions in support of a global minimum wage.

5.5.2 A Global Minimum Wage

The underlying intuition here is that a good response to the race to the bottom challenge is to raise the floor. The standard argument against keeping national wages high, whether by minimum wage legislation or other devices, is that it promotes capital flight—and that this becomes easier as the rate of capital mobility outstrips that of labor. No doubt this argument can be exaggerated.[77] Wages are often more downwardly sticky than the standard economic models imply, enabling countries like Germany to maintain full employment and high wages simultaneously.[78] But protecting national wages through minimum wage legislation is hard politically because it pits local capital against local labor. Alternatives such as the Earned Income Tax Credit (EITC) in the United States avoid this difficulty by subsidizing low wages with tax credits, but that pits low-income workers against taxpayers.[79] This is not to deny that these battles are worth fighting. Indeed, as I note below, the conflicts between capital and labor over minimum wages in the developed countries have been exaggerated. But we should not expect too much from national strategies in an era when obstacles to the mobility of capital have atrophied so much. Given the interests arrayed on the other side, on their own national strategies are unlikely to keep pace with the challenge in ways that will produce structural change.[80] By contrast, pressing for a global minimum wage has a better chance to avoid opposition from taxpaying voters or powerful sectors within the developed economies.

Of course, not everyone will support it. As the resistance to the May 2014 worldwide minimum wage strike against fast-food corporations underscored, minimum wage campaigns will always provoke opposition.[81] Even in that case, however, while striking workers talked about a global minimum wage, they were in fact pressing for increases in national minimum wages. A true global minimum, if instituted, would not put corporations at a competitive disadvantage or increase taxes. From this perspective, what looks like a conflict between capital and labor is really a collective action problem among firms. Everyone would be better off with a global minimum that bought industrial peace and freedom from the public relations opprobrium of running sweatshops, not to mention contented workers with more to spend. Indeed, economists like Thomas Palley argue that the delinking of wages from productivity growth in recent decades fed the inordinate reliance on debt and asset price inflation to spur demand that culminated in the 2008 financial crisis. A higher global minimum wage system, he contends, would counteract this trend, stimulating the global economy while tempering the acceleration of inequality.[82] But until the global minimum is established, every firm is better off resisting increases in local minimums where they do business.[83]

The history of minimum wage legislation in the United States supports this conjecture. Peter Swenson has shown that employer opposition to minimum wages during the 1920s and 1930s was lukewarm and, once legislation passed, many employers supported it. Moreover, when courts began striking down minimum wage legislation, businesses and business groups—including the less than progressive National Association of Manufacturers (NAM)—often came out in support of the minimum wages. The result was that by the mid-1930s, New Dealers could reasonably bet that "minimum standards legislation would enjoy considerable post facto, if not always immediate business support."[84] This is partly why minimum wage legislation survived the political and judicial assaults on other New Deal legislation, including the Supreme Court's striking down the National Industrial Recovery Act in 1935.[85] Prominent businessmen organized effective lobbying efforts to protect wage and hours legislation, garnering support from significant peers. Swenson adduces compelling evidence that even when groups like NAM formally opposed labor standards legislation, as they did in 1938, their official contrarian stance "masked a strong and steady undercurrent of approval" among their members. For some employers the appeal of minimum labor standards legislation was partly that labor groups like the American Federation of Labor initially opposed it as an alternative to collective bargaining. But organized labor's opposition was also temporary and tepid. Whatever the mixes of motives, and despite the subsequent challenges to maintaining the value of minimum wages that I discuss in section 4.3.2, it seems clear that the idea of a floor was established and preserved by a widespread, if not comprehensive, recognition of its advantages.[86]

Comparable logic applies to the idea of a global minimum wage. Efforts to export minimum wages have been gathering steam in recent decades in response to the increased mobility of capital, which, as Jason Hickel says, "has been globalized while the rules that protect people from it have not."[87] Organized labor, human rights groups, the ILO, and international NGOs have sought to protect wages through legislation, trade agreements, transnational strikes, and public relations campaigns. This is a predictable response to both the acceleration in capital mobility since the 1980s and the concomitant wage stagnation in both developed and middle-income economies.

Much of the effort has been geared toward bolstering national minimum wages. Countries like the UK, which had dismantled them in the neoliberal heyday of the 1980s, reversed course in 1999. Most developed economies either instituted or increased minimum wages in the first decade of the new century, and many developing countries followed suit—particularly high-growth middle-income countries like Brazil, China, and South Africa. These interventions meant that minimum wages kept pace with average wages globally and with per capita GDP in the advanced countries. But minimum wages have been falling when compared with per capita GDP globally, reflecting the reality that increased productivity does not produce wage gains at the bottom of the labor market.[88] Unskilled and, increasingly, semiskilled workers are price-takers when capital can easily pack up and move. Nike can relocate plants from China to Vietnam.[89] South African textile jobs can hemorrhage to Lesotho.[90] To forestall such outcomes, a global minimum is needed to drag up the floor in the poorest countries.

As with the U.S. minimum wage, many who do not advocate reform might not oppose it with much gusto. Setting a global minimum wage would impose costs, to be sure, but the extent of the costs is debatable, and in any case they would not ultimately be borne by workers or employers. Rather, they would be borne by consumers and by the unemployed in poor countries that became less attractive to investors, leading to fewer jobs at the margin. It is hard to imagine consumers overcoming the collective action obstacles to resisting a global minimum wage. As for the employment cost in poor countries, this would be substantially mitigated if cheaper labor were not on offer elsewhere. There is no race to the bottom when you are already there.

Champions of a global minimum wage recognize the value of starting small. Any feasible minimum would be substantially below wages in the developed economies and, indeed, most middle-income economies, leaving plenty of scope for global competition for cheap labor. Yet even an exceedingly modest global minimum would make a big difference at the bottom. After the April 2013 Savar tragedy in Bangladesh, in which 1,127 workers were killed by a collapsing sweatshop, Nobel Prize winner Muhammad Yunus called for a 50-cents-an-hour global minimum. At one-fifteenth of the U.S. minimum wage, that is scarcely a number to make investors, or even economists, tremble. But it would double the pay of sweatshop workers in Bangladesh.[91]

Alternatives to Yunus's 50-cent minimum are on offer. Palley has proposed a global minimum wage system in which each country's minimum is set at 50 percent of its median income.[92] Hickel has argued for an additional constraint that no country's national minimum should fall below its poverty line.[93] There is value to such proposals, but their effectiveness in combating domination will ultimately depend on establishing a meaningful minimum in the world's poorest economies. Whether Yunus's 50-cent proposal is the right place to start can be debated, but some global minimum makes sense as a proximate goal. It is friendly to political coalition building: it blunts conflicts of interest between labor in poor countries and labor in wealthier ones, and it creates the possibility of the kind of business acquiescence, if not support, that Swenson describes in the 1930s United States. Individual firms might oppose it at the margin, but they are unlikely to fight that hard individually and they will find it difficult to organize opposition to a global minimum campaign. Moreover, once a global minimum becomes established and relatively institutionalized, businesses will have incentives to support it, lest they become vulnerable to illicit competition from cheaters. A global minimum is also a morally appealing goal, focused, as it is, on the condition of the most vulnerable.

Focusing on the bottom and then ratcheting up also has encouraging precedents. When the ILO was founded in 1919, it began by outlawing slavery and all forms of coerced labor, thereby codifying the results of the century-and-a-half struggle for abolition. This was followed by a series of conventions outlawing child labor and affirming basic workplace rights and protections, and, eventually, rights against employment discrimination. These "core" protections were codified in the 1998 "Declaration on Fundamental Principles and Rights at Work." Since then, they have become widely accepted as part of international customary law.[94] The ILO has made recommendations for an international wage base that would be sensitive to local variations in the cost of living, and in 1996 they proposed a global minimum wage of $435 per month for the class of maritime workers known as Able Seamen.[95]

Even with core protections, the real challenge is enforcement. Here, too, the history of international labor standards is instructive. Created as a branch of the League of Nations by the Treaty of Versailles, the ILO has no enforcement power. Initially it worked by persuading many of the forty-four signatories to adopt its conventions against forced labor. It got a boost when the United States joined in 1934 as part of the Roosevelt administration's search for an internationally coordinated response to the Depression. Today the ILO is part of the UN. It has the power to establish conventions that have the force of treaties.[96] Most of them therefore depend on ratification by member states, but because the meaning of compliance is determined by the states themselves, in practice this makes the behavior of powerful players such as the United States vital.

The historical record supplies grounds for hope, if not optimism. Since the McKinley Act of 1890, which restricted imports produced by prison labor, the United States has a considerable, if uneven, record of linking foreign trade to meeting minimum labor conditions. Following the General Agreement on Tariffs and Trade (GATT), which recognized the right of nations to restrict products of forced labor in 1947, labor standards have been incorporated into much U.S. trade law.[97] The 1974 Trade Act empowered the government to grant trade preferences to developing countries that met basic labor standards enunciated by the ILO. A decade later, Congress limited the president's authority to grant tariff relief, excluding countries that fail to recognize basic labor standards embodied in the ILO conventions.[98] In the next seven years, thirty-three countries were reviewed under this provision. Nicaragua, Romania, and the Sudan were removed from the program, and Chile, Paraguay, the Central African Republic, Burma, and Liberia were suspended.[99] The 1983 Caribbean Basin Economic Recovery Act and the 1985 congressional reauthorization of the Overseas Private Investment Corporation (which insures investors in less developed countries) require similar measures.[100]

The Clinton administration took a step backward when negotiating the labor side-agreements to the North American Free Trade Agreement (NAFTA) in 1993. It provided for trade sanctions of up to $20 million (or suspension of equivalent NAFTA trade benefits) for countries that persistently fail to embrace labor standards and minimum wage requirements, but only the country's own requirements.[101] Legislation in 2002 and 2007 has been more proactive. Violators can be sanctioned for failing to incorporate internationally recognized labor standards and for reducing established protections in their domestic law.[102] The various ILO conventions and declarations do not explicitly mention minimum wages among the "core" labor protections, but U.S. trade agreements routinely require "acceptable conditions of work with respect to minimum wages, hours of work, and occupational safety and health" for a country to qualify for preferential status.[103] The more robust enforcement regimes created since 2007 have yet to be fully tested, but there is some evidence that countries have improved their practices in the shadow of possible sanctions.[104]

The campaign against slavery reminds us that sustained public pressure is another vital ingredient of success. Here, too, a start has been made on the global minimum wage front. Yunus's campaign for the 50-cents-an-hour minimum is the tip of an iceberg. NGOs like the International Convention for a Global Minimum Wage, explicitly modeled on the antislavery campaigns, work to create public pressure.[105] High-profile campaigns against egregious violators can have demonstrable effects on their conduct. Indeed, there is evidence that public campaigns can be more effective than pressure from powerful trading partners. One study of Indonesia in the 1990s found that U.S. threats to withdraw tariff privileges for Indonesian exports if the government continued to allow workplace abuses produced a doubling in the Indonesian real minimum wage. But a combination of grassroots campaigns, negative publicity, and consumer awareness campaigns in the footwear and apparel industries produced even greater improvements in these industries in the same period. Because the wages in these sectors were so low to begin with, subcontractors hired by Nike could implement significant increases before approaching the average Indonesian manufacturing wage. Moreover, because the goods were produced for high-end retail markets in which profit margins are large and brand identity is vital, the firms could improve wages and working conditions significantly with negligible cost to their profitability or market share.[106]

High-visibility companies like Nike and Gap are logical targets for public campaigns for these reasons, but also because they are most likely to influence the behavior of other firms. Here the example of the Sullivan principles, conceived by the U.S. pastor and civil rights activist Leon H. Sullivan in the mid-1970s to pressure American multinationals during South African apartheid, is instructive. Sullivan used his position as a board member of General Motors to persuade virtually all U.S. companies with South African interests to adopt the principles in 1984, and subsequently to divest in 1987 in the face of continuing South African government intransigence. The principles themselves eventually achieved the status of a kind of moral minimum that it would be costly for companies to be seen to flout.[107] In 1999, Sullivan and UN Secretary General Kofi Annan jointly unveiled the "Global Sullivan Principles," again to focus attention on companies that were exploiting workers in countries lacking basic human rights protections. The Global Sullivan Principles have since been endorsed by hundreds of companies, including such major multinationals as General Motors, Royal Dutch Shell, Chevron, Colgate Palmolive, Sunoco, and Sodexo.[108]

This focus on high-visibility corporations had a discernible impact only once it began affecting their bottom lines. As the antisweatshop campaign ramped up in the 1990s, companies like Levi Strauss, Gap, and Nike responded with a mix of evasion, denial, and cosmetic remedies that failed to quell, and may even have fueled, additional protests and boycotts— particularly on American college campuses.[109] Declining sales amid relentless criticism eventually led Nike to face the reality that its product had, as the company's CEO Philip Knight admitted in 1998, "become synonymous with slave wages, forced overtime, and arbitrary abuse."[110]

Nike agreed to raise the minimum age in shoe factories to eighteen and their other plants to sixteen, adopt U.S. Occupational Safety and Health standards worldwide, and allow outsiders from labor and human rights groups to join independent auditors to interview workers and assess working conditions in their Asian factories. The following year they helped create the Fair Labor Association (FLA), a nonprofit consisting of corporations and human rights and labor representatives to establish independent monitoring and a code of conduct including a minimum age and a sixty-hour workweek. By 2004 they had performed some 600 audits, and even the human rights activists acknowledged that they had dealt with some of the worst problems. Nike also became significantly more transparent, publishing audits and detailed reports on conditions in its factories and complete inventories of its subcontractors.[111]

Despite the improvements, even mainstream business publications such as *Bloomberg Businessweek* have noted that neither "Nike nor any other businesses have come close to solving the sweatshop problem."[112] Nike wages remain low by global standards, and basic worker protections are still absent in countries such as China and Vietnam where Nike shoes and apparel are produced. Moreover, although companies like Mattel and Adidas have set up monitoring systems comparable to Nike's, FLA president Auret Van Heerden has candidly described their work as "a drop in the ocean." Most of the 90,000 or so factories that export to the United States lag far behind even firms such as these.[113] As was the case with slavery, the public campaigns can help mobilize activists and create pressure, but in the end it will take a coordinated effort in the powerful countries to sustain a global minimum wage system and then begin ratcheting it up from the bottom. The campaigns are vital to that effort as well, because they provide the ideological glue that is needed to keep political coalitions together in the face of efforts to pull them apart. The history of the U.S. minimum wage reminds us that resisting those efforts need not be futile, and that it might garner support from unexpected quarters. Tough as the battle is, I have sought to show here that it is the kind of effort that offers plausible prospects for success. In any case, it stands as a better approach to combatting economic domination across borders than the various projects for world government that have been, or are likely to be, proposed.

CHAPTER SIX

RESISTING DOMINATION ACROSS BORDERS

With world government off the table, how should we think about the place of national boundaries in resisting domination? The challenges are legion. Aggressive leaders unleash attacks to seize territory or subjugate populations, as Napoleon and Hitler sought to do in much of Europe, Saddam Hussein tried in Kuwait, and some believe Vladimir Putin hopes to do with nations comprising the former USSR. Secessionist movements push to dismember states. This can be straightforward and benign, as with Czechs and Slovaks, Scottish nationalists, and Canada's Québécois. But separatists can harbor more unsettling plans. Catholics in Northern Ireland want to leave the United Kingdom, but they also want to reunite with the Irish Republic against the wishes of the more numerous Northern Irish Protestants. Kurds in Iran, Iraq, and Turkey want to carve a Kurdish state out of those countries. Such aspirations inevitably conflict with other visions of national identity embraced by defenders of the status quo. The Israeli-Palestinian conflict is a paradigm, if chronic, illustration. There are many more peoples than nations, not to mention conflicting understandings of the aspirations of the same peoples. In much of the Middle East today, Sunnis and Shiites battle among themselves and with one another over whose account will prevail, just as Catholics and Protestants frequently did in seventeenth-century Europe. The nation-state system—any nation-state system—is bound to collide with these realities.

Sometimes, but only sometimes, people seek to change national boundaries democratically. Scottish nationalists tried that unsuccessfully in 2014, but it can succeed. Czechs and Slovaks separated democratically in 1992. The East Timorians left Indonesia after winning a referendum in 1999. South Sudan voted to leave Sudan in 2011. Nationalist Québécois hoped to win their independence referendums in 1980 and 1995, yet they accepted defeat in both—in the latter by a mere 1 percent of the vote. That is rare. Often, democratic failure fuels insurrection and civil war. This happened in the American South after the 1860 election, when Lincoln declared that the U.S. Constitution does not permit secession.[1] Indeed, violence can be the strategy of first resort. The Islamic State of Iraq and the Levant (ISIL) plans to manufacture a Sunni caliphate out of eastern Syria, western Iraq, and perhaps parts of Lebanon, Jordan, and North Africa as well. They are willing to go to any lengths, including ethnic cleansing, mass murder, and even genocide, to achieve their goals.

Stopping gambits of this kind can be difficult, sometimes impossible. Indeed, the presumption of nonintervention that became embedded in the international system after World War II loads the dice against trying. And the presumption is stronger when states are well established, with their immunity from interference enshrined in treaties and conventions. When the Rwandan genocide erupted in 1994, denunciations and handwringing abounded. Yet no outside power made a serious effort to stop it. Ethnic cleansing and genocidal killing might have been with us since time immemorial, but the nation-state system supplies few tools to combat it—let alone prevent it. That is bound to concern anyone who sees resisting domination as the primary challenge of politics.

These examples capture two kinds of circumstance in which national borders are implicated in domination: when they are violated in order to perpetrate domination, and when they must be compromised in order to resist it. The first, my subject in section 6.2, deals with forcible transgression of boundaries or attempts to redraw them. These are invariably problematic for partisans of nondomination, not because there is anything sacrosanct about the existing nation-state system, but rather because the arbitrary character of inherited boundaries does not justify forcibly compromising them or replacing them with new ones that would also be arbitrary from some defensible point of view. This stance creates a bias toward the global status quo, to be sure, because those who oppose it might be unable to achieve the change they want democratically. But that just means that people cannot always have what they want and that nondomination, just like every normative stance, is not neutral among competing visions of the good life.[2]

Opposing domination across borders includes straightforward self-defense, as when countries respond to attacks of the sort Hitler prosecuted against many European countries and the Japanese launched against the United States at Pearl Harbor in 1941. But resisting cross-border domination often includes defending others. Thirty-four countries joined the U.S.-led Operation Desert Storm to oust Iraq from Kuwait in 1991.

The NATO Charter requires signatories to come to the aid of any fellow member who is attacked. Whether by ad hoc arrangement or treaty obligation, such agreements commit countries to combat aggression against third parties. This possibility is enshrined in the UN Charter, which affirms the "sovereign equality" of all members and empowers the Security Council to authorize "suppression of acts of aggression or other breaches of the peace."[3] A central challenge, we will see, is to determine what this can defensibly mean given that those with the capacity to suppress aggression invariably harbor debatable—if not dubious—motives and often have dirty hands as well.

Crossing borders to prevent domination also presents this challenge, but the stakes are higher. In 1999 NATO began bombing Kosovo to protect Albanian Muslims from ethnic cleansing by Serb paramilitaries and armies, an intervention that would famously be declared "illegal but legitimate" after the fact by the Independent International Commission on Kosovo.[4] The Kosovo operation sharpened debates that had been brewing at the Organization of African Unity—replaced by the African Union (AU) in 2001—and at the UN since the Rwandan genocide. It led to the AU's asserting in 2002 the right to intervene in a member state to prevent war crimes, genocide, and crimes against humanity, and the UN General Assembly's embrace of the "Responsibility to Protect" (R2P) doctrine three years later.[5] R2P declares all governments responsible for shielding their populations from genocide, crimes against humanity, war crimes, and ethnic cleansing, and empowers the Security Council to authorize intervention when they do not. I take up this ambitious escalation in Security Council authority in section 6.3. There I argue that the authorizing mechanism is wanting, and that R2P intervention should face notably higher hurdles than intervention to combat cross-border domination—not least because it risks creating new failed states in which forces bent on serious forms of domination will predictably run rampant.

This leads to the question underscored by NATO's 2011 intervention in Libya: Under what conditions, if any, should outsiders overthrow, or help overthrow, oppressive regimes? I take this up in section 6.4, arguing that intervening to overturn regimes is defensible only when there is an indigenous democratic opposition that offers a viable alternative and whose leaders actively seek external assistance. Minimally favorable economic conditions should also be present. Otherwise, regime change should be the strategy of absolute final resort, attempted only if there is no other way to prevent the extreme kinds of domination proscribed by R2P. Recent efforts at regime change in Afghanistan, Iraq, and Libya have failed this test, I argue, weakening Security Council authority and damaging the international legitimacy of the United States and other intervening powers. Finally, I turn to the ISIL menace that mushroomed in Syria and Iraq in 2014, identifying the approach that offers the best chance to avoid replicating the recent failures. As a prelude to defending these claims, I begin, in section 6.1, by arguing that the challenges they present are best understood by reference to a version of the doctrine of containment developed by George Kennan in the 1940s. This builds on my earlier critique of the Bush Doctrine that was adopted after the al-Qaeda attacks on the United States in September 2001 and invoked to justify the 2003 invasion of Iraq.[6] But here I offer a more general account of containment than in my earlier book, defending it as the best approach to resisting domination across borders, and to crossing them in order to prevent it.

6.1 Why Containment?

Kennan's case for containment might seem an unlikely candidate to do this heavy lifting. It was, after all, not intended as a general theory. Famously skeptical of grand thinking, Kennan championed containment as a particular response to a particular threat at a particular time: it was, he argued, the best way for the United States to face down the military hazard posed by Soviet Union during the Cold War. Kennan was convinced that the USSR's flawed economic system, combined with its unsustainable global ambitions, would cause its leaders eventually to give up, if the system did not collapse first. "For no mystical, messianic movement—and particularly not that of the Kremlin—can face frustration indefinitely without eventually adjusting itself in one way or another to the logic of that state of affairs."[7] More ambitious strategies, such as the "rollback" pressed by John Foster Dulles and others in the Eisenhower administration, were unnecessary and imprudent.[8] Sustaining domestic political support for protracted conflict with the USSR seemed to Kennan to be a tall order in the era of public exhaustion and fiscal austerity after World War II. Better to hem the Soviets in and wait them out.

6.1.1 Minimize Dependence on Coercion

Rooted as it was in these particular considerations, Kennan's logic nonetheless offers useful resources to think more generally about transnational domination. A central insight concerns keeping the use of force to a minimum. Aside from the budgetary considerations of the late 1940s, Kennan recognized that in a democracy, war is fraught with electoral peril. Your side might win quickly, boosting your popularity. But wars often drag on, taking unpredictable twists and turns. If the conflict is a war of choice rather than necessity and the costs mount, eventually the electorate is bound to sour. This concern led Kennan to oppose the Vietnam War in the early 1960s, presciently as it turned out. Four decades later, when the United States was gearing up to invade Iraq, the ninety-eight-year-old Kennan invoked it again, no less wisely, warning that in war "you know where you begin. You never know where you are going to end."[9] Leaders who offer electorates little more than blood, toil, tears, and sweat had better be sure that the case for war is overwhelming.[10] Exaggerating the threat, relying on debts rather than taxes, and deploying volunteer forces and mercenaries instead of a draft might stave off the day of reckoning for a while. But eventually voters will pull the plug. Indeed, as George W. Bush's father learned to his cost in 1992, even a quick, successful war will not save you from an electorate focused on pocketbook issues and the bottom line.[11]

Unlike those, such as Dulles, for whom the best defense is invariably a good offense, Kennan's stance was to do what is needed, but only what is needed, to face down threatening aggression. Minimizing the use of force did not, however, mean abjuring it, or even waiting passively for an adversary's collapse. Kennan was confident, as he said at the National War College in March 1947, that the Soviets lacked the means to dominate Europe or the Middle East, but he insisted that this was not a reason to let them try. After all, the Visigoths who sacked Rome could not consolidate their conquest of Italy, but they did trigger the demise of the Roman Empire and usher in "centuries of ignominy for the city which was its heart and soul." The Soviets had a dynamic view of their historical role as the vanguard of the world socialist movement. Kennan was confident that they would fail as the Visigoths did, but their efforts to export their system and subjugate new populations still had to be resisted. In short, we know that floodwaters "must—by the laws of nature—some day subside," but we should still take measures to contain them in view of the damage they can do in the meantime.[12]

This is why Kennan distinguished containment so sharply from appeasement, despite relentless efforts by his critics to conflate the two. Containment means doing only what is needed to frustrate attempts at domination, but it does mean doing it. Kennan was confident that the Soviet leaders would never accept peaceful coexistence, partly because they believed that there is an "innate antagonism between capitalism and socialism," and partly for the reasons I spelled out in section 5.3: their political authority depended, as Kennan put it, on cultivating the "semi-myth of implacable foreign hostility." American leaders should not be deceived by occasional signs of compromise; these tactical retreats would invariably be replaced by "pressure, unceasing constant pressure, toward the desired goal" of a global communist order led by the USSR.[13] Efforts at Soviet expansion must meet implacable resistance.[14]

But we should not overreach needlessly. Kennan opposed the formation of NATO partly out of general skepticism of alliances, but also because he thought it would militarize the standoff in Europe unnecessarily by encouraging a siege mentality among Soviet leaders, who would then conclude their own military pact—as they indeed did in 1955 following West Germany's integration into NATO.[15] Holding containment steady made better sense than unilateral ratcheting up, for Kennan. We might think of containment as what I described in section 1.4 as a restorative tit-for-tat strategy. Ratcheting up is a response to defection by the other side, but it should be kept to a minimum and accompanied, where possible, by face-saving opportunities for the aggressor to back down. It is a way of forestalling what international relations theorists describe as a security dilemma, where actions taken to increase a state's security, such as joining alliances or engaging in military buildups, end up reducing its security by initiating a spiraling arms race of escalating responses.[16]

Kennan played no role in managing the 1962 Cuban missile crisis, but President Kennedy's conduct of it stands as a model of successful containment thus conceived. Having been badly burned by the advice of his generals at the Bay of Pigs the previous year, Kennedy resisted them this time. He refused to invade the island, quarantining it instead, a fortuitous choice as it turned out. We now know that Soviet troops stationed there were armed with battlefield nuclear weapons and instructions to deploy them in the event of an American invasion. This would have sparked the unthinkable: a nuclear exchange between the superpowers.[17] Kennedy had to confront the Soviets' aggressive action, but he did so in a way that allowed them to deescalate by returning to the status quo ante: to pack up and leave. His secret agreement to remove what were in any case superfluous Jupiter nuclear missiles from Italy and Turkey within six months of the Soviet departure gave Khrushchev his face-saving way out.[18] This was calculated resolve, not appeasement: Khrushchev did indeed back down and nuclear war was avoided.

Kennan's admonition to economize on the use of force travels well into the post–Cold War world. George H. W. Bush was roundly criticized by neoconservatives—the closest thing to modern champions of rollback—for failing to remove Saddam Hussein following Iraq's expulsion from Kuwait in 1991. In section 6.2, I make the case that, despite some flaws, the policy Bush put in place then was a model for the post–Cold War use of containment to prevent cross-border domination—until it was undone by his son's gamble on gratuitous regime change there in 2003. The downstream costs of that disastrous gambit continue accumulating across the globe more than a decade later, but notable among them was depletion to the point of near exhaustion of the U.S. capacity to resist cross-border threats of serious domination.

The depletion began with the initial decision, taken in mid-2002, to invade Iraq. It meant redeploying forces from Afghanistan before defeating al-Qaeda, whose fighters escaped into the White Mountains following the inconclusive battle of Tora Bora the previous December. The redeployment added to the decade-long delay in hunting down Bin Laden in Pakistan and ending the Afghanistan war. And this is to say nothing of the Iraq operation itself, which the Bush administration predicted would be over in the summer of 2003 and sold to Congress on the grounds that the $30 billion total cost of the preceding dozen years of containment had been too high. A decade and $1.6 trillion later, the United States finally departed—leaving behind a freshly minted failed state.[19]

By then, the American public was so jaded by the two longest wars in the country's history that President Obama found himself hamstrung when a genuinely serious threat erupted. ISIL forces, already in control of much of Syria, stormed western Iraq, and the vestiges of Iraq's military collapsed overnight. Many of its officers, casualties of America's ill-considered de-Baathification program in the mid-2000s, were now fighting for ISIL, deploying American weapons captured from the army that the United States had tried to reconstitute during its occupation.[20] Having unwisely declared that Syrian president Bashar Hafez al-Assad "must go" in August 2011, Obama had already been embarrassed by his lack of domestic political support to make that happen—not even when it appeared that Assad had unleashed chemical weapons on rebels in the Ghouta suburbs of Damascus two years later.[21] After ISIL transitioned from mass slaughter of Syrian and Iraqi prisoners to decapitating Western journalists on YouTube in 2014, Congress finally authorized Obama to bomb ISIL. But he could get the necessary votes only by foreclosing the possibility of American boots on the ground, even though his former defense secretary and his current chairman of the Joint Chiefs quickly went on record contradicting Obama's confident insistence that this would be sufficient.[22]

Obama's ISIL policy exhibited some good features that I discuss in section 6.2, but his declared limits to it undermined its effectiveness. Containment depends for its efficacy on the aggressor's expectation that you will ratchet things up as needed to stop him; that is what gives him the incentive to ratchet aggression down. If you reveal at the start that there are costs you are unwilling to incur, you give him an incentive to keep escalating. Obama's need to turn up his cards in this way for domestic political reasons deflated his declaration to the UN General Assembly in September 2014 that "there can be no reasoning—no negotiation—with this brand of evil," and his stern admonition that "those who have joined ISIL should leave the battlefield while they can."[23]

Obama was stepping on his own feet. For reasons that follow from my account of the role of uncertainty in iterated prisoner's dilemmas in section 1.4, containment does best when an aggressor cannot count on your ever giving up. You should never ratchet up unnecessarily and never by more than is necessary, but you have to signal your resolve to ratchet up as much as necessary. By revealing that you lack the resources for tit-for-tat in the face of indefinite defection, you turn defection into your adversary's dominant strategy. Instead of announcing limited means to pursue an unachievable goal, Obama should have announced an achievable goal and then committed the U.S.-led coalition to do whatever would be needed to achieve it. Rather than declare it to be U.S. policy to "degrade, and, ultimately, destroy ISIL," Obama should have committed the U.S.-led coalition to do whatever would be needed to expel ISIL from Iraq. That coalition could have included countries in the region threatened by ISIL: most obviously Jordan and Lebanon, with at least acquiescence from Iran and the Gulf states. What the policy should have been with respect to the Syrian civil war is taken up in section 6.3.

6.1.2 Avoid Destroying Villages in Order to Save Them[24]

Kennan's conviction that Soviet attempts at domination would fail was partly based on his analysis of the soulless and unappealing character of what they themselves had to offer. In Europe, he thought, people were drawn less by ideological conviction, or even illusions about Soviet communism's authentic character, than by a "bandwagon effect": a sense that communism was "the coming thing," an unstoppable "movement of the future." This lack of passion would erode Soviet influence and authority over time, he believed, making the leadership increasingly dependent on the decreasingly attractive use of force. Still less would the Soviets be able to dominate Muslim peoples. Getting them to subordinate their religious convictions to Soviet ideology would require direct and continuous reliance on Soviet military power.[25] This is why waiting the Soviets out made sense; eventually the chickens would come home to roost.[26]

The trump card would be the magnetic appeal of prosperous democracies. Kennan saw no reason for the United States to trade ideological banter with Soviet leaders who were surely beyond persuasion. Rather, he had in mind what is known today as the battle for hearts and minds. This is why he supported the Marshall Plan for Europe and swift reconstitution of Japan, and why he judged the prevailing focus on rearmament and military alliances in 1948 a "regrettable diversion" from the more important "struggle for economic recovery and internal political stability."[27] Rather than repeat the mistakes that had been made after World War I, the United States should ensure that democratic capitalism would thrive at home and among its allies. Soviet pretensions to being the harbinger of the future appealed to formulaic narratives about the "palsied decrepitude of the capitalist world."[28] Confronted with the actual differences between flourishing democratic capitalism and authoritarian communism, the populations that the Soviets sought to control, including—eventually—their own, would resist.

For the strategy to succeed, however, it was vital that the United States and its allies not erode the quality of their own institutions, lest they start resembling those whom they sought to contain. The democracies must be beacons of "spiritual vitality." They should be countries that were obviously coping with their problems and holding their own "among the major ideological currents of the time." To get people to see how "sterile and quixotic" the Soviet model was, Kennan insisted, the United States must "measure up to its own best traditions and prove itself worthy of preservation as a great nation."[29] America must be, as Ronald Reagan would later often put it, a shining city on a hill.[30]

This possibility was never more real than at the Cold War's end, but American governments have since squandered it. Far from living up to America's best traditions, George W. Bush's administration dissipated the moral capital the nation accumulated due to its restraint during the 1990s and as a result of the 9/11 attacks. The global outpouring of support after the twin towers fell went far beyond America's traditional allies and even the former communist countries. Almost every Muslim political and religious leader condemned the attacks, including Hosni Mubarak, Yasser Arafat, Muammar Gaddafi, Bashar al-Assad, Pervez Musharraf, and even Iran's Mohamed Khatami—despite the fact that the United States had backed their enemy in the bitter Iran-Iraq war of the 1980s. But the neoconservatives in the Bush administration saw no advantage in this as they ramped up America's new unilateralist foreign policy. They spurned Khatami's offer to help bring the 9/11 perpetrators to justice and included

Iran, along with Iraq and North Korea, in the president's "Axis of Evil" in his 2002 State of the Union address. Their hubris, summed up by Bush's "Mission Accomplished" speech in May 2003[31] and his advisor Karl Rove's insistence the following October that on the world stage "we create our own reality,"[32] would eventually be unmasked by their failures—but not before they had done great damage to American credibility as an honest broker and force for good in the world. Secretary of State Colin Powell would later concede that his risible "demonstration" to the UN Security Council that Iraq had weapons of mass destruction left a permanent blot on his record.[33]

Considerably more than Powell's reputation had been ruined. The spurious invasion rationale damaged America's image, but this paled by comparison with Abu Ghraib. In late 2003 the press reported extensive violations of Iraqi prisoners' human rights by American soldiers there, including physical and sexual humiliation, torture, rape, sodomy, and murder.[34] Vivid photographs of the appalling abuse soon went viral, as opinion polls chronicled the accelerating collapse of America's standing across the Arab world.[35] Abu Ghraib quickly became such a damaging symbol that President Bush promised to demolish it the following year; but he failed. It was left to the Iraqis to close it a decade later, after the Americans had left.[36]

Obama ran for office in 2008 insisting that it was past time to restore America's moral capital. Echoing Reagan's shining city on a hill, candidate Obama promised "to show the world that America is still the last, best hope on Earth." Among other things, this meant closing the Guantánamo Bay prison in Cuba, where alleged enemy combatants had languished beyond the limits of American due process for years.[37] But Obama's executive order to close Guantánamo within a year, issued on his first day in office, fared no better than had Bush's promise to demolish Abu Ghraib.[38] Five years later, the only thing the State Department had closed was the office tasked with decommissioning the prison. Obama had by then given up on getting the detainees tried in U.S. courts, and the Guantánamo authorities were force-feeding hunger-striking prisoners. Many of the prisoners still had no prospect of trial or release, and the administration was fighting a losing battle to keep the grotesque details out of the public eye.[39] This has been costly, because Kennan was surely right that visibly getting one's own house in order is a vital part of defeating a competitive ideological threat.

During Obama's second term it became increasingly difficult to distinguish his policies in this area from those of his predecessor. The Marine major general who had been responsible for setting up Guantánamo called it a mistake, noting that most of the inmates should never, in any case, have been sent there. Thirty-one retired military officers went on record declaring that as long it remained, "Guantánamo will undermine America's security and status as a nation where human rights and the rule of law matter."[40] The Obama administration ignored their advice, however, and in 2012 the Justice Department closed the book on accountability by abandoning, without charging anyone, the only two remaining investigations into detainees who had died during interrogation.[41] Now no one would ever be held to account for the torture, even though the Bush administration's claims that its "enhanced interrogation" techniques had yielded useful intelligence had by then been debunked.[42] Releasing the Senate report on the CIA's detention and interrogation program in December 2014 was a small step in the right direction, but the United States was still a long way away from measuring up to its best traditions.[43]

6.1.3 Stopping the Bully

Kennan's advice to bet on the attractiveness of Western institutions to win over the populations behind the Iron Curtain was about the closest he ever came to developing a normative case for containment. But there are compelling arguments for containment that flow from a bedrock commitment to nondomination. Insisting that force be proportionate to the present threat and that war be a strategy of last resort both enjoy venerable histories in just war theory.[44] They reflect the widespread appeal of the idea that coercion is legitimate only to the extent that it is needed to repel unjustified aggression. Like Machiavelli's dictum that it is better to give power to those who want to avoid domination than to those who seek to dominate, containment draws part of its rationale from the idea that people are unlikely to bestow legitimacy on institutions that have been forced on them. There are rare exceptions to this that I take up when discussing regime change in section 6.4, but generally coercion is hard to justify unless its goal is to forestall unwarranted aggression.

Containment embodies the principle that one should do what is needed, but only what is needed, to stop the bully. This makes evident tactical sense; it reminds us to husband scarce coercive resources. And it makes sound strategic sense, as Kennan intimated, in the battle for hearts and minds. In this connection it is notable that containment did substantially better than rollback during the Cold War. Although Eisenhower ran on rollback during the 1952 campaign, once in office he quickly ditched the policy in Europe, relying instead on classic containment.[45] Europe today is a continent of democracies. In the Middle East, by contrast, the United

States toppled Iran's democratically elected government, judged too friendly to the Soviets, in 1953—installing the more agreeable Mohammad Reza Shah Pahlavi in its place. That was no more propitious in the medium run than were the attempts at rollback in Southeast Asia that extended through the Kennedy, Johnson, and Nixon administrations.

Beyond these tactical and strategic considerations, containment also makes normative sense in foreswearing the gratuitous use of force. Otherwise the enterprise of stopping the bully inevitably morphs into bullying—certainly in the eyes of others and perhaps also as a matter of objective fact. This has been the great cost of U.S. national security policy since 2003, as I am about to argue. To be sure, forswearing bullying will not gain much purchase with those, like Nietzscheans, who glorify domination. But as I intimated in Chapter 1, this book is not for them.

6.2 Containing Cross-Border Domination

The simplest case for war is in the face of an actual or imminent threat. People whose survival is at stake can be mobilized to fight and pay for wars. Wars of aggression and imperial expansion lie at the opposite pole of the continuum, though it is noteworthy that even they are often sold as integral to survival. Populations were mobilized to fight on all sides of World War I on the grounds that they were responding to aggression from others.[46] Even Adolf Hitler's *Mein Kampf* trumpets an alarmist vision of the Aryan race as locked in an inexorable fight in which only the strongest will survive.[47] The Cold War was seen in the West as a response to Soviet aggression in Eastern Europe and elsewhere, but behind the Iron Curtain it was portrayed as vital to resisting the encroaching threat of capitalist imperialism.[48] In the 1990s and early 2000s, al-Qaeda claimed to be prosecuting a "defensive jihad," geared exclusively to getting the United States and its allies out of the Middle East.[49]

6.2.1 The Importance of Imminent Threats

As these examples illustrate, such claims are often debatable—if not manifestly false. Advocates of the Vietnam War invoked a domino theory, according to which defeat would lead to a communist takeover of East Asia. They turned out to be wrong. Soviet leaders embraced an equally flawed domino theory that steered them into their Afghanistan gambit in the 1980s. They were convinced that if the pro-Soviet regime in Kabul fell, their own Asiatic republics with large Muslim populations—long believed to be the USSR's vulnerable underbelly—would revolt.[50] Afghanistan did fall, yet the predicted knock-on disaster did not eventuate. Ironically, when the dominos finally started toppling, they were unanticipated, in Europe, and had nothing to do with Islam. François Truffaut is famous for the quip that life has more imagination than us.[51] It surely has more imagination than confident proponents of the unknowable.

Better to avoid war against threats that are less than imminent. The costs of flouting this injunction were well illustrated by the national security doctrine developed by the G.W. Bush administration to justify its 2003 invasion of Iraq.[52] President Bush and his national security advisor, Condoleezza Rice, argued that they could not afford to wait until the smoking gun became "a mushroom cloud."[53] Instead the administration embraced the need for military action against alleged "gathering threats," and even the so-called "1 percent doctrine." As Vice President Cheney elaborated, the administration would treat threats with a 1 percent probability of occurring as 100 percent certainties "in terms of our response."[54] Setting aside the sheer nuttiness of this view, which assumes that governments have inexhaustible resources for national defense, it courts exactly the risk I discussed earlier: crying wolf in the face of what turn out to be phantom threats sours electorates when their support is needed in the face of genuine ones.

Even in the face of actual or imminent attack, the constraints of necessity and proportionality make sense from the standpoint of nondomination. This is true not only for the strategic reasons discussed in section 6.1.1 in connection with the Cuban missile crisis, but also because doing more than necessary can drag you into unsustainable foreign occupations and might in any case be objectionable on its own merits. For instance, after the 9/11 attacks the U.S. government was surely justified—even obliged—to pursue the al-Qaeda perpetrators wherever they might be. But little attention was devoted to the necessary scope of the response or its likely downstream implications.

Consider a path not taken when the Taliban government refused to turn over al-Qaeda forces in Afghanistan. Rather than overthrow the regime, the United States could simply have pursued al-Qaeda while ignoring the government in Kabul. This is what the Obama administration eventually did when they learned that Bin Laden was holed up in Abbottabad, knowing that, by then, Pakistan would be unlikely to cooperate. As some military leaders proposed in 2001, the United States could simply have declared that any Taliban interference would be met with devastating force.[55] Devoting U.S. troops to hunting down Bin Laden and al-Qaeda would have taken more than the few dozen Special Operations forces they deployed, but the actual course followed was penny wise and pound foolish. Estimates of how many U.S. troops would have been needed vary, but the generals on the ground at the time believed it could be done with fewer than the 3,000 who were then available in the region and that the logistical challenges, while formidable, were surmountable.[56] Successful hot U.S. pursuit of Bin Laden might also have required cooperation from Pakistan, demanded by President Bush in the wake of 9/11. President Musharraf overruled internal opposition in his government, fired the religiously conservative head of his intelligence services and his cronies who were opposed, and promised cooperation.[57] His willingness to do this reminds us that, in the atmosphere after the 9/11 attacks, when *Le Monde* was declaring "Nous sommes tous Américains!" and traditional adversaries like Libya, Russia, and Iran were lining up to pledge help, the United States could have secured extensive support to do almost anything in pursuit of Bin Laden and al-Qaeda.[58]

But the Bush administration wanted to do Afghanistan on the cheap. After the 9/11 attacks, senior U.S. officials quickly became obsessed with attacking Iraq, making the prospect of major troop commitments in Afghanistan unattractive.[59] The path of least resistance was therefore to ally with the Northern Alliance in the civil war that it had for some time been losing against the Taliban government.[60] The decision to take sides in this war was doubly costly. On the one hand, the fact that the Northern Alliance and other anti-Taliban militias were losing the civil war should have been a red flag about their capacity to become a viable government that could quell the inevitable insurgencies without long-term propping up by the United States.[61] On the other hand, the Northern Alliance turned out to be fickle allies, whose mixed loyalties played into the failure at Tora Bora. They proved unable or unwilling to corner Bin Laden's fighters, forcing U.S. commanders, who had only a few dozen American and British special forces troops at their disposal, to rely on local warlords instead.[62] Meanwhile, the Afghan militias, who also had mixed loyalties, engaged in stalling tactics including phony surrender negotiations that enabled Bin Laden and hundreds of al-Qaeda fighters to escape to Pakistan, where they soon became the nucleus of the insurgency.[63]

The Americans ended up with the worst of both worlds. They failed to get Bin Laden or destroy al-Qaeda, but having forced Mullah Omar and Taliban from power, they were stuck with the responsibility of trying to build a viable regime in Afghanistan. As Colin Powell said, "If you break it, you own it."[64] Indeed, they subordinated the war aim of defeating Bin Laden and al-Qaeda to this Sisyphean nation-building agenda. Lieutenant General Michael DeLong, number two to Central Command General

Tommy Franks, conceded as much to the Senate Foreign Relations Committee staff, saying that the real reason they refused to send U.S. troops to Tora Bora was that "we didn't want to have U.S. forces fighting before [Hamid] Karzai was in power. We wanted to create a stable country and that was more important than going after Bin Laden at the time."[65]

Nor was it the last missed opportunity to avoid rekindling the insurgency. By the mid-2000s, several commentators were arguing that the Taliban should have been included in the power-sharing agreement negotiated in Bonn at the end of 2001.[66] But the Americans were convinced that the Taliban, now defeated, dispersed, or over the border in Pakistan, could be ignored.[67] This was costly, as Anand Gopal and Carlotta Gall both point out, because rejecting overtures from former Taliban and mujahedeen leaders—who were often gratuitously attacked or mistakenly imprisoned, sometimes for years—led many of them eventually to join the insurgency.[68] The United States compounded this error with its Disarmament, Demobilization, and Reintegration (DDR) program, which Gall likens to the United States' 2003 de-Baathification and disarmament program in Iraq that fueled that country's collapse into chaos. Unlike the Taliban, many mujahedeen were generally pro-Western and favored the new order. DDR disabled Karzai's rivals, but it also sidelined and alienated tens of thousands of former fighters and created a power vacuum—especially in the south. Once the insurgency ramped up, this made the Taliban's return easier and provided them with additional fighters.[69]

The U.S. response to the 9/11 attacks was thus doubly disproportionate. It was insufficient in that the administration refused to commit the resources needed to apprehend and destroy the terrorist group that perpetrated the 9/11 attacks. But unrealistic assumptions about what could be accomplished on the cheap, when combined with the administration's aggrandizing goals of remaking the political map of the Middle East, committed them to a program of gratuitous regime change. They undermined their own efforts and ignored obvious evidence that their agenda would not likely be sustainable. When the United States finally ended combat operations in 2014, after more than 5,500 U.S. soldiers plus military contractors, and between 56,000 and 68,000 Afghans, had been killed and more than $1 trillion had been spent to little avail, Afghanistan was still broken.[70] Some 5,000 Afghan security forces had been killed in the final year of the occupation, eclipsing all previous years. Outgoing Lieutenant General Joseph Anderson described the situation as "not sustainable, and neither are the astounding desertion rates."[71] Afghanistan remained, by any plausible measure, a failed state, and the government in Kabul was facing the most effective Taliban insurgency since Bin Laden and his fighters had escaped to Pakistan thirteen years earlier. By then, as Rory Stewart noted, the only real choice facing incoming president Ashraf Ghani was whether to reach an accommodation with the Taliban or face resumption of full-blown civil war.[72]

6.2.2 Intervention to Protect Third Parties

Difficult as these issues are when you are defending yourself, they are even more so when you are defending a third party who is not even part of some postulated chain of dominoes with you at the wrong end of it. These challenges have become more common in the post–Cold War world, because proxy conflicts no longer map onto superpower standoffs in any predictable way. It is a world in which my enemy's enemy might well turn out to be my enemy, as has become most strikingly evident in the Middle East.

Three years after the war in which the United States had backed Saddam Hussein against Iran, America was expelling Iraq from Kuwait. Between the 1990s and 2001 the Afghan mujahedeen mutated from allies to foes, as we have seen. Decades of albeit ambivalent U.S. cooperation with Syria to stabilize Lebanon was abandoned when the United States began revamping its Middle East policy in the run-up to invading Iraq in 2003.[73] Obama went further, recasting Assad as an enemy who "must go" following his repression of insurgents in 2011, a decision that would widely be second-guessed once ISIL reared its head in 2013. That development also transformed rump Iraqi and Syrian militias, long objects of U.S. suspicion, into potential "moderates," to be courted, trained, and armed to fight ISIL, even at the risk that this would again wind up strengthening new enemies if they were overrun or switched sides. Iran, long demonized by Israel and the United States for its support of Hezbollah and Hamas and its nuclear program, began to look decidedly more benign than traditional U.S. ally Saudi Arabia, whose rich citizens, if not its royal family, were funneling support to ISIL as part of its gambit for regional hegemony.[74] By late 2014 the *Wall Street Journal* was describing U.S.-Iranian relations in the language of détente.[75] Lord Palmerston's dictum to the effect that nations have no permanent friends or allies, only permanent interests, might have receded in significance during the Cold War.[76] But it has since returned with a vengeance.

In this world, military action to resist cross-border domination should pass substantial thresholds of authorization and implementation. Flawed as it was, the U.S.-led coalition to force Saddam Hussein out of Kuwait in 1991 is the closest thing we have to a viable template. In the four months after Iraq's August 1990 invasion, the Security Council passed a dozen resolutions demanding Iraq's immediate and unconditional withdrawal, culminating in Resolution 678, which authorized member states to use "all necessary means" to enforce the resolutions and "restore international peace and security in the area" unless Iraq complied by January 15, 1991.[77] The coalition that the United States assembled when Iraq failed to comply was large and diverse. The major Western powers were among its thirty-four members, but most Arab countries made significant commitments as well. Even Bangladesh sent 6,000 troops.[78] The coalition did not overreach. President Bush resisted considerable pressure to "go to Baghdad" and topple Saddam Hussein. Instead he scrupulously observed the terms of Resolution 678 and subsequent Security Council resolutions that subjected Iraq to a rigorous containment regime that remained in place—rendering the Iraqi regime unable to threaten outsiders—until the United States destroyed it twelve years later. The 1991 action thus combined international authorization with the enforcement of proportionately appropriate goals.

This is not to defend everything the United States did in Iraq in 1990. For one thing, in the weeks before the invasion the Bush administration sent mixed diplomatic signals, which Hussein interpreted as a green light for moving into Kuwait.[79] For another, in the wake of Iraq's expulsion from Kuwait, the Bush administration actively encouraged Shiites in southern Iraq to rebel against Saddam Hussein, fostering expectations of U.S. support that then failed to materialize.[80] The result was brutal suppression by the Baathist regime, at the cost of at least 100,000 lives—perhaps many more.[81] Whether the U.S. encouragement was unconscionable or merely irresponsible can be debated, but surely it was unwise. Active support for the Sha'aban Intifada would have embroiled the United States in the kind of civil war that has been so costly in Afghanistan. Indeed, a keen awareness of the major challenges posed by regime change disciplined the administration to resist pressure from hawks at home to take Baghdad.[82] But in that posture, Washington had no business promoting the rebellion. It was also unwise for reasons I discuss further in section 6.4: there was no evidence that the rebels had democratic credentials or aspirations.

That said, Desert Storm met three key criteria for intervention better than any subsequent international operation has done. These are: invitation by the legitimate government of the invaded country, supplemented, where possible, by authorization in a credible international forum; enforcement by a large and diverse coalition; and proportional restraint to limit the intervention to what is needed to achieve the authorized objective.

These criteria merit more detailed consideration as the basic requirements for international intervention, both when countries attack one another and when governments attack their own populations or fail to protect them from others who threaten genocide, crimes against humanity, war crimes, or ethnic cleansing.

Countries that are attacked or under imminent threat of attack are bound to defend themselves regardless of what others do. Security Council resolutions or other forms of international support will often be welcome, but they are not essential. The United States would thus have been justified in pursuing al-Qaeda in the wake of the 9/11 attacks even if the Security Council resolutions endorsing its actions had not been forthcoming.[83] But once the focus shifts from self-defense to defending third parties, additional kinds of authorization are needed.

One reason is that vital national interests are no longer at stake. When George Bush senior assembled the coalition to force Saddam Hussein out of Kuwait, neither the United States nor the great majority of its members had any vital interest at stake. To be sure, they had major interests at stake—chief among them access to cheap oil. There was a credible concern that, were Iraq not expelled from Kuwait, Saddam Hussein would enjoy a potential stranglehold on large swaths of the world's crude oil reserves.[84] Billions of dollars, perhaps even trillions over time, were arguably at stake. But large interests should not be conflated with basic or vital ones.[85] Indeed, a substantial increase in world oil prices would arguably have been a good thing for the advanced economies, accelerating their search for alternative energy technologies. The Kuwaitis were, to be sure, in a different position, even if it is not obvious that they would have been any less subject to domination living in Iraq's nineteenth province rather than in their—not notably democratic—independent Kuwait. But for reasons that I spell out in section 6.4, the invasion could not have qualified as a war of liberation even if Hussein had claimed that it was—which he did not. It was simply a unilateral land grab on his part. Lacking the power to repel Saddam Hussein's domination, Kuwait would have to be rescued by third parties or not at all.

Just because third-party interveners do not have basic interests at stake, their motives are bound to be suspect. True, they might be acting for altruistic reasons. But they might be pursuing their own aggrandizing ambitions, trying to garner favor with stronger countries, or doing the bidding of powerful interests at home. Democratic accountability offers some protection against such abuses, but we saw in sections 4.3.2 and 4.3.3 that these protections are less than perfect. Even when they limit abuse, they do nothing to legitimize intervention in the eyes of people who are not voters in the authorizing country. More important will be requests from the legitimate government of the targeted country and, secondarily, international authorization. The former might be secured ad hoc, as happened with the guarantee Poland received from Britain in 1939 and with the Kuwaiti government in exile's request for international help in 1990.[86] Alternatively, security guarantees might be embedded in treaties like the NATO Charter, Article V of which declares that an attack on any member "shall be considered an attack against them all" that triggers any necessary measures "including the use of armed force" to repel the attack. Article V actions do not require UN approval, but the treaty does require that they be reported to the Security Council immediately and terminated when NATO "has taken the measures necessary to restore and maintain international peace and security."[87]

This genuflecting toward the Security Council reflects the legitimacy deficit that inevitably rears its head when nations go to war on behalf of others. Lacking any third-party enforcement, treaties are often fragile window-dressing for power politics. Even within NATO, there is always the possibility that weaker countries are being strong-armed by more powerful ones for their own purposes.[88] Moreover, beleaguered governments of liberated countries, not to mention governments in exile, are inherently vulnerable, as the Poles learned at the end of World War II when the Roosevelt administration backtracked on its commitments to Stanislaw Mikolajczyk's provisional government in London, acquiescing—for its own geopolitical reasons—in the Soviet installation of its puppet Lublin government instead.[89] Occupations can be challenging to end even when they have been internationally authorized, as exemplified by the many decades it took to get South Africa to leave South West Africa even though the UN revoked its mandate and the International Court of Justice declared its occupation illegal.[90]

International authorization is in any case an imperfect substitute for a request from a legitimate government. This is because those on whose behalf the intervention is being undertaken, and who must live with its consequences, do not do the authorizing. Rather, the value of international authorization stems from deflecting, or at least blunting, charges of self-interest on the part of an intervening power. It is also flawed for this purpose, however, because the available international institutions are neither elected nor representative. They are disproportionately influenced by major powers, or, in the case of the Security Council, powers that were major at the end of World War II. Especially but not only in the eyes of audiences in the global South, Security Council authorization needs supplementing by other measures if it is to counter charges that third-party intervention is really being pursued to serve the interests of interveners.

The best supplement is an intervening coalition made up of countries with diverse interests. It helped in Iraq in 1991 that, as well as the major Western powers, support emanated from all parts of the world and significant military contributions came from every Arab country except Jordan.[91] In 2003, by contrast, although the United States extracted nominal commitments of support from some thirty-nine countries, almost all of them contributed nothing and combat assistance came only from Australia and the UK, plus a tiny Polish contingent.[92] Lacking both international authorization and a diverse coalition, the invasion was easily and widely portrayed as a rogue action by America in pursuit of its own agenda—even before its allegations about weapons of mass destruction and the security threat posed by Iraq were unmasked as untrue.[93]

Proportionality matters for the reasons discussed in section 6.2.1, but also to legitimate intervention. Limiting force to that which is needed to face down the threat at hand lends credence to the claim that the intervening country is containing aggression, not pursuing another agenda—stopping the bully without becoming one. Here, too, Desert Storm is a model, which unfortunately was not followed twelve years later when UN weapons inspectors' requests for additional time to determine whether Saddam Hussein in fact posed any threat were brushed aside by a Bush administration bent on war.[94] Lack of proportionality has also marked interventions to prevent domination within countries since the Cold War, as will become plain in section 6.3. Note for now that proportionality might well imply not invading militarily at all.

The 2014 Russian move into Ukraine is a case in point. On the one hand, Russia clearly violated Ukrainian sovereignty when its troops took control of Crimea and then annexed it following a local referendum of dubious legitimacy.[95] On the other hand, those events were triggered by a coup in Ukraine the previous month, as a result of which the president fled the country. The new government in Kiev—also, therefore, of dubious legitimacy—moved quickly to sign agreements with the EU. This raised the specter of a civil war in which ethnic Russians in eastern Ukraine might be in danger as well as the risk that Russia could lose access to its only warm-water naval base, on the Black Sea at Sevastopol.[96]

There were also intermittent suggestions that Ukraine might either join NATO or place itself under NATO's umbrella.[97] This was particularly irksome for the Russians, who believed, not without reason given recent history, that Western declarations about limits to NATO expansion were worthless. In 1990 the United States promised that including the newly unified Germany would not become a precedent.[98] Since then, three waves of expansion have added all the former Warsaw Pact countries and the former Soviet Baltic states of the USSR—ignoring strong Russian objections.[99] Russian skepticism that NATO is a defensive alliance is therefore understandable. There is no USSR or Soviet bloc, no Cold War, and no communist threat against which to defend. NATO's raison d'être has evaporated. It is scarcely surprising, therefore, that Putin invoked NATO's continued eastward expansion as requiring the Russian move in Crimea.[100]

None of this legitimates the Russian action, but it does suggest that the European and American caution displayed in dealing with it was warranted. No doubt this was partly due to the lack of agreement among the European governments, several of which are heavily dependent on Soviet oil and gas, and partly because it was obvious that the Obama administration would not risk starting World War III over Crimea. This, in turn, reflected awareness—if not recognition—of Russia's long involvement there. Crimea had become an autonomous republic in the new USSR in 1922, incorporated into the Russian Federation in 1945 after two years of Nazi occupation, and then transferred to the Ukrainian Soviet Republic in 1954. With the breakup of the USSR, Crimea had—somewhat uneasily—become an autonomous republic within the new Ukraine. Fifty-four percent of Crimeans voted for Ukrainian independence in 1991, but with a 60 percent turnout this meant that only 37 percent of the Crimean electorate actually voted for independence from Russia.[101] And with Russians representing some 67 percent of the population at that time, it seems clear that the great majority of the votes came from the 26 percent who were Ukrainian, the small number of Crimean Tartars who had survived Stalin's ethnic cleansing in 1944, and other small ethnic groups.[102]

The Western response was therefore to try to stop the Crimean annexation, which the Russians saw as necessary to vindicate a vital interest, from escalating. NATO beefed up its military presence in Poland, Romania, the Baltics, and the Black Sea, but refrained from providing military assistance to Ukraine.[103] The main strategy was economic sanctions, designed to make the Russian government pay a price sufficiently heavy that it would not consider grabbing more of Ukraine or moving elsewhere in Eastern Europe.[104] Whether this strategy would succeed in stabilizing the new status quo was unclear, not least because the outcome of the fighting in Ukraine remained in doubt. But the Western response amounted to the best available application of containment in circumstances where there were no good options. Escalation might come in any case, but no other feasible strategy offered the prospect of doing better. Given the stakes of a military confrontation between Russia and the United States, the exceptional history of Russia's relationship with Crimea, the weak legitimacy claims on all sides, and the absence in any case of agreement within NATO or beyond on a more aggressive response, it was the best that could be done. Putin's subsequent bristling against the West's use of containment against him suggested that it was working.[105]

6.3 Crossing Borders to Prevent Domination

As important as authorization, proportionality, and diverse coalitions are to preventing domination across borders, they are even more so when crossing borders to prevent domination. The reason is twofold. First, the best kind of authorization, invitation from a legitimate government, will almost always be unavailable. There are exceptions, as when the Nigerian government briefly accepted U.S. military help in 2014 to pursue Boko Haram terrorists who were selling girls kidnapped in Borno into slavery.[106] But more often the question will be whether to intervene when a government fails to protect significant sectors of its population from ethnic cleansing or murderous forms of political repression, or the government is itself the perpetrator. In these circumstances outsiders must act unilaterally, in coalitions, or via authorization from an international entity such as the UN or the AU. Imperfect as these are in authorizing resistance to transnational aggression, they become even more so when invading a country to protect a population from its own government.

The other consideration arises from the real possibility that intervention will make things worse. Think of it as the political equivalent of the physicians' imperative, often inaccurately attributed to Hippocrates: "First, do no harm."[107] Taking on a national government on its own territory might well mean taking it out, inevitably raising the question: What comes next? People might hope for improvements, but there is always the chance that the next regime will be worse, or that there will be a failed state governed by warlords, militias, and criminal gangs. This might be less of an issue in an ongoing civil war where the state is already collapsed or semicollapsed, but even then outsiders are all too easily manipulated by local protagonists in ways that undermine peacemaking and state building. Gopal documents in depressing detail how extensively this happened in Afghanistan, where U.S. forces became tools in local conflicts in ways that undermined their own mission and the Karzai government they were trying to support.[108] Michael Doyle is therefore persuasive that a precondition for intervening in civil wars should be credible plans for peacemaking and state building, and that these are not easily come by.[109] This is not least because peacekeeping and state building are expensive, and voters in the intervening states are unlikely to commit billions of dollars over long periods of time in situations where they have no vital interest at stake.

Sobering as these issues are in collapsed states, they are even more so when taking on a viable government. The 2011 intervention in Libya is a case in point. A supporter of terrorists in the 1980s and early 1990s, Gaddafi had since come in from the cold. In 1996 the State Department's report on global terrorism noted a sharp reduction in Libyan sponsorship of terrorism.[110] Three years later Gaddafi agreed to extradite the Pan Am 104 hijackers for trial in The Hague and pay compensation to the victims of this and other terrorist attacks in which Libya had been implicated.[111] He was also one of the first Arab leaders to condemn the 9/11 attacks, calling the Taliban "Godless promoters of political Islam."[112] In 2002 Libya signed the 1999 Convention for the Suppression of the Financing of Terrorism and the 1991 Convention on the Marking of Plastic Explosives for the Purpose of Detection. In December 2003 Gaddafi agreed to dismantle his nuclear weapons program to get sanctions removed.[113] Gaddafi moved quickly to normalize relations with the West. He expanded oil exports to Europe, consorted frequently with Nicolas Sarkozy, Silvio Berlusconi, and Tony Blair, bought a share of Juventus, Italy's most successful football team, and sent his son to the London School of Economics.[114] This was consistent with Gaddafi's behavior at home over the preceding decade, where he had become distinctly less oppressive. As Alan Kuperman notes, all the major human rights abuses reported in Amnesty International's 2010 report on Libya took place before the turn of the century.[115] By 2010 he had become a run-of-the-mill autocrat, not notably worse than others in the Middle East who had good relations with the West.

Attitudes changed after the advent of the Arab Spring. Revolutions swept from North Africa to Yemen, capturing Western public imaginations and rattling the longtime cozy relations between their governments and Middle East autocrats. In Libya, events moved rapidly. Violent uprisings erupted in the eastern part of the country in February 2011. The rebels made rapid gains, seizing the entire coastline from the oil-exporting port at Ras Lanuf to the Egyptian border. They soon took Misurata on the central coast, Zawiya and Zuwara just west of Tripoli, and major towns in the mountains to the southwest. By early March they controlled at least half the country's populated areas and six of Libya's nine largest cities. But their success depended mainly on surprise, and the insurgency quickly fell apart in the face of a major counteroffensive by Gaddafi's forces. It took less than two weeks for Gaddafi to regain control of almost all populated areas west of the rebel stronghold of Benghazi. The rebels were on the verge of total defeat there when the UN authorized the NATO bombing that began on March 19. For the next eight months, NATO bombed Gaddafi's forces and supplied the rebels with weapons, training, logistical support, and supplies. They finally took control of the country following the killing of Gaddafi in his native Sirte in October.[116]

For the European leaders, the change in policy may partly have emanated from early predictions that Gaddafi was finished and the felt need to keep the oil flowing under what would be the new order. Whatever the reason, the French in particular bet early on the self-appointed Transitional National Council led by recent defectors from the Gaddafi regime. None of them had democratic histories or credentials.[117] Their attack on the regime was at the head of an armed movement, not a democratic uprising as had been the case in Tunisia and Egypt. In fact, the insurgents, not Gaddafi's forces, perpetrated the bulk of the violence.[118] When Gaddafi gained the upper hand in early March, the insurgents trumpeted alarmist claims—later revealed as somewhere between wildly exaggerated and flat out false—about actual and imminent slaughter of unarmed civilians at Benghazi. Western governments affirmed these claims, as did the media, almost without exception.[119] This triggered calls across the region for the enforcement of a no-fly zone against the Libyan air force and the passage of Security Council Resolution 1973, authorizing the NATO intervention "to protect civilians and civilian populated areas under threat of attack."[120]

U.S. enthusiasm for the mission was spurred by the belief, which had fast become orthodox, that the Arab Spring revolutions would sideline al-Qaeda. The empirical basis for this conviction remains puzzlingly elusive, not least because, as Daveed Gartenstein-Ross has noted, jihadist leaders saw the Arab Spring revolutions, and especially the prospect of Gaddafi's fall, as an opportunity.[121] He had been in the forefront of the fight against them for a decade, and they were quick to sign up, along with other fundamentalist clerics, with the "rebels" fighting Gaddafi.[122] For their own purposes they were happy to play along with the fiction of a popular uprising. How much Western governments believed their own narrative about this, and how much they were trapped by their early conviction—which they then felt obliged to salvage—that Gaddafi was destined for defeat, is hard to tell. The contemporaneous evaluations remain classified. It is clear from Defense Secretary Robert Gates's account that his and other skeptical voices were swept aside in the rush to intervene.[123]

The Libyan debacle is a model of how not to intervene. Kuperman notes that the initial justification for intervention was based on reports that exaggerated the death toll by a factor of ten. Claims that Gaddafi was targeting civilians came from less-than-credible sources: principally an opposition that was hoping to get external support in a civil war that it was losing.[124] In fact, there was no indiscriminate targeting of civilians, and— also contrary to contemporaneous claims by rebel groups—Gaddafi's forces did not engage in reprisals in cities as they retook them. Even in Misurata, a city of 400,000 where the fighting was most intense, a total of 257 were killed and 949 wounded on all sides of the conflict, of whom 22 were women and eight were children. The story in Tripoli was comparable. Of the 200 corpses observed by Human Rights Watch in the city's morgue, all were adults and only two were women—numbers that do not support charges of indiscriminate civilian slaughter.[125] Kuperman notes that some of the exaggerated press accounts of killing during the uprising can be traced to a French physician in Benghazi who extrapolated from a tiny sample in one hospital to claim that more than 2,000 deaths had occurred there by February 21, when in reality Human Rights Watch could identify only 233 deaths in the entire country by that date.[126] But for the most part, the deceptive claims and numbers were taken largely on trust from rebel sources when there were good reasons to be skeptical of them.

Security Council Resolution 1973 had called only for a no-fly zone to prevent civilian casualties and it had prohibited the introduction of foreign troops. But it rapidly became obvious that toppling Gaddafi had been the goal all along. Indeed, France recognized the Transitional National Council as Libya's government before the UN Security Council resolution passed, led the diplomatic campaign to get the United States on board, and started bombing Gaddafi's forces on the day Resolution 1973 was adopted.[127] Cease-fire proposals from Gaddafi and the AU were brushed aside, insurgents were trained, supported, and buttressed in many parts of the country and abroad, and Gaddafi's forces were bombed even in places—notably Sirte—where the civilian population supported the regime. The sustained NATO campaign eventually enabled the rebels to topple Gaddafi, but at the cost of prolonging the war by eight months and increasing the death toll, Kuperman calculates, by seven to ten times.[128]

The legacy was disastrous. Radical Islamists, long suppressed by Gaddafi, refused to disarm after the war and prospered as they had expected to. Ironically, they mounted successful attacks on the French embassy in Tripoli and the U.S. embassy in Benghazi—killing the U.S. ambassador and three other embassy staff. The secular moderate coalition government elected in July 2012 quickly fell apart in acrimonious regional rivalries, and the central government was unable to reestablish anything remotely resembling a Weberian state. The result was continuing militia battles over control of the major cities, airports, and government buildings, and new footholds for jihadist militias in Libya and neighboring countries.[129] By late 2014 even ISIL had moved into Libya, seizing control of Derna near the Egyptian border.[130]

The worst regional fallout from Gaddafi's fall was in Mali, hitherto one of West Africa's few stable democracies. Malian ethnic Tuareg fighters in Gaddafi's security forces fled home with their weapons and launched a rebellion, triggering a military coup. The Tuareg rebellion was then hijacked by local Ansar Dine Islamists, who quickly gained control of large swaths of northern Mali, imposed sharia law, and displaced hundreds of thousands of people, producing a humanitarian catastrophe. France intervened, sending 4,000 troops when the rebels were advancing on the capital city, Bamako. Paris planned for a brief operation, after which UN peacekeepers from Chad and elsewhere would take over. But the peacekeepers failed to materialize, and although the French drove the rebels deep into the mountains on the Algerian border, they were not defeated before France pulled out most of its troops. The result was a series of failed peace agreements between the government and the rebels, who continued pressing for an Islamic state in the north of the country at a minimum.[131]

The regional fallout was not limited to Mali. A 2013 UN Security Council report documented extensive weapons flows from the remnants of Gaddafi's arsenals to Islamist rebels across North Africa. Fifteen thousand man-portable surface-to-air missiles, capable of shooting down civilian airliners, were never recovered. Some fell into the hands al-Qaeda's North African affiliates; some went to Boko Haram in Niger and Northern Nigeria; and some ended up with Hamas in Gaza. Both Kuperman and Marc Lynch noted evidence of fallout in Syria as well, where the moral hazard of intervention kicked in. Comparatively peaceful protesters against Bashar al-Assad's regime saw the NATO intervention in Libya turn the tide against Gaddafi and then turned to violence themselves, anticipating that the predictable crackdown from Assad would bring NATO into Syria as well.[132] Kuperman and Gartenstein-Ross are surely right that the Libyan intervention was a strategic failure for the United States and NATO. It increased civilian deaths, left Libya as a failed state, and had damaging fallout across the region. Some of the most ardent cheerleaders for the intervention would eventually be forced admit this.[133]

Curiously, though, some did not. Robert Pape, who is generally skittish about R2P and instead favors a "pragmatic" standard for humanitarian intervention, maintains that the Libya operation was a success. It is illuminating to consider the limitations of his account from the nondomination perspective defended here.

Pape's threshold for intervention is threefold. It requires the existence of an ongoing campaign of mass killing sponsored by the local government, "near zero" prospect of casualties for the intervening force, and a "workable strategy for creating long-lasting local security." Collectively, he argues, they are preferable to R2P, which "sets the bar for intervention so low that that virtually every instance of anarchy or tyranny—or, indeed, every potential instance—represents an opportunity for the international community to violate the sovereignty of states." Pape also believes that his three-pronged test is better than the conventional requirement of ongoing genocide, which, he agrees with Kuperman, is so stringent that it will not likely have a significant impact even on major genocides such as the Rwandan one.[134]

Pape believes that the Libyan intervention was a success partly because he accepts as "credible" contemporaneous estimates of the number of civilians who had been killed or were in imminent danger in early 2011, numbers that we now know to have been wildly inflated. He also ignores the estimated casualties that Kuperman computes as having resulted from the eight-month prolongation of the war caused by the intervention. To some extent these differences are inherently speculative, depending, as they must do, on counterfactual estimates. But there are deeper reasons to reject Pape's "pragmatic" test as too permissive that have been well-illustrated by the way in which the Libyan intervention has played out.

The central difficulty with Pape's view is that, on the one hand, he claims that it implies no commitment to regime change but, on the other, his requirement of keeping casualties of the intervening force to a minimum means that it must team up with, and—indeed—strengthen, antigovernment forces. "With significant opposition on the ground," he argues about Libya, the interveners could reduce their risk to near zero by relying on cruise missiles, unmanned aerial vehicles, and other over-the-horizon measures. The purpose of arming the rebels was to enable them "to decide their own fate."[135] But as my discussion of Afghanistan in section 6.2.1 underscores, intervening on the cheap by teaming up with insurgents in a civil war inevitably ties you to their agenda.

Pape evades this problem by saying that it would be up to the rebels to decide, ultimately, whether "to cut a deal with Gaddafi."[136] But how plausible is that? NATO repeatedly attacked government forces, even in areas where no civilians were threatened, and its forces armed, trained, and supported the rebels. Yet at no point did NATO pressure rebel groups to explore possibilities of a cease-fire or other accommodation, which would surely have been appropriate, as Kuperman notes, if minimizing civilian casualties had been the goal.[137] Moreover, the NATO forces made it clear that they would keep up their campaign—as they indeed did—until the rebels prevailed. In such circumstances, why would defectors from Gaddafi's cabinet and security forces have any interest in reaching an accommodation with him?[138]

Pape's commitment to teaming up with local insurgents to keep casualty costs of the intervening force close to zero also lives in tension with his third criterion for intervention: that there be a "workable strategy for creating long-lasting local security." As happened with the Northern Alliance in Afghanistan, the intervening forces in Libya were supporting what had become the losing side in a civil war. This will often be so; it verges on being true by definition that if an insurgency could win without outside support it, would not be losing. Backing them therefore creates the danger that John Stuart Mill worried about in "A Few Words on Non-Intervention" in 1859, to wit, that if rebels are unable to overthrow oppressors on their own, "the liberty which is bestowed on them by other hands" will be "nothing real, nothing permanent."[139] Pape's assertion that Libya was "not descending into the kind of chaos and violence that would fundamentally undermine the goals of the intervention" had already become wishful thinking by the time he made it in mid-2012. By then it was obvious, as he conceded, that many of the militias "have refused to disarm, and some regions have been reluctant to cede authority to the National Transitional Council."[140] The puzzle is why he, or anyone, would have expected anything different.

The Libyan lesson on this point is the same as the Afghan one: there is no effective foreign intervention on the cheap. Moreover, in a world in which failed states are toxic breeding grounds for transnational terrorist movements, intervention is unlikely to be cheap in the end anyway. Failed states generate their own dynamics, often pulling the intervening powers back in at tremendous cost in hopes of sustaining the new regime. In inflation-adjusted dollars, the United States has spent more in Afghanistan since 2001 than it did on the Marshall Plan.[141] Yet almost none of it has been spent on building a viable country. Gopal reports that a mere 5.4 percent of the $557 billion that Washington spent in Afghanistan between 2001 and 2011 went to development or governance. The vast majority went toward military expenditures, significant chunks of which wound up in coffers of regional strongmen who were actually fighting against the Karzai regime that the Americans were trying to sustain.[142] This, too, was due to intervening on the cheap. Because the Afghan military did not control vast sectors of the country where the U.S. military was operating, the choice was either to pay many millions of dollars to the regional strongmen, euphemistically described as "private security companies," to protect U.S. supply lines, or bring in many thousands of additional soldiers to replace the subcontractors, which would cause the American body count to skyrocket.[143] By the end of 2014 the Obama administration was being forced in that direction anyhow. Spooked by how inept Iraqi forces had been in confronting the ISIL insurgency after the U.S. departure without a status of forces agreement in 2011, the Obama administration was once again beefing up its military commitments to Afghanistan.[144]

The full cost of the Libyan intervention in lives, dollars, discredited NATO leadership, and regional fallout will not be known for decades. But by late 2014, Libya was undeniably a failed state. The U.S. State Department had abandoned claims that it was transitioning to democracy, calling it as a "terrorist safe haven" instead, and Libya's interim government acknowledged that "the majority of the ministries, institutions, and associations" in the capital were no longer under its control.[145] Enough had unfolded to make it clear that the wiser course would have been to limit the intervention to what the Arab League called for, what Security Council Resolution 1973 authorized, and what other regional players were at least passively willing to endorse: destruction of the offensive capabilities that Gaddafi was deploying against Benghazi, followed by fact-finding on the ground and support for one of the peace initiatives that the AU and other groups were pressing at the time.[146] This would have been the nondomination move, a proportionate response to the threat that Gaddafi actually posed.

NATO's contribution to Libya's joining the ranks of failed states raises the issue of whether it should ever intervene militarily when no NATO member is threatened. This new role goes back to NATO's 1999 action in Kosovo, ambiguously validated after the fact as "illegal but legitimate" by the Swedish government's ad hoc commission. But Kosovo created unrealistic expectations about NATO's potential as a roving global police force. For one thing, the wars and civil wars that followed Yugoslavia's collapse had not produced a consolidated state in Kosovo, so that the downside risk of destroying it by intervening did not arise. For another, there was overwhelming evidence that the Serbs—though not only the Serbs—had committed major war crimes and were engaged in ethnic cleansing, and that Kosovo's Albanian Muslims were in imminent danger.[147] Third, neither the United States nor any other NATO country had significant geostrategic stakes in Kosovo, lending color to the contention that they were not pursuing a self-interested agenda. Having suffered extensive criticism for failing to act in Rwanda six years earlier, Bill Clinton and other Western leaders might have seen in Kosovo an opportunity to redeem their legacies. They had little else to gain, and it helped, for non-Western audiences, that NATO forces were intervening in Kosovo to protect a Muslim population that was in grave danger. Last and perhaps most important, the Kosovo intervention preceded the huge hit that U.S. and UK credibility would soon take in Iraq. All this buttressed a narrative of benign intentions, but this turned out to be a high point rather than a precedent.

In any case, NATO leaders blew any chance that their Libyan intervention would repair the damage done to their reputations by their conduct of the Afghan and Iraq wars. The mission creep—really mission leap—from protecting civilians to toppling Gaddafi brought swift condemnation from the Arab League, which had backed creating no-fly zones to protect civilians.[148] The AU, which had never recognized Libya's Transitional National Council, followed suit, pressing for a negotiated settlement. The deteriorating conflict triggered widespread condemnation from opinion leaders across the African continent.[149] Russia and China, whose abstentions had facilitated adoption of Security Council Resolution 1973, condemned the regime-change agenda as unauthorized.[150] Having been played for suckers in Libya, they would remain intransigent in resisting imposing significant costs on Syria despite the regime's manifest and escalating humanitarian abuses.[151] Who could be surprised?

The West has fallen a long way since George H. W. Bush's call for a New World Order in the run-up to the 1991 expulsion of Iraqi forces from Kuwait.[152] Had his model of combining credible authorization with large and diverse coalitions to do only what is needed to face down imminent threats—to stop bullies without bullying—prevailed, things might have evolved differently. If the next several conflicts had been managed according to that script, a common law of acceptable norms for resisting domination across borders just might have begun to emerge. It would have taken levels of restraint and leadership that are rare in international politics, and almost unheard of on the kind of sustained basis that is needed to weave new norms into the fabric of international conduct. As with governments voluntarily giving up power when they lose elections, the hardest part is getting the benign dynamic going.[153] In the event, the 1991 Iraq intervention turned out to be an outlier, and any global claim to moral leadership that the United States enjoyed between then and the aftermath of the 9/11 attacks has since been squandered.

There is a related difficulty with R2P authorizations that undermines their legitimacy.[154] R2P obliges governments to protect their populations from genocide, crimes against humanity, war crimes, and ethnic cleansing, and it empowers the Security Council to authorize intervention when they fail to do so. It does not, however, oblige the Security Council to authorize intervention. Nor does it oblige members to enforce a Security Council resolution triggered by R2P considerations. In practice, this means that intervention is most likely when a permanent Security Council member decides to push for intervention, as France did, with American acquiescence, in Libya in 2011. This means that others will inevitably see R2P as a tool for permanent members to intervene when it suits them, rather than when the situation calls for it. During Israel's Operation Protective Edge in July 2014, there were repeated allegations that R2P violations were occurring in Gaza.[155] Valid or not, there was no chance that intervention would be authorized or attempted, given the prevailing array of interests and alliances.

NATO is in a similar boat. Its new self-appointed role as humanitarian policeman in no way obviates the reality that it is a military alliance geared to protecting its members' interests. R2P interventions will always be subject to that constraint, and therefore perceived by others as partisan. This makes NATO a poor instrument for humanitarian intervention, particularly when acting alone, and especially in places where NATO members have major strategic or commercial interests. When the UN approved intervention in Somalia in 2006 to protect the interim government against Islamic militants, it authorized a seven-nation regional group but explicitly excluded Ethiopia, Djibouti, and Kenya because they were perceived to have stakes in the outcome.[156] AU interventions generally exclude neighboring countries for the same reason. This echoes the tradition dating back to the Cold War, by which UN peacekeeping forces excluded superpowers and neighbors. Yet in Libya, the Security Council authorized unspecified "member states" to intervene "acting nationally or through organizations or arrangements"—in effect giving NATO carte blanche to do what it did.[157]

There is, of course, a trade-off between getting the benefit of essential street-level knowledge that neighbors and other interested players bring to an intervention, and avoiding the perception of bias that they inevitably bring as well. The best way to manage the resulting tension is by creating diverse coalitions that include credible whistle-blowers to keep the interested players honest, and make it less likely that they will exceed their authorized mandates. Part of the reason George H. W. Bush did not go to Baghdad in 1991 is that many of the Arab countries would have dropped their support for Desert Storm had he done so.[158] There is no strict recipe for the composition of intervening forces; what is best will always depend on many contingencies. But the more that powerful players act unilaterally, flout authorized mandates, and violate the principle of proportionality, the less legitimacy they will garner for crossing borders to prevent bullying. Others will rightly see them, instead, as bullies.[159]

6.4 Installing Democracy

Setting aside R2P considerations and attacks across borders, what about intervening to promote democracy where currently it is lacking? If democracy is, as I argued in earlier chapters, the best political system for combating domination, then helping it spread makes sense. Moreover, one of the more serviceable generalizations of political science is that democracies tend not to go to war with each other. This is not true without qualification, and its robustness might be eroding in an era when funding wars with debt and fighting them with volunteer soldiers, military contractors, and drones has weakened the electoral constraints on reckless decisions by democratic governments to fight. But there is still some basis to agree with Kant that democracies are less likely than other regimes to try to subjugate one another by force.[160] This makes democracy promotion doubly worthwhile from the standpoint of resisting domination.

But successful examples of installing democracy from outside a country are few and far between. The seminal examples are Japan and West Germany after World War II, but they exhibited three features that that are as propitious as they are rare: democratic legacies that preceded the authoritarian takeover; a devastated population, many of whom blamed their own government for their catastrophic defeat and accepted— however grudgingly—the legitimacy of foreign occupation; and intervening powers that were willing to make huge investments, for many decades, in buttressing the new order both institutionally and economically.[161] Trying to install democracy from outside when any of these features is missing is vastly more challenging, if it is possible at all, as recent experiences in Iraq, Afghanistan, and now Libya underscore.

Promoting regime change in Iraq became U.S. policy with the adoption of the Iraq Liberation Act in 1998.[162] President Clinton signed the bill under heavy pressure from neoconservatives, in effect abandoning the prevailing containment policy—at least officially.[163] Some of those who lobbied for the law's passage were moved by watching the return of democracy to much of Eastern Europe after 1989. They thought that instigating regime change in Iraq would be easy and that it would have a domino effect—spreading democracy across the region.[164] Remove the repressive autocrat, the history lesson seemed to be, and democracy will blossom. But the Eastern European countries had considerably more in common with postwar Japan and West Germany than they did with Iraq. Their populations remembered prewar democratic institutions that had been crushed by Hitler, the USSR, or Soviet puppet regimes after 1945, and in 1989 they were looking forward to economic benefits of integration into the new Europe.

Advocates of regime change for Iraq would have been better advised to look at the former Asiatic republics of the USSR for models of how things would likely go in a country with no democratic history, an oil-based rentier economy, and a population that was ill-disposed toward the United States as a potential liberator. In Iraq, the Sunni minority's privileges depended on Saddam Hussein; they had little to gain from his departure or, obviously, from a democracy in which Shiites would predominate. Many Shiites felt betrayed by the United States during the 1991 Sha'aban Intifada; trusting America as a democratic liberator would be a tough sell. President Clinton, who evidently understood this, added a signing statement to the bill to make it clear that the United States did not intend to oust Saddam Hussein by force.[165] But signing it was unwise nonetheless. It fed the image of the United States as a regional meddler and supplied cover for the subsequent Bush administration to deny that its regime-change agenda in Iraq was the radical departure that it was.

Democratic transformations can be helped along from the outside where democracy has not previously been well established, but only at the margin. For one thing, democracy is unlikely to be sustainable, however it is instituted, unless the economy is reasonably robust and diversified. Przeworski et al. find that democracy becomes stable when per capita income (PCI) reaches $6,000 measured in 1985 dollars (about $13,300 in 2015 dollars).[166] Democracy becomes vulnerable as PCI falls below that threshold, and the farther it falls, the more vulnerable democracy becomes. There are exceptions, India being the principal outlier, but democracy almost never endures in poor countries.[167] Lack of economic diversification also threatens democracy even when PCI is otherwise sufficient. If the principal access to prosperity is via resources controlled by the state, those in power are unlikely to give it up, and those who lack power will grab it if they can. And without economic diversification there will not be a middle class possessed of the wherewithal to put pressure on the regime to democratize. This means that even if a transition could be effectuated in any of the oil-rich countries of the Middle East, it would be hard-pressed to survive.[168] Oil is not always a curse, but it will be one when the economy consists of little else. This will not change unless external pressure to democratize comes with major and sustained economic development programs.

But economics is only part of the story. External help is unlikely to be effective unless there is already an indigenous opposition that is plausibly democratic and sufficiently organized to be a credible government-in-waiting. Moreover, the request for external help needs to come from the indigenous opposition, lest it starts being seen as the puppet of the outside power. Potentially viable democratic oppositions are not likely, therefore, to request armed intervention, which they will see as undermining their legitimacy. They are more likely to call for weapons, training, and financial help; or for boycotts and sanctions against the regime. South Africa during the struggle against apartheid is an example. The ANC was a well-organized opposition that had been fighting for democracy for decades when it called for external sanctions to weaken the apartheid regime.[169] Burma arguably fell into this category as well during the 1990s and 2000s.[170] But a government that depends on foreign troops will eventually find itself in the catch-22 of Hamid Karzai's government in 2009, when only a huge surge of U.S. troops could save him from being engulfed by the Taliban insurgency. Yet as Gall put it: "Bringing in more foreign troops to counter the insurgency would further undermine the legitimacy of his government. His administration would be seen as a puppet government, and the Taliban would be seen as fighting on the right side, for independence and religion."[171]

It also matters that the democratic opposition is indigenous. This is partly because of the legitimacy considerations just mentioned, but also because it helps judge the veracity of opposition claims. Expatriates who turn out to be wrong can continue their lives abroad. Indigenous oppositions will have to pay the price. This makes their claims more credible. There are exceptions, as with the provisional governments of countries like Norway, France, and Poland in Britain during World War II. There was little doubt about their democratic bona fides, or their ability to govern if Hitler could be defeated and they could return to power. The ANC in exile maintained close contact with imprisoned leadership in South Africa, and there was never any doubt that Nelson Mandela would lead its first government. Things quickly become problematic, however, when expatriate oppositions are disconnected from indigenous struggles. Ahmad

Chalabi's Iraqi National Congress provided much of what turned out to be false claims about weapons of mass destruction in Iraq, not to mention confident but wrong predictions that American soldiers would be greeted in the streets as liberators. The fact that Chalabi, who lived in London, had not been to Iraq for decades should have been a red flag for the Bush administration. Yet they relied on his avowals and were dragged into an untenable morass as a result.[172] There was no plausible democratic opposition in Iraq, which left the United States in the hopeless position of running an occupation while trying to render its puppet regime legitimate.

In this area as well, since the Cold War successive U.S. governments seem to have displayed a learning curve with a negative slope. Having failed to heed the lessons of Afghanistan and Iraq, and having provoked the Syrian escalation through its actions in Libya in March 2011, as we have seen, the Obama administration then demanded Bashar al-Assad's resignation and escalated sanctions against Syria in hopes of bringing this about.[173] This was unwise, not only because the United States lacked the capacity to topple Assad given Obama's prohibition of American boots on the ground, but also because there was no reason to believe that there was an organized opposition that could overthrow Assad and govern the country—let alone ensure the transition to democracy that he was demanding. William Polk wrote at the end of 2013, "If the opponents of the regime are fighting for some form of democracy, they have yet to make their voices heard."[174] Of the hundreds of opposition groups seeking Assad's ouster, outside observers were finding it hard to identify any that seemed genuinely interested in moving Syria toward a democracy.[175]

In fact, the Syrian conflict was no more an Arab Spring uprising than the Libyan one had been. Instead, the civil war resulted from years of catastrophic droughts that began in 2006.[176] They stripped hundreds of thousands of farmers of their livelihoods and crippled the economy. Destitute farmers streamed into towns and cities in search of nonexistent employment. In 2008 the Syrian minister for agriculture declared that the economic and social fallout from the drought "beyond our capacity as a country to deal with," but USAID declined their requests for assistance. In 2010, UN observers estimated that between two and three million rural Syrians had been reduced to extreme poverty. The situation continued deteriorating, prompting escalating demonstrations and eventually the government crackdown and civil war. As Polk says, "what had begun as a water issue gradually turned into a political and religious issue."[177]

The United States has a history of undermining the Syrian regime, dating at least to its support for the Hama uprising in 1982.[178] But to what end? Before the onset of the water crisis in 2006, Syrian per capita income stood at about $5,000—less than half the minimum needed to sustain democracy. By 2010 it had fallen to $2,900.[179] Yet as radical Islamists consolidated themselves into ISIL, the Obama administration remained committed to the idea that, besides taking them on, the United States should identify and train "moderate" Syrians to attack the Assad regime.[180] It was as if the Western Allies had decided in the middle of Operation Barbarossa that the time had come to get rid of Stalin.[181] The Syrian conflict was at least as multifaceted as the ongoing Afghan one, in which the United States had repeatedly been manipulated in local conflicts, confused allies with enemies, and strengthened the Taliban insurgency it was fighting.[182] In Syria, Obama added the challenge of fighting on two major fronts of what was at least a three-sided civil war, when the prospects of replacing the Assad regime with a viable democracy were no more plausible than they had been in Afghanistan or Libya. It was obvious by then that any suggestion that democracy was blossoming across the Middle East was no more plausible than the Bush administration's democratic domino theory had been a decade earlier.

To be sure, things other than democracy promotion have shaped much of the animosity between the United States and Syria. Competition with the Soviets for regional influence, the U.S. alliance with Israel, and Syria's links to Iran during and since the Iran-Iraq war all played their roles. To some extent such proxy conflicts were understandable during the Cold War, though even then they often played out in unpredictable ways. The Eisenhower administration's decision to topple Iran's elected government in 1953 came back to haunt Americans when the Shah's repressive regime provoked the Islamic revolution of 1979. The mujahedeen militias that the United States backed against the Soviets in Afghanistan in the 1980s became a source of major headaches for the U.S. occupation after 2002. In any case, whatever might have been the strategic wisdom of such proxy battles during the choreographed conflicts of the Cold War, they make little sense in the multifaceted world of the twenty-first century, as I noted in section 6.2.2. Propping up strongmen who are judged friendly is too fraught with uncertainty to yield networks of reliable allies. It is more likely to breed a reputation for opportunism, and it fails to supply others any incentive to support democracy.[183]

Some will call this naive. Countries invariably pursue their interests, helping allies and undermining adversaries as they go. They do, but that is not at issue here. Rather my argument is a variant of Alexis de Tocqueville's "self-interest, rightly understood."[184] The logic behind Kennan's defense of containment that I endorsed in section 6.1 was that trying to dominate the global security environment would be self-defeating over time, and that the better course is to work for a security environment that no one can dominate. This, in turn, will be more likely if democracy spreads. Supporting democratic movements therefore makes sense when there is a plausible case that they are authentic and viable, when they seek external help, and when economic conditions are at least minimally hospitable to the enterprise. But toppling oppressive regimes where these conditions are absent is unwise. They might well be replaced by something at least as bad, or by a failed state in which terrorists and armed militias proliferate.

The same logic applies to movements for national liberation. Historically many of these were anticolonial groups that fought against the denial of democratic freedoms and for their national ambitions. In the contemporary world they often oppose some sort of neocolonialism or occupation, or they might, like the Kurds, be ethnic minorities in several countries seeking to consolidate their own nation-state. But nationalism is one thing and democracy another. Without credible evidence that people are both committed and able to deliver the latter, there is no good reason to intervene on their behalf from the standpoint of nondomination. Whether it is Kurdish opposition parties, Hamas in Gaza and the West Bank, or the Chechen separatists seeking independence from Russia, the question cannot only be whether others, who embrace different national ambitions, frustrate theirs and oppress them. Just as the strength of claims for multicultural accommodation within countries depends on how their proponents themselves treat vulnerable minorities, those who seek liberation from an oppressive national order should pass a comparable test.[185] We should not prop up their oppressors, but nor should we be complicit in knocking them off unless there are good grounds to believe that, once in power, the insurgent opposition forces would themselves be less oppressive of others.[186]

That does not mean doing nothing in circumstances like those that prevailed in Syria and northern Iraq in 2014. But intervention should be constrained by what is feasible and calibrated to real threats. As Kuperman notes, the United States' limited military actions to prevent the slaughter of Turkmen in Amerli and the Yazidi on Mount Sinjar in northern Iraq in 2014 are appropriate models.[187] They are the kind of actions that intervening powers should have pursued at Benghazi in March 2011. More extensive involvement in Syria should have been geared to dealing with ISIL in collaboration with regional powers along the lines discussed in section 6.1.1. Pushing the jihadists out of Iraq would have made it easier to choke off funds they were earning from black-market sales of oil, much of it stolen from Kirkuk.[188] The goal would be to weaken them to the point where they could plausibly be dealt with by the Syrian military. This, in turn, assumes that the United States would not simultaneously be bent on destabilizing the Syrian state. The prospects of establishing democracy in Syria in the near term being slim to none, the appropriate goal is to focus on the major threat posed by ISIL. If and when a plausibly democratic Syrian opposition emerges, then the question of what assistance to provide will be well put. In the meantime, the more constructive course would be humanitarian assistance for Syrian farmers and refugees, geared to building the kind of economy in which democracy might eventually become viable. By the end of 2014 these considerations had, unfortunately, taken a backseat to the regime-change agenda.[189]

In February 2015 the Obama administration published its second *National Security Strategy* report, the first in five years.[190] Much of the report consists of the usual boilerplate typical of documents composed by many hands to satisfy many constituencies. But the report contained one notable summary statement:

> The use of force should not be our first choice, but it will sometimes be the necessary choice. The United States will use military force, unilaterally if necessary, when our enduring interests demand it: when our people are threatened; when our livelihoods are at stake; and when the security of our allies is in danger. In these circumstances, we prefer to act with allies and partners. The threshold for military action is higher when our interests are not directly threatened. In such cases, we will seek to mobilize allies and partners to share the burden and achieve lasting outcomes. In all cases, the decision to use force must reflect a clear mandate and feasible objectives, and we must ensure our actions are effective, just, and consistent with the rule of law. It should be based on a serious appreciation for the risk to our mission, our global responsibilities, and the opportunity costs at home and abroad. Whenever and wherever we use force, we will do so in a way that reflects our values and strengthens our legitimacy.[191]

How should we evaluate this? On the one hand, it includes core elements of the antibullying outlook I have advocated here. True, there is no mention that force used be proportionate or that it should be a last resort in response to an imminent threat. Nor does it say that third-party interventions should be internationally authorized where possible. Those are major omissions, though requiring U.S. actions to be consistent with justice and the rule of law could be said to imply all three.[192] That aside, the statement is arguably a good start. It is principled, limiting the use of force to when it is "necessary," and insisting that the trigger be a threat to basic interests—"our livelihoods"—or the security of allies. There is no mention of preemption, a defining feature of the George W. Bush's declared policy.[193] There is a clear preference for acting with "allies and partners," and the statement recognizes the need for higher thresholds to justify third-party military interventions. The statement insists on clear mandates and feasible objectives, and it requires that U.S. actions be just and consistent with the rule of law. It highlights the need for serious consideration of the risks and opportunity costs of intervention at home and abroad, and, echoing Kennan's insistence that U.S. national security policy must "measure up to its own best traditions and prove itself worthy of preservation as a great nation,"[194] it acknowledges the importance of acting in ways that reflect American values and strengthen its legitimacy.

On the other hand, the Obama administration flouted these principles so thoroughly across the Middle East since 2011 that is hard to know whether to take its affirmation of them seriously. The Libyan fiasco was not triggered by any plausible threat threshold, let alone a heightened one. Within weeks, if not days, the intervening forces had violated the Security Council mandate. Gaddafi was toppled with no plan as to what would come next, let alone attention to the conditions for a lasting outcome. There was little, if any, consideration of the likely effect on the Syrian conflict, not to mention the regional fallout across North Africa. Worse, the administration seemed not to learn from, or even acknowledge, these failures. Toppling Assad remained administration policy as though none of this had happened and without any evidence of attention to what would follow in Syria, despite the rise of ISIL and the flood of books detailing the failure of U.S. attempts, spanning more than a decade, to achieve sustainable regime change in Afghanistan.

A more hopeful reading of the 2015 *National Security Strategy* report would be that by 2015 the administration had finally started learning some of the right lessons from its mistakes, even if it could not admit to them publicly. Media reports began to surface suggesting that the United States was no longer serious about toppling Assad, and was perhaps even working with him against ISIL behind the scenes.[195] In Yemen the administration was openly supporting the Saudis in what had become a proxy war against Iran for regional influence, but at least they were avoiding direct U.S. military participation in the civil war that erupted following their client Ali Abdullah Saleh's departure from office in 2012.[196] Perhaps the Obama administration was finally starting to live up to the line often attributed to Churchill that the United States can always be counted on to do the right thing, but only after having exhausted every other possibility.[197]

6.5 Conclusion

John Locke famously held that we are obliged to preserve others so long as this "comes not in competition" with the need to preserve ourselves. That claim was embedded in his belief that, as God's creations, human beings are "made to last during his, not one another's pleasure."[198] Locke's natural law argument is not relevant to us here, but my argument in this chapter suggests that aspects of his thinking travel beyond their theological moorings. They suggest reasons to connect our interest in resisting domination to working toward a world that no one can dominate.

By prioritizing self-preservation, Locke did not mean that one's own life is more important than those of others.[199] The better, if anachronistic, gloss on his lexical logic is suggested by the standard airline safety injunction to put on your own oxygen mask before helping others. Compromising one's capacity to resist domination in hopes of saving others courts the danger that no one will end up adequately protected. If democratic institutions are the best available guard against domination, as I have argued, it is not worth compromising one's own democracy in hopes of preserving or creating others. Indeed, as I have argued here, the two enterprises are linked.

Similar thinking informed Kennan's warnings against adopting authoritarian practices at home in the name of resisting them abroad. The danger of destroying villages in order to save them achieved currency during the Vietnam era, but we saw in section 6.1 that it has survived the Cold War with a vengeance, time and again undermining America's exceptionalist pretentions. Overreach after 9/11 resulted in failed foreign interventions. They jaded the American public as the costs, in blood and treasure, exceeded by orders of magnitude the 1991–2003 price tag for containing Saddam that the second Bush administration complained was unacceptably high. More serious was the nation's failure to live up to what Kennan called its best traditions. The chance to work and lead toward a post–Cold War order based on self-restraint and proportionality in facing down aggression was compromised by waging preemptive war, efforts to export democracy at the barrel of a gun, and indulging in torture shrouded in euphemisms that succeeded only in tarnishing what remained of America's image as a shining city on a hill.[200] None of this bodes well for the medium term, but as I argued in section 1.3, there are reasons to remain hopeful even when there are few grounds for optimism.

Stop the bully without becoming one has been my central message. Whether we consider efforts at foiling domination across borders or crossing them in order to thwart it, the goal is to empower those who resist domination without themselves seeking to dominate. This argument is continuous with my defense of combating domination within countries, but there is a difference that stems from the reality that democracy, the best means to institutionalize nondomination within countries, is unavailable here. International institutions can sometimes help mitigate cross-border domination, but frequently they are oversold. Inevitably subject to the agendas of powerful states and alliances, they all too often become captured instruments of those agendas. Instead I have sought to develop an account that not only is compatible with the interests of powerful democracies, "rightly understood," but also serves those interests better than the going alternatives. It comes from an unlikely source in that George Kennan was not much interested in democracy or theoretical argument. Yet the logic that underlies his defense of containment in the 1940s remains the best available basis to advance the cause of nondomination beyond the nation-state, whether in response to domination that crosses borders or when they must be crossed in order to forestall it.

CHAPTER SEVEN

POLITICS AGAINST DOMINATION

WE HAVE A central interest avoiding domination. People have many other interests as well, but avoiding being dominated offers the best hope and basis for pursuing them. It underlies their other commitments; indeed, it often motivates them and gives them their point. Some contend that ideals such as equality, freedom, or impartiality are more fundamental, but Michael Walzer noted long ago that we typically sort innocuous inequalities from malevolent ones based on whether they facilitate domination, and I have argued the same about freedom and impartiality elsewhere.[1] The heart of the matter is escaping, combating, or reducing domination, understood as the illicit use of power that threatens people's basic interests. There is more to the meaning of domination, and to opposing it, than that; but my concern here has been to explore its meaning for major arenas of political action and institutions. It remains to take stock of the book's main arguments, and spell out their implications for politics going forward.

Adapting against domination shares affinities with pragmatism, but it is more than just muddling through. Lacking blueprints for a just social order, partisans of the antidomination enterprise can nonetheless be inspired by the well-founded hope that practices and institutions that will militate against domination can be devised and gain traction. Successes are often partial and they cannot be entrenched forever; nothing can in the shifting sands of politics. Rather than fetishize particular arrangements, our allegiance to them should always be conditional—informed by what we learn about changing circumstances and possibilities. Resisting domination is like fighting a chronic ailment. The better we understand it, the better we can combat it. We know there is no permanent cure, but we have tools and capacities to prevent its becoming completely disabling or terminal. Not trying is scarcely an option, not least because some ways of managing it are better for us than others. We have an interest in discovering what they are and pursuing them.

7.1 National Politics

Politics never begins or ends. Ironically, John Locke, so often associated with constitutionalism and founding moments, supplies some of the best political insights about this. Locke's social contract started from a different place than those of contemporary contractarians who frame the root question of politics as some variant of: When is collective action warranted? Locke's question was: When can a government legitimately be resisted? The ubiquitous nature of collective life and the monopoly character of power combine to mean that our rights cannot be asserted against the state selectively. Unless we are willing to overthrow the government, whatever the majority either decides by itself or delegates to a monarch or other governing body is binding. Someone always prevails in politics; the question is, who? When push comes to shove, for Locke, the answer is always the majority. Majority rule is what will happen and what should happen. Majorities will rule because a body must "move that way whither the greater force carries it." Indeed, even revolution will succeed only when the majority turns out to favor it. And majorities should rule because "the act of the majority" embodies "the law of nature and reason."[2] It beats the going alternatives.

Locke's reasoning anchors a wiser approach to majority rule than the better-known tradition Rousseau spawned eight decades later. Confusing from its inception, Rousseau's account requires us to start from the "sum of particular wills," deduct the "pluses and minuses which cancel each other out," and then the remaining "sum of the differences" constitutes the general will.[3] Whether this merely amounts to an elaborate game of Where's Waldo? or instead comes down to chasing a mirage over the horizon has been debated by social choice theorists for centuries. Theorists in the Lockean tradition do not care. They start from the reality that power will be exercised willy-nilly and then ask: How can people best manage it so as to minimize the prospects for domination? Majority rule wins that prize. It is this Lockean tradition, summed up in Winston Churchill's dictum that democracy is the worst system except for the rest, that I have defended here as providing the best resources to resist domination in politics.[4] We have learned since Locke's time that it is possible to reduce the risk that it will lead to domination by multiplying cleavages, reducing stakes, and institutionalizing uncertainty of outcomes.

Some critics remain unconvinced. They insist that majority rule should be hemmed in by some kind of constitutional corset, or they opt instead for a variant of benign authoritarianism. But benign authoritarian regimes seldom stay that way for long. Either they democratize fully or they revert to hard-line authoritarianism.[5] As for constitutional corsets, there is no omniscient or disinterested seamstress to do the job. People who make constitutions are fighting particular battles, and their efforts are constrained by what they understand about politics. Constitutions and bills of rights are, in any case, parchment barriers: at best superfluous when they seem to work, and in any case ineffective when they are truly needed.

The same holds for consociational and other supermajority constraints on majority rule. Part of the issue here is that systems meant to protect vulnerable minorities are all too easily hijacked by powerful ones. But we saw that the problems run deeper. Electoral incentives shape the fault lines along which people are mobilized, so that systems designed to protect minorities often end up balkanizing politics—undermining the competition that is democracy's lifeblood. Madison's most productive insight is that it is better to diversify the polity by expanding it, making it harder for majorities to identify and act on common interests. This strategy militates against the very idea of identifying a common interest that motivates the Rousseauist enterprise. Duped by Rousseau's definition of the problem, rational choice theorists since Kenneth Arrow have been searching for stable orderings of collective preferences when this is the enemy of social stability.[6] If they found it, it would ossify exactly the kind of "majority faction" Madison dreaded; those in the minority might as well reach for their guns.

But for Madisonian pluralism to foster the right kinds of uncertainty in politics, it is vital that the stakes remain low enough for people to be able to live with the risk of losing particular political battles. That is most likely when divisible goods underpin society's politicized cleavages. The majority-rule divide-a-dollar logic can operate only if there are multiple ways to divide up the costs and benefits of collective decisions. If goods are not divisible, people find themselves pressed in the direction of winner-take-all politics—which is also, by definition, loser-lose-all politics. We should have learned from seventeenth-century European history that whenever there is religious or even denominational pluralism, creating official religions invites zero-sum conflict over the commanding heights of the state. This does not mean banishing religion or any subject from politics, but it does underscore the unwisdom of creating incentives to politicize indivisible goods. For people to be able to split political differences, there must be something to split.

Among the advantages of two large parties competing for diverse constituencies is the inevitable policy bundling it requires. Assembling winning electoral platforms will likely involve submerging conflicts over indivisible goods. Republican Party platforms in the United States routinely include language, demanded by conservative activists, proposing pro-life prohibition of all abortions and pro-life constitutional amendments. Few people expect them to be acted on in the event of a Republican victory. The same was true of Clause Four the British Labour Party's constitution, which called for nationalization of the means of production. It had ceased to be a serious political prospect decades before Tony Blair insisted on its removal in 1995. Yet the Clause Four fundamentalists remained in the Labour Party just as anti-abortion fundamentalists remain with the Republicans, because the party is closest to their ideal on other issues. In PR systems, which foster party proliferation, by contrast, single-issue groups can form their own parties and then extract huge premiums if they turn out to be pivotal to a winning coalition.

Are these differences exaggerated? After all, two-party systems involve coalitions within parties before elections, whereas multiparty systems require them among parties after elections.[7] This is true, but misses what is at stake here. The uncertainty we should want is the uncertainty needed to keep people committed to the process, not uncertainty about what elected parties will seek to do in government. When the coalition agreements are fought out within parties before elections, the party that will become the government will be held responsible for what that government does. In a multiparty system, by contrast, all bets are off until the results are in and the coalitions form. Moreover, coalition members can finger-point and blame one another for unpopular government policies, arguing that their hands were tied—which they might in fact have been.[8] Opposition parties are equally fragmented. They can take potshots at the government from their different points of view, but they have no incentive—or even opportunity—to articulate the alternative platform that would be on offer should the governing coalition fall.[9]

More serious issues are at stake concerning political mobilization. Multiparty systems supply leaders and other political entrepreneurs with incentives to mobilize people around narrow platforms and even single issues. Indivisible goods, particularly those linked to religious and other forms of identity politics, are often prime candidates. Even when goods are divisible in principle, supporters will likely be intensely committed to narrow platforms as the raison d'être for the party's existence and their commitment to it. This makes compromise harder than when people are mobilized over the broad arrays of issues in a catchall party and must weigh them against a competing array in another catchall party. In short, single-issue mobilization contributes to segmented electorates. The benefits of centralized competition are foregone, and politicians are rewarded for engaging in the kinds of mobilization that tend to polarize electorates.

True, sometimes voters remain intensely attached to their attitudes and commitments regardless of what politicians do.[10] But to the extent that political commitments are malleable, systems that supply politicians with incentives to ramp up intense commitments to narrow platforms push things in the wrong direction. Single-issue mobilization can be valuable to get subjects onto the political agenda. Abolition of the slave trade in British politics, the suffragist agenda, and civil rights in the United States are all good examples as we saw in section 5.5. But the impact will most likely be sustained only if the issue is absorbed into major party platforms, as these all eventually were, rather than remain the preserve of intense minority groups that find themselves fortuitously placed in coalitions that might collapse or be torn apart.

Single-issue politics appeals to some because it carries the whiff of direct democracy and grassroots activism. But partisans of nondomination should be suspicious of the instruments of direct democracy. They might be dreamed up by the disempowered, but once established they become available for the powerful and well-resourced as well. This has been the story of primaries, ballot initiatives, and much social movement politics.[11] Nondomination theorists like Philip Pettit, who put their faith in such groups, cherry-pick the ones they find appealing—in his case the women's movement, the green movement, the gay rights movement, and activists for ethnic minorities and indigenous peoples.[12] Of these, it is notable that the groups that have been most effective in U.S. politics are those whose agendas have been absorbed into electoral politics: the women's movement and, more recently, the gay rights movement.

When we think about grassroots groups that have been effective outside of electoral politics, they include many Pettit would likely find less congenial: the movement to enact Proposition 13 slashing property taxes in California, the estate tax repeal coalition, and groups fighting to cut back on abortion rights and affirmative action. Perhaps the most effective grassroots group in recent memory has been the Tea Party movement, formed in 2009 to hobble Barack Obama's agenda on economic stimulus, environmental and financial regulation, health care reform, and immigration.[13] The Tea Party stands in illuminating contrast to Occupy Wall Street, a grassroots group that emerged two years later but has since faded away without leaving any imprint on elections or legislation.[14] This is scarcely surprising. Effective political action requires the organized deployment of resources. If anyone is going to achieve that outside the realm of electoral politics, it is most likely to be those who can generate them.

This is the tip of an iceberg. Partisans of resisting domination who cleave to republican theories often miss how counterproductive their recommendations are. This goes back to the American founders at least. We saw in Chapter 4 that Madison's insightful, if rudimentary, remarks about the advantages of diverse factions were not matched by his prognostications about institutions. He and the other founders constructed intersecting webs of veto players to hem in the phantom monster of majority tyranny, but they produced, instead, a system beset by chronic institutional inertia that is too easily milked by powerful interests. The irony is that, far from reducing the "mischiefs of faction" that had so worried Madison in *Federalist* #10, this strengthens the kinds of financial elites who would begin alarming him and Jefferson once the fault lines of political conflict began solidifying in the early 1790s. By then the most important institutional die had been cast.

Contemporary republicans should know better than the founders, who lacked experience of democratic politics on a large scale, yet commentators like Pettit seem not to. Despite professed worries about the malevolent effects of private power, he endorses bicameralism, supermajority requirements, separation of powers, judicial review, federalism, appeals processes against administrative decisions, ex-ante measures to limit their effects, independent banks, exemptions and special treatment for minority cultures, turning politically charged matters over to "professionally informed bodies," and deploying gag rules to limit the writ of electoral politics.[15] This is to say nothing of his faith in deliberative and other forums to contest unwelcome majority decisions. In his vision of democracy it is essential that people be "able to contest decisions at will and, if the contest establishes a mismatch with their relevant interests or opinions, [be] able to force an amendment."[16] Appealing as such forums might sound, we have seen that they all too easily place bargaining chips in the hands of veto players.[17]

Majoritarian democracy is the best system yet devised to combat domination in national politics. This not to say that conditions to make it effective are always present. Prevailing conflicts might follow religious or other identity-based fault lines instead of crosscutting cleavages underpinned by divisible goods. Patterns of migration and misguided reforms can erode the representativeness of constituencies—undermining political competition. There might be conditions of actual or imminent civil war that can be defused only by power-sharing agreements that threaten to take balkanization into the postwar order. We saw this with the 1995 Dayton agreement that ended the war in Bosnia and Herzegovina and in the power sharing in South Africa's transitional constitution adopted in 1993.[18] Such developments are scarcely novel; many of the consociational elements in the U.S. Constitution were inspired by a vain attempt to head off a civil war over slavery. In any case, the Constitution would not have been adopted without them. Its authors were in their Donegal, with neither a road nor a compass to get themselves to Dublin.

This is almost always true to some degree. But I have resisted the dichotomy between ideal and second-best theory that has been fashionable among political philosophers since Rawls. In reality, we fashion ideals where we find ourselves and recalibrate them when we see how they work out in practice—as Madison did, once faced with the realities of politics without political parties in the 1790s. But fallible and incomplete as our knowledge is, it cumulates. We know more about political dynamics and institutions than was known in the eighteenth century, and we also know more about the costs of compromising with recalcitrant facts of political life. Just because institutions and embedded practices themselves create incentives, we should be leery of entrenching particular arrangements under pressure of the exigencies of the moment.[19] The South Africans were wise to abandon constitutionally mandated power sharing in the final 1996 constitution; they will be better off still when the ANC breaks up and there can be meaningful political competition. If anything should be entrenched, it should be the essentials of democratic politics. But entrenching anything can be overrated. We saw that the Westminster system is a product of evolution, not architectonic design. The lack of a written constitution might well have helped this along. Written constitutions and entrenched clauses can, in any case, be ignored. A Hitler, a Mussolini, or an Idi Amin will see them for the parchment barriers that they are.

7.2 Global Politics

Centralized competition is best for national politics, but it is not an option beyond national borders. The disjunction is rooted in different possibilities for and limitations on the exercise of power in the two settings. National governments must monopolize legitimate coercion within their borders in order to be effective, but this is impossible in the world as a whole. Whether the realists are right that the global system is pure anarchy, or their critics are convincing that norms and institutions partly shape it, need not detain us here.[20] The decisive fact is that there is not going to be a global political system with anything remotely approaching monopoly control over the use of lethal force. Moreover, all available sources of international legitimacy are tainted. The democratic deficit that people complain about in such institutions as the EU is even worse in international bodies that aspire to authorize coercive force. The Security Council is democratic in neither composition nor process, and the General Assembly is laughably democratic in enfranchising dictatorships along with democracies.

Some think that the answer is to make international institutions more representative in order to enhance their legitimacy, setting us on the path—however halting and gradual—toward world government. But just as we rejected Rousseau's principal-agent lens on representation at the national level, starting instead with a Lockean focus on power, so we should do the same here. If a global power-monopoly is unavailable, as I have argued, then the question of how best to manage said monopoly does not arise. States, or coalitions of states, could not compete for temporary control of something that does not exist. The idea that there could be global political parties is no less far-fetched, and not just because of the less than prepossessing experience with transnational parties in the EU. National governments are not going to cede control of their militaries to international institutions, however constituted.

For the foreseeable future, the world system will operate in large measure as realists characterize it. Governments act in what they see as their interests on the international stage. They might encumber themselves with treaties, alliances, and commitments to international norms and institutions to a degree, but when the chips are down, their sense of their vital interests trumps. Interests less than vital often trump these encumbrances as well, as political leaders inevitably juggle principles, convenience, costs, allies, and domestic politics, among other considerations. It is better to develop strategies to combat domination while acknowledging this reality than either to wish it were not so or to predict, implausibly, that it is on the way out.

Nor is the reality all bad. Inequalities often lead to domination, but there are few reasons to think that a world state would reduce them—whether or not it was democratic. Advocates of world government try to shift the burden of persuasion onto skeptics, but this is not plausible in light of the historical record within countries and the failure of anyone to describe institutions or mechanisms that would operate differently on a world scale. It is perhaps not surprising that most partisans of world government are philosophers; few who have studied actual political conflicts or institutions would take their arguments seriously.

Proposals for global constitutionalism are less extravagant than plans for world government, but their apparent appeal trades on exaggerated assumptions about the beneficial role of constitutionalism in domestic politics. Attention by scholars like Michael Doyle and Mark Mazower to the operation of such institutions of global constitutionalism as the International Criminal Court lends credence to the realist case that they are largely instruments by which powerful countries work their way in world politics.[21] My discussion in Chapter 6 of the abuse of quasi-constitutional authorizing mechanisms for humanitarian intervention such as the Security Council reinforces that conclusion. To be sure, the fact that institutions have been abused is not, by itself, an impeachment of them; but it is hard to see where the impetus to prevent abuse will come from in international politics.

This is not to give up on fighting domination across borders. Expanding the extraterritorial jurisdiction of national courts can make sense, especially when perpetrators would otherwise get away with practices that are illegal at home. This is one way to resist the race to the bottom that so often facilitates domination, but we saw in Chapter 5 that it is also worth trying to pull the floor up. The international campaign against slavery showed that sometimes people can build coalitions to achieve improbable outcomes, especially when they focus on proximate goals and are buttressed by moral narratives that are sufficiently compelling to hold the coalition together long enough to get the job done. The campaign for a global minimum wage is a plausible, if challenging, next step.

Democratic options are not available internationally, but "stop the bully without becoming one" is available. Whether for countries operating alone or in conjunction with others, it offers the best guidance for decisions on the margin as well as for shaping norms of international conduct. Establishing and sustaining them depends on convincing electorates at home and partners and adversaries abroad that the alternatives are either unsustainable or self-defeating. This takes creative effort and leadership of the sort George H. W. Bush displayed but which, we saw, his successors have lacked. By expanding NATO onto Russia's doorstep after the collapse of the USSR, the Clinton and second Bush administrations missed a chance to nudge international politics in better directions—increasing the odds that someone with Vladimir Putin's proclivities would come to power in Russia.[22] George W. Bush's preemptive unilateralism was a major setback for the possibility of establishing a nondomination regime in the post–Cold War world. But the goal remains worth pursuing despite the setbacks. It offers the best available combination of principle and strategy to combat domination internationally.

Getting "stop the bully without becoming one" widely embraced as a norm of international conduct has more the flavor of a collective action problem than of a profound conflict of interest: everyone would be better off if it were universally adhered to, but individual countries have incentives to violate its imperatives in particular situations. With no possibility of third-party enforcement, establishing it will likely depend on a decision to do so by a few significant players—what Russell Hardin has referred to as a K group—for whom it is worth providing the collective good in question even if others elect to free ride.[23] This creates an opportunity for the United States to lead. But along with diplomacy, cajoling, and pressure, successive U.S. governments will have to lead by example if they are to have any prospect of enduring success. This means showing restraint when they can get away with not doing so, and making it clear that they expect the same of partners and allies. President Obama's failure of leadership in Libya is a case in point. Instead of being cajoled by partners and allies into participating in gratuitous regime change, albeit by "leading from behind," he should have restrained them as Secretary Gates and others were recommending at the time.

Originally I made the case for this kind of U.S. leadership in *Containment*. That book was a response to George W. Bush's invasion of Iraq, but it was just as much a critique of the Democrats for failing to propose an alternative. In fact, the book grew out of a talk I gave at the Yale Club of Tokyo in the run-up to the 2004 U.S. election, when I was asked to expound on what an incoming Kerry administration's foreign policy would likely be. I argued that there was not going to be a Kerry administration, partly on the grounds that you can't beat something with nothing. No doubt Kerry lost for many reasons, but I argued that his inability to formulate an alternative post-9/11 vision to Bush's—already manifestly failing—strategy in Afghanistan and Iraq played a significant part. By the time I published the book in 2007, the failures were so extensive and the administration so unpopular that it seemed a good bet that the Democrats would take back the White House, even though neither of the leading candidates, Senators Barack Obama and Hillary Clinton, had done any better than Kerry at articulating America's national security interests or a strategy for vindicating them. I worried, in the conclusion to that book, that if the Democrats stumbled into the White House without a principled strategic vision, they risked being manipulated by others in ways that would undermine America's security and make the world worse.[24]

We have seen here that my worries were well founded. The Obama administration's national security policy has been telling testimony to the difference between muddling through and policies that, while adaptable to changing events, are informed by strategic decisions rooted in a coherent outlook that is geared to resisting domination. Muddlers inevitably respond to strong personalities, loud voices, well-funded interest groups, and the pressing crisis du jour. These are ever present, part of the rough and tumble of politics that confronts every administration. It is for just that reason that a principled strategy is needed; otherwise people are bound to lose their bearings in the daily maelstrom of crisis management, when "the urgent" crowds out "the merely important." The strategy need not be detailed or complex. Indeed, there are good reasons to think that in uncertain environments simple rules, rooted in hands-on experience, do better than the complex decision models often pressed by self-styled experts.[25] Stop the bully without becoming one is one such rule.

7.3 Acting against Domination

But that cannot be the last word. In this book, I have made the case for an adaptive approach to combating domination that takes account of political reality without capitulating to it. The hardest questions for this view concern knowing what the limits of the possible are, and how best to push against them. I noted at the outset that Rousseau insists that "the bounds of the possible in moral matters are less narrow than we think," yet he does not explain how we can know how wide they are.[26] Rawls, likewise, advocates a "realistically utopian" outlook that "extends what are ordinarily thought of as the limits of practical possibility" without telling us how to recognize or extend those limits.[27]

This problem is not limited to Rousseau and Rawls. Marx said that human beings make their own history though not in circumstances of their own choosing, but he was famously elusive on how to reconcile his determinism with even that constrained affirmation of human agency.[28] Subsequent debates among Marxists explored various more nuanced formulations, but left us with the problem that if economic interests determine outcomes "in the last instance," as Louis Althusser put it, we do not know in particular situations whether or not that point has been reached.[29] Anthony Giddens argues, plausibly enough, that agents and social structures shape one another, but he offers little guidance about when and how agents can aspire to reshape structures.[30] Contemporary political scientists put great weight on the ways in which institutions, and the incentives embedded in them, constrain what individuals can expect to achieve in politics, but they have little to say about when people can change or overcome them.

We should not be surprised. The scope for human agency in politics varies, often unpredictably. Just as evolution is sometimes gradual and sometimes punctuated by rapid shifts, apparently stable politics can suddenly become fluid before solidifying into new patterns. This can occur for a single issue, as with the rapid change over the prospects for legalizing gay marriage in the United States between 2012 and 2015; for a whole policy landscape, as with FDR's New Deal between 1933 and 1938 or the rapid expansion of the British welfare state after World War II; or for basic rules of the political game, as in the late 1770s in the United States, after 1989 in Eastern Europe, or between 1990 and 1994 in South Africa. If there are rules about when politics becomes fluid in these ways, no one has identified them. Obviously unsustainable situations can stagger on for decades or even longer, so that predicting when change will come or what form it will take often carries the whiff of forecasting earthquakes or calling the top of a bull market. The best we can do is try to be as well informed as possible, so as not to miss opportunities to create better institutions and practices when opportunities arise.

The same is true in international politics. The lack of a global political system means that opposing domination often involves single-issue politics, where the most important considerations have to do with identifying feasible proximate goals and building sustainable coalitions to achieve them. It might be hard, even impossible, to know when there will be opportunities to do this. But when the openings do occur, it will be important to know what makes coalition politics more and less successful. This means grasping what is at stake in the differences between divisible and indivisible goods, and understanding the opportunities and challenges built into the divide-a-dollar logic (section 3.1.2). It means seeing the advantages of reducing the stakes for one's potential adversaries (section 1.4) and understanding the role of moral narratives in holding coalitions together and motivating their members (section 5.5.1). None of this guarantees success for any given effort—nothing does. But attending to these factors improves the odds.

The openings for governments to alter international dynamics in positive directions also expand and contract like an accordion. George Kennan judged the decision to create NATO a missed opportunity to avoid the militarized Cold War that set in when President Truman ignored his advice in 1949. Whether or not Kennan was right, the accordion surely contracted shortly thereafter—leaving few opportunities until 1989. Then it expanded again, though the Clinton and second Bush administrations failed to take good advantage of this, as we have seen. When President Obama took office in January 2009, he faced fewer degrees of freedom than any president in living memory.[31] The American electorate had soured on the bad decisions that had long since been made and implemented in Afghanistan and Iraq, the battle for hearts and minds in those countries had been lost, and surviving the effects of the financial crisis at home was more pressing. Obama had been elected on a platform to end the wars, and that is what he sought to do.

Obama was not constrained by past decisions when the Arab Spring erupted, however, yet he chose poorly. He and his key advisors assumed that the accordion had expanded when both experience and the available evidence suggested that it had not. They made fatally flawed decisions over Libya and Syria, as we have seen, decisions that could have been avoided had Obama paid more attention to veterans of the Afghan and Iraq conflicts in his administration than to others with less experience, and had he been better informed concerning what political scientists know about democratic regime change and civil wars. He and the advisers who prevailed believed, perhaps, that they were on a moral mission to combat domination and usher in a better future.[32] In fact there was little doubt that the Libya effort would fail and a good chance that it would make things worse—as it did. The fact that Obama could be cajoled into committing the United States to regime change in Libya and Syria in stark conflict with the platform he had campaigned on, against the advice of his most experienced national security staff, and when there was no reason to believe that the outcomes would be any better than they had been in Afghanistan or Iraq, stands as compelling testimony to how hard it is to remain on course if you lack a principled strategic outlook.

It also illustrates why having such an outlook matters. Without one, adaptation does indeed risk morphing into muddling through. This can go in bad directions as well as good ones, and there will always be people trying to influence outcomes who either have no interest in limiting domination or whose reach exceeds their grasp. For leaders, as for the rest of us, adapting against domination depends on principled realism about goals and limitations. The realism matters because "ought" does indeed entail "can." Our obligations are constrained by what is feasible, which makes it important to know what really is feasible. That is why combatting domination, though not a science, should be governed by principles that are informed by science. There will inevitably be imponderables and hard calls. Then people must take leaps into the dark, hoping that the cards fall the right way. But acting hopefully is not acting recklessly. There is no recipe to avoid confusing the one with the other, but the more we know about politics, the more likely we are to choose well.

NOTES

INDEX

NOTES

Preface

1. Ian Shapiro, *Democracy's Place* (Cornell University Press, 1996), 1–16, 220–262; *Democratic Justice* (Yale University Press, 1999), 1–63; and "On Non-domination," *University of Toronto Law Journal* 62 (2012): 293–335.
2. Jonathan Wolff, review of Brian Barry's two-volume *Essays in Political Theory, Mind* 101, no. 402 (April 1992): 355–357.
3. My main disagreements with Barry are set out in Shapiro, "Against Impartiality," *Journal of Politics* 78, no. 2 (April 2016).

1. Adapting against Domination

1. Hobbes insisted that the sovereign's right to govern "cannot be maintained by any Civill Law, or terrour of legall punishment." Thomas Hobbes, *Leviathan*, ed. Ian Shapiro (Yale University Press, 2010), 202. In his history of the English civil war Hobbes elaborates that "the power of the mighty hath no foundation but in the opinion and belief of the people." Hobbes, *Behemoth or the Long Parliament* (University of Chicago Press, 1990), 16. For further discussion of this subject, see David Dyzenhaus, "Hobbes's Constitutional Theory," in Hobbes, *Leviathan*, 453–480.
2. Edmund Burke, *Reflections on the Revolution in France*, ed. J. C. D. Clark (Stanford University Press, 2001), 220.
3. Obituary of Pieter William Botha (1916–2006), South African History online, http://www.sahistory.org.za/pages/people/bios/botha-pw.htm.
4. See Ian Shapiro, *The Real World of Democratic Theory* (Princeton University Press, 2011), chap. 3.
5. *Concise Report on the World Population Situation in 2014*, UN Department of Economic and Social Relations (United Nations, 2014), 5,

http://www.un.org/en/development/desa/population/publications/pdf/trends
/Concise%20Report%20on%20the%20World%20Population%20
Situation%202014/en.pdf.

6. For much of the twentieth century the conventional academic wisdom was
that those identities would diminish in political significance. See Seymour
Martin Lipset, "Some Social Requisites of Democracy: Economic Development and Political Legitimacy," *American Political Science Review* 53, no. 1
(1959): 69–105; David E. Apter, *The Politics of Modernization* (University
of Chicago Press, 1967); and Seyla Benhabib, Ian Shapiro, and Danilo
Petranović, eds., *Identities, Affiliations, and Allegiances* (Cambridge
University Press, 2007).

7. See Jerome Bruner, *Actual Minds, Possible Worlds* (Harvard University
Press, 1987).

8. Wittgenstein noted that games all share features with some other games
but that they lack a universally shared feature. This does not prevent our
knowing what games are, or explaining this to others. Ludwig Wittgenstein,
Philosophical Investigations (Blackwell, 1953), §§66–67, pp. 27*–28*. This
did not commit Wittgenstein to the view that there are no universals, as is
sometimes supposed, only to recognizing that there are comprehensible
descriptive terms that do not depend on universals.

9. See Jean-Jacques Rousseau, "Discourse on the Origin and Foundations
of Inequality among Men," in *The Discourses and Other Early Political
Writings*, ed. Victor Gourevitch (Cambridge University Press, 1997); Karl
Marx, "Estranged Labor," in *The Economic and Philosophic Manuscripts
of 1844* (Prometheus Books, 1988), 69–84; and Karl Marx and Frederick
Engels, *The Communist Manifesto* (Yale University Press, 2012), 72–84,
99–101.

10. John Rawls, *The Law of Peoples* (Harvard University Press, 1999), 6.

11. Kant's actual formulation was: "For since pure reason commands that such
actions ought to occur, they must also be able to occur." Immanuel Kant,
Critique of Pure Reason (Hackett, 1996), 737.

12. Rousseau, *Discourses*, 151.

13. Jean-Jacques Rousseau, *Of the Social Contract*, bk. 3, chap. 12, in *The
Social Contract and Other Later Political Writings*, ed. Victor Gourevitch
(Cambridge University Press, 1997), 111.

14. Casiano Hacker-Cordón, "Global Injustice and Human Malfare" (PhD
diss., Yale, 2002).

15. The ANC stuck with nonviolent resistance for almost five decades, from its
founding in 1912 until it turned to armed struggle a year after the Sharpeville massacre of 1960, when the USSR and its allies offered training and
support. Once that support began to disappear in the mid-1980s, the ANC
began exploring other possibilities, including negotiations, even though the
apartheid government showed no interest until the late 1980s. The ANC
did not suspend the armed struggle until the government released political

prisoners and unbanned all opposition movements in 1990. Even then, the ANC refused to decommission its military wing, Umkhonto we Sizwe, and they continued to make tactical use of violence during the transition negotiations. Eventually it was merged into the South African Defense Force, helping render the transition irreversible. See Courtney Jung and Ian Shapiro, "South Africa's Negotiated Transition: Democracy, Opposition, and the New Constitutional Order," in Ian Shapiro, *Democracy's Place* (Cornell University Press, 1996), 174–219; and Stephen Ellis, "The Genesis of the ANC's Armed Struggle in South Africa, 1948–1961," *Journal of Southern African Studies* 34, no. 4 (July 2011): 657–676.

16. Raymond Geuss, *Philosophy and Real Politics* (Princeton University Press, 2008), 10.

17. Immanuel Kant, *The Contest of Faculties,* in *Kant's Political Writings,* ed. Hans Reiss, trans. H. B. Nisbet (Cambridge University Press, 1970), 183–184.

18. Karl Marx, *Critique of the Gotha Programme* (Foreign Languages, 1972 [1875]), 10.

19. Marx and Engels, *Communist Manifesto,* 26. It would have been truer to the spirit of Marx's argument if he had said instead that the free development of all should be the condition for the free development of each.

20. G. A. Cohen, "Self-Ownership, World-Ownership, and Equality, Part I," in *Justice and Equality Here and Now,* ed. Frank Lucash (Cornell University Press, 1986), 117.

21. G. A. Cohen, *Karl Marx's Theory of History: A Defense* (Princeton University Press, 1980), 306–307.

22. Anthony Trollope, *The Fixed Period* (Norilana Books, 2008).

23. John Rawls, *A Theory of Justice,* 2nd ed. (Harvard University Press, 1999 [1971]), 226.

24. Ibid., 118–119.

25. See John Harsanyi, "Can the Maximin Principle Serve as a Basis for Morality? A Critique of John Rawls's Theory," *American Political Science Review* 69, no. 3 (1975): 594–606. Rawls's assumptions about risk aversion are pretty extreme, given the low probability of winding up the worst off and the fact that he would insist on this principle even if it came at huge costs for other groups or for the overall rate of economic growth. See Ian Shapiro, *The Evolution of Rights in Liberal Theory* (Cambridge University Press, 1986), 218–233.

26. Ian Shapiro, "On Non-domination," *University of Toronto Law Journal* 62 (2012): 296–297.

27. Some will object that my argument here underestimates the Rawlsian device of reflective equilibrium. After all, reflective equilibrium is an invitation to get the reader to rethink moral intuitions and the opinions based on them by holding them up to scrutiny in light of the thought experiment posed by the original position. The idea is to get us back and forth between our moral intuitions and the choice problem until we see why our intuitions

should be revised along the lines that Rawls suggests. Notice, however, that reflective equilibrium does not extend to the characterization of the original position itself, or to the assumptions about human psychology and the causal operation of the world embodied in it. The "laws of psychology and economics" and the "general facts" about society as Rawls stipulates these—moderate scarcity, grave risks, etc.—are not meant to be objects of revision through the process of reflective equilibrium. On the contrary, Rawls deploys the assumptions about them in hopes of getting people to rethink their moral intuitions. For further discussion, see Ian Shapiro, *The Moral Foundations of Politics* (Yale University Press, 2003), 124–126, 139–141.

28. John Rawls, "Justice as Fairness: Political not Metaphysical," in John Rawls, *Collected Papers,* ed. Samuel Freeman (Harvard University Press, 1999), 388–414.

29. Cass Sunstein, "Incompletely Theorized Agreements," *Harvard Law Review* 108, no. 7 (May 1995): 1733–1772.

30. Amartya Sen, *The Idea of Justice* (Harvard University Press, 2009), 54–58.

31. It is not entirely clear how Rawls determined what counts as "basic." For instance, in *A Theory of Justice* he excluded the family, even though major thinkers in the Western tradition from Plato and Aristotle through Locke, Rousseau, Tocqueville, Mill, Dewey, and many contemporary feminists have seen child rearing and the family as central to politics. Partly in response to feminist criticism, Rawls eventually conceded that the family should be included, at least for some purposes. This did not buy him much from the critics, however, because he excluded the "internal life" of the family from consideration. See "The Idea of Public Reason Revisited," in Rawls, *Collected Papers,* 595–601. In doing this he was partly trying to head off another difficulty: once civic associations are included in the basic structure, it is difficult to see what should be excluded. See Ruth Abbey, "Back toward a Comprehensive Liberalism? Justice, Gender, and Families," *Political Theory* 35, no. 1 (February 2007): 5–28. Rawls also declared his theory to be agnostic between capitalism and socialism on the grounds that it is unclear which of these systems, or possibly some hybrid, best meets its requirements. Rawls, *Theory of Justice,* 234–242. That would seem to make the definition of basic structure basic to the point of irrelevance to the vast majority of what concerns people in actual politics.

32. In "The Idea of Public Reason" he asserted that "any reasonable balance" of the values of "due respect for human life, the ordered reproduction of political society over time, including the family in some form, and finally the equality of women as citizens" would guarantee women a right to first-trimester abortions. "The reason for this is that at this early stage of pregnancy the political value of the equality of women is overriding, and this right is required to give it substance and force." Rawls was less confident about post-first-trimester abortions, but he was sure that at least in the first trimester "other values" would not be sufficient to overcome that right. Rawls, *Political Liberalism* (Columbia University Press, 1993), 243.

33. Ibid., lv–lvi.

34. Thus Rawls asserts that "the present system woefully fails in public financing for political elections, leading to a grave imbalance in fair political liberties; it allows a widely disparate distribution of income and wealth that seriously undermines fair opportunities in education and in chances of rewarding employment, all of which undermine economic and social equality; and absent also are provisions for important constitutional essentials such as health care for many who are uninsured." Ibid., 407.

35. See Rawls, *Theory of Justice*, 198.

36. I take up the tensions between free speech and political competition in §4.3.3.

37. See my discussion in *Evolution of Rights*, 218–234.

38. See Rawls, *Political Liberalism*, 245.

39. The Constitutional Court refused to order the dialysis that was being sought, throwing its hands up in the face of scarcity. See *Soobramoney v. Minister of Health* (November 27, 1997), 13, http://www.escr-net.org/usr _doc/Soobramoney_Decision.pdf.

40. De Klerk promised white South Africans that power sharing would never be given away; when it was, the ANC was in control and there was nothing they could do about it. See Jung and Shapiro, "South Africa's Negotiated Transition," 197–204.

41. Christopher Lasch, *The True and Only Heaven: Progress and Its Critics* (Norton, 1991), 81.

42. "Yes, I am personally the victim of deferred dreams, of blasted hopes, but in spite of that I close today by saying I still have a dream, because, you know, you can't give up in life. If you lose hope, somehow you lose that vitality that keeps life moving, you lose that courage to be, that quality that helps you go on in spite of all. And so today I still have a dream." Martin Luther King Jr., "A Christmas Sermon on Peace," Ebenezer Baptist Church, Atlanta, December 24, 1967, http://www.ecoflourish.com/Primers/education /Christmas_Sermon.html.

43. Gerard Manley Hopkins, "No Worst, There Is None," in *Selected Poems* (Oxford University Press, 2008), 66.

44. Letter from Thomas Hardy to Henry Rider Haggard, undated but written sometime in 1891. In *The Collected Letters of Thomas Hardy*, ed. R. L. Purdy and Michael Millgate (Oxford University Press, 1985), 1:135.

45. Hardy's remark is shocking also because of the lack of empathy, bordering on callousness, that it displays.

46. Martin Luther King Jr., *Strength to Love* (Walker, 1984 [1963]), 97.

47. George Bernard Shaw, *Caesar and Cleopatra* (1901), act 4 (Players Press, 1991), 68.

48. "Eternity Road," The Moody Blues, track nine on *To Our Children's Children's Children* (Polydor, 1969).

49. Karl Popper had proposed in *The Open Society and Its Enemies* (Princeton University Press, 1962), 1:235, that the utilitarian greatest-happiness maxim

be replaced by an imperative that we should ensure "the least amount of avoidable suffering for all." Smart pointed out that this would entail an obligation to destroy the entire human race if this could be done painlessly, because it is "empirically certain that there would be some suffering before all those alive on any proposed destruction day were to die in the natural course of events." R. N. Smart, "Negative Utilitarianism," *Mind* 67, no. 268 (October 1958): 542–543.

50. The Latin proverb has variously been translated to mean that fortune favors the brave, the bold, or the strong; in common use it is used to encourage effort in the face of uncertainty or adversity.

51. See James Read and Ian Shapiro, "Transforming Power Relationships: Leadership, Risk, and Hope," *American Political Science Review* 108, no. 1 (February 2014): 40–54.

52. This is not to be confused with the situation, taken up in §7.2, where for a subset of the players the benefits are big enough that it will be worth it to them to supply a collective good, even if they know that others will free-ride. This is what Russell Hardin defines as a K group, where K is the size of any subgroup that "just barely stands to benefit from providing the good, even without cooperation from other members of the whole group." See Hardin, *Collective Action* (Johns Hopkins University Press, 1982), 41.

53. See Melissa Lane, "Uncertainty, Action and Politics: The Problem of Negligibility," in *Political Thought and the Environment*, ed. Katrina Forrester and Sophie Smith (Cambridge University Press, 2015).

54. See Martha Finnemore and Kathryn Sikkink, "International Norms Dynamics and Political Change," *International Organization* 4, no. 4 (Autumn 1998): 887–917.

55. See Susanne Lohmann, "The Dynamics of Informational Cascades: The Monday Demonstrations in Leipzig, East Germany, 1989–91," *World Politics* 47, no. 1 (October 1994): 42–101.

56. Thanks to Robert Lane for the term *timid rebel.*

57. Finnemore and Sikkink, "International Norms Dynamics," 902–904. It is possible to characterize all motivations as self-interested at some level, but this comes at the price of rendering one's explanation trivially true. See Donald Green and Ian Shapiro, *Pathologies of Rational Choice Theory: A Critique of Applications in Political Science* (Yale University Press, 1994), 13–32.

58. Robert Axelrod, *The Complexity of Cooperation: Agent-Based Models of Competition and Collaboration* (Princeton University Press, 1997), 6. Axelrod is here building on a line of scholarship that goes back to Herbert Simon, "A Behavioral Model of Rational Choice," *Quarterly Journal of Economics* 69 (1955): 99–118; and James March, "Bounded Rationality, Ambiguity, and the Engineering of Choice," *Bell Journal of Economics* 9 (1978): 587–608. See also Green and Shapiro, *Pathologies,* 13–32, 47–71; and Green and Shapiro, "Revisiting the Pathologies of Rational Choice

Theory," in Ian Shapiro, *The Flight from Reality in the Human Sciences* (Princeton University Press, 2005), 51–99.

59. A prisoner's dilemma game involves two players who must decide whether to cooperate or defect without knowing what the other will do. Defection yields a higher payoff than cooperation no matter what the other player does, but if both defect then both do worse than they would have done had both cooperated. An iterated prisoner's dilemma involves repeated play of the same game in which both know what the other has done in the past and do not know in advance which round will be the last. Axelrod ran a series of tournaments in which strategies for the prisoner's dilemma devised by game theorists were tested against one another by computers over 200 iterations in each tournament. Robert Axelrod, *The Evolution of Cooperation* (Basic Books, 1984).

60. Jianzhong Wu and Robert Axelrod, "How to Interpret Noise in the Iterated Prisoner's Dilemma," in Axelrod, *Complexity of Cooperation*, 33–39.

61. A useful summary of various nice and nasty strategies can be found in Richard Dawkins, *The Selfish Gene*, 3rd ed. (Oxford University Press, 2006), 202–233. See also Philip Ball, *Critical Mass: How One Thing Leads to Another* (Farrar, Straus and Giroux, 2006).

62. See Ross Thompson and Susan Limber, "'Social Anxiety' in Infancy: Stranger and Separation Reactions," in *Handbook of Social and Evaluation Anxiety*, ed. Harold Leitenberg (Plenum, 1990), 85–138; and Paul Bloom, "Horrible Children," in *The Development of Social Cognition*, ed. Mahzarin M. R. Banaji and S. A. Gelman (Oxford University Press, 2012).

63. Comparative research suggests that people in industrialized countries are more likely to be generous in ultimatum games (when a unilateral offer to divide a sum of money is accepted or rejected) than people in poorer, less market-integrated countries. See Joseph Henrich, Steven Heine, and Ara Norenzayan, "The Weirdest People in the World?," *Behavioral and Brain Sciences* 33, nos. 2–3 (June 2010): 65–67. Because ultimatum games are generally one-shot, they are not directly relevant to my discussion here, but Henrich et al.'s finding is a wise caution against inferring very much from what comparatively affluent North American undergraduates do in experimental settings. Their cooperativeness and generosity might be artifacts of the trivial stakes.

64. Experimental research on public goods games shows that people learn that hope is sometimes not warranted. People contribute anonymously to a collective fund, which is then multiplied by some factor before being divided equally among them. All would be better off if everyone contributed all their resources to the fund, but the standard game theory prediction is that no one contributes. In fact, most people start by contributing substantially. But if the game is iterated, they realize that there are some free riders, and contributions quickly decline—and can be restored only if players punish free riders. See Marco Janssen and T. K. Ahn, "Learning, Signaling, and

Social Preferences in Public-Good Games," *Ecology and Society* 11, no. 2 (2006), art. 21, http://www.ecologyandsociety.org/vol11/iss2/art21/.

65. J. Glen Gray, *The Warriors: Reflections on Men in Battle* (Bison Books, 1998 [1959]), 225.

66. John Locke, "The Second Treatise: An Essay Concerning the True Original, Extent, and End of Civil Government," in Locke, *Two Treatises of Government and A Letter Concerning Toleration,* ed. Ian Shapiro (Yale University Press, 2003), §225, p. 199.

67. "Where the body of the people, or any single man, are deprived of their right, or are under the exercise of a power without right, having no appeal on earth they have a liberty to appeal to Heaven whenever they judge the cause of sufficient moment." Locke, "Second Treatise," §168, p. 175. See also Richard Ashcraft, *Locke's Two Treatises of Government* (Allen and Unwin, 1987), 60–80.

68. Computer programs can still (for the moment) be beaten by teams of grandmasters, but such programs as Deep Junior or even more readily available programs like Fritz are unbeatable by ordinary players.

69. See Max Albert, "Bayesian Rationality and Decision-Making: A Critical Review," *Analyse & Kritik* 25 (2006): 101–117; and Mike Oaksford and Nick Chater, *Bayesian Rationality: The Probabilistic Approach to Human Reasoning* (Oxford University Press, 2007).

70. Robert H. Frank, Thomas Gilovich, and Dennis T. Reagan, "Does Studying Economics Inhibit Cooperation?," *Journal of Economic Perspectives* 7, no. 2 (Spring 1993): 159–171.

71. See Daniel Kahneman and Amos Tversky, "Prospect Theory: An Analysis of Decisions under Risk," *Econometrica* 47 (1979): 262–291.

72. See Shapiro, *Real World of Democratic Theory,* 27–31.

73. Max Weber, *Economy and Society,* ed. Guenther Roth and Claus Wittich (University of California Press, 1968 [1914]), 53.

74. Philip Pettit, *Republicanism: A Theory of Freedom and Government* (Oxford University Press, 1997), 52–58.

75. I am indebted to Rebecca Trupin for this example.

76. Michael Foucault, *Power/Knowledge: Selected Interviews and Other Writings* (Vintage, 1972).

77. "We call that which is in itself worthy of pursuit more final than that which is worthy of pursuit for the sake of something else, and that which is never desirable for the sake of something else more final than the things that are desirable both in themselves and for the sake of that other thing, and therefore we call final without qualification that which is always desirable in itself and never for the sake of something else." Aristotle, *Nichomachean Ethics,* in *The Complete Works of Aristotle,* ed. Jonathan Barnes (Princeton University Press), vol. 2, bk. 1, chap. 7, p. 1734.

78. Aristotle identified the most final good as eudemonia, generally translated as happiness or flourishing. He believed there was universal agreement

about this (a view that would be disputed today), though he recognized that people disagree about what this consists in and about what other final goods can be identified. Aristotle, *Nichomachean Ethics*, bk. 1, chap. 1, p. 1722.

79. Rawls, *Theory of Justice*, 78–81.

80. Pettit, *Republicanism*, 90.

81. Ronald Dworkin, *Sovereign Virtue: The Theory and Practice of Equality* (Harvard University Press, 2000), 65–121; Amartya Sen, "Capability and Well-Being," in *The Quality of Life*, ed. Martha Nussbaum and Amartya Sen (Oxford University Press, 1993), 30–53; and Martha C. Nussbaum, *Women and Human Development: The Capabilities Approach* (Cambridge University Press, 2000), 84–86. Elsewhere Sen describes his as a "midfare" view rather than a purely resourcist one, because it is concerned with the development of human capabilities. It shares the advantages of resourcist views that I identify here in that it assumes a comparatively undetermined conception of welfare.

82. John Locke, "The First Treatise: The False Principles and Foundation of Sir Robert Filmer," §42, in Locke, *Two Treatises of Government*, 30.

83. Ian Shapiro, *Democratic Justice* (Yale University Press, 1999), 85–99, 134–136; and Shapiro, *Real World of Democratic Theory*, 253–264.

84. Even my comparatively capacious account is not exhaustive. A closet homosexual or someone who is having a secret affair is vulnerable to blackmail. No doubt there are other reasons to outlaw blackmail, but a commitment to nondomination would proscribe it as well.

85. See Shapiro, *Democratic Justice*, 12, 80–81, 93, 116, 132.

86. Martin Heidegger, *Being and Time* (Harper, 1962).

87. A different tack, taken by Philip Pettit, is to treat nondomination as the political mechanism to realize the philosophical ideal of freedom. I think this undersells nondomination's importance as a normative ideal in its own right rather than as an instrument to achieve some other benefit. Moreover, I worry about a defense of nondomination that makes it hinge on our first buying a particular contestable view of freedom. Pettit contends that nondomination is the best available instrument to realize his theory of freedom as "discursive control." Some elements of this account of freedom are appealing to me; others I find problematic. In particular I am leery of any conception of freedom that requires a prior commitment to agreement and shared goals. Philip Pettit, *A Theory of Freedom* (Oxford University Press, 2001), 67ff. See also his *Republicanism*. For my discussion, see my "On Non-domination," 309–311, 321–332.

88. David Hume, "Of the First Principles of Government," in Hume, *Essays Moral, Political, and Literary* (Liberty Fund, 1987 [1741]), 32.

89. Friedrich Nietzsche, *The Genealogy of Morals* [1887], in Nietzsche *The Birth of Tragedy and the Genealogy of Morals*, trans. Francis Goldberg (Anchor Books, 1956), 211.

90. Friedrich Nietzsche, *The Will to Power* (Digireads.com, 2010), §685; see also §§660, 674, 677, 707, 721 776, 784. Darwin's *On the Origin of Species* was published in 1859.
91. Joseph Hamburger, *James Mill and the Art of Revolution* (Yale University Press, 1964).
92. Adam Smith, *The Wealth of Nations* (Modern Library, 1937 [1776]), 670.
93. See my discussion in Ian Shapiro, *The State of Democratic Theory* (Princeton University Press, 2005), 104–145.
94. See Kevin Narizny, "Anglo-American Primacy and the Global Spread of Democracy," *World Politics* 64, no. 2 (April 2012): 341–373.
95. India was a notable exception, but the failures buttressed what became the conventional view that democracy would not spread much further. See Samuel Huntington, "Will More Countries Become Democratic?," *Political Science Quarterly* 99, no. 2 (1984): 193–218.
96. Postcommunist democratic triumphs in Eastern Europe and Russia were not matched in the former USSR's Asiatic republics. Brutal dictatorships have remained in China, Burma, and North Korea. Democracy's fortunes in the Middle East have been halting at best since democracy was toppled in Iran, with American help, in 1953.
97. See Adam Przeworski, ed., *Democracy in a Russian Mirror* (Cambridge University Press, 2015).
98. See Robert Dahl, *On Political Equality* (Yale University Press, 2006), 81–83; Ronald Dworkin, *Is Democracy Possible Here?* (Princeton University Press, 2006), 123–129; and Bruce Ackerman, *Before the Next Attack: Preserving Civil Liberties in an Age of Terrorism* (Yale University Press, 2006), 1–76.
99. See Shapiro, *Real World of Democratic Theory,* 1–38.
100. Hobbes, *Leviathan,* 76.
101. Christopher Boehm, *Hierarchy in the Forest* (Harvard University Press, 1999), 43–63.
102. Ibid., 172.
103. On democracy's advantages in this regard, see David Runciman, *The Confidence Trap: A History of Democracy in Crisis from World War I to the Present* (Princeton University Press, 2013).
104. Niccolò Machiavelli, *Discourses on Livy* (Penguin, 1970), §1.6, p. 116.
105. It is worth noting that Nietzsche's defense of the will to power is not an account of the desire to dominate others so much as to behave with utter indifference toward them. Indeed, he blamed the democratic turn for the political and social domination—such as barbaric punishments—that he identified around him. He had contempt for the individualism of his day, but this was because he saw it as a perversion of the romantic individualism, marked by the single-minded pursuit of greatness, that he treasured. Nietzsche, *Genealogy of Morals,* 158–229. Arguably this takes self-absorption to the point of narcissism, which is perhaps one reason

Nietzsche so often appeals to teenagers when they first dabble in political philosophy but seems puerile to more mature minds.

106. Lord Acton, letter to Bishop Mandell Creighton, 1887. In Lord Acton, *Essays in Freedom and Power* (Ludwig von Misses Institute, 2010), 364.

107. Perhaps the most recent is Francis Fukuyama, *The End of History and the Last Man* (Free Press, 1992).

108. See J. G. A. Pocock's discussion of the civic humanist tradition in *The Machiavellian Moment* (Princeton University Press, 1974), 243, 285, 300–303, 317.

2. Power and Majority Rule

1. See Ian Shapiro, *Democratic Justice* (Yale University Press, 1999).

2. Philip Pettit, *Republicanism: A Theory of Freedom and Government* (Oxford University Press, 1997); Pettit, *On the People's Terms: A Republican Theory and Model of Democracy* (Cambridge University Press, 2012). For my discussion of Pettit's views, see Ian Shapiro, "On Non-domination," *University of Toronto Law Journal* 62 (2012): 321–332.

3. See Shapiro, *Democratic Justice,* 10, 20, 115; and Shapiro, "On Non-domination," 313–335.

4. Aristotle, *Nicomachean Ethics*, bk. 3, §5, in *The Complete Works of Aristotle,* ed. Jonathan Barnes (Princeton University Press, 1984), 2:1758–1760. I think Aristotle's claim is overblown in that people do deliberate about ends and can change them. But I agree with such contemporary Aristotelians as Alasdair MacIntyre that there is no reason to think the government, or any other outsider to a civil institution or social practice, is in as good a position as insiders to determine what those ends should be. Shapiro, *Democratic Justice,* 92, 116, 180–181.

5. Max Weber, *Theory of Social and Economic Organization* (Free Press, 1947), 156; and Robert Nozick, *Anarchy, State, and Utopia* (Basic Books, 1974), 23–24.

6. Plato, *The Republic,* part 7, bk. 6, §4 (Penguin, 1987), 232–239.

7. Something is a public good if no one can be excluded from its benefits and if one person's enjoyment of them does not prevent others from enjoying them as well. Clean air is the standard example for economists.

8. Nozick, *Anarchy, State, and Utopia,* 108–118. Nozick's conceit was a thought experiment in which associations selling protection in a state of nature find that they cannot protect their members without marginalizing or coopting competing protection associations. At the time, it was widely criticized as a contrived philosopher's example, but his point is illustrated in the instability that permeated Lebanon in the 1980s, Colombia in the 1990s, and Afghanistan, Iraq, and Libya more recently.

9. Actual compensation would generate moral hazards. There would be incentives to refuse to join and be compensated rather than to join and pay dues. See Shapiro, *Evolution of Rights in Liberal Theory* (Cambridge University Press, 1986), 169–176.

10. Ibid., 169–178.

11. Because it follows, a fortiori, that no other state meets his test either, Nozick might nonetheless try to salvage things by insisting that the minimal state is the state that is the closest possible to a legitimate one. But there is no way to evaluate that claim, because comparing the minimal state to other possible regimes from the standpoint of even a single independent requires the paternalistic judgments that Nozick shuns. Remember his hardboiled insistence that there is never a "*social entity* with a good that undergoes some sacrifice for its own good. There are only individual people, different individual people, with their own individual lives." Nozick, *Anarchy, State, and Utopia,* 32–33, Nozick's italics.

12. Ibid., 4.

13. This is not to say that Locke had an account of democratic procedures or institutions, or to deny that his natural rights are prior to all institutions. Rather, as I have argued at length elsewhere, it is to say that he affirmed a conception of political legitimacy that was fundamentally democratic and he held that majority rule offers the only viable basis to protect our natural rights in this world. See Ian Shapiro, "John Locke's Democratic Theory," in *The Real World of Democratic Theory* (Princeton University Press, 2012), 39–67.

14. John Locke, "The Second Treatise: An Essay Concerning the True Original, Extent, and End of Civil Government," in Locke, *Two Treatises of Government and A Letter Concerning Toleration,* ed. Ian Shapiro (Yale University Press, 2003), §96, p. 142.

15. Ibid., §97, p. 142.

16. Ibid., §225, p. 199.

17. Ibid., §149, p 166.

18. Ibid., §98, pp. 142–143.

19. Ibid., §99, p. 143.

20. Lincoln won 39.82 percent of the national popular vote in a four-way race, giving him a plurality over Stephen Douglas (29.56 percent), John Breckenridge (18.10 percent), and John Bell (12.62 percent). David Leip, "1860 Presidential Election Results," http://uselectionatlas.org/USPRESIDENT/GENERAL/pe1860.html.

21. Jean-Jacques Rousseau, *The Social Contract* (Penguin, 1968 [1762]), 72–74.

22. Adam Przeworski, "Minimalist Conception of Democracy: A Defense," in *Democracy's Value,* ed. Ian Shapiro (Cambridge University Press, 1999), 48.

23. As late as the Preliminary Emancipation Proclamation of September 22, 1862, Lincoln was still offering rebel states the right to maintain slavery if

they returned to the Union by year's end. http://www.archives.gov/exhibits
/american_originals_iv/sections/transcript_preliminary_emancipation.html;
and Allan Nevins, *Ordeal of the Union*, vol. 6, *War Becomes Revolution,
1862–1863* (Scribner's, 1960), 231–245.

24. James H. Read, "'The Only True Sovereign of a Free People': Lincoln and
Majority Rule," paper presented at the 2013 American Political Science
Association, Chicago, August 2013.

25. Charles Francis Adams, ed., *Memoir of John Quincy Adams* (J. B. Lippincott
& Co, 1875), 5:210. Adams's observation was prompted by the adoption of
the Missouri Compromise, which staved off the eventual conflict by ushering
in an era during which admission of slave states to the Union was paired
with the admission of free states. Like Lincoln, Adams would have judged
such a war as warranted: "[I]ts result might be the extirpation of slavery
from this whole continent; and, calamitous and desolating as this course of
events in its progress must be, so glorious would be its final issue, that, as
God shall judge me, I dare not say that it is not to be desired."

26. Lincoln, "First Inaugural Address," *Speeches and Writings, 1859–1865*
(Library of America, 1989), 221.

27. Read, "'Only True Sovereign,'" 3.

28. Locke, "Second Treatise," §99, p. 143.

29. Barry Day, ed., *Oscar Wilde: A Life in Quotes* (Metro Books, 2000), 238.

30. James Buchanan and Gordon Tullock, *The Calculus of Consent* (University
of Michigan Press, 1962), 63–77.

31. Lincoln, "First Inaugural Address," 221.

32. Brian Barry, *Political Argument,* 2nd ed. (Harvester Wheatsheaf, 1990
[1965]); Douglas Rae, "The Limits of Consensual Decision," *American
Political Science Review* 69 (1975): 1270–1294; and Norman Schofield,
"Is Majority Rule Special?," in *Probability Models of Collective Decision
Making,* ed. Richard Niemi and H. F. Weisberg (Merrill, 1972), 60–82.

33. Rae, "Limits of Consensual Decision." Perhaps the limiting case of real-
world pathologies generated by decision rules that privilege the status quo
was the liberum veto, in place in the Polish-Lithuanian Commonwealth
from the mid-sixteenth to the late eighteenth century. Any member of the
Sejm could nullify all legislation passed in the current session by yelling *Nie
pozwalam!* (literally: "I do not allow!"). Conceived as a way to limit royal
power, it rendered the Sejm hostage to conservative opponents of change,
whom foreign powers often bribed to cast vetoes. William Bullitt, *The
Great Globe Itself: A Preface to World Affairs* (Scribner's, 1946), 42–43;
and George W. Carey, *The Political Writings of John Adams* (Regnery,
2000), 242. The liberum veto was gradually abandoned and eventually
replaced by majority rule in the 1791 Constitution.

34. Nolan McCarty, Keith Poole, and Howard Rosenthal, *Political Bubbles:
Financial Crises and the Failure of American Democracy* (Princeton
University Press, 2013), 251–273.

35. Locke, "Second Treatise," §§96–97, p. 142.
36. Plato likened the manipulators of the people to mutinous sailors who use flattery to sucker others into supporting their power grabs, or to people who study the "moods and wants" of a large animal in order to better know what will "soothe or annoy it" so that they can humor it enough to control it. Plato, *The Republic*, part 7, bk. 6, §3, pp. 220–232; James Madison, *Federalist* #10, in Alexander Hamilton, James Madison, and John Jay, *The Federalist Papers*, ed. Ian Shapiro (Yale University Press, 2009), 50.
37. Alexis de Tocqueville, *Democracy in America*, ed. J. P. Mayer (Doubleday, 1969 [1835]), 12–13.
38. This has been partly, though not wholly, the result of European Union membership. See Vernon Bogdanor, "Constitutional Reform in Britain: The Quiet Revolution," *Annual Review of Political Science* 8 (2005): 73–98.
39. Robert Dahl, *A Preface to Democratic Theory* (University of Chicago Press, 1956), 26; and Jeremy Waldron, "The Core of the Case against Judicial Review," *Yale Law Journal* 115 (2006): 1346–1409.
40. J. G. A. Pocock, *The Ancient Constitution and the Feudal Law: A Study of English Historical Thought in the Seventeenth Century* (Cambridge University Press, 1957); and Pocock, *The Machiavellian Moment: Florentine Political Thought and the Atlantic Republican Tradition* (Princeton University Press, 1974), 340–389, 404–458.
41. Buchanan and Tullock, *Calculus of Consent*, 14; and John Rawls, *A Theory of Justice*, 2nd ed. (Harvard University Press, 1999 [1971]), 172.
42. Article 18 of the Confederation provided for a perpetual union that could be altered only if changes were agreed by Congress and "afterwards confirmed by the legislatures of every state." Hamilton, Madison, and Jay, *Federalist Papers*, 452–453. Of course, the Articles of Confederation were not the product of unanimous agreement on the part of everyone bound by them either.
43. Lincoln, *Speeches and Writings*, 217–218, 255–257.
44. Some social contract theorists—notably Hobbes and Rawls—try to elide this difficulty by arguing that there is only one rational constitutional choice for people to make, so that it is the appeal to rationality rather than to agreement that does the heavy lifting in their arguments. But it is easily shown that these arguments depend on debatable assumptions about human psychology, such as people's vulnerability to fear or their propensity for risk. See Chap. 1, §1.2, and Ian Shapiro, *The Moral Foundations of Politics* (Yale University Press, 2003), 109–115.
45. Antonin Scalia and Bryan Garner, *Reading Law: The Interpretation of Legal Texts* (West, 2012), 84–85.
46. Not even him, according to Richard Posner. See Posner, "The Incoherence of Antonin Scalia," *New Republic*, August 24, 2012, http://www.tnr.com/article/magazine/books-and-arts/106441/scalia-garner-reading-the-law-textual-originalism.

47. See Christopher Wolfe, *The Rise of Modern Judicial Review from Constitutional Interpretation to Judge-Made Law* (Rowman and Littlefield, 1994); and Wolfe, *How to Read the Constitution* (Rowman and Littlefield, 1996). Taking a different tack on this theme, H. Jefferson Powell argues that the Founders intended subsequent generations to revise the Constitution. Powell, "The Original Understanding of Original Intent," *Harvard Law Review* 93, no. 5 (March 1985): 885–948. For one recent attempt, see Jack Balkin, *Living Originalism* (Harvard University Press, 2011).

48. Scalia and Garner, *Reading Law,* 88, 407–408. For similar objections to Balkin's "living originalism," see Stephen Sedley, "Construct or Construe," *London Review of Books,* August 30, 2021, http://www.lrb.co.uk/v34/n16/stephen-sedley/construct-or-construe. For an earlier version of this debate in a British idiom, see Patrick Devlin's invocation of the values of "the man on the Clapham omnibus" to inform judicial interpretation, in Devlin, *The Enforcement of Morals* (Oxford University Press, 1965), 1–25; and H. L. A. Hart, "Immorality and Treason," in *The Philosophy of Law,* ed. Ronald Dworkin (Oxford University Press, 1977), 83–89.

49. Locke, "Second Treatise," §119, pp. 152–153.

50. Someone who has "by actual agreement, and any express declaration, given his consent to be of any commonwealth, is perpetually and indispensably obliged to be, and remain unalterably a subject to it." Ibid., p. 153.

51. Troy Bickham, *The Weight of Vengeance: The United States, the British Empire, and the War of 1812* (Oxford University Press, 2012), 31–36, 59–62, 183–184, 217–218, 272–273. As Hume had pointed out in his own discussion of the right to leave, "A company of men, who should leave their native country, in order to people some uninhabited region, might dream of recovering their native freedom; but they would soon find, that their prince still laid claim to them, and called them as his subjects, even in their new settlement. And in this he would but act comfortably to the common ideas of mankind." David Hume, "Of the Original Contract," in *Essays, Moral, Political, and Literary,* ed. Eugene Miller (Liberty Fund, 1985), 476.

52. Locke says that such a person "is at liberty to go and incorporate himself into any other commonwealth; or to agree with others to begin a new one, in *vacuis locis,* in any part of the world they can find free and unpossessed." Locke, "Second Treatise," §121, p. 153.

53. See Adam Tooze, *The Wages of Destruction: The Making and Breaking of the Nazi Economy* (Penguin, 2006), 74–75, 89–90, 274–277.

54. Nozick, *Anarchy, State and Utopia,* 287.

55. Locke, "Second Treatise," §119, pp. 152–153.

56. What should we make of Locke's comments about express consent, and particularly his insistence that one who by "express declaration" has given "his consent to be of any commonwealth, is perpetually and indispensably obliged to be, and remain unalterably a subject to it, and can never be again in the liberty of the state of nature; unless, by any calamity, the government

he was under comes to be dissolved, or else comes some public acts, cuts him off from being any longer a member of it"? Ibid., §119, pp. 153–154. Notice that Locke did not think it the typical case, given that most people never make express declarations of allegiance. Nor does express consent extinguish the right to resist, which is rooted in natural law and indefeasible. To the extent that Locke was thinking about an actual case, it might have been the Engagement Controversy. Cromwell's government had insisted on oaths of allegiance, which Hobbes had famously maintained royalists were free to swear because, following the execution on Charles I in 1649, they were no longer protected by the monarchy (for discussion, see my introduction to Hobbes's *Leviathan* [Yale University Press, 2010 (1651)], x–xii). Like Hobbes, I suspect, Locke would have said that such declarations were binding only so long as government delivered basic protections. A more complex question is whether Locke's comments in §119 mean that someone who had made a declaration of express consent could be prohibited from leaving to escape persecution. More sharply put, what would Locke have made of the Nazi case, modified by postulating that the Jews in question had sworn allegiance to the German state, or of Soviet Jews who might have sworn allegiance to the USSR? Locke is clear that people do not have to accept confiscation of their property in violation of law even from legitimate authorities (see "Second Treatise," §139, p. 162). It is in any case hard to imagine Locke siding with Hitler or Stalin in these examples, because even with express consent, one is subordinate not to the government but to majority rule. Hitler and Stalin had both usurped power and engaged in tyranny, so that Locke would have discerned no obligation to obey them. There is always theoretical possibility that a legitimately constituted majority could tyrannize over a minority in the ways that Hitler and Stalin did, in which case Locke is clear that in extremis the appeal is to heaven. A fortiori, people confronting such tyranny would surely be entitled to leave—though they would have to live with the costs in this life, deferring the benefits to the next.

57. According to Ackerman, the three constitutional moments that have punctuated U.S. political history since the Founding were Reconstruction, the New Deal, and the Civil Rights Revolution. See Bruce Ackerman, *We the People,* vol. 1, *Foundations* (Harvard University Press, 1993); *We the People,* vol. 2, *Transformations* (Harvard University Press, 1998), and *We the People,* vol. 3, *The Civil Rights Revolution* (Harvard University Press, 2014).

58. Thomas Jefferson, letter to James Madison from Paris (September 6, 1789), http://teachingamericanhistory.org/library/index.asp?document=2220.

59. As we saw in §2.2, even that view is vulnerable if circumstances change, undermining the original rationale. A limiting case is what lawyers describe as adhesion contracts, where holding people to the terms of agreements produces severe injustice. Similar arguments are embraced when courts

refuse to enforce prenuptial agreements that would leave a spouse destitute at divorce, or decline to hold borrowers to the terms of predatory loans.

60. On the Leveller demand for annual parliaments, see Michael Mendel, *The Putney Debates of 1647: The Army, the Levellers and the English State* (Cambridge University Press, 2001), 114. For discussion of Burgh's argument, see Jackson Turner Main, *The Antifederalists: Critics of the Constitution, 1781–1788,* 2nd ed. (University of North Carolina Press, 2012), 12. On the Progressives and recall elections, see John M. Allswang, *The Initiative and Referendum in California, 1898–1998* (Stanford University Press, 2000), 1–29.

61. Sen used this phrase to describe the Indian government's search for a theory to explain the great Bengal famine of 1943. See his "Starvation and Exchange Entitlements: A General Approach and Its Application to the Great Bengal Famine," *Cambridge Journal of Economics* 1, no. 1 (1977): 53.

3. The Stakes of Political Conflict

1. See Paul Gauguin's Tahitian painting *D'où Venons Nous/Que Sommes Nous/Où Allons Nous,* usually translated as "Where do we come from? What are we? Where are we going?" (1897), Boston Museum of Fine Arts, http://www.picturalissime.com/g/gauguin_ou_que_l.htm.

2. Stephen Sedley, "Construct or Construe," *London Review of Books,* August 30, 2012, 19–20, http://www.lrb.co.uk/v34/n16/stephen-sedley /construct-or-construe.

3. "Hunger, Poverty Rates in Egypt Up Sharply over the Last Three Years—UN Report," UN News Center (May 21, 2013), http://www.un.org /apps/news/story.asp?NewsID=44961#.UjDiYMxSbx4; and "Egypt Q&A: Why Is the Country Once Again in Turmoil," CTVNews Canada (July 2, 2013), http://www.ctvnews.ca/world/egypt-q-a-why-is-the-country-once -again-in-turmoil-1.1350228.

4. Hobbes insists in chap. 21 of *Leviathan,* "The end of Obedience is Protection," explaining that the "Obligation of Subjects to the Soveraign, is understood to last as long, and no longer, than the power lasteth, by which he is able to protect them." This is because "the right men have by Nature to protect themselves, when none else can protect them, can by no Covenant be relinquished." Thomas Hobbes, *Leviathan,* ed. Ian Shapiro (Yale University Press, 2010), 114.

5. James Madison, *Federalist* #51, in Alexander Hamilton, James Madison, and John Jay, *The Federalist Papers,* ed. Ian Shapiro (Yale University Press, 2009), 264.

6. Madison, *Federalist* #10, 48. Madison's anxiety echoes verbatim Rousseau's, a quarter of a century earlier, that if "sectional associations are

formed at the expense of the larger association, the will of each of these groups will become general in relation to its members and private in relation to the state." Jean-Jacques Rousseau, *Of the Social Contract*, bk. 2, chap. 3, in *The Social Contract and Other Later Political Writings*, ed. Victor Gourevitch (Cambridge University Press, 1997), 73. There is no evidence that Madison ever read Rousseau; he seems more likely to have been influenced by Hume's earlier declaration, "Though it is more difficult to form a republican government in an extensive country than in a city; there is more facility, once when it is formed, of preserving it steady and uniform, without tumult and faction. It is not easy, for the distant parts of a large state to combine in any plan of free government." Moreover, in a large government, "there is compass and room enough to refine the democracy, from the lower people, who may be admitted into the first elections or first concoction of the commonwealth, to the higher magistrates, who direct all the movements. At the same time, the parts are so distant and remote, that it is very difficult, either by intrigue, prejudice, or passion, to hurry them into any measures against the public interest." David Hume, "Idea of a Perfect Commonwealth" [1754], in Hume, *Essays Moral, Political, and Literary* (Liberty Fund, 1985), 527–588. For discussion of Hume's influence on Madison, see Mark G. Spencer, "Hume and Madison on Faction," *William and Mary Quarterly*, 3rd ser., 59, no. 4 (October, 2002): 869–896.

7. "But it could not be less folly to abolish liberty," he continued "which is essential to political life, because it nourishes faction, than it would be to wish the annihilation of air, which is essential to animal life, because it imparts to fire its destructive agency." Madison, *Federalist* #10, 48.

8. Ibid., 49.

9. Ibid., 52.

10. See William Riker, *Liberalism against Populism: A Confrontation of Democracy and the Theory of Social Choice* (W. H. Freeman, 1982). For criticism, see Ian Shapiro, *The State of Democratic Theory* (Princeton University Press, 2003), 12–13, 65–66.

11. In April 2008, candidate Barack Obama described Pennsylvanian voters as "clinging to their guns and religion." See Katharine Seelye and Jeff Zeleny, "On the Defensive, Obama Calls His Words Ill-Chosen," *New York Times*, April 13, 2008, http://www.nytimes.com/2008/04/13/us/politics/13campaign.html?pagewanted=all. In September 2012, candidate Mitt Romney, at a fund-raiser in which he was surreptitiously recorded, said that 47 percent are "takers, not makers." See Ezra Klein, "Romney's Theory of the 'Taker Class,' and Why It Matters," *Washington Post*, September 17, 2012, http://www.washingtonpost.com/blogs/wonkblog/wp/2012/09/17/romneys-theory-of-the-taker-class-and-why-it-matters/.

12. William Golding, *Lord of the Flies* (Perigree Books, 1959 [1954]).

13. I have explored elsewhere the implications of this for distributive politics. See Shapiro, *State of Democratic Theory*, 104–145; and Shapiro, *Democracy and Distribution* (Princeton University Press, forthcoming).

14. As Madison elaborated: "The most common and durable source of factions has been the various and unequal distribution of property. Those who hold and those who are without property have ever formed distinct interests in society. Those who are creditors, and those who are debtors, fall under a like discrimination. A landed interest, a manufacturing interest, a mercantile interest, a moneyed interest, with many lesser interests, grow up of necessity in civilized nations, and divide them into different classes, actuated by different sentiments and views." Madison, *Federalist* #10, 49.

15. See Susan Dunn, *Jefferson's Second Revolution: The Election Crisis of 1800 and the Triumph of Republicanism* (Houghton Mifflin, 2004), 624–626. This partly explains why huge majorities can become liabilities. In 1936, FDR swept forty-six out of forty-eight states in an unprecedented landslide that gave Democrats supermajorities in both houses (75 of 98 in the Senate, and 334 of 435 in the House), leading the *New York Times* to declare that "President Roosevelt's word will be law." In fact, his most ambitious New Deal legislation was already behind him. Future administration bills splintered FDR's coalition, and he had his head handed to him by his own party over his court-packing plan the following year. See Ira Katznelson, *Fear Itself: The New Deal and the Origins of Our Time* (W. W. Norton, 2013), 265–266.

16. Nolan McCarty, Keith Poole, and Howard Rosenthal, *Political Bubbles: Financial Crises and the Failure of American Democracy* (Princeton University Press, 2013), 50–51. The exception was race, which operated as a second dimension during the 1950s and 1960s. See McCarty, Poole, and Rosenthal's earlier book, *Polarized America* (MIT Press, 2006), 15–70.

17. The exception was Bosnia-Herzegovina, in which there was no majority ethnic group.

18. Roger Hayden, "Imagined Communities and Real Victims: Self-Determination and Ethnic Cleansing in Yugoslavia," *American Ethnologist* 23, no. 4 (November 1996): 783–801.

19. Karin Tamar Schafferman, "Participation, Abstention, and Boycott: Trends in Arab Participation in Israeli Elections," Israel Democracy Institute (April 21, 2009), http://en.idi.org.il/analysis/articles/participation-abstention -and-boycott-trends-in-arab-voter-turnout-in-israeli-elections/.

20. This view is traceable to Hobbes's *Leviathan,* but its canonical statement in the contemporary literature is Samuel P. Huntington's *Political Order in Changing Societies* (Yale University Press, 1968).

21. This is not to mention disagreement about what constitutes the basic structure, as feminist critics of Rawls's disinclination to include the family have noted. See Susan Moller Okin, *"Political Liberalism,* Justice, and Gender," *Ethics* 95, no. 1 (1994): 23–43.

22. See Shannon O'Neil, "Mexico," in *Pathways to Freedom: Political and Economic Lessons from Democratic Transitions,* ed. Isobel Coleman and Terra Lawson-Remer (Council on Foreign Relations, 2013), 42–44.

23. Giovanni Carbone and Vincenzi Memoli, "Does Democratization Foster State Consolidation? Democratic Rule, Political Order, and Administrative

Capacity," *Governance* 28, no. 1 (January 2015): 5–24. On the deepening of institutional capacities in response to the demands of democratic politics in the United States, see Stephen Skowronek, *Building a New American State: The Expansion of National Administrative Capacities, 1877–1920* (Cambridge University Press, 1982).

24. See Frances McCall Rosenbluth and Michael F. Thies, *Japan Transformed: Political Change and Economic Restructuring* (Princeton University Press, 2010), 95–122.

25. See Vernon Bogdanor, "Constitutional Reform in Britain: The Quiet Revolution," *Annual Review of Political Science* 8 (2005): 73–98.

26. James Harrington, *The Commonwealth of Oceana [1656] and A System of Politics [c. 1661]*, ed. J. G. A. Pocock (Cambridge University Press, 1992).

27. Adam Przeworski, "Self-Enforcing Democracy," in *The Oxford Handbook of Political Economy*, ed. Donald Wittman and Barry Weingast (Oxford University Press, 2006), 312.

28. Dunn, *Jefferson's Second Revolution*, 95–152.

29. Pauline Maier, *From Resistance to Revolution: Colonial Radicals and the Development of American Opposition to Britain, 1765–1776* (W. W. Norton, 1992).

30. See Seymour Martin Lipset, *Political Man: The Social Bases of Politics* (Doubleday, 1960); David E. Apter, *The Politics of Modernization* (University of Chicago Press, 1967); Barrington Moore Jr., *The Social Bases of Dictatorship and Democracy: Lord and Peasant in the Making of the Modern World* (Beacon Press, 1966); and Dietrich Ruechemeyer, Evelyn Huber Stephens, and John Stephens, *Capitalist Development and Democracy* (University of Chicago Press, 1992).

31. Adam Przeworski, Michael E. Alvarez, Jose Antonio Cheibub, and Fernando Limongi, *Development and Democracy: Political Institutions and Well-Being in the World, 1950–1990* (Cambridge University Press, 2000), 78–141.

32. Lipset, *Political Man*, 51.

33. Jess Benhabib and Adam Przeworski, "The Political Economy of Redistribution under Democracy," *Economic Theory* 29, no. 2 (2006): 271–290. Przeworski speculates that democracy might have better prospects for survival in poor countries if they are egalitarian due to the dearth of wealthy people whose assets could be expropriated in a revolution. Przeworski, "Self-Enforcing Democracy," 312–328. Apart from the difficulties attending this reasoning raised in the next paragraph, it fails to account for democracy's survival in India, whose Gini coefficient is comparable to those of New Zealand, France, and the United Kingdom. See "Global Gini Index (Distribution of Family Income) Ranking by Country," *CIA Factbook 2010*, January 2010. http://www.mongabay.com/reference/stats/rankings /2172.html.

34. Shapiro, *State of Democratic Theory*, 104–145.

35. Niccolò Machiavelli, *Discourses on Livy* (Penguin, 1970), §1.5, p. 116.

36. See Rudy Abramson, *Spanning the Century: The Life of W. Averell Harriman, 1891–1986* (William Morrow, 1992); and Ralph Miliband, *The State in Capitalist Society* (Quartet Books, 1973).

37. See Isobel Coleman and Terra Lawson-Remer, eds., *Pathways to Freedom: Political and Economic Lessons from Democratic Transitions* (Council on Foreign Relations, 2013), 35–38, 59–62, 83–89, 136–141.

38. Coleman and Lawson-Remer, *Pathways to Freedom,* 162–168, 206–213; and "The Status of Poverty and Food Security in Egypt: Analysis and Policy Recommendations, May 2013," World Food Program, May 21, 2013, http://www.wfp.org/content/egypt-status-poverty-food-security-analysis-policy-recommendations-may-2013.

39. See Ken Wells and Ari Levy, "Gore Is Romney-Rich with $200 Million after Bush Defeat," Bloomberg, May 6, 2013, http://www.bloomberg.com/news/articles/2013-05-06/gore-is-romney-rich-with-200-million-after-bush-defeat.

40. See Adam Przeworski, "Acquiring the Habit of Changing Governments through Elections," *Comparative Political Studies* 48, no. 1 (August 2014): 101–129.

41. See Ian Shapiro and Kahreen Tebeau, *After Apartheid: Reinventing South Africa?* (University of Virginia Press, 2011), 1–4. This was not alternation of government, because the ANC remained in power, but in a single-party-dominant democracy it is the next best thing.

42. See, for instance, the Thabo Mbeki African Leadership Institute, http://www.unisa.ac.za/Default.asp?Cmd=ViewContent&ContentID=23684; the Thabo Mbeki Foundation http://www.thabombekifoundation.org.za/SitePages/Home_New.aspx; IC Publications board list at http://www.icpublications.com/en/our-advisory-board.html; and Murtala Opoola, "Africa 2012: Thabo Mbeki, African of the Year 2012," AllAfrica, May 26, 2013, http://allafrica.com/stories/201305260191.html.

43. Dunn, *Jefferson's Second Revolution,* 218–272.

44. See Stanley Elkins and Eric McKitrick, *The Age of Federalism: The Early American Republic, 1788–1800* (Oxford University Press, 1993), 163–194. This is not to deny that the American regime was scarred by contingencies in its early years. Bruce Ackerman makes a powerful case that the rise of presidentialism was aided by, among other things, the Federalist suppression of the Republican press in the Sedition Act of 1798 and Jefferson's debatably legal decision, as sitting vice president, to declare himself the winner of the electoral college vote in February 1801. See Bruce Ackerman, *The Failure of the Founding Fathers: Jefferson, Marshall and the Rise of Presidential Democracy* (Harvard Belknap, 2007).

45. This suggests a different perspective on some recent democratic transitions. Soviet elites have been attacked as corrupt for seizing state assets on the way out of power, but the price might have been worth paying for the

peaceful demise of the USSR. Good things do not always go together. In the Arab spring, the fates of Muammar Gaddafi and Hosni Mubarak were no doubt duly noted by leaders in Riyadh, Sanaa, Rabat, and Amman in their responses to their own uprisings.

46. Przeworski et al. find that democracies survive indefinitely once PCI reaches about $6,000 measured in 1985 dollars (about $13,200 2014 dollars). See Przeworski et al., *Development and Democracy,* 78–141. I discuss this further in §6.3.

47. Democracy can survive in countries with some of the highest Gini coefficients in the world, such as South Africa at 63.1 and Brazil at 55.1 (World Bank data, http://data.worldbank.org/indicator/SI.POV.GINI). It survives in India despite a PCI below $1,500 per year (World Bank data, http://data .worldbank.org/indicator/NY.GDP.PCAP.CD).

48. Amartya Sen, *The Idea of Justice* (Harvard University Press, 2009), 338–345, 388–390.

49. McCarty, Pool, and Rosenthal, *Political Bubbles,* 228–239.

50. E. E. Schattschneider, *The Semi-Sovereign People: A Realist's View of American Politics* (Holt, Reinhart, and Winston, 1960), 35.

51. James Buchanan and Gordon Tullock, *The Calculus of Consent* (University of Michigan Press, 1962), 125–130. Robert Dahl flirted with the notion that attending to intensity might be desirable from the standpoint of political stability, though he was skeptical that it could be measured.

52. Robert Dahl, *A Preface to Democratic Theory* (University of Chicago Press, 1956), 90–123.

53. Vilfredo Pareto, *Manual of Political Economy* (Augustus Kelley, 1979 [1909]), 49.

54. David Goldfield, *America Aflame: How the Civil War Created a Nation* (Bloomsbury Press, 2011), 483–505.

55. Katznelson, *Fear Itself,* 131–194.

56. James Patterson, *The Eve of Destruction* (Basic Books, 2012), 96–106, 137–138, 173–174, 178–179, 226–227.

57. Guinier defended cumulative voting schemes that provide for voters to cast more than one vote for a single candidate in an election to fill more than one seat—reflecting intense support. Lani Guinier, *The Tyranny of the Majority: Fundamental Fairness in Representative Democracy* (Free Press, 1994), 41–70, 119–156. Cumulative voting is often used in corporate governance, has been used in various state and local elections in the United States, and arguably is less intrusive than gerrymandering to create majority minority districts. See my *State of Democratic Theory,* 96–98. Nonetheless, when Clinton pulled Guinier's nomination, he disavowed her views on representation, insisting, "Had I read them before I nominated her I would not have done so." David Lauter and Sam Fullman III, "Clinton Withdraws Guinier as Nominee for Civil Rights Job," *Los Angeles Times,* June 4, 1993, http://articles.latimes.com/1993–06–04/news/mn-43163_1_lani-guinier.

58. I defer to §§6.2 and 6.3 discussion of the circumstances under which war is justified.

59. Scott Clement, "Ninety Percent of Americans Want Background Checks on Guns—Why Isn't This a Political Slam Dunk?," *Washington Post,* April 3, 2013, http://www.washingtonpost.com/blogs/the-fix/wp/2013/04/03/90-percent-of-americans-want-expanded-background-checks-on-guns-why-isnt-this-a-political-slam-dunk/. Generally, see Paul Barrett, *Glock: The Rise of America's Gun* (Broadway Books, 2012).

60. Michael Graetz and Ian Shapiro, *Death by a Thousand Cuts: The Fight over Taxing Inherited Wealth* (Princeton University Press, 2005), 239–252.

61. Frank Rich, "The Billionaires Bankrolling the Tea Party," *New York Times,* August 28, 2010, http://www.nytimes.com/2010/08/29/opinion/29rich.html?_r=0. See also McCarty, Poole, and Rosenthal, *Political Bubbles,* 242.

62. Banking interests spent some of the largest amounts ever to finance hundreds of lobbyists to limit the impact of financial reform. Over $150 million was spent in each of 2009, 2010, and 2011. See Jennifer Liberto, "Banking Interests Pay Big to Influence Washington," CNN Money, January 31, 2012, http://money.cnn.com/2012/01/31/news/economy/wall_street_influence/index.htm.

63. Cass Sunstein, "The Law of Group Polarization," *Journal of Political Philosophy* 10, no. 2 (June 2002): 175–195.

64. Daniel Kahneman, *Thinking, Fast and Slow* (Farrar, Straus and Giroux, 2011), 245–254.

65. In fact it was reinstated in 2013, albeit with a $5 million threshold. See Matthew Dalton, "Permanent Estate Tax Ends Decades of Uncertainty," *Tax Notes Today,* January 3, 2013, http://services.taxanalysts.com/taxbase/tnt3.nsf/(Number/2013+TNT+2-4?OpenDocument.

66. Graetz and Shapiro, *Death by a Thousand Cuts,* 51–52, 154–167, 221–238.

67. Morris Fiorina, Samuel Abrams, and Jeremy Pope, *Culture War? The Myth of Polarized America,* 3rd ed. (Longman, 2010).

68. McCarty, Poole, and Rosenthal, *Polarized America,* 15–70.

69. Daniel Walker Howe, *What Hath God Wrought: The Transformation of America, 1815–1848* (Oxford University Press, 2009), 147–160.

70. Hence Jefferson's remark to his son-in-law in 1820 that a female slave who has a child every other year is "more valuable than the best man of the farm." Letter from Thomas Jefferson to John W. Eppes, June 30, 1820, quoted in Steven Deyle, "The Irony of Liberty: Origins of the Domestic Slave Trade," *Journal of the Early Republic* 12, no. 1 (1992): 51.

71. Steven Deyle, *Carry Me Back: The Domestic Slave Trade in American Life* (Oxford University Press, 2005), 14–39.

72. Howe, *What Hath God Wrought,* 149.

73. Arend Lijphart, "Consociational Democracy," *World Politics* 21, no. 2 (January 1969): 216. Generally, see Lijphart, *Democracy in Plural Societies* (Yale University Press, 1977).

74. Lijphart, "Prospects for Power-Sharing in South Africa," in *Election 94,* ed. Andrew Reynolds (St. Martin's Press, 1994). Power sharing had been in part mandated in the provisional constitution that came into force in 1994, but Lijphart's recommendation to entrench it in the final constitution was not followed. See Ian Shapiro, *Democracy's Place* (Cornell University Press, 1996), 180, 216–217.

75. Shapiro and Tebeau, *After Apartheid,* 1–6. There has been xenophobic violence directed at foreigners, but that would have been unaffected by Lijphart's recommendations.

76. Donald Horowitz, *Ethnic Groups in Conflict,* 2nd ed. (University of California Press, 1985), 572; Brian Barry, "Political Accommodation and Consociational Democracy," *British Journal of Political Science 5,* no. 4 (1975): 477–505; and Barry, "The Consociational Model and Its Dangers," *European Journal of Political Research* 3, no. 4 (1975): 393–412.

77. Donald Horowitz: *A Democratic South Africa? Constitutional Engineering in a Divided Society* (University of California Press, 1992), 32.

78. Lijphart seems to think that this difficulty is avoided so long as the particular ethnic groups are not designated in advance. See Arend Lijphart, *Power-Sharing in South Africa,* Institute for International Studies, University of California, Policy Paper no. 21 (1985), 58, 81. But as Horowitz and others have pointed out, he never explains why politicians who are rewarded by appealing to inherited sectarian antipathies will not continue to mobilize people along those lines. Horowitz, *Democratic South Africa?,* 143; Horowitz, *Ethnic Groups in Conflict,* 569–576; and Shapiro, *Democracy's Place,* 100–105, 216–217.

4. Democracy against Republicanism

1. John Dewey, *The Public and Its Problems* (Henry Holt, 1927), 84–85.

2. Robert Dahl, *How Democratic Is the American Constitution?* (Yale University Press, 2003), 9–39.

3. Stanley Elkins and Eric McKitrick, *The Age of Federalism: The Early American Republic, 1788–1800* (Oxford University Press, 1993), 263–270.

4. Dahl, *How Democratic?,* 37.

5. Juan Linz, "Presidential or Parliamentary Democracy: Does It Make a Difference?," in *The Failure of Presidential Democracy,* ed. Juan J. Linz and Arturo Vanenzuela (Johns Hopkins University Press, 1994); and José Cheibub and Fernando Limongi, "Democratic Institutions and Regime Survival: Parliamentary and Presidential Regimes Reconsidered," *Annual Review of Political Science* 5 (2002): 151–179.

6. This is known as Duverger's law. See Maurice Duverger, *Political Parties: Their Organization and Activity in the Modern State,* 3rd ed. (Methuen 1964), 216–255. Duverger's law will only apply if constituencies are

heterogeneous. If they are internally homogeneous regionally but different, as in India, then parties can proliferate. In any case, it can take a long time for these dynamics to kick in. For instance, in South Africa the path-dependent effects of the ANC's organizational power have not yet been upset by the logic of proportional representation, which will eventually erode its single-party dominance. Party proliferation under PR can be limited up to a point by manipulating district magnitude. See Douglas Rae, "Using District Magnitude to Regulate Political Party Competition," *Journal of Economic Perspectives* 9, no. 1 (1995): 65–75; and John Carey and Simon Hix, "The Electoral Sweet Spot: Low Magnitude Proportional Election Systems," *American Journal of Political Science* 55, no. 2 (April 2011): 383–397.

7. Guido Tabellini, Torsten Persson, and Gérard Roland, "How Do Electoral Rules Shape Party Structures, Government Coalitions and Economic Policies?," *Quarterly Journal of Political Science* 2, no. 2 (2007): 155–188; and Kathleen Bawn and Frances Rosenbluth, "Coalition Parties vs. Coalitions of Parties: How Electoral Agency Shapes the Political Logic of Costs and Benefits," *American Journal of Political Science* 50, no. 2 (2006): 251–266.

8. See Ian Shapiro, *Democracy and Distribution* (Princeton University Press, forthcoming), 104–145.

9. It surely is a debatable claim, if only by reference to slavery and the racial history of the franchise, but that does not stop people from making it. See "The United States: Fulfilling the Promise of the American Dream," Thomas White International, http://www.thomaswhite.com/world-markets/the-united-states-fulfilling-the-promise-of-the-american-dream/.

10. James Madison, "Majority Government," in *Letters and Other Writings of James Madison,* vol. 4 (J. P. Lippincott, 1865), 332. For additional discussion, see Ian Shapiro, *The Real World of Democratic Theory* (Princeton University Press, 2011), 38–67.

11. Albert Hirschman, *Exit, Voice, and Loyalty: Responses to Decline in Firms, Organizations, and States* (Harvard University Press, 1970), 3–44.

12. Indeed American reluctance to accept Jews from Germany aggravated their plight. See Adam Tooze, *The Wages of Destruction: The Making and Breaking of the Nazi Economy* (New York: Penguin, 2006), 74–75, 89–90, 274–277.

13. See Scott Sayre, "Socialists Denounce Gérard Depardieu for Leaving France," *New York Times,* December 12, 2012, http://www.nytimes.com/2012/12/13/world/europe/gerard-depardieu-called-pathetic-for-leaving-france.html?_r=0. Prohibiting Depardieu's departure is surely unappealing, but the French authorities should adopt the Lockean stance discussed in §5.2, insisting that he exchange the benefits of French residence and citizenship for whatever comes with the more favorable Russian tax treatment for millionaires that he seeks—in effect increase his exit costs. Selective exit should not be an option.

14. See Ian Shapiro, *Democratic Justice* (Yale University Press, 1999), 190–195.

15. According to Carles Boix, *Democracy and Redistribution* (Cambridge University Press, 2003), 36–59, once the economy moves from fixed assets like oil to those that depend on more mobile capital, economic elites can embrace democracy. Credible threats to leave insulate them from redistributive taxation.

16. See Adam Przeworski and Michael Wallerstein, "Structural Dependence of the State on Capital," *American Political Science Review* 82, no. 1 (1988): 11–29.

17. Elkins and McKitrick, *Age of Federalism*, 4–33.

18. James Madison, *Federalist* #48, in Alexander Hamilton, James Madison, and John Jay, *The Federalist Papers,* ed. Ian Shapiro (Yale University Press, 2009), 252–254.

19. See §1.6.

20. Comparable fears led John Stuart Mill to propose a second vote for bankers, merchants, foremen, entrepreneurs, and university graduates to temper the influence of society's lower orders. John Stuart Mill, *Considerations on Representative Government* (Prometheus Books, 1991), 183.

21. Madison, *Federalist* #51, 263.

22. Dahl, *A Preface to Democratic Theory,* 2nd ed. (University of Chicago Press, 2005 [1956]), 30–32.

23. See David Goldfield, *America Aflame: How the Civil War Created a Nation* (New York: Bloomsbury Press, 2011), 194–200, 214.

24. Keith Whittington, *Political Foundations of Judicial Supremacy: The Presidency, The Supreme Court, and Constitutional Leadership in U.S. History* (Princeton University Press, 2007).

25. Ira Katznelson, *Fear Itself: The New Deal and the Origins of Our Time* (New York: Norton, 2013), 337.

26. Katznelson, *Fear Itself,* 339–342.

27. In *Korematsu v. United States,* 323 U.S. 214 (1944), the Court upheld Executive order 9066 providing for the internment of U.S. citizens of Japanese descent. Notably, in the present context, the Court never reversed this decision. Rather, it was, the Executive branch which—in 2011!—finally filed official notice conceding that the government's stance in *Korematsu* had been an error. See Neal Katyal, "Confession of Error: The Solicitor General's Mistakes During the Japanese Internment Cases," U.S. Department of Justice blog (May 20, 2011), http://blogs.justice.gov/main/archives /1346.

28. Katznelson, *Fear Itself,* 441, 443–444.

29. John Ferejohn and Rick Hills, "Blank Checks, Insufficient Balances," NYU Law School, mimeo 2013.

30. Southern Democrats were in the vanguard of the early New Deal, strongly supporting such measures as the creation of the National Recovery

Administration in 1933 and the Wagner Act in 1935. Buyer's remorse set in after 1936, as they came to fear that a powerful Washington bureaucracy and the increasingly muscular union movement would threaten the Southern racial order. As a result, they supported measures to decentralize administration of the New Deal programs to the states and a series of measures to weaken the Wagner Act, culminating in the Taft-Hartley Act of 1947, which was passed over President Truman's veto with their support in alliance with almost all Republicans. See Katznelson, *Fear Itself,* 227–275, 367–402.

31. See Goldfield, *America Aflame,* 138–140.

32. *Bush v. Gore,* 531 U.S. 98 (2000). See Howard Gillman, *The Votes that Counted: How the Court Decided the 2000 Presidential Election* (University of Chicago Press, 2003); and Geoffrey R. Stone, "Equal Protection? The Supreme Court's Decision in Bush v. Gore," *Fathom Archive,* http://fathom .lib.uchicago.edu/1/777777122240/.

33. For a celebratory interpretation, see Eric Posner and Adrian Vermeule, *The Executive Unbound* (Oxford University Press, 2010).

34. Donald Horowitz notes that the other main features of the American model such as the electoral system, federalism, and independently elected presidents have been much less widely imitated. "*The Federalist* Abroad in the World," in Hamilton, Madison, and Jay, *The Federalist Papers,* 502–531.

35. Hamilton, *Federalist #78,* 391–397; and Alexander Bickel, *The Least Dangerous Branch* (Bobbs-Merrill, 1962).

36. For the flavor, see Dworkin's many contributions to the *New York Review of Books,* http://www.nybooks.com/contributors/ronald-dworkin-2/.

37. *Dred Scott v. Sandford,* 60 U.S. 393 (1857), held that blacks, whether free or slave, were not citizens and therefore lacked standing to sue in in federal court. *Plessy v. Ferguson,* 163 U.S. 537 (1896), coined the euphemism "separate but equal" to sanctify racial segregation in schools and public facilities. *The Slaughter-House Cases,* 83 U.S. 36 (1873), crafted a narrow reading of the Fourteenth Amendment, immunizing the states' police powers, and *The Civil Rights Cases,* 109 U.S. 3 (1883), held that the Amendment's enforcement provisions did not empower Congress to outlaw racial discrimination by private individuals and organizations—only by state and local governments.

38. Melvin Urofsky, *The Warren Court: Justices, Rulings, and Legacy* (ABC-CLIO, 2001), 264.

39. See Kevin T. McGuire and James Stimson, "The Least Dangerous Branch Revisited: New Evidence on Supreme Court Responsiveness to Public Preferences," *Journal of Politics* 66 (2004): 1018–1035; Michael W. Giles, Bethany Blackstone, and Rich Vining, "The Supreme Court in American Democracy: Unraveling the Linkages between Public Opinion and Judicial Decision-making," *Journal of Politics* 70 (2008): 293–306; Nathaniel Persily, Jack Citrin, and Patrick Egan, eds., *Public Opinion and Constitutional Controversy* (Oxford University Press, 2008); and Barry Friedman,

The Will of the People: How Public Opinion Has Influenced the Supreme Court and Shaped the Meaning of the Constitution (New York: Farrar, Straus and Giroux, 2010).

40. Patrick Devlin, *The Enforcement of Morals* (Oxford University Press, 1965), 15.
41. *Bowers v. Hardwick,* 478 U.S. 186 (1986), upheld as constitutional Georgia's proscription of homosexual conduct between consenting adults. It was reversed by *Lawrence v. Texas,* 539 U.S. 558 (2003), which struck down a Texas sodomy law and granted constitutional protection to same-sex sexual activity legal in all U.S. jurisdictions.
42. Most famously, Ruth Bader Ginsberg. See Shapiro, *Real World of Democratic Theory,* 238–241.
43. Gerald A. Rosenberg, *The Hollow Hope: Can Courts Bring About Social Change?,* 2nd ed. (University of Chicago Press, 2008).
44. Robert Dahl, *A Preface to Democratic Theory* (University of Chicago Press, 1956); and Dahl, "Decision-Making in a Democracy: The Supreme Court as National Policy-Maker," *Journal of Public Law* 6 (1957): 279–295.
45. See Mark Tushnet, *Taking the Constitution Away from the Courts* (Princeton University Press, 1999); and Ran Hirschl, *Towards Juristocracy: The Origins and Consequences of the New Constitutionalism* (Harvard University Press, 2007).
46. Ran Hirschl, "The Political Origins of Judicial Empowerment through Constitutionalization: Lessons from Four Constitutional Revolutions," *Law and Social Inquiry* 25, no. 1 (January 2000): 91–147.
47. The Parliament Act of 1911 entirely denied the Lords the power to veto money bills and left them with the power to delay other legislation by up to two years. Donald Shell, *The House of Lords* (Philip Allan, 1988), 9.
48. Gordon Wood, *The Creation of the American Republic: 1776–1787* (W. W. Norton, 1969), 559.
49. Madison, *Federalist* #63, 321.
50. United States Constitution, Article I, §3, as modified by the Seventeenth Amendment, provides that "The Senate of the United States shall be composed of two Senators from each State, elected by the people thereof." http://www.archives.gov/exhibits/charters/constitution_amendments_11–27 .html#17. This produces the anomaly that there are seven states (Alaska, Delaware, Montana, North Dakota, South Dakota, Wyoming, and Vermont) whose populations are so small that they qualify for only a single House representative, yet each has two senators. http://usgovinfo.about.com/od /uscongress/a/abouthouse.htm.
51. The Senate is also an independent brake on the president because Article II, §2, provides that "advice and consent" of two-thirds of the senate is needed to ratify treaties, and a majority must approve appointment of "ambassadors, other public Ministers and Consuls, Judges of the supreme Court, and all other Officers of the United States." http://www.archives.gov/exhibits /charters/constitution_transcript.html.

52. Samuel Smucker, *The Life and Times of Thomas Jefferson* (J. W. Bradley, 1859), 82. Madison also had an elevated view of the Senate, defending its thirty-years-old age and nine-year minimum citizenship limitations as needed to generate the requisite "senatorial trust," which required greater "stability of character" than needed in the House of Representatives. Madison, *Federalist #62*, 313.

53. Alexis de Tocqueville, *Democracy in America,* ed. J. P. Mayer (Anchor Books, 1969 [1835, 1840]), 200–201.

54. Terence Samuel, *The Upper House: A Journey behind Closed Doors* (Palgrave Macmillan, 2010), 68.

55. It is true that there were also plenty of Southern veto players in the House, often ensconced as chairs of key committees by the seniority system, but the combination of the same seniority rules in the Senate and the filibuster rule (which was two-thirds rather than the 60 votes that it has been since 1975) made the Senate the more powerful blocking force. Katznelson, *Fear Itself,* 156–194.

56. Ibid., 166–168.

57. This is true despite the fact that the threshold was reduced from two-thirds to three-fifths (usually 60 votes) in 1975. On the history of the filibuster, see Gregory Koger, *Filibustering: A Political History of Obstruction in the House and Senate* (University of Chicago Press, 2012).

58. Walter Bagehot, *The English Constitution* (Oxford University Press, 2001 [1867]), 88.

59. Donald Shell, *The House of Lords,* 152–174; and Meg Russell, *The Contemporary House of Lords: Westminster Bicameralism Revisited* (Oxford University Press, 2013), 45–46, 271–272. See also Vernon Bogdanor, *The New British Constitution* (Hart, 2009), 16–18, 145–173, 222–225, 278–289.

60. The House of Lords Act of 1999 reduced the membership from 1,330 to 699 and got rid of all but 92 of the hereditary peers who were allowed to remain on an interim basis and ten who were made life peers. On the recent evolution, see Russell, *Contemporary House of Lords,* 13–35, 258–284.

61. Ibid., 138, 239–242.

62. Ibid., 245, 254.

63. See Meg Russell, "Is the House of Lords Already Reformed?," *Political Quarterly* 74, no. 3 (July 2003): 311–318.

64. Heredity peerages are no longer created, and since the 1999 reform only 92 of the 762 lords sit as heredity peers (though a few more heredity peers sit there on a basis other than their heredity title). Russell, *Contemporary House of Lords,* 72–73.

65. Ibid., 254–255.

66. Frank Vilbert, *The Rise of the Unelected: Democracy and the New Separation of Powers* (Cambridge University Press, 2007).

67. Bruce Ackerman, "The New Separation of Powers," *Harvard Law Review* 113 (2000): 633–729, 723.

68. Ibid., 718.
69. There are separate commissions for England, Scotland, Wales, and Northern Ireland. There are four members of each commission (including the Speaker of the House of Commons ex officio). With some minor exceptions, each constituency must be within 5 percent of the UK electoral quotas and no constituency can be larger than 13,000 square kilometers. See Ron Johnston and Charles Pattie, "From the Organic to the Arithmetic: Redistricting/Redistribution Rules in the United Kingdom," *Election Law Journal* 11, no. 1 (2012): 70–89.
70. Base-closing commissions were established by the U.S. Congress to avoid inefficient logrolling among members who would be loath to lose bases in their constituencies. A Base Realignment and Closure Commission makes a report that Congress can accept or reject but not amend. See David Lockwood and George Siehl, "Military Base Closures: A Historical Review form 1988 to 1995," Congressional Research for Congress Report, October 2004, Order Code 97-305 F. "Ulysses and the Sirens" refers to a voluntary choice to bind one's hands in advance to foreclose the possibility of making a tempting destructive choice. It gets its name from the pact Ulysses made with his men when he wanted to hear the beautiful voices of the Sirens, which he knew would render him incapable of rational action. He put wax into his men's ears and had them tie him to the ship's mast to prevent his jumping into the sea at the sound of the Sirens' voices until the danger was past. See Jon Elster, *Ulysses and the Sirens: Studies in Rationality and Irrationality* (Cambridge University Press, 1998).
71. The Bank of England Act of 1998 gave the bank sole responsibility for setting interest rates to meet the government's inflation target of 2.5 percent. "Key Monetary Policy Dates since 1990," Bank of England website, http://web.archive.org/web/20070629143630/http://www.bankofengland.co.uk/monetarypolicy/history.htm.
72. See Alexander Mihailov, "Operational Independence, Inflation Targeting, and UK Monetary Policy," University of Essex discussion paper, 2006, http://www.essex.ac.uk/economics/discussion-papers/papers-text/dp602.pdf.
73. Halah Touryali, "Why Wall Street Is Winning Right Now and Everyone Else Seems to Be Losing," *Forbes,* March 6, 2013, http://www.forbes.com/sites/halahtouryalai/2013/03/06/why-wall-street-is-winning-right-now-and-everyone-else-seems-to-be-losing/.
74. Ironically, in the United States it is the extreme-right libertarians who try to argue that the Federal Reserve violates the Constitution. See Ron Paul, *End the Fed* (Grand Central, 2009), chap. 12. It seems unlikely that a court would agree with him, but you never know.
75. As James Vreeland has shown, governments of developing countries sometimes ask institutions like the IMF to insist on more austere conditions for loans than the institutions themselves deem necessary, in order to take

hard choices off the table in their domestic politics. See James Vreeland, *The IMF and Economic* Development (Cambridge University Press, 2003).

76. Joseph Schumpeter, *Capitalism, Socialism, and Democracy* (Harper, 1942), 250–273.

77. See Benjamin Barber, *Strong Democracy: Participatory Politics for a New Age,* 2nd ed. (University of California Press, 2003), 139–162, 213–260; and Carol Pateman, *Participation and Democratic Theory* (Cambridge University Press, 1970), 3–29, 40, 103, 110.

78. Adam Przeworski, "Minimalist Conception of Democracy: A Defense," in *Democracy's Value,* ed. Ian Shapiro and Casiano Hacker-Cordón (Cambridge University Press, 1999), 23–55.

79. Schumpeter, *Capitalism, Socialism, and Democracy,* 269–273.

80. Unlike supporters of single-issue parties in PR systems (such as Israel's religious parties), Britain's Liberal Democrats are to the left of the Tories on most questions, and there was no intensely desired pound of flesh that they could extract for joining the government besides the referendum on the alternative vote, which they lost anyway. Their supporters were left feeling used and ignored, which—for the most part—they were. Andrew Grice, "Lib Dem Support Approaches All Time Low," *Independent,* January 5, 2011, http://www.independent.co.uk/news/uk/politics/lib-dem-support -approaches-alltime-low-2176158.html.

81. The alternative vote (AV) system (also known as instant runoff, transferable vote, ranked choice voting, or preferential voting) lets voters rank their preferences over three or more candidates for a particular seat, with the first-choice votes for the least preferred candidate being redistributed to their second and subsequent choices until some candidate wins an absolute majority. It is often said to maximize voters' chances of getting a winning candidate who comes as close as possible to reflecting their views without resorting to strategic voting. The demerit from our point of view here is that it undermines Duverger's law by giving small parties incentives to stay in the game, making single-member-district systems in effect more like PR. In the referendum held on May 5, 2011, British voters decisively rejected AV (by 68 to 32 percent with a 42.2 percent turnout). See "Vote 2011: U.K. Rejects Alternative Vote," BBC Online (May 6, 2011), http://www.bbc.co .uk/news/uk-politics-13297573.

82. John Stuart Mill, *On Liberty* (Hackett, 1978 [1859]), 50–52.

83. Andrew Rehfeld, *The Concept of Constituency: Political Representation, Democratic Legitimacy, and Institutional Design* (Cambridge University Press, 2005), 209–239.

84. Ibid., 119–124.

85. Ibid., 227.

86. Rehfeld does suggest (ibid., 237–238) that "descriptive" diversity could be achieved in Congress by reserving specified numbers of constituencies for African American or female candidates, but he never explains who would

do the specifying or how they would agree on what the appropriate quotas would be. His proposes reserving 20 percent of seats for African Americans and 40 percent for women, but he never tells how people would be persuaded that these—or any others—are the right numbers. He also ignores the fact that if the median voter were a racist, then minority candidates would have to vie against one another as Uncle Toms. If the median voter were a sexist, then female candidates would have to vie as sultry champions of traditional gender roles.

87. Former U.S. treasury secretary and Harvard president Lawrence Summers is famous for self-confidence bordering on arrogance. In 2013 it cost him his coveted appointment as chairman of the Federal Reserve. See Michael Hirsh, "The Case against Larry Summers," *National Journal,* September 12, 2013, http://www.nationaljournal.com/magazine/the-case-against-larry-summers-20130912.

88. Rehfeld, *Concept of Constituency,* 180–198, 214–215.

89. Here I ignore the corrupting imperatives to respond to organized interests and money, taken up in §4.3.2 and §4.3.3, respectively, as they are not germane to my disagreement with Rehfeld.

90. Phillip Pettit, *On the People's Terms: A Republican Theory and Model of Democracy* (Cambridge University Press, 2012).

91. "Full Transcript of the Mitt Romney Secret Video," *Mother Jones,* September 19, 2012, http://www.motherjones.com/politics/2012/09/full-transcript-mitt-romney-secret-video.

92. Hamilton, Madison, and Jay, *Federalist Papers,* 49.

93. Elkins and McKitrick, *Age of Federalism,* 257–302.

94. Ibid., 266–270.

95. "Hunger, Poverty Rates in Egypt Up Sharply over the Last Three Years—UN Report," UN News Center (May 21, 2013), http://www.un.org/apps/news/story.asp?NewsID=44961#.UjDiYMxSbx4; and "Egypt Q&A: Why Is the Country Once Again in Turmoil," CTVNews Canada (July 2, 2013), http://www.ctvnews.ca/world/egypt-q-a-why-is-the-country-once-again-in-turmoil-1.1350228.

96. See Keith Feiling, *A History of the Tory Party* (Clarendon Press, 1924); and J. R. Jones, *The First Whigs: The Politics of the Exclusion Crisis* (Oxford University Press, 1961).

97. Archibald Foorde, *His Majesty's Opposition, 1714–1830* (Clarendon Press, 1964).

98. 2015 provided a stark illustration of what is at stake. The United Kingdom Independence Party (UKIP) cried foul when their 3.9 million votes (12.6 percent of the vote) translated into a single seat in the Commons, whereas the Tories won 331 seats and an absolute majority with 11.4 million votes (36.9 percent of the vote). Under proportional representation (PR), UKIP would have had many more seats, giving the Tories a choice to combine either with the UKIP or with the Liberal Democrats and other

minor parties to cobble together a government. Labour won 9.3 million votes (30.4 percent) and the Scottish Nationalists 1.4 million (4.7 percent), meaning that they would also have depended on minor parties to form a government in the event that the Tories failed. This would have given the minor parties leverage comparable to the extreme religious parties in Israel, where, on the day before the British election, Benjamin Netanyahu was forced to form a government well to the right of Israel's median voter. See "Election 2015: What Difference Would Proportional Representation Have Made?," BBC News online (May 9, 2015), http://www.bbc.com /news/election-2015-32601281; and Jodi Rudorin, "Netanyahu Forms Government with Minutes to Spare," *New York Times,* May 6, 2015, http://www.nytimes.com/2015/05/07/world/middleeast/netanyahu-israel -coalition-government.html. The contrasting outcomes underscore the fact that PR is more representative at the electoral stage, but often not at the government formation stage. But at the end of the day what matters is the government.

99. Eugene Boyd and Michael Fauntroy, "American Federalism, 1776–2000: Significant Events," Congressional Research Service, November 2000, http://congressionalresearch.com/RL30772/document.php?study =AMERICAN+FEDERALISM+1776+TO+2000+SIGNIFICANT +EVENTS.

100. Katznelson, *Fear Itself,* 133–224.

101. Charles Black, *Structure and Relationship in Constitutional Law* (LSU Press, 1969), 67–98.

102. Katznelson, *Fear Itself,* 367–402.

103. Nolan McCarty, Keith Poole, and Howard Rosenthal, *Polarized America: The Dance of Ideology and Unequal Riches* (MIT Press, 2006), 47–50. See also Jowei Chen and Jonathan Rodden, "Unintentional Gerrymandering," *Quarterly Journal of Political Science* 8 (2013): 239–269; and Dan Baltz, "Red, Blue States Move in Opposite Directions in New Era of Single Party Control," *Washington Post,* December 28, 2013, http://www.washington post.com/politics/red-blue-states-move-in-opposite-directions-in-a-new-era -of-single-party-control/2013/12/28/9583d922-673a-11e3 -ae56-22de072140a2_story.html.

104. McCarty, Poole, and Rosenthal, *Polarized America,* 15–70. See also Morris Fiorina, Samuel Adams, and Jeremy Pope, *Culture Wars? The Myth of Polarized America* (Longman, 2010).

105. Because Democratic voters are disproportionally concentrated in cities, they tend to have more surplus or "wasted" votes per constituency than do Republicans. Chen and Rodden, "Unintentional Gerrymandering," 239–269.

106. Abby Philip, "Republicans and Tea Party Activists in 'Full Scale Civil War,' " ABC News online, December 12, 2013, http://abcnews.go.com /Politics/republicans-tea-party-activists-full-scale-civil-war/story?id =21194296.

107. Some believe that the answer to extremist domination of party primaries is to move to "open" primaries, in which voters can choose which party's primary to vote in, or nonpartisan "blanket" primaries in which the two candidates with the most votes are selected for runoffs regardless of their party affiliation. The obvious potential for strategic voting in such situations should give us pause, particularly in view of the impossibility of limiting political expenditures discussed in §4.3.3. As with ballot initiatives and other mechanisms of enhancing grassroots participation, they would easily be hijacked by the well resourced. Open or blanket primaries would be magnets for untold sums of money, much of it anonymous and from outside the constituency, with predictable effects.

108. *Gaffney v. Cummings,* 412 U.S. 735 (1973).

109. In *Davis v. Bandemer,* 478 U.S. 109 (1986), the Court held that partisan gerrymandering (when the party controlling the state legislature shapes congressional districts to its advantage) could be challenged, but this was cut back by *Vieth v. Jubelirer,* 541 U.S. 267 (2004), which refused to hold partisan gerrymandering claims justiciable.

110. Samuel Issacharoff, "Surreply: Why Elections," *Harvard Law Review* 116 (2002): 694.

111. Samuel Issacharoff, "Gerrymandering and Political Cartels," *Harvard Law Review* 116 (2002): 600.

112. Desmond King and Rogers Smith, *Still a House Divided: Race and Politics in Obama's America* (Princeton University Press, 2011), 172–173.

113. Voting Rights Act of 1982, sec. 2, title 42, chap. 20 (1A)(b), U.S. Department of Justice website, http://www.justice.gov/crt/about/vot/42usc/subch_ia.php. Congress was responding to the Court's decision in *Mobile v. Bolden* two years earlier, which declared acceptable laws with racially discriminatory effects; discriminatory intent was needed to establish a constitutional violation. *Mobile v. Bolden,* 446 U.S. 55 (1980).

114. The 1982 VRA reforms passed by 389–24 in the House and 85–8 in the Senate. Shortly thereafter, in *Rogers v. Lodge,* 458 U.S. 613 (1982), the Court struck down a Georgia at-large constituency that had never elected a black candidate. Four years later, in *Thornburgh v. Gingles,* 478 U.S. 30 (1986), the Justices spelled out criteria to identify unacceptable vote dilution in multimember districts even when there was no intent to discriminate—backtracking on *Mobile v. Bolden.* For discussion, see King and Smith, *Still a House Divided,* 177–180.

115. *Shaw v. Reno* affirmed the strict scrutiny test in 1993, using it to strike down a North Carolina plan to create a single predominantly black district that was geographically "so bizarre on its face" as to be inexplicable "on grounds other than race." 509 U.S. 630, 664 (1993). Two years later the Justices employed similar logic to strike down as a "geographic monstrosity" a new Georgia MMD created in response to the 1990 decennial census, which had been taken to imply that, with 27 percent of

the population, blacks were entitled to an additional district. *Miller v. Johnson*, 515 U.S. 900, 909 (1995). The next year they struck down a Texas plan on the grounds that because race was the predominant factor in the creation of MMDs, Texas had not carried the strict scrutiny burden of showing it to be narrowly tailored to a compelling governmental interest. *Bush v. Vera*, 517 U.S. 952 (1996). In 2003 they struck down a Georgia plan for focusing "too heavily on the ability of the minority group to elect a candidate of its choice in the [safe] districts." *Georgia v. Ashcroft*, 539 U.S. 461, 490 (2003). Three years later they held that the VRA did not require creation of an MMD to prevent minority vote dilution unless the minority population in the proposed constituency would exceed 50 percent. *Bartlett v. Strickland*, 556 U.S. 1 (2009).

116. Clarence Thomas and Antonin Scalia complain that by allowing remedies that segregate voters "into racially designated districts to ensure minority electoral success," the Court has "collaborated in what may aptly be termed the racial 'balkaniz[ation]' of the Nation." Concurrence in *Holder v. Hall*, 512 U.S. 874, 892 (1994).

117. Thus, in antidiscrimination and affirmative action law we have the anomaly that racial classifications are subject to "strict scrutiny" that requires remedies to be narrowly tailored to a compelling state interest, whereas gender-based classifications require only "intermediate scrutiny" that mandates only a rational relationship to a legitimate governmental objective. *Craig v. Boren*, 429 U.S. 190 (1976). See Rosalie Berger Levinson, "Gender-Based Affirmative Action and Reverse Gender Bias: Beyond *Gratz, Ricci*, and *Parents Involved*," *Harvard Journal of Law and Gender* 34 (2011): 8–10.

118. I sidestep the debates over the extent, if any, to which the move to create MMDs resulted from an unholy alliance between the Congressional Black Caucus and the Reagan Justice Department and the extent, if any, to which this contributed to the Republican takeover of the South. For a useful discussion of the literature and evidence, concluding that both claims have been exaggerated, see King and Smith, *Still a House Divided*, 168–191.

119. Code of Good Practices in Electoral Matters, http://www.venice.coe.int /webforms/documents/?pdf=CDL-AD%282002%29023-e (2002). Issacharoff defends such an approach in "Beyond the Discrimination Model on Voting," *Harvard Law Review* 127 (2013): 117.

120. Critics of Issacharoff, like Nathaniel Persily, defend partisan gerrymandering on the grounds that it maximizes "consumer welfare" by giving more voters a representative they prefer than in highly competitive districts—where almost half the voters vote for the losing candidate. His complaint that competitive districts "make the greatest number of voters unhappy with the election outcome" betrays the extent to which, like Rehfeld, he is trapped by the principal-agent view of representation, which

in any case fails to produce governments that are accountable to voters for the policies they adopt. Nathaniel Persily, "In Defense of Foxes Guarding Henhouses: The Case for Judicial Acquiescence to Incumbent-Protecting Gerrymanders," *Harvard Law Review* 116 (2002): 668.

121. Madison, *Federalist* #10, 48; #62, 317.
122. Susan Dunn, *Jefferson's Second Revolution: The Election Crisis of 1800 and the Triumph of Republicanism* (Houghton Mifflin, 2004), 50–58.
123. Elkins and McKitrick, *Age of Federalism,* 282–292.
124. James Madison, "Parties," *National Gazette,* January 23, 1792, http://www.constitution.org/jm/17920123_parties.txt.
125. McCarty, Poole, and Rosenthal, *Polarized America,* 7–9, 71–138.
126. Shapiro, *Real World of Democratic Theory,* 6–9.
127. See Paul Pierson, *Dismantling the Welfare State? Reagan, Thatcher, and the Politics of Retrenchment* (Cambridge University Press, 1995).
128. Contributions of current workers pay the benefits of current retirees, whose own contributions paid for the previous generation of retirees. This practically entrenches the system, as its would-be privatizers in the George W. Bush administration learned in 2005. Their plans would have required double funding for a generation: payments to existing retirees who have already paid in as well as contributions to fund the new "private" accounts—virtually an impossible political sell. As FDR recalled to Luther Gulick in 1941, "We put those pay roll contributions there so as to give the contributors a legal, moral, and political right to collect their pensions and their unemployment benefits. With those taxes in there, no damn politician can ever scrap my social security program." Research Note #23, Social Security Administration website, July 1, 2005, http://www.ssa.gov/history/Gulick.html.
129. Jeremy Seekings and Nicoli Nattrass, *Class, Race, and Inequality in South Africa* (Yale University Press, 2007), 271–299, 340–375; and Jeremy Seekings, "Poverty and Inequality in South Africa, 1994–2007," in *After Apartheid: Reinventing South Africa?,* ed. Ian Shapiro and Kahreen Tebeau (University of Virginia Press, 2011), 21–51.
130. Torben Iversen and Frances Rosenbluth, *Women, Work, and Politics* (Yale University Press, 2010), xiv, 62, 102, 105–106, 135, 140–142.
131. See Katznelson, *Fear Itself,* 372–402.
132. A federal minimum wage (FMW) was first set in 1938 at $0.25 an hour, or $4.00 in 2012 dollars. By that benchmark the highest was $10.51 in 1968. The FMW is congenitally eroded by inflation until Congress can be induced to raise it (as it last did in 2009). In 2012 the FMW stood at $7.25, the real level reached in 1960. See "Minimum Wage History," Oregon State University, http://oregonstate.edu/instruct/anth484/minwage .html; Lawrence Mishel, "Declining Value of the Federal Minimum Wage as a Major Factor Driving Inequality," Report for the Economic Policy Institute, February 21, 2013, http://www.epi.org/publication/declining

-federal-minimum-wage-inequality/; and McCarty, Poole, and Rosenthal, *Polarized America,* 166–169.

133. Internal Revenue Code, sec. 55(d), as amended by section 104(b)(1) of the American Taxpayer Relief Act of 2012 (January 2, 2013).

134. Matthew Dalton, "Permanent Estate Tax Ends Decade of Uncertainty, *Tax Notes Today,* January 3, 2013, http://www.taxanalysts.com/www/website .nsf/Web/RequestInformation?OpenDocument&trial=FTN&dn=2013-106 &title=Permanent%20Estate%20Tax%20Ends%20Decade%20of%20 Uncertainty.

135. On the ways in which capture exacerbates inequality, see "Working for the Few: Political Capture and Economic Inequality," Oxfam Briefing Paper no. 178, January 20, 2014, http://www.oxfam.org/en/policy/working-for -the-few-economic-inequality.

136. The hundreds of millions of dollars spent by financial lobbies while the bill was moving through Congress and regulations were being written swamped anything that could be put together on the other side. See Gary Rivlin, "How Wall Street Defanged Dodd-Frank," The Investigative Fund, April 30, 2013, http://www.theinvestigativefund.org/investigations /politicsandgovernment/1778/how_wall_street_defanged_dodd-frank/. One economist who worked on Dodd-Frank in the White House remarked that, knowing that it would be impossible to get any effective bill after 2010 midterms (in which the Democrats would surely lose seats in Congress and would perhaps lose control of the Senate), they had to take what they could get, even though it was less than optimal and less effective than the Financial Services Act that was would eventually be passed in the UK. Andrew Metrick interview with the author, April 18, 2013.

137. Alan S. Blinder, *After the Music Stopped: The Financial Crisis, the Response, and the Work Ahead* (Penguin, 2013), 290–319.

138. Ibid., 315–316. Even when the 867-page rule was finally adopted (more than two years late) in December 2013, it was still beset by more than 1,800 outstanding questions and what even *Forbes* magazine described as hundreds of pages "full of loopholes for the well-paid lawyers from Sullivan & Cromwell, Cleary Gottlieb, Skadden Arps and the other $1,400 an hour attorneys to interpret favorably for Goldman Sachs and J. P. Morgan Chase." Robert Lenzer, "The 867 Page Volcker Rule Is Unfathomable and a Plague on Markets," Forbes online, December 10, 2013, http://www.forbes.com/sites/robertlenzner/2013/12/10/the-credit -markets-are-broken-due-to-the-disastrous-867-page-volcker-rule/.

139. Blinder, *After the Music Stopped,* 313.

140. Kate Davidson, "CFPB Exodus: Brain Drain or Growing Pains?," Politico, June 13, 2013, http://www.politico.com/story/2013/06/consumer-financial -protection-bureau-brain-drain-92120.html.

141. Kathleen Bawn and Frances Rosenbluth, "Short versus Long Coalitions: Electoral Accountability and the Size of the Public Sector," *American*

Journal of Political Science 50, no. 2 (2006): 251–265; and Torsten Persson, Gerard Roland, and Guido Tabellini, "Electoral Rules and Government Spending in Parliamentary Democracies," *Quarterly Journal of Political Science* 20 (2007): 1–34.

142. Mayling Birney, Ian Shapiro, and Michael Graetz, "The Political Uses of Public Opinion: Lessons from the Estate Tax Repeal," in *Divide and Deal: The Politics of Distribution in Democracies,* ed. Ian Shapiro, Peter Swenson, and Daniela Donno (NYU Press, 2008), 298–340.

143. Blinder, *After the Music Stopped,* 306–309.

144. Nolan McCarty, Keith T. Poole, and Howard Rosenthal, *Political Bubbles: Financial Crises and the Failure of American Democracy* (Princeton University Press, 2013), 31–89.

145. On housing, see Gretchen Morgenson and Joshua Rosner, *Reckless Endangerment: How Outsized Ambition, Greed, and Corruption Led to Economic Armageddon* (Times Books, 2011). On the meat-packing industry, see Timothy Pachirat, *Every Twelve Seconds: Industrialized Slaughter and the Politics of Sight* (Yale University Press, 2011), 162–232.

146. George Stigler, "The Theory of Economic Regulation," *Bell Journal of Economics and Management Science* 2, no. 3 (1971): 3–21. This dovetails my discussion in §6.2 of what happens when mass preferences are not intense.

147. Willem H. Buiter, "Lessons from the North Atlantic Financial Crisis," paper presented at conference, The Role Money Markets, Federal Reserve Bank of New York, May 29–30, 2008, 35–38.

148. Stephen Labaton, "The Reckoning: Agency's '04 Rule Let Banks Pile Up New Debt," *New York Times,* October 3, 2008, http://www.nytimes.com /2008/10/03/business/03sec.html.

149. "Greenspan Concedes Error on Regulation," *New York Times,* October 23, 2008, http://www.nytimes.com/2008/10/24/business/economy /24panel.html?_r=1&scp=1&sq=october%202008%20greenspan&st=cse.

150. In return for the reserve requirement exemption, the investment banks had agreed to open their books to the SEC. But with seven inspectors responsible for tracking assets in excess of $4 trillion, working in an office that for much of the time lacked even a director, few inspections were performed. As late as March 2008 (by which time Paulson had become treasury secretary), SEC chairman and former congressman Christopher Cox was reassuring Congress that the SEC had "a good deal of comfort about the capital cushions" of the banks. Six months later Lehman Brothers was bankrupt, and soon thereafter the other major investment banks had to be rescued with multibillion-dollar bailouts to stop a systemic meltdown. Labaton, "The Reckoning."

151. *Buckley v. Valeo,* 424 U.S. 1, 48, 39 (1976).

152. *Buckley v. Valeo,* 424 U.S. 1, 59 (1976).

153. *Citizens United v. Federal Election Commission,* 558 U.S. 310 (2010).

154. *SpeechNow.org v. Federal Election Commission,* 599 F.3d 686, 689 (D.C. Cir. 2010).

155. As of July 2013, Super PACs had reported total receipts of $828,224,595 and total independent expenditures of $609,417,654 in the 2012 cycle. Open Secrets, Center for Responsive Politics, http://www.opensecrets.org /pacs/superpacs.php. See also "Koch-Backed Political Network, Designed to Shield Donors, Raised $400 Million in 2012," *Washington Post,* January 6, 2014, http://www.washingtonpost.com/politics/koch-backed -political-network-built-to-shield-donors-raised-400-million-in-2012 -elections/2014/01/05/9e7cfd9a-719b-11e3-9389-09ef9944065e_story .html.

156. *McCutcheon v. Federal Election Commission,* 134 S. Ct. 1434 (2014).

157. Stephen Engelberg and Kim Barker, "Flood of Secret Campaign Cash: Its Not All *Citizens United,*" ProPublica (August 23, 2012), http://www .propublica.org/article/flood-of-secret-campaign-cash-its-not-all-citizens -united.

158. *Davis v. Federal Election Commission,* 554 U.S. 724 (2008).

159. *Buckley v. Valeo,* 424 U.S. 1, 259, 265, 266.

160. Ibid., 288. Surprisingly, Marshall did not dissent from the rest of the *Buckley* holding.

161. Ibid., 253.

162. Ibid., 19.

163. *Red Lion Broadcasting Co. v. Federal Communications Commission,* 359 U.S. 367, 390 (1969).

164. *Citizens United v. Federal Election Commission,* 588 U.S. 310, 480 (2010).

165. *Buckley v. Valeo,* 424 U.S. 19, n. 18.

166. See *Bowman v. United Kingdom,* which held that a British law limiting independent political expenditures during election campaigns to £5 violates the European Convention on Human Rights, 1998-I Eur. Ct. H.R. at 188 (1998) and *VgT Verein gegen Tierfabriken v. Switzerland,* which suggested that any ban on political advertising in the broadcasting media might contravene Article 10 of the European Charter on Human Rights. 2001-VI Eur. Ct. H.R. 243 (2001). Generally, see Samuel Issacharoff, "The Constitutional Logic of Campaign Finance Regulation," *Pepperdine Law Review* 35 (2008–2009): 373–393.

167. Paul Hirschkorn, "The $1 Billion Presidential Campaign," CBS News, October 21, 2012, http://www.cbsnews.com/news/the-1-billion -presidential-campaign/.

168. McCarty, Poole, and Rosenthal, *Political Bubbles,* 269–273.

169. See Katznelson, *Fear Itself,* 156–194, 227–275, 367–402.

170. See Rudy Abramson, *Spanning the Century: The Life of W. Averell Harriman, 1891–1986* (William Morrow, 1992), 236–265.

171. McCarty, Poole, and Rosenthal, *Polarized America*, 8–9.

172. Douglas Rae, "Democratic Liberty and the Tyrannies of Place," in *Democracy's Edges*, ed. Ian Shapiro and Casiano Hacker-Cordón (Cambridge University Press, 1999), 165–192. See also Ian Shapiro, *The State of Democratic Theory* (Princeton University Press, 2003), 135–136.

173. Graetz and Shapiro, *Death by a Thousand Cuts*, 85–98, 312–318. There is some evidence that the "think tank gap" has narrowed somewhat in recent years, as activist think tank spending on the political left has increased. See Hans Gutbrod, "How Did Leading U.S. Think Tanks Fare in 2012? Analysis by the Numbers," thinktank.org http://onthinktanks.org/2013/09 /12/how-did-leading-us-think-tanks-fare-in-2012-analysis-by-numbers/, and Andrew Rich and Kent Weaver, "Think Tanks in the U.S. Media," *International Journal of Press/Politics* 5, no. 4 (2000): 96–97. However, there might be less to this than meets the eye. The huge growth in contributions to right-wing PACs and, now, Super PACs may indicate that conservative groups have found that they get more bang for the buck this way than by contributing to activist think tanks. See "Total Outside Spending by Election Cycle, Excluding Party Committees," Center for Responsive Politics, January 2014, http://www.opensecrets.org/outside spending/cycle_tots.php. See also "Koch-Backed Political Network."

174. Graetz and Shapiro, *Death by a Thousand Cuts*, 88–89, 242.

175. Activist think tanks routinely have liaisons on the Hill who work closely with lobbyists to avoid the appearance of lobbying themselves. Ibid., 241–243.

176. See William Bigelow, "New GOP Report Highlights White House Connection to IRS Scandal," Breitbart (June 17, 2014), http://www.breitbart.com /Big-Government/2014/06/17/New-GOP-Report-Highlights-White-House -Connection-to-IRS-Scandal; and Noam Scheiber, "Notes on a Trumped Up Scandal," *New Republic*, May 15, 2013, http://www.newrepublic.com /article/113217/irs-tea-party-scandal-conservative-political-correctness -action#.

177. Melanie Sloan and Anne Weisman, "The IRS's Latest Misstep on the 5019 (C)(4) Front," The Hill, June 27, 2013, http://thehill.com/blogs/congress -blog/economy-a-budget/308035-the-irss-latest-misstep-on-the-501c4 -front.

178. The irony is that if the Equal Rights Amendment, which provided that "equality of rights under the law shall not be denied or abridged by the United States or by any State on account of sex," had been ratified by the required three-quarters of the states after it was adopted in Congress in 1972, affirmative action for women would face strict scrutiny from the Court, when now it does not.

5. Against World Government

1. See Sebastian Mallaby, *More Money than God: Hedge Funds and the Making of a New Elite* (Penguin, 2010), 156–170, 197–219.
2. Francisco Vitoria, *Relectiones Theologicae,* lectures 5 and 6, Salamanca, 1538–1539. Bavarian State Library 1586, digitized 2009, http://books .google.co.za/books/about/Relectiones_theologicae.html?id=bwk8AAAA cAAJ&redir_esc=y; and Pope Benedict, "Address of His Holiness Pope Benedict XVI to participants in the Plenary Assembly of the Pontifical Council for Justice and Peace" (December 3, 2012), Roman Curia, http://www.vatican.va/roman_curia/pontifical_councils/justpeace/index.htm.
3. Ian Shapiro, *Democratic Justice* (Yale University Press, 1999), 38–39.
4. Alexander Wendt, "Why a World State Is Inevitable," *European Journal of International Relations* 9, no. 4 (2003): 505–508.
5. Bertrand Russell, *Towards World Government* (Thorney House, 1947), 4–5.
6. Ibid., 5.
7. See David Thatcher, "Conflicting Values in Community Policing," *Law and Society Review* 33, no. 4 (2001): 765–798; and Archon Fung, *Empowered Participation: Reinventing Urban Democracy* (Princeton University Press, 2004).
8. Max Weber, "Politics as a Vocation," in *The Vocation Lectures* (Hackett, 2004 [1919]), 38.
9. See Fernand Braudel, *The Mediterranean and the Mediterranean World in the Age of Philip II,* vol. 1 (University of California Press, 1996), 53–59; Braudel, *Civilization and Capitalism, 15th to 18th Century,* vol. 3 (Harper and Row, 1984); James Scott, *Weapons of the Weak* (Yale University Press, 1985); and Scott, *Domination and the Arts of Resistance* (Yale University Press, 1990).
10. See David Dyzenhaus, "Hobbes's Constitutional Theory," in Thomas Hobbes, *Leviathan,* ed. Ian Shapiro (Yale University Press, 2010), 453–480.
11. The high costs of transnational enforcement might partly explain why Hobbes did not see the international system as beset by the same kind of dangers as a return to the state of nature within one country would entail. For discussion, see Noel Malcolm, "Hobbes's Theory of International Relations," in *Aspects of Hobbes,* ed. Noel Malcolm (Oxford University Press, 2002), 432–456.
12. Gregory Kavka, "Nuclear Weapons and World Government," *Monist* 70, no. 3 (1978): 304.
13. Wendt, "Why a World State Is Inevitable," 509.
14. G. W. F. Hegel, *Phenomenology of Spirit* (Oxford University Press, 1976 [1807]), 115–126.

15. Mark Mazower, *Governing the World: The History of an Idea, 1815 to the Present* (Penguin, 2012), 214–342.

16. Wendt, "Why a World State Is Inevitable," 508.

17. In addition to the nineteen countries manufactured out of the former USSR and Yugoslavia between 1989 and 1992, we saw the creation of Namibia and the unifications of Yemen and Germany in 1990; independence for the Marshall Islands and Micronesia in 1991; creation of the Czech Republic, Slovakia, and Eritrea in 1993; Palau in 1994; East Timor in 2002; Montenegro and Serbia in 2006; Kosovo in 2008; and South Sudan in 2011. See Matt Rosenberg, "New Countries in the World," http://geography.about .com/cs/countries/a/newcountries.htm.

18. In 1945 there were some 75 countries in the world, including occupied states. http://en.wikipedia.org/wiki/List_of_sovereign_states_in_1945. In 2014 there were 196, of which 193 were members of the United Nations. http://geography.about.com/cs/countries/a/numbercountries.htm.

19. Tony Judt, *Postwar* (Penguin, 2005), 731–745.

20. See "Europe Goes to the Polls" and "Elected, but Strangely Unaccountable," *Economist,* May 17–23, 2014, 11, 21–22; and Peter Spiegel, "Anti-EU Parties Celebrate Election Success," *Financial Times,* May 26, 2014, http://www.ft.com/intl/cms/s/2/783e39b4-e4af-11e3-9b2b-00144feabdc0 .html#slide0.

21. For a powerful critique of Scheuerman's interpretations of the mid-twentieth-century realists, see the review by Georg Sorensen in *Perspectives on Politics* 11, no. 3 (September 2013): 895–897.

22. William Scheuerman, *The Realist Case for Global Reform* (Polity Press, 2011), 3–14, 150–153.

23. Ibid., 155.

24. Ibid., ix; and William Scheuerman, "Globalization, Constitutionalism, and Sovereignty," *Global Constitutionalism* 3, no. 1 (2014): 116.

25. Scheuerman, *Realist Case,* 154, 162. Likewise, in response to the worry that a world state might distribute the negative externalities of globalization to "the poor and working classes," he insists there "is simply no sound basis for excluding the long-term prospect of a less divided global economy and thereby a thicker supranational society" (167).

26. Scheuerman, *Realist Case,* 156.

27. Ibid., 164.

28. Cohen, *Globalization and Sovereignty: Rethinking Legality, Legitimacy, and Constitutionalism* (Cambridge University Press, 2012), 312–313.

29. Ibid., 173–178, 266–319. I take up aspects of these issues in §6.3.

30. Perry Anderson, *Lineages of the Absolutist State* (Schocken Books, 1979).

31. David Held, *Democracy and the Global Order: From the Modern State to Cosmopolitan Governance* (Polity Press, 1995). This does not mean, of course, that centralized authoritarian states necessarily democratize as the modernization theorists believed. See Seymour Lipset, "Some Social

Requisites of Democracy: Economic Development and Political Legitimacy," *American Political Science Review* 53, no. 1 (1959): 69–105; and David Apter, *The Politics of Modernization* (University of Chicago Press, 1967). Just as authoritarian regimes can survive in national states, the same problem might arise with a world state.

32. David Held, "The Transformation of Political Community: Rethinking Democracy in the Context of Globalization," in *Democracy's Edges,* ed. Ian Shapiro and Casiano Hacker-Cordón (Cambridge University Press, 1999), 84–111.

33. Juan Linz and Alfred Stepan, *The Breakdown of Democratic Regimes: Latin America* (Johns Hopkins University Press, 1978).

34. Max Edling, *A Revolution in Favor of Government: Origins of the U.S. Constitution and the Makings of the American State* (Oxford University Press, 2008).

35. See Carles Boix, *Democracy and Redistribution* (Cambridge University Press, 2003), 112–118.

36. On the role of war, see John Ferejohn and Frances Rosenbluth, *Forged through Fire: Military Conflict and the Democratic Bargain* (Norton Liveright, 2016). On external imposition, see Ian Shapiro, *Containment: Rebuilding a Strategy against Global Terror* (Princeton University Press, 2007), 102–118.

37. Robert Dahl, "Can International Organizations Be Democratic? A Skeptic's View," in Shapiro and Hacker-Cordón, *Democracy's Edges,* 19–36.

38. Kant therefore favored working for well-governed national states that would participate in a global federation. See Immanuel Kant, "Idea for a Universal History with a Cosmopolitan Purpose" and "Perpetual Peace: A Philosophical Sketch," in *Political Writings*, trans. H. B. Nisbet, ed. Hans Reiss, 2nd ed. (Cambridge University Press, 1991), 41–53, 93–130.

39. The Lisbon Treaty, which came into force in 2009, grants the European Parliament power over the entire EU budget, makes its legislative powers coequal to the Council's in most areas, and links the appointment of the European president to the outcome of European elections. See "The European Union," Europa: A Constitution for Europe, http://europa.eu/scadplus/constitution/parliament_en.htm.

40. The phrase *democratic deficit* seems originally to have been coined by the Young European Federalists in their 1977 manifesto to call attention to the failures of European national governments. See Peter Matjašič, "Democratic Deficit: A Federalist Perspective," The New Federalist (October 17, 2010), http://www.thenewfederalist.eu/Democratic-deficit-a-federalist-perspective. It was first deployed, as it conventionally is today, to criticize the European Economic Community (forerunner of the European Union) by David Marquand in 1979. See Marquand, *Parliament for Europe* (Jonathan Cape, 1979), 64.

41. Mazower, *Governing the World,* 421.
42. I define basic interests by reference to the wherewithal to survive and thrive in the economy that can reasonably be expected to operate over the course of one's lifetime and in the polity governed as a democracy. See §1.5 and Shapiro, *Democratic Justice,* 85–90.
43. For additional discussion, illustrated by the flawed deliberative sessions of the reform of Oregon's health care system in the early 1990s, see Ian Shapiro, *The State of Democratic Theory* (Princeton University Press, 2003), 23–28.
44. For additional discussion, see Shapiro, *Democratic Justice,* 219–229.
45. In 1985, a U.S. District Court in the Southern District of New York declined to hear the case, invoking the common law doctrine of *Forum non conveniens* ("forum not agreeing") to support the conclusion that the plaintiffs could pursue their case more conveniently in India, an unfortunate decision in view of the eventual settlement with the Indian government, which had intervened to declare itself the representative of all the plaintiffs, of a mere $470 million. The decision to refer the case to the Indian courts attracted trenchant criticism and might not occur in similar circumstances today. See Jamie Cassals, *The Uncertain Promise of Law: Lessons from Bhopal* (University of Toronto Press, 1993).
46. See *Sosa v. Alvarez-Machain,* 542 U.S. 692 (2004).
47. See *Kiobel v. Royal Dutch Petroleum Company,* 133 S.Ct. 1659 (2013); and Gregory Fox and Yunjoo Goze, "International Human Rights Litigation after *Kiobel,*" *Michigan Bar Journal* (November 2013), https://www.michbar .org/journal/pdf/pdf4article2288.pdf.
48. The Court had been expected to rule on this question in *Kiobel,* a case in which Nigerian citizens alleged that Royal Dutch/Shell had aided and abetted the Nigerian government's brutal suppression of peaceful opposition to oil development in the Ogoni Niger River Delta. But the Justices never reached the issue, holding that the matter at hand did not "touch and concern the territory" of the United States. See Keith Gibson, "Did the Supreme Court's Kiobel Decision Revive Corporate ATS Cases in the Second Circuit?," Product Liability Monitor (April 30, 2014), http://product -liability.weil.com/alien-tort-statute/did-the-supreme-courts-kiobel-decision -revive-corporate-ats-cases-in-the-second-circuit/.
49. The Foreign Corrupt Practices Act, adopted by Congress in 1977, provides for prosecution of individuals and corporations that are registered in the United States or are required to file U.S. reports under the Securities and Exchange Act. It governs payments, which can be nonmonetary, not only to foreign officials, candidates, and parties, but to any other recipient if part of the bribe is ultimately attributable to a foreign official, candidate, or intermediaries. The OECD Convention on Combatting Foreign Bribery, which creates similar avenues for prosecution throughout the OECD, came into force in 1999. For an overview of enforcement of these laws, see Trace

Global Enforcement Report 2012, http://www.traceinternational.org/data
/public/GER_2012_Final-147966-1.pdf.

50. See Thomas Pogge, *Realizing Rawls* (Cornell University Press, 1989); and
Charles Beitz, *Political Theory and International Relations* (Princeton
University Press, 1999).

51. Michael Doyle, *The Question of Intervention: John Stuart Mill and the
Responsibility to Protect* (Yale University Press, 2015), 32.

52. Mazower, *Governing the World,* 191–214, 273–304, 378–405. I take up
these developments in §6.3.

53. The extent of this atrophy can be overstated. See Geoffrey Garrett, *Partisan
Politics in the Global Economy* (Cambridge University Press, 1998).

54. See Shelly Kagan, *The Limits of Morality* (Oxford University Press, 1991);
and Peter Singer, *One World: The Ethics of Globalization* (Yale University
Press, 2004).

55. As Casiano Hacker-Cordón and I note elsewhere: "A chicken-and-egg problem
thus lurks at democracy's core. Questions relating to boundaries and membership seem in an important sense prior to democratic decision-making, yet
paradoxically they cry out for democratic resolution." *Democracy's Edges,* 1.

56. For a review of the literature, see Ian Shapiro, *The State of Democratic
Theory* (Princeton University Press, 2003), 104–145.

57. James Galbraith "Inequality and Economic and Political Change," UTIP
Working Paper no. 51 (September 2008), http://utip.gov.utexas.edu/papers
/Utip_51.pdf.

58. Philippe Van Parijs does maintain that in order to sustain an equal right
to get married, if marriageable men are relatively scarce, every woman
should be entitled to an equal tradable share in the pool of eligible single
men and have to bid for whole partnership rights, in effect generating
compensation from married women to those who cannot find a husband.
Van Parijs, *Real Freedom for All* (Clarendon Press, 1995), 127–130. That
only goes to show that there is no proposition that some political philosopher somewhere will not defend. What would Van Parijs say to
polygamists?

59. Steven Pinker, *The Better Angels of Our Nature: Why Violence Has
Declined* (Penguin, 2011), 75–78, 235–244.

60. Benedict Anderson, *Imagined Communities,* 2nd ed. (Verso, 2006), 145–158.

61. Seymour Drescher, *Econocide: British Slavery in the Era of Abolition,* 2nd
ed. (University of North Carolina Press, 2010), 113–186.

62. Dissenting Christians who had separated from the Church of England
provided much of the leadership and grassroots support for the abolitionist
cause. David Brion Davis, *Slavery and Human Progress* (Oxford University
Press, 1986), 139.

63. Steven Deyle, *Carry Me Back: The Domestic Slave Trade in American Life*
(Oxford University Press, 2005), 14–39. The Constitution protected the
slave trade until 1808.

64. Chaim Kaufmann and Robert Pape, "Explaining Costly International Moral Action: Britain's Sixty-Year Campaign against the Atlantic Slave Trade," *International Organization* 53, no. 4 (1999): 631–668.

65. The exceptions were Ceylon, St. Helena, and some territories possessed by the British East India Company.

66. For the financial conversion rate, see Sanchez Manning, "Britain's Colonial Shame: Slave Owners Given Huge Payouts after Abolition," *Independent*, February 24, 2013, http://www.independent.co.uk/news/uk/home-news /britains-colonial-shame-slaveowners-given-huge-payouts-after-abolition -8508358.html.

67. See Kaufmann and Pape, "Explaining Costly International Moral Action," 650–653.

68. Roger Anstey, "Religion and British Slave Emancipation," in *The Abolition of the Atlantic Slave Trade: Origins and Effects in Europe, Africa and the Americas*, ed. David Eltis and James Wavlin (University of Wisconsin Press, 1981), 38–41; Kaufmann and Pape, "Explaining Costly International Moral Action," 650–653.

69. Kaufman and Pape, "Explaining Costly International Moral Action," 661. This was five years before the Tories split over free trade in the fight over the repeal of the Corn Laws. Cheryl Schonhardt-Bailey, *From the Corn Laws to Free Trade* (MIT Press, 2006), 19–33, 191–292.

70. Other campaigns for social change support this conjecture. In the American battle against slavery, to corral the votes needed to secure House passage of the Thirteenth Amendment in January 1865, radicals like Thaddeus Stevens had to repudiate any defense of racial equality. See the memorable portrayal by Tommy Lee Jones in the film *Lincoln*. https://www.youtube.com/watch ?v=QTwKOCILJl0. For a less dramatic, if historically more accurate, account, see Doris Kearns Goodwin, *Team of Rivals: The Political Genius of Abraham Lincoln* (Simon and Schuster, 2005), 684–696. Social Security and the other basic New Deal economic protections could also be secured only by avoiding any challenge to Jim Crow, as we saw in §3.2. The battle for women's suffrage in the United States was won by explicit dissociation from the race question, even though this caused soul searching by some feminists. See Sidney Bland, "New Life in an Old Movement: Alice Paul and the Great Suffrage Parade of 1913 in Washington, D.C.," *Records of the Columbia Historical Society* 71/72 (1971–1972): 657–678; Jen McDaneld, "White Suffragist Dis / Entitlement: The Revolution and the Rhetoric of Racism," *Legacy* 30, no. 2 (2013): 243–264; Garth Pauley, "W. E. B. Du Bois on Woman Suffrage: A Critical Analysis of His Crisis Writings," *Journal of Black Studies* 30, no. 3 (2000): 383–410; and Suzanne Marilley "Frances Willard and the Feminism of Fear," *Feminist Studies* 19, no. 1 (1993): 123–146. The civil rights revolution, by contrast, virtually ignored women. Indeed, one of the few mentions of sex discrimination in the Civil Rights Act was inserted into Title VII at the last minute by Congressman

Howard Smith of Virginia, a vigorous foe of integration who hoped to turn it into a wedge issue to derail the legislation. It provoked jokes on the Senate floor and was not included in Johnson's implementing legislation creating the EEOC. See James Patterson, *The Eve of Destruction* (Basic Books, 2012), 209–212.

71. Utopian ventures can become more realistic because of the inadvertent actions of their opponents. In 1896 a near-unanimous U.S. Supreme Court handed down *Plessy v. Ferguson,* endorsing "separate but equal," a decision that is often vilified as a fig leaf that shielded Southern segregation. 163 U.S. 537. But by affirming the principle of racial equality, *Plessy* helped shape the future terrain of American racial politics, creating the possibility, after decades of discriminatory segregation, of *Brown*'s insistence that separate educational facilities "are inherently unequal." 347 U.S. 495. Even though *Plessy* was meant to blunt demands for racial equality, it thus became a way station on the road to *Brown*.

72. "Petitioning and Lobbying Parliament," The Abolition Project, http:// abolition.e2bn.org/campaign_16.html. The 1801 Census would put England's population at 8.3 million. Office of Population Censuses and Surveys (OPCS) (1993), 1991 Census: Historical Tables, Great Britain. http://web.archive.org/web/20080630070408/http://www.chronology.ndo .co.uk/1800–1849.htm. The 1832 Reform Act would increase the electorate from 400,000 to about 650,000. John A. Phillips and Charles Wetherell, "The Great Reform Act of 1832 and the Political Modernization of England," *American Historical Review* 100, no. 2 (1995): 413–414.

73. David Goldfield, *America Aflame: How the Civil War Created a Nation* (Bloomsbury Press, 2011), 17–41; and David Brion Davis, *The Problem of Slavery in the Age of Revolution, 1770–1823* (Cornell University Press, 1975), 523–556.

74. Dorina Outram, *The Enlightenment,* 2nd ed. (Cambridge University Press, 2005), 60–76.

75. Goldfield, *America Aflame,* 483–505.

76. David Brion Davis, *Inhuman Bondage: The Rise and Fall of New World Slavery* (Oxford University Press, 2006), 331.

77. Market fundamentalists advert reflexively to the race to the bottom, but it is worth noting that the evidence is debatable. See Drusilla Brown, Alan Dearorff, and Robert Stern, "Labor Standards and Human Rights: Implications for International Trade and Investment," University of Michigan IPC Working Paper no. 119 (August 2011), 23–39, http://ipc.umich.edu /working-papers/pdfs/ipc-119-brown-deardorff-stern-labor-standards -human-rights-international-trade-investment.pdf; and John Schmitt, "Why Does the Minimum Wage Have No Discernible Effect on Employment?," Center for Economic and Policy Research (February 2013), http://www.cepr .net/documents/publications/min-wage-2013–02.pdf.

78. Generally, see Schmitt, "Why Does the Minimum Wage Have No Discernible Effect?"

79. The Earned Income Tax Credit is a refundable tax credit, first introduced in the Ford administration, that in effect subsidizes low wages. See Michael Graetz and Jerry Mashaw, *True Security: Rethinking American Social Insurance* (Yale University Press, 1999), 49–55, 287–296; and Christopher Howard, *The Hidden Welfare State: Tax Expenditures and Social Policy in the United States* (Princeton University Press, 1997), 14–15, 139–160, 184–188.

80. See my discussion of failures to index minimum wage legislation in the United States in §4.3.2.

81. Christine Owens, "The Fight for a Global Minimum Wage," Reuters (May 15, 2014), http://blogs.reuters.com/great-debate/2014/05/15/the-fight-for-a-global-minimum-wage/.

82. Thomas Palley, "A Global Minimum Wage System," *Financial Times,* July 18, 2011.

83. In this it parallels the collective actions that firms face with respect to the provision of employment benefits, such as health insurance, that could instead be provided through taxpayer-funded national health insurance. See Shapiro, *Democratic Justice,* 182–195.

84. Peter Swenson, *Capitalists against Markets: The Making of Labor Markets and Welfare States in the United States and Sweden* (Oxford University Press, 2002), 197–201.

85. Ira Katznelson, *Fear Itself: The New Deal and the Origins of Our Time* (W. W. Norton, 2013), 245–267.

86. Swenson, *Capitalists against Markets,* 200–201.

87. Jason Hickel, "Its Time for a Global Minimum Wage," London School of Economics (June 14, 2013), http://blogs.lse.ac.uk/indiaatlse/2013/06/14/its-time-for-a-global-minimum-wage/.

88. *Minimum Wages and Collective Bargaining: Global Wage Report 2008/09,* International Labour Organization, Geneva (November 2008), 35.

89. On a visit to the Nike plant outside Ho Chi Minh City in March 2011, a floor manager explained to me why Nike had been relocating plants from China to Vietnam: "Vietnamese workers argue less and work harder than Chinese workers. And if the Vietnamese start to argue, we go to Cambodia."

90. Nicoli Nattrass and Jeremy Seekings, "Job Destruction in Newcastle: Minimum Wage Setting and Low-Wage Employment in the South African Clothing Industry," *Transformation,* no. 84 (2014): 1–30.

91. Indeed, if the 50 cents were passed on to consumers, they would scarcely notice, given the enormous markups in the textile industry. Muhammuad Yunus, "After the Savar Tragedy, Time for a Global Minimum Wage," *Guardian,* May 12, 2013, http://www.theguardian.com/commentisfree/2013/may/12/savar-bangladesh-international-minimum-wage.

92. Thomas Palley, *From Financial Crisis to Stagnation: The Destruction of Shared Prosperity and the Role of Economics* (Cambridge University Press, 2012), 174–175.

93. Hickel, "Its Time for a Global Minimum Wage."

94. See Leslie Deak, "Customary International Labor Laws and Their Application in Hungary, Poland, and the Czech Republic," *Tulsa Journal of Comparative and International Law* 2, no. 1 (1994): 1–44, http:// digitalcommons.law.utulsa.edu/cgi/viewcontent.cgi?article=1123 &context=tjcil; and Leslie Carrington, "Corporate Liability for Violation of Labor Rights under the Alien Tort Claims Act," *Iowa Law Review* (2009): 1402–1413, http://www.uiowa.edu/~ilr/issues/ILR_94-4 _Carrington.pdf.

95. Rex Zachofsky, "An International Minimum Wage: Can a Historical Solution Solve a Modern Day Problem?" *Journal of International Business and Law* 3, no. 1 (2004): 213–215, http://scholarlycommons.law.hofstra .edu/jibl/vol3/iss1/11/. The $435 figure was intended to be a figure that most developing countries could meet without drastic cost to their national economies, though, as Zachofsky notes, India and China were among those that denounced it as too high.

96. "Origins and History," International Labour Organization, http://www.ilo .org/global/about-the-ilo/history/lang—en/index.htm.

97. Robert Rogowsky and Eric Cbyn, "U.S. Trade Law and FTAs: A Survey of Labor Requirements," *Journal of International Commerce and Economics,* web version (July 2007), http://www.ilocarib.org.tt/trade/documents/other _agreements/trade_law_ftas.pdf.

98. Harlan Mandel, "In Pursuit of the Missing Link: International Worker Rights and International Trade?," *Columbia Journal of Transnational Law* 27 (1989): 443–482.

99. Mark Barenberg, "Federalism and American Labor Law: Toward a Critical Mapping of the 'Social Dumping' Question," in *Harmonization of Legislation in Federal Systems,* ed. Ingolf Pernice (Nomos Verlagsgesellschaft, 1996), 106.

100. Ibid., 106–107.

101. See Barenberg, "Federalism and American Labor Law," 107.

102. Mary Jane Bolle, "Overview of Enforcement Issues in Free Trade Agreements," Congressional Research Service Report (January 29, 2014), http://fas.org/sgp/crs/misc/RS22823.pdf.

103. Rogowsky and Cbyn, "U.S. Trade Law and FTAs," 4.

104. Timothy Wedding, "The Evolution and Enforcement of Labor Provisions in U.S. Free Trade Agreements," http://apps.americanbar.org/labor /intlcomm/mw/papers/2010/pdf/wedding.pdf. See also Rogowsky and Cbyn, "U.S. Trade Law and FTAs," 8–22.

105. See International Convention for a Global Minimum Wage, http://www .international-convention-for-minimum-wage.org/.

106. Ann Harrison and Jason Scorse, "Moving Up or Moving Out? Anti-Sweatshop Activists and Labor Market Outcomes," NBER Working Paper no. 10492 (May 2004), http://www.nber.org/papers/w10492.

107. The Sullivan Principles required "(1) nonsegregation of the races in all . . . facilities; (2) equal and fair employment practices for all employees; (3) equal pay for . . . equal or comparable work for the same period of time; (4) . . . development of training programs that will prepare, in substantial numbers, blacks and other nonwhites for supervisory, administrative, clerical, and technical jobs; (5) increasing the number of blacks and other nonwhites in management and supervisory positions; (6) improving the quality of life for blacks and other nonwhites outside the work environment in . . . housing, transportation, school, recreation, and health facilities; and (7) working to eliminate laws and customs that impede social, economic, and political justice" (added in 1984). The Sullivan Principles, 1977, http://www.marshall.edu/revleonsullivan/principles.htm.

108. Philip H. Rudolph, "The Global Sullivan Principles of Corporate Social Responsibility," in Ramon Mullerat, *Corporate Social Responsibility: Corporate Governance in the Twenty-First Century* (Kluwer Law International, 2005), 221–224.

109. See Sharon Beder, "Nike's Greenwashing Sweatshop Labor," Organic Consumer's Association (April 2002), http://www.organicconsumers.org/clothes/nikesweatshop.cfm.

110. John Cushman, "Nike Pledges to End Child Labor and Apply U.S. Standards Abroad," *New York Times,* May 13, 1998, http://www.nytimes.com/1998/05/13/business/international-business-nike-pledges-to-end-child-labor-and-apply-us-rules-abroad.html.

111. Max Nisen, "How Nike Solved Its Sweatshop Problem," Business Insider (May 9, 2013), http://www.businessinsider.com/how-nike-solved-its-sweatshop-problem-2013–5.

112. "Online Extra: Nike's New Game Plan for Sweatshops," Bloomberg Business Magazine (September 19, 2004), http://www.businessweek.com/stories/2004-09-19/online-extra-nikes-new-game-plan-for-sweatshops.

113. Ibid.

6. Resisting Domination across Borders

1. Abraham Lincoln, *Speeches and Writings, 1859–1865* (Library of America, 1989), 217–218, 255–257.

2. Ian Shapiro, "On Non-domination," *University of Toronto Law Journal* 62 (2012): 304–306.

3. Ian Shapiro and Joseph Lampert, eds., *Charter of the United Nations together with Scholarly Commentaries and Essential Historical Documents* (Yale University Press, 2014), 15.

4. The Independent International Commission on Kosovo was an ad hoc commission appointed by the Swedish government on the initiative of Prime Minister Göran Persson in 1999. For its findings, see their *Kosovo Report* (Oxford University Press, 2001), 3–4.

5. See Article 4(h) of the Constitutive Act of the African Union, http://www.au .int/en/sites/default/files/ConstitutiveAct_EN.pdf; and 2005 UN General Assembly Agenda items 46 and 120 (October 24, 2005), http://www.un.org /womenwatch/ods/A-RES-60–1-E.pdf.

6. Ian Shapiro, *Containment: Rebuilding a Strategy against Global Terror* (Princeton University Press, 2007).

7. [George Kennan], "The Sources of Soviet Conduct," *Foreign Affairs,* July 1947, http://www.foreignaffairs.com/articles/23331/x/the-sources-of-soviet -conduct.

8. Advocates of rollback wanted to confront communism across the globe and push the Soviets out of Eastern Europe at the start of the Cold War. For discussion, see Shapiro, *Containment,* 8–9, 34–35.

9. Albert Eisele, "At 98, Veteran Diplomat Declares Congress Must Take Lead on War with Iraq," *The Hill,* September 25, 2002, https://www.mtholyoke .edu/acad/intrel/bush/kennan.htm.

10. "I would say to the House, as I said to those who have joined this Government: I have nothing to offer but blood, toil, tears and sweat." Winston Churchill's first speech to the House of Commons as prime minister, May 13, 1940, http://hansard.millbanksystems.com/commons/1940/may/13 /his-majestys-government-1.

11. Gallup polls show that Bush's approval rating fell from 89 percent in March 1991 to 33 percent in October 1992, a month before the election he lost to Bill Clinton. See http://www.gallup.com/poll/124922/presidential -approval-center.aspx.

12. George F. Kennan, "Comments on the National Security Problem," in *Measures Short of War: Lectures at the National War College, 1946–1947,* ed. Giles Harlow and George Maerz (National Defense University Press, 1991), 166–167.

13. [Kennan], "Sources of Soviet Conduct."

14. Even this judgment had to be calibrated by informed analysis of particular cases. For instance, Kennan thought that the Carter administration overreacted to the Soviet invasion of Afghanistan, which he saw as a hopeless last-ditch effort to save the collapsing Marxist regime there. He thought it posed no danger to American interests and that the Soviets would soon be seeking a way out. See John Gaddis, *George F. Kennan: An American Life* (Penguin, 2011), 642–644. Kennan turned out to be right, though it took longer than he expected. The Soviets did not finally give up until their entire world began collapsing in 1989.

15. George F. Kennan, "Considerations Affecting the Conclusion of a North Atlantic Security Pact," in *Foreign Relations of the United States,*

vol. 3, U.S. Department of State (U.S. Government Printing Office, 1948), 153–153. See also Kennan, *Memoirs, 1925–1950* (Pantheon, 1967), 409–412.

16. See John Herz, *Political Realism and Political Idealism: A Study in Theories and Realities* (University of California Press, 1951).

17. See James Blight and Janet Lang, *The Fog of War: Lessons from the Life of Robert S. McNamara* (Rowman and Littlefield, 2005), 59; and James Blight, Bruce Allyn, and David Welch, *Cuba on the Brink: Castro, the Missile Crisis, and the Soviet Collapse* (Rowman and Littlefield, 2002), 53–318.

18. See Dominic Johnson and Dominic Tierny, *Failing to Win: Perceptions of Success and Failure in International Politics* (Harvard University Press, 2006), 94–126. In one respect it was not adequately face-saving for Khrushchev. Part of the reason Khrushchev was ousted by the Soviet leadership two years later was their perception that he had bungled the missile crisis, embarrassing them. See William Taubman, *Khrushchev: The Man and His Era* (W. W. Norton, 2004), 579.

19. On the projections and war costs, see Shapiro, *Containment*, 48–49.

20. Ben Hubbard and Eric Schmidt, "Military Skill and Terrorist Technique Fuel Success of ISIS," *New York Times*, August 28, 2014, http://www .nytimes.com/2014/08/28/world/middleeast/army-know-how-seen-as-factor -in-isis-successes.html.

21. Michael Gordon et al., "Forensic Details in U.N. Report Point to Assad's Use of Gas," *New York Times*, September 16, 2013, http://www.nytimes .com/2013/09/17/world/europe/syria-united-nations.html?pagewanted=all &module=Search&mabReward=relbias%3Ar. Obama was further humiliated by Putin's triumphant *New York Times* editorial after the United States began talks to implement a Russian-Syrian agreement to monitor Syria's chemical weapons stockpile. See Vladimir Putin, "A Plea for Caution from Russia," *New York Times*, September 11, 2013, http://www.nytimes.com /2013/09/12/opinion/putin-plea-for-caution-from-russia-on-syria.html ?pagewanted=all&_r=0.

22. Zach Beauchamp, "Obama's Top General Says We Might Need 'Boots on the Ground' in Iraq After All," Vox, September 16, 2014, http://www.vox .com/2014/9/16/6226401/iraq-ground-troops-obama; and Ed Morrissey, "No 'Hope of Success' against ISIS without Boots on the Ground," Hot Air, September 17, 2014, http://hotair.com/archives/2014/09/17/gates-no -hope-of-success-against-isis-without-boots-on-the-ground/comment -page-1/.

23. Barack Obama, speech to the United Nations General Assembly, September 24, 2014, http://www.washingtonpost.com/politics/full-text-of -president-obamas-2014-address-to-the-united-nations-general-assembly /2014/09/24/88889e46-43f4-11e4-b437-1a7368204804_story.html.

24. The phrase originated with a U.S. Army major's explanation to journalist Peter Arnett during the Vietnam War of why commanders bombed and shelled a town to rout the Vietcong regardless of civilian casualties: "It became necessary to destroy the town to save it." See "Major Describes Move," *New York Times,* February 8, 1968, 14.

25. Kennan, "Comments on the National Security Problem," 163, 165.

26. [Kennan], "Sources of Soviet Conduct."

27. As he elaborated in his memoirs: "Intensive rearmament represented an uneconomical and regrettable diversion of their [American and West European leaders] effort—a diversion that not only threatened to proceed at the cost of economic recovery but also encouraged the impression that war was inevitable and thus distracted attention from the most important tasks." Kennan, *Memoirs,* 410.

28. [Kennan], "Sources of Soviet Conduct."

29. Ibid.

30. Reagan was paraphrasing John Winthrop's words spoken in 1630: "We will be as a city upon a hill. The eyes of all people are upon us, so that if we deal falsely with our God in this work we have undertaken and so cause Him to withdraw His present help from us, we shall be made a story and a byword throughout the world." There is some irony to this, since Winthrop was not famous for his religious tolerance and he despised democracy as "the meanest and worst of all forms of government" and believed that it contravened the Fifth Commandment. See "'A Shining City upon a Hill': Troubling Information about a Famous Quote," World Future Fund, http://www.worldfuturefund.org/wffmaster/reading/religion/john%20 winthrop.htm.

31. Bush, decked out as a U.S. fighter pilot, delivered the speech on the USS *Lincoln,* flanked by an enormous "Mission Accomplished" banner. See George W. Bush, "Address Announcing the End of Major Combat Operations in Iraq," http://www.johnstonsarchive.net/terrorism/bushiraq4.html.

32. Rove elaborated: "And while you're studying that reality—judiciously, as you will—we'll act again, creating other new realities, which you can study too, and that's how things will sort out. We're history's actors . . . and you, all of you, will be left to just study what we do." Quoted in Ron Suskind, "Faith, Certainty, and the Presidency of George W. Bush," *New York Times Magazine,* October 17, 2004, http://www.nytimes.com/2004/10/17/magazine /17BUSH.html?ex=1255665600&en=890a96189e162076&ei=5090 &partner=rssuserland&_r=0.

33. Powell laid his credibility on the line by deploying satellite images of supposed WMD programs and intelligence to establish that Iraq was developing WMD programs "in order to project power, to threaten, and to deliver chemical, biological and, if we let him, nuclear warheads." See Shapiro, *Containment,* 21–22.

34. Charles Hanley, "AP Enterprise: Former Iraqi Detainees Tell of Riots, Punishment in the Sun, Good Americans and Pitiless Ones," Associated Press, November 1, 2003, http://legacy.utsandiego.com/news/world/iraq /20031101-0936-iraq-thecamps.html; and Seymour Hersh, "Torture at Abu Ghraib," *New Yorker* (May 10, 2004), http://www.newyorker.com /magazine/2004/05/10/torture-at-abu-ghraib.

35. Marc Lynch, "Anti-Americanisms in the Arab World," in *Anti-Americanisms in World Politics,* ed. Peter Katzenstein and Robert Keohane (Cornell University Press, 2007), 196–225.

36. Duraid Adnan and Tim Arango, "Iraq Shuts Down Abu Ghraib Prison, Citing Security Concerns," *New York Times,* April 15, 2014, http://www .nytimes.com/2014/04/16/world/middleeast/iraq-says-abu-ghraib-prison-is -closed.html?_r=0.

37. George W. Bush might occupy the White House, said Obama, "but for the last six years the position of leader of the free world has remained open . . . We're not a country that runs prisons which lock people away without ever telling them why they're there or what they're charged with." Senator Barack Obama, "Turn the Page," speech to the California Democratic Convention, April 28, 2007, http://obamaspeeches.com/120-Obama-Turn -The-Page-Speech-California-Deomcratic-Convention.htm.

38. "Executive Order—Review and Dispose of Individuals Detained at the Guantánamo Bay Naval Base and Closure of Detention Facilities," White House, January 22, 2009, http://www.whitehouse.gov/the_press_office /Closure_Of_Guantanamo_Detention_Facilities.

39. See Charlie Savage, "Judge Orders Disclosure of Guantánamo Videos," *New York Times,* October 3, 2014, http://www.nytimes.com/2014/10/04/us /judge-orders-disclosure-of-guantanamo-videos.html?_r=0, which describes the legal battle over the videos of force-feeding in the prison.

40. Marina Koren, "Five Years after Obama Promised to Shut It Down, Guantánamo Remains Open," *National Journal,* January 22, 2014, http://www.nationaljournal.com/defense/five-years-after-obama-vowed-to -shut-it-down-guantanamo-bay-remains-open-20140122. On force-feeding, although the U.S. courts have said they lack the authority to end it, federal district court judge Gladys Kessler refused Obama administration requests to keep hearings on the matter secret and urged the administration to end the "painful, humiliating, and degrading" practice. Anne Marimow, "Obama Can Halt 'Degrading' Force Feeding at Guantánamo, Judge Says," *Washington Post,* July 8, 2013, http://www.washingtonpost.com/world /national-security/obama-can-halt-degrading-force-feeding-at-guantanamo -federal-judge-says/2013/07/08/2102041c-e80e-11e2-aa9f-c03a72e2d342 _story.html; and Charlie Savage, "Guantánamo Inmate's Case Reignites Fight over Detentions," *New York Times,* May 23, 2014, http://www .nytimes.com/2014/05/24/us/judge-allows-military-to-force-feed -guantanamo-detainee.html.

41. Glen Greenwald, "Obama's Justice Department Grants Final Immunity to Bush's CIA Torturers," *Guardian*, August 31, 2012, http://www.theguardian.com/commentisfree/2012/aug/31/obama-justice-department-immunity-bush-cia-torturer.

42. Vice President Cheney's repeated assertions that waterboarding had yielded actionable intelligence were contradicted by the interrogators themselves, former CIA directors Leon Panetta and Mike Hayden, and Deputy National Security Director John Brennan, as well as numerous Republican and Democratic senators who had access to classified intelligence. See "Torture Did Not Reveal Bin Laden's Whereabouts," Human Rights First Fact Sheet, http://www.humanrightsfirst.org/wp-content/uploads/pdf/Torture-Did-Not-Reveal-Bin-Laden-Whereabouts.pdf. President Bush's contention that waterboarding had produced actionable intelligence was also refuted by Prime Minister David Cameron. Hélène Mulholland, "David Cameron Challenges George Bush's Claim about Waterboarding," *Guardian*, November 11, 2010, http://www.theguardian.com/politics/2010/nov/11/david-cameron-challenges-george-bush-waterboarding.

43. See Senate Select Committee on Intelligence, "Committee Study of the Central Intelligence Agency's Detention and Interrogation Program," December 3, 2014, http://www.documentcloud.org/documents/1376748-sscistudy1.html.

44. See Michael Doyle, *The Question of Intervention: John Stuart Mill and the Responsibility to Protect* (Yale University Press, 2014), 25–26, 71.

45. Shapiro, *Containment*, 34, 37, 59–60.

46. Alexander Watson, *Ring of Steel: Germany and Austria-Hungary in World War One* (Basic Books, 2014), 53–103.

47. Adolf Hitler, *Mein Kampf* (Jaico, 2007 [1925]). For elaboration see Tim Snyder, *Black Earth: The Holocaust as History and Warning* (Random House, 2016).

48. On Western perceptions, see Winston Churchill's Iron Curtain speech delivered at Westminster College in Fulton, Missouri, on March 5, 1946, The History Channel, http://www.history.com/this-day-in-history/churchill-delivers-iron-curtain-speech. On Soviet perceptions, see Samuel H. Baron and Nancy W. Heer, "The Soviet Union: Historiography since Stalin," in *International Handbook of Historical Studies: Contemporary Research and Theory*, ed. Georg Iggers and Harold Parker (Greenwood Press, 1979), 281–294.

49. Michael Scheuer, *Imperial Hubris: Why the West Is Losing the War on Terror* (Potomac Books, 2004), 7–18, 77–82, 129–141.

50. William Maley quotes Soviet foreign minister Andrei Gromyko as surprised by the 1979 insurgency's scale but insisting nonetheless that "under no circumstances may we lose Afghanistan." Maley, *The Afghanistan Wars* (Palgrave Macmillan, 2002), 30–31. See also Gregory Feifer, *The Great Gamble: The Soviet War in Afghanistan* (Harper, 2010), 9–54; and

Alexandre Bennigsen and Marie Broxup, *The Islamic Threat to the Soviet Union* (Routledge, 1993), 5–54, 88–123.

51. "Life has more imagination than we do." François Truffaut, *The 400 Blows* (1959), Criterion Collection, http://www.criterion.com/films/151-the-400 -blows.

52. Shapiro, *Containment*, 15–31.

53. See Wolf Blitzer, "Search for the 'Smoking Gun,'" *CNN*, January 10, 2003,http://www.cnn.com/2003/US/01/10/wbr.smoking.gun/.

54. Cheney as quoted in Suskind: "If there's a 1% chance that Pakistani scientists are helping al-Qaeda build or develop a nuclear weapon, we have to treat it as a certainty in terms of our response. It's not about our analysis . . . It's about our response." Ron Suskind, *The One Percent Doctrine* (Simon and Schuster, 2006). On the "gathering threat" logic, see my *Containment*, 19–22.

55. Listen to Colonel Lawrence Wilkerson, Colin Powell's chief of staff: "I think the smart strategy, and there were those who advocated this at the time, . . . was to go in, pound the hell out of al-Qaeda, try to get bin Laden and his leadership. If you didn't, so be it. You'd keep hunting. You'd do it mostly with special operation forces and the CIA, you would pound the Taliban a little bit and as you left you would tell them, 'Do it again, and we'll do it again.' That was a very formidable, persuasive, strategic brief and the president rejected it. I shouldn't say that. The vice president rejected it." Interview of Lawrence Wilkerson published in the *Cairo Review*, October 19, 2014, http://www .washingtonpost.com/blogs/monkey-cage/wp/2014/10/20/a-fighting-season-to -remember-in-afghanistan/?wpisrc=nl-cage&wpmm=1.

56. For a detailed battle plan, see Peter Krause, "The Last Good Chance: A Reassessment of U.S. Operations at Tora Bora," *Security Studies* 17 (2008): 644–684, http://web.mit.edu/polisci/people/gradstudents/papers /PKrause%20The%20Last%20Good%20Chance.pdf. Some estimates of what would have been needed at the time were around 10,000 troops. See "Tora Bora Reconsidered: How We Failed to Get Bin Laden and Why It Matters Today," report to the Senate Foreign Relations Committee, November 30, 2009, 17–19, http://www.foreign.senate.gov/imo/media/doc /Tora_Bora_Report.pdf. As Carlotta Gall notes, by 2010 there would be 140,000 coalition troops in Afghanistan (two-thirds of whom were Americans). Gall, *The Wrong Enemy: America in Afghanistan, 2001–2014* (Houghton Mifflin, 2014), 76.

57. See Benjamin Runkle, "Tora Bora Reconsidered: Lessons from 125 Years of Strategic Manhunts," *Joint Force Quarterly* 70, no. 3 (2013): 45, http://ndupress.ndu.edu/Portals/68/Documents/jfq/jfq-70/JFQ-70_40-46 _Runkle.pdf.

58. Editorial, *Le Monde*, September 13, 2001, http://langlois.blog.lemonde.fr /2013/01/25/leditorial-du-monde-du-13-septembre-2001/.

59. Indeed, it would become conventional wisdom to account for the failures by reference to the pivot to Iraq. As Deputy Secretary of State Richard

Armitage put it: "The war in Iraq drained resources from Afghanistan before things were under control." Seth Jones, *The Graveyard of Empires: America's War in Afghanistan* (W. W. Norton, 2009), 127. Anand Gopol makes a powerful case, however, that U.S. forces in Afghanistan were so lacking in street-level knowledge, and so extensively manipulated by local warlords in local conflicts they did not understand, that they probably would have failed at securing regime change anyhow. Gopal, *No Good Men among the Living: America, the Taliban, and the War through Afghan Eyes* (Metropolitan Books, 2014), 101–119. This is not a surprise to political scientists who have extensively documented the reality that civil wars that appear to revolve around a few ethnic or religious cleavages invariably become enmeshed in multifaceted local conflicts that will likely be opaque to outsiders. See Stathis Kalyvas, *The Logic of Violence in Civil War* (Cambridge University Press, 2006).

60. There had been few illusions about this in Washington before the 9/11 attacks. In 2000, Northern Alliance lobbyists seeking weapons and other support had been fobbed off as hopelessly unrealistic. The conventional view was summed up by the U.S. ambassador to Pakistan, Bill Milam, and the CIA's section chief in Islamabad, both of whom reported that "the Northern Alliance could not govern Afghanistan and that, secondly, they probably couldn't beat the Taliban anyway." Steve Coll, *Ghost Ward: The Secret History of the CIA, Afghanistan, and Bin Laden, from the Soviet Invasion to September 10, 2001* (Penguin, 2004), 520–521, 571–572.

61. This is to say nothing of the Northern Alliance's lack of democratic credentials or history that might have made Afghanistan a plausible candidate for externally imposed regime change of the sort discussed in §6.4. See Human Rights Watch backgrounder on the United Front / Northern Alliance, October 2001, http://www.rawa.org/na.htm; Edith Lederer, "Afghan Women's Representative Says Northern Alliance as Bad as Taliban," Associated Press, November 21, 2001, http://lang.sbsun.com/socal /terrorist/1101/21/terror04.asp; and Ken Silverstein, "Our Scary New Best Friends," Salon (September 25, 2001), http://www.salon.com/2001/09/25 /united_front/.

62. U.S. Central Command rejected repeated requests from field commanders to send U.S. troops to seal off Tora Bora and defeat Bin Laden. One of the reasons subsequently given was that they were uncertain that Bin Laden was in fact at Tora Bora, but the report to the Senate Foreign Relations Committee (13–20) makes it clear that the United States knew that he was there.

63. Runkle, "Tora Bora Reconsidered," 41.

64. Colin Powell, "Chaos in Baghdad," *Newsweek*, May 13, 2012, http://www .newsweek.com/colin-powell-bush-administrations-iraq-war-mistakes -65023.

65. Senate Foreign Relations Committee report, 9.

66. Among others, veteran Algerian diplomat and peacemaker Lakhdar Brahimi, who chaired the UN mission to Afghanistan, concluded that it had been a mistake to spurn the surrender plans the Taliban had been offering in the north of the country. Reported in an interview with Gall, *Wrong Enemy*, 36–37.

67. The CIA station chief in Pakistan, Robert Grenier, admitted that because the Taliban were defeated more quickly than expected, he considered them "a spent force." Bruce Geidel, a former CIA official who wrote a strategic review of Afghanistan for the incoming Obama administration, also said that the Americans "considered the Taliban irrelevant once they were defeated." Gall, *Wrong Enemy*, 82.

68. Gopal, *No Good Men*, 118–148; and Gall, *Wrong Enemy*, 72–74. On the resilience of the Taliban, see also Gilles Dorronsoro, *Revolution Unending: Afghanistan, 1979 to the Present* (Columbia University Press, 2005), 312–356.

69. Gall, *Wrong Enemy*, 121–124.

70. See Catherine Lutz and Neta Crawford, "Direct War Death in Afghanistan, Iraq, and Pakistan October 2001–April 2014," Costs of War Project, Watson Institute for International Studies, Brown University, http://www .costsofwar.org/sites/default/files/Direct%20War%20Death%20Toll%20 in%20Iraq,%20Afghanistan%20and%20Pakistan%20since%20 2001%20to%20April%202014%206%2026.pdf; and Geoff Dyer and Chloe Sorvino, "$1tn Cost of Longest U.S. War Hastens Retreat from Military Intervention," *Financial Times*, December 14, 2014, http://www .ft.com/intl/cms/s/2/14be0e0c-8255-11e4-ace7-00144feabdc0 .html#slide0.

71. Azam Ahmed, "U.S. General Has Misgivings as Afghan Mission Ends," *New York Times*, December 8, 2014, http://www.nytimes.com/2014/12/09 /world/asia/us-general-joseph-anderson-mission-in-afghanistan.html.

72. Rory Stewart, "Afghanistan: 'A Shocking Indictment,'" *New York Review of Books*, November 6, 2014, http://www.nybooks.com/articles/archives /2014/nov/06/afghanistan-shocking-indictment/.

73. On U.S.-Syria cooperation before 2003, see Shapiro, *Containment*, 98–100.

74. Lori Boghardt, "Saudi Funding of ISIS," Policywatch 2275, Washington Institute, June 23, 2014, http://www.washingtoninstitute.org/policy-analysis /view/saudi-funding-of-isis. On Iran's strained relations with Hamas, see Nidal al-Mughrabi, "Hamas Says Its Iran Ties Worsen over Syrian Civil War," Reuters, June 19, 2013, http://www.reuters.com/article/2013/06/19/us -syria-crisis-hamas-idUSBRE95I0W220130619.

75. Jay Solomon and Maria Abi-Habib, "U.S.-Iran Relations Move to Détente," *Wall Street Journal*, October 29, 2014, 1, http://online.wsj.com/articles/u-s -iran-relations-move-to-detente-1414539659.

76. "Therefore I say that it is a narrow policy to suppose that this country or that is to be marked out as the eternal ally or the perpetual enemy of England. We have no eternal allies, and we have no perpetual enemies. Our

interests are eternal and perpetual, and those interests it is our duty to follow." Viscount Palmerston, speech to the House of Commons, on the Treaty of Adrianople, March 1, 1848, http://hansard.millbanksystems.com /commons/1848/mar/01/treaty-of-adrianople-charges-against.

77. UN Security Council Resolution 678, November 29, 1990, http://daccess -dds-ny.un.org/doc/RESOLUTION/GEN/NR0/575/28/IMG/NR057528.pdf ?OpenElement.

78. "Operation Desert Storm: Military Presence, Allied Forces," http://www .desert-storm.com/War/nations.html.

79. Eight days before the invasion, as Iraqi troops were massing on the border with Kuwait, U.S. ambassador April Glaspie told the Iraqi government that Washington had "no opinion on the Arab-Arab conflicts, like your border disagreement with Kuwait." Elaine Sciolino and Michael Gordon, "Confrontation in the Gulf: U.S. Gave Iraq Little Reason Not to Mount Kuwait Assault," *New York Times,* September 23, 1990, http://www.nytimes.com /1990/09/23/world/confrontation-in-the-gulf-us-gave-iraq-little-reason-not -to-mount-kuwait-assault.html [11/1/2014).

80. See President Bush's speech at the Raytheon Missiles plant in Andover, Massachusetts, on February 15, 1991, http://www.gpo.gov/fdsys/pkg/PPP -1991-book1/html/PPP-1991-book1-doc-pg148.htm.

81. John Burns, "Uncovering Iraq's Horrors in Desert Graves," *New York Times,* June 5, 2006, http://www.nytimes.com/2006/06/05/world/middleeast /05grave.html?_r=0.

82. Listen to Defense Secretary Dick Cheney's prescient, though subsequently forgotten, words in April 1991: "If you're going to go in and try to topple Saddam Hussein, you have to go to Baghdad. Once you've got Baghdad, it's not clear what you do with it. It's not clear what kind of government you would put in place of the one that's currently there now. Is it going to be a Shia regime, a Sunni regime or a Kurdish regime? Or one that tilts toward the Baathists, or one that tilts toward the Islamic fundamentalists? How much credibility is that government going to have if it's set up by the United States military when it's there? How long does the United States military have to stay to protect the people that sign on for that government, and what happens to it once we leave?" See "Echoes from the Past," History News Network, http://hnn.us/articles/631.html. The concern was not new. Here is British Prime Minister Herbert Asquith wondering what will happen if Britain defeats the Turks in World War I: "Taking on Mesopotamia, for instance, means spending millions in irrigation and development with no immediate or early return; keeping up quite a large army white and coloured in an unfamiliar country; tackling every kind of tangled administrative question, worse than we ever had it in India, with a hornet's nest of Arab tribes, and even if that were set right having a perpetual menace to our flank in Kurdistan." Charles Townshend, *Desert Hell: The British Invasion of Mesopotamia* (Harvard University Press, 2011), 81–82.

83. Immediately following the attacks, the Security Council adopted Resolution 1368, which "calls on all States to work together urgently to bring to justice the perpetrators, organizers and sponsors of these terrorist attacks." http://daccess-dds-ny.un.org/doc/UNDOC/GEN/N01/533/82/PDF/N0153382.pdf?OpenElement. A few weeks later the Security Council adopted Resolution 1373, which authorized measures to prevent terrorism, such as suppressing of terror financing and recruitment and information sharing. http://www.un.org/en/sc/ctc/specialmeetings/2012/docs/United%20Nations%20Security%20Council%20Resolution%201373%20%282001%29.pdf.

84. See Paul Aarts and Michael Renner, "Oil and the Gulf War," *Middle East Report* 21 (July/August 1991), http://www.merip.org/mer/mer171/oil-gulf-war.

85. Ian Shapiro, *Democratic Justice* (Yale University Press, 1999), 85–86; and Shapiro, "On Non-domination," *University of Toronto Law Journal* 62 (2012): 294–295, 314–316, 323–335.

86. See Churchill's statement to the House of Commons on March 31, 1939, http://avalon.law.yale.edu/wwii/blbk17.asp. On the Kuwaiti government in exile's request for help, see Eric Ridge, "Civil Affairs in Desert Shield/Storm," Center for Strategic and International Studies Working Paper, 2014, 4, http://csis.org/files/media/csis/pubs/090129_desert_shield_desert_storm_study.pdf.

87. NATO Charter, Article 5, http://www.nato.int/cps/en/natolive/official_texts_17120.htm.

88. For an account of the U.S. pressure to get participation in the 2003 Iraq invasion, see John Ferejohn and Frances Rosenbluth, *Forged through Fire: Military Conflict and the Democratic Bargain* (Norton Liveright, 2016).

89. See Norman Graebner, Richard Dean Burns, and Joseph M. Siracusa, *America and the Cold War, 1941–1991: A Realist Interpretation* (Praeger, 2010), 37–64.

90. See Jean Krasno, "Namibian Independence: A UN Success Story," in Shapiro and Lampert, *Charter of the United Nations*, 174–192.

91. "Operation Desert Storm: Military Presence, Allied Forces."

92. See "The U.S. Coalition against Iraq (2003)," European Institute for Research, http://www.medea.be/en/countries/iraq/us-led-coalition-against-iraq-2003/. Many nominal supporters were unceremoniously strong-armed into signing. See Sarah Anderson, Phyllis Bennis, and John Cavanaugh, "Coalition of the Willing or Coalition of the Coerced?," Institute for Policy Studies (February 26, 2003), http://www.tni.org/sites/www.tni.org/archives/mil-docs/coalition.pdf.

93. See my discussion in *Containment*, 21–22, 32–53, 61–63, 122–123.

94. See Hans Blix, *Disarming Iraq: The Search for Weapons of Mass Destruction* (Bloomsbury, 2004), 195–253.

95. Ilya Somin, "The Dubious Crimean Referendum on Annexation by Russia," *Washington Post*, March 17, 2014, http://www.washingtonpost

.com/news/volokh-conspiracy/wp/2014/03/17/the-dubious-crimean
-referendum-on-annexation-by-russia/.

96. Andrew Higgins and David Herszenhorn, "Defying Russia, Ukraine
Signs E.U. Trade Pact," *New York Times,* June 27, 2014, http://www
.nytimes.com/2014/06/28/world/europe/ukraine-signs-trade-agreement
-with-european-union.html?_r=0.

97. In 2008 NATO had announced that it looked forward to the accession of
both Georgia and Ukraine. See "Final Communiqué," press release from
the meeting of the North Atlantic Council at the level of foreign ministers
held at NATO headquarters in Brussels (December 3, 2008), http://www
.nato.int/cps/en/natolive/official_texts_46247.htm; and Stephen Brown
and Missy Ryan, "Ukraine Crisis: West and Russia Accuse Each Other of
'Coercing' Unstable Ukraine," NBC News (February 1, 2014), http://
worldnews.nbcnews.com/_news/2014/02/01/22533424-ukraine-crisis-west
-and-russia-accuse-each-other-of-coercing-unstable-nation?lite.

98. Joshua Shifrinson, "Put It in Writing: How the West Broke Its Promise to
Moscow," *Foreign Affairs,* October 29, 2014, http://www.foreignaffairs
.com/articles/142310/joshua-r-itzkowitz-shifrinson/put-it-in-writing.

99. NATO homepage, member countries as of August 20, 2013, http://www
.nato.int/cps/en/natolive/topics_52044.htm.

100. "When the infrastructure of a military bloc is moving toward our borders,
it causes us some concerns and questions. We need to take some steps in
response . . . NATO ships would have ended up in the city of Russian navy
glory, Sevastopol." Vladimir Putin quoted in "Putin Says Annexation of
Crimea Partly in Response to NATO Enlargement," Reuters, April 17,
2014, http://www.reuters.com/article/2014/04/17/us-russia-putin-nato
-idUSBREA3G22A20140417.

101. Andrew Wilson, *Ukrainian Nationalism in the 1990s: A Minority Faith*
(Cambridge University Press, 1996), 129.

102. Paul Kolstoe, *Russians in the Former Soviet Republics* (Indiana University
Press, 1995), 191–199.

103. Paul Belkin, Derek Mix, and Steven Woehrel, "NATO: Response to the
Crisis in Ukraine and Security Concerns in Central and Eastern Europe,"
Congressional Research Service report, April 16, 2014, http://fas.org/sgp
/crs/row/R43478.pdf.

104. James Kanter and David Herszhensorn, "U.S. and Europe Back New
Economic Sanctions against Russia," *New York Times,* September 11,
2014, http://www.nytimes.com/2014/09/12/world/europe/eu-pushes
-forward-with-tougher-sanctions-on-russia.html.

105. James Marson and Andrey Ostroukh, "Putin Blasts West's 'Containment'
Policy," *Wall Street Journal,* December 5, 2014, A7, http://online.wsj.com
/public/resources/documents/print/WSJ_-A007-20141205.pdf.

106. "U.S. Team in Nigeria to Aid Search for Kidnapped Girls," Voice of
America, May 8, 2014, http://www.voanews.com/content/five-countries-to

-help-nigeria-find-kidnapped-girls/1910259.html; and Sani Tokur, "Nigeria Cancels U.S. Military Training as Relations between Both Nations Worsen," *Sahara Reporters* (December 1, 2014), http://saharareporters.com/2014/12/01/nigeria-cancels-us-military-training-relations-between-both-nations-worsen.

107. In fact it appears to have been coined by Thomas Inman in 1860. See James Morrison, "Heroic Treatment," *Academic Medicine* 83, no. 12 (December 2008): 1166–1167.

108. Gopal, *No Good Men,* 184–236. See also Astri Suhrke, *When More Is Less: The International Project in Afghanistan* (Columbia University Press, 2011), 19–72.

109. Doyle, *Question of Intervention,* 147–185.

110. "Patterns of Global Terrorism," U.S. State Department, April 1996, http://www.fas.org/irp/threat/terror_96/overview.html.

111. Shapiro, *Containment,* 96–97.

112. Andrew Solomon, "Circle of Fire: Libya's Reformers Dream of Rejoining the World," *New Yorker,* May 8, 2006, http://www.newyorker.com/fact/content/articles/060508fa_fact3.

113. Shapiro, *Containment,* 97.

114. Tobias Vanderbruck, "Gaddafi's Legacy of Libyan Oil Deals," Oil-Price.Net, October 21, 2011, http://www.oil-price.net/en/articles/gaddafi-legacy-of-libya-oil-deals.php.

115. Alan Kuperman, "A Model Humanitarian Intervention? Reassessing NATO's Libya Campaign," *International Security* 38, no. 1 (Summer 2013): 126.

116. Ibid., 116–118.

117. The leaders of the "revolution" included Gaddafi's former justice minister Abdul Jalil, his former ambassador to India Ali Aziz, and one of his top economic advisors (with close links to the oil multinationals), Mahmoud Jebril. Among the leaders of the "rebel" military council were Omar Hariri, who lacked any democratic credentials, and former Interior Ministry head General Abdul Fattah Younis, who had a long history, dating back to 1969, of repressing democratic movements. See James Petras and Henry Veltmeyer, *Beyond Neoliberalism: A World to Win* (Ashgate, 2011), 194–195.

118. Kuperman, "A Model Humanitarian Intervention?," 107–113.

119. The BBC was one of the few media organizations to note that footage purporting to show protesters fleeing live gunfire from Gaddafi's troops in February 2011 was misleading. See "Libya Protests: Second City Benghazi Hit by Violence," BBC News Africa, February 16, 2011, http://www.bbc.co.uk/news/world-africa-12477275.

120. UN Security Council Resolution 1973 (March 17, 2011), http://www.un.org/en/ga/search/view_doc.asp?symbol=S/RES/1973%282011%29.

121. Daveed Gartenstein-Ross, "Successes and Failures of the U.S. and NATO Intervention in Libya," testimony before the House Committee on

Oversight and Government Reform, Washington, D.C., May 1, 2014, 2–3, http://www.defenddemocracy.org/content/uploads/documents/Libya _testimony_final_4_30_2014.pdf.

122. Petras and Veltmeyer, *Beyond Neoliberalism,* 195.

123. Gates strongly opposed the intervention, along with Vice President Biden, Chairman of the Joint Chiefs Mike Mullen, National Security Advisor Tom Donilon, White House Chief of Staff Bill Daley, Deputy National Security Advisor John Brennan, and Deputy National Security Adviser Denis McDonough. UN Ambassador Susan Rice, Special Assistant for Human Rights Samantha Power, Deputy Advisor Ben Rhodes, and Secretary of State Hillary Clinton favored the intervention. Robert M. Gates, *Duty: Memoirs of a Secretary of State at War* (W. H. Allen, 2014), 518. Clinton had been skeptical, but was persuaded on a visit to Paris by President Nicolas Sarkozy and the dubiously credible former Libyan justice minister Abdul Jilal. Steven Erlanger, "By His Own Reckoning, One Man Made Libya a French Cause," *New York Times,* April 1, 2011, http://www.nytimes.com/2011/04/02/world /africa/02levy.html?_r=0. She became the decisive voice in persuading President Obama in what he said privately to Gates was a 51/49 call. Gates, *Duty,* 519. Emails from advisor Sidney Blumenthal to Hilary Clinton released by the House Select Committee on Benghazi in October 2015 suggest that the prospect of oil concessions indeed played a role. In an email dated May 15, 2011, for example, Blumenthal, who was himself pursuing business interests in Libya, complains to Clinton about the "French economic grab" of promised oil concessions. Letter from committee chair Congressman Trey Gowdy to Democratic ranking member Congressman Elijah Cummings dated October 7, 2015, 10–12. https://benghazi.house.gov /sites/republicans.benghazi.house.gov/files/TG%20letter%20to%20 EEC%2010.7.15.pdf, pp. 10–12

124. One widely reported claim that Gaddafi's air force was indiscriminately bombing and strafing civilians in Tripoli and Benghazi was not exposed as false until after the war ended, when the International Crisis Group's Africa Project leader admitted as much. Hugh Roberts, "Who Said Gaddafi Had to Go?," *London Review of Books,* November 2011, 8–18.

125. Kuperman, "A Model Humanitarian Intervention?," 111–112.

126. Ibid., 110–111.

127. Erlanger, "By His Own Reckoning."

128. Kuperman, "A Model Humanitarian Intervention?," 116–123.

129. Gartenstein-Ross, "Successes and Failures," 4–5.

130. David Stout, "ISIS Now Controls the Libyan City of Derna and Is Aiming to Expand West," *Time,* November 17, 2014, http://time.com/3593885/isis -libya-iraq-syria-terrorism-derna/. This is to say nothing of the cascading refugee crisis that would eventually spill into the Mediterranean, spawning humanitarian disasters and vicious anti-immigration politics across southern Europe. See Franziska Brantner, "The Libyan Context of the

Migration Crisis," European Council of Foreign Relations, May 22, 2015, http://www.ecfr.eu/article/commentary_the_libyan_context_of_the _migration_crisis3040.

131. Kuperman, "A Model Humanitarian Intervention?," 129–130; and "Talks without Hope," *Economist*, August 26, 2014, http://www.economist.com /node/21613924/print.

132. Kuperman, "A Model Humanitarian Intervention?," 134–135; and Marc Lynch, "Reflections on the Arab Uprisings," *Washington Post*, November 17, 2014, http://www.washingtonpost.com/blogs/monkey-cage/wp/2014/11/17 /reflections-on-the-arab-uprisings/.

133. See Lynch's recantation in "Reflections on the Arab Uprisings."

134. Robert Pape, "When Duty Calls: A Pragmatic Standard for Humanitarian Intervention," *International Security* 37, no. 1 (Summer 2012): 43; and Alan Kuperman, *The Limits of Humanitarian Intervention* (Brookings Institute, 2001), 14–22.

135. Pape, "When Duty Calls," 66–67.

136. Ibid., 67.

137. Kuperman, "A Model Humanitarian Intervention?," 113–116.

138. Pape is in any case unconvincing that the intervening forces did not intend regime change. Resolution 1973 would never have been adopted by the Security Council or supported by the Arab League without its proscription of introducing foreign troops onto Libyan soil. But from the start NATO did everything it could to reverse the course of the civil war and ensure that Gaddafi would lose. Pape says that the "newly formed" Transitional National Council declared that Libya had been liberated on October 23, 2011 ("When Duty Calls," 68–69). But it was not newly formed—it had been recognized as Libya's legitimate government by France in early March, even before Resolution 1973 was adopted. Pape seems innocent of the French role as described by Erlanger in "By His Own Reckoning." Even more oddly, Pape contrasts the Libyan intervention on this score with Desert Storm, in which, he alleges, there was a "major effort to decapitate Saddam Hussein's government" (69). Once Saddam's armies had been decimated in Kuwait, it would have been child's play for the half-a-million-plus troops on the ground to roll into Baghdad. As I noted in §6.2.2, it was diplomatic and strategic considerations that led the Bush administration to resist the considerable pressure to do exactly that.

139. Mill elaborates: "The only test possessing any real value, of a people's having become fit for popular institutions, is that they, or a sufficient portion of them to prevail in the contest, are willing to brave labour and danger for their liberation . . . if they have not sufficient love of liberty to be able to wrest it from merely domestic oppressors, the liberty which is bestowed on them by other hands than their own, will have nothing real, nothing permanent. No people ever was and remained free, but because it

was determined to be so; because neither its rulers nor any other party in the nation could compel it to be otherwise." John Stuart Mill, "A Few Words on Non-Intervention" [1859], reprinted in Doyle, *Question of Intervention,* 122–124.

140. Pape, "When Duty Calls," 69.

141. The Marshal Plan delivered $103 billion in 2014 dollars to sixteen European countries between 1948 and 1952 as compared with $109 billion Congress appropriated for Afghanistan reconstruction between 2002 and 2014. Special Inspector General for Afghanistan Reconstruction, *Quarterly Report to the United States Congress* (July 30, 2014), 5, http://www.sigar.mil/pdf/quarterlyreports/2014-07-30qr.pdf.

142. Gopal, *No Good Men,* 273. Much of the rest vanished due to corruption. Ibid., 273–274.

143. Gopal elaborates: "In 2013, there were, by some estimates, 60,000 to 80,000 armed private security employees in the country, almost all of them working for Afghan strongmen. Add to this 135,000 Afghan army soldiers, 110,000 police and tens of thousands of private militia men working directly for the Afghan government, the U.S. special forces, or the CIA, and you have more than 300,000 armed Afghan men all depending on U.S. patronage. You can't help but wonder: What happens when the troops leave, the bases close, and the money dries up?" Gopal, *No Good Men,* 276.

144. Mark Mazzetti and Eric Schmidt, "In Shift, Obama Extends U.S. Role in Afghan Combat," *New York Times,* November 22, 2015, 1, http://www.nytimes.com/2014/11/22/us/politics/in-secret-obama-extends-us-role-in-afghan-combat.html?ref=todayspaper&_r=0.

145. See Christopher Blanchard, "Libya: Transition and U.S. Policy," Congressional Research Service, September 8, 2014, http://fpc.state.gov/documents/organization/231785.pdf.

146. Alex Dewall, "The African Union and the Libya Conflict of 2011," World Peace Foundation, December 29, 2012, http://sites.tufts.edu/reinventingpeace/2012/12/19/the-african-union-and-the-libya-conflict-of-2011/.

147. See Norman Naimark, *Fires of Hatred: Ethnic Cleansing in Twentieth-Century Europe* (Harvard University Press, 2002), 139–184.

148. See Edward Cody, "Arab League Condemns Broad Bombing in Libya," *Washington Post,* March 20, 2011, https://www.washingtonpost.com/world/arab-league-condemns-broad-bombing-campaign-in-libya/2011/03/20/AB1pSg1_story.html.

149. Andrew Meldrum, "African Leaders Criticize Bombing of Libya," GlobalPost, March 22, 2011, http://www.globalpost.com/dispatches/globalpost-blogs/africa-emerges/african-leaders-voice-support-gaddafi.

150. "Russia and China Team Up against NATO Libya Campaign," *Forbes,* June 17, 2011, http://www.forbes.com/sites/kenrapoza/2011/06/17/russia-and-china-team-up-against-nato-libya-campaign/.

151. "Russia, China, Warn West Not to Intervene in Syria, Following U.S. Threat," *Haaretz,* August 21, 2012, http://www.haaretz.com/news/middle -east/russia-china-warn-west-not-to-intervene-in-syria-following-u-s-threat -1.459709.

152. President George H. W. Bush, address before a joint session of the U.S. Congress, September 11, 1990, http://millercenter.org/president/bush /speeches/speech-3425.

153. See Adam Przeworski, "Acquiring the Habit of Changing Governments through Elections," *Comparative Political Studies* 48, no. 1 (August 2014): 101–129.

154. The argument developed in this paragraph and the next applies to Pape's "pragmatic" account as well, because his threefold test deals with necessary conditions for intervention. He does not argue that his triggering criteria mandate intervention.

155. See, for instance, Jack Guez, "French Lawyer Files Complaint against Israel at ICC," *France 24,* August 25, 2014, http://www.france24.com/en /20140725-israel-icc-war-crimes-gaza-complaint-filed/.

156. Maggie Farley, "UN Approves Troops for Somalia," *Los Angeles Times,* December 7, 2006, http://articles.latimes.com/2006/dec/07/world/fg -somalia7.

157. UN Security Council Resolution 1973, March 17, 2011, http://daccess-dds -ny.un.org/doc/UNDOC/GEN/N11/268/39/PDF/N1126839.pdf ?OpenElement.

158. Kenneth Katzman, "Iraq: Post-Saddam Governance and Security," Congressional Research Service Report for Congress 7-5700 (June 8, 2009), 3, http://fas.org/sgp/crs/mideast/RL31339.pdf.

159. Mark Mazower tells a comparable story about the International Criminal Court. Nonsignatories to the Court, such as the United States, China, Russia, and India, have no difficulty backing resolutions to refer figures like Gaddafi and Omar-al-Bashir of Sudan to the Court for prosecution, yet the United States has made its participation in peacekeeping operations conditional on explicit exemptions from possible prosecution. Mazower, *Governing the World: The History of an Idea, 1815 to the Present* (Penguin, 2012), 399–402.

160. See James Ray, "Does Democracy Cause Peace?," *Annual Review of Political Science* 1 (1998): 27–46; John Owen, "Democratic Peace Research: Whence and Whither," *International Politics,* no. 41 (2004): 605–617; Alan Dafoe, "Statistical Critiques of the Democratic Peace: Caveat Emptor," *American Journal of Political Science* 55, no. 2 (April 2011): 247–262; and Allan Dafoe, John Oneal, and Bruce Russett, "Democratic Peace: Weighing the Evidence and Cautious Inference," *International Studies Quarterly* 57 (2014): 201–224.

161. See Alexander Downes and Jonathan Morten, "Forced to Be Free? Why Foreign-Imposed Regime Change Rarely Leads to Democratization,"

International Security 37, no. 4 (Spring 2013): 90–131. At p. 94 Downes and Morten note that people frequently overlook the fact that bringing down the German and Japanese states was in itself enormously expensive, even ignoring the costs of reconstruction. In addition to economic development and prior experience with democracy, they also contend, more debatably in my judgment, that ethnic homogeneity matters when intervening to install democracy. If they are right, this would be yet another strike against the prospects for Iraq, Afghanistan, Libya, and Syria.

162. Iraq Liberation Act of 1998, H.R.4655.ENR, http://thomas.loc.gov/cgi-bin /query/z?c105:H.R.4655.ENR. The Act specified seven antiregime groups that were eligible to receive up to $97 million in U.S. funding.

163. See Nick Ritchie and Paul Rogers, *The Political Road to War with Iraq: 9/11 and the Drive to Overthrow Saddam* (Routledge, 2006), 36–52.

164. For claims about the democratic domino effect from senior Bush administration officials, see Paul Reynolds, "The Democratic Domino Theory," BBC News, April 10, 2003, http://news.bbc.co.uk/2/hi/middle_east /2935969.stm.

165. "Statement on Signing the Iraq Liberation Act, October 31, 1998," *Public Papers of the Presidents of the United States, William J. Clinton, 1998*, vol. 2 (U.S. Government Printing Office), 1938.

166. See Adam Przeworski, Michael E. Alvarez, Jose Antonio Cheibub, and Fernando Limongi, *Democracy and Development: Political Institutions and Economic Well-Being in the World, 1950–1990* (Cambridge University Press, 2000), 78–141.

167. There are various explanations for democracy's survival in India. Perhaps the most convincing is the advantages derived from decades of direct rule during the colonial period, during which a groundwork for democratic politics was laid and indigenous elites with strong commitments to democracy developed. But other factors, such as unusual luck in its early leaders, must also have played a role in view of the fact that Pakistan did not harvest similar benefits from the indirect-rule legacy. See Ian Shapiro, *The State of Democratic Theory* (Princeton University Press, 2003), 87–88.

168. See my chapter 16 in the second edition of Robert Dahl, *On Democracy* (Yale University Press, 2015), 191–199.

169. The African National Congress waged a nonviolent struggle from its inception in 1911 until the Sharpeville massacre of 1960, after which they took up arms on the grounds that peaceful change was no longer possible. In 1990, three months after the National Party government released all political prisoners and unbanned all political organizations, the ANC suspended the armed struggle unilaterally. See Ian Shapiro, *The Real World of Democratic Theory* (Princeton University Press, 2012), 151–153.

170. Just as the ANC had resisted calls for "constructive engagement" instead of sanctions against the apartheid regime in South Africa until the regime

freed political prisoners and legalized the opposition in 1990, Aung San Suu Kyi's National League for Democracy called for sanctions against Burma to be maintained until the regime made comparable moves there. On the ANC, see Oliver Tambo, "Statement at the International Conference on Sanctions against South Africa," Paris, France, May 21, 1981, http://www.anc.org.za/show.php?id=4236. On Burma, see David Pilling, "Suu Kyi Says Burma Sanctions Should Remain," *Financial Times,* January 28, 2011, http://www.ft.com/intl/cms/s/0/c6d7a6bc-2b0f-11e0-a65f-00144feab49a.html#axzz3MS7HZNjo; and Steven Myers, "Myanmar's Opposition Leader Urges End to Sanctions," *New York Times,* September 18, 2012, http://www.nytimes.com/2012/09/19/world/asia/myanmars-opposition-leader-aung-san-suu-kyi-begins-visit-to-us.html?_r=0.

171. Gall, *Wrong Enemy,* 220.
172. Jane Mayer, "The Manipulator," *New Yorker,* June 7, 2004, http://www.newyorker.com/magazine/2004/06/07/the-manipulator.
173. See the White House blog for August 18, 2011, http://www.whitehouse.gov/blog/2011/08/18/president-obama-future-syria-must-be-determined-its-people-president-bashar-al-assad.
174. William Polk, "Understanding Syria: From Pre-Civil War to Post-Assad," *Atlantic,* December 10, 2013, 16, http://www.theatlantic.com/international/archive/2013/12/understanding-syria-from-pre-civil-war-to-post-assad/281989/.
175. See "Syria's War More Complex than Ever as Both Sides Face Internal Divisions," *Guardian,* September 19, 2013, http://www.theatlantic.com/international/archive/2013/12/understanding-syria-from-pre-civil-war-to-post-assad/281989/.
176. Peter Gleick, "Water, Drought, Climate Change and Conflict in Syria," *Weather, Climate, and Society* 6, no. 2 (July 2014): 331–341.
177. Polk, "Understanding Syria," 14–15.
178. Ibid., 12. In fact this was an ambivalent policy, because since the 1970s the United States had often found it convenient to cooperate with Syria to stabilize Lebanon. See Shapiro, *Containment,* 98–100.
179. Polk, "Understanding Syria," 14.
180. Michael Eisenstadt and Jeffrey White, "An Enhanced Train-and-Equip Program for the Moderate Syrian Opposition," Policy 2280, The Washington Institute, July 8, 2014, http://www.washingtoninstitute.org/policy-analysis/view/an-enhanced-train-and-equip-program-for-the-moderate-syrian-opposition.
181. Operation Barbarossa, named for the medieval Holy Roman emperor Frederick Barbarossa, was the code name for Germany's invasion of the Soviet Union that began in June 1941. See Adam Tooze, *The Wages of Destruction: The Making and Breaking of the Nazi Economy* (Penguin Books, 2006), 420–512.

182. Alex van Linschoten and Felix Kuehn, *An Enemy We Created: The Myth of the Taliban–Al Qaeda Merger in Afghanistan* (Oxford University Press, 2014); and Gopal, *No Good Men,* 101–150, 183–186. On the shifting alliances within and among Afghan insurgent groups, see Fotini Christia, *Alliance Formation in Civil Wars* (Cambridge University Press, 2012), 47–147.

183. The same is true of backing elections only when the outcomes are deemed favorable. The United States pushed for elections in Lebanon in 2005 and in Gaza and the West Bank in 2006 as part of the campaign to show that regime change in Iraq was having its hoped-for domino effect. But the results strengthened Hezbollah and Hamas, an unwelcome outcome for Israel and many of its supporters in the United States. Elsewhere I have argued that refusing to recognize the Hamas victory was a tactical blunder, particularly when coupled with their proposal for a government of national unity with the PLO and a ten-year truce with Israel. It offered the best basis for a negotiated settlement since Yitzhak Rabin's assassination a decade earlier. Shapiro, *Containment,* 80–89. Regardless of that claim, it surely undermined American claims to be supporters of democracy. Better to not call for elections than to refuse to recognize the results after the fact.

184. Alexis de Tocqueville, *Democracy in America,* vol. 2, ed. J. P. Mayer (Harper and Row, 1969 [1840]), 528–530.

185. For elaboration of the argument that multicultural accommodation should be conditioned on the treatment of minorities within the minority cultures seeking accommodation, see Sarah Song, *Justice, Gender, and the Politics of Multiculturalism* (Cambridge University Press, 2007).

186. In this connection it is worth noting that President Jimmy Carter signed a secret directive to support the nascent Afghan mujahedeen against the Soviet-backed government in the summer of 1979, six months before the Soviet invasion. See van Linschoten and Kuehn, *An Enemy We Created,* 41. The future might have been exceedingly different without that action.

187. In August 2014, a U.S. bombing campaign broke a three-month siege of Amerli by ISIL extremists, allowing the residents to escape with the help of Iraqi troops. In the same month U.S. and British forces helped Yazidi stranded on Mount Sinjar escape imminent slaughter. Alan Kuperman interview, BBC World Service *Newshour,* September 27, 2014, http:// alanjkuperman.podomatic.com/entry/2014-09-27T16_13_59-07_00.

188. See "ISIS Sells Stolen Kirkuk Oil at $20 a Barrel," Reuters, November 9, 2014, http://endthelie.com/2014/11/09/isis-sells-stolen-kirkuk-oil-20-per -barrel-iraq-finance-ministry/.

189. See Henry Ridgwell, "Rights Group: International Community Not Taking Refugees," Voice of America, December 6, 2014, http://www.voanews.com /content/rights-group-international-community-not-takin-in-syrian

-refugees/2547600.html#hash=relatedInfoContainer; Oxfam, "A Fairer Deal for Syrians," 190 Oxfam Briefing Paper (September 9, 2014), http://www.oxfam.org/sites/www.oxfam.org/files/file_attachments/bp190 -fairer-deal-syrians-090914-en.pdf; and Sarah Lazare, "U.S. and Western Allies Turn Backs on Refugee Crisis in Syria and Iraq," *Common Dreams*, November 12, 2014, http://www.commondreams.org/news/2014/11/12/us -and-western-allies-turn-backs-refugee-crisis-syria-and-iraq.

190. The Goldwater-Nichols Defense Department Reorganization Act of 1986 requires administrations to submit an annual National Security Strategy Report to Congress along with a budget, a schedule that no administration since Reagan has met. See National Security Strategy Archive, http://nssarchive.us/.

191. The White House, *National Security Strategy* (February 2015), 8, https://www.whitehouse.gov/sites/default/files/docs/2015_national_security _strategy.pdf.

192. The requirements of proportionality and last resort are conventional elements of just-war theory. See Doyle, *Question of Intervention,* 19–50. The Security Council, as provided for in the UN charter, to which the United States is a signatory, reserves the right to authorize third-party interventions. Since 2002 the African Union has also assumed that it, too, can authorize interventions in member countries. See Article 4(h) of the Constitutive Act of the African Union, http://www.au.int/en/sites/default /files/ConstitutiveAct_EN.pdf; and 2005 UN General Assembly Agenda items 46 and 120 (October 24, 2005), http://www.un.org/womenwatch /ods/A-RES-60–1-E.pdf.

193. See Shapiro, *Containment,* 15–31.

194. [Kennan], "Sources of Soviet Conduct."

195. Anne Barnard and Somini Sengupta, "U.S. Signals Shift on How to End Syrian War," *New York Times,* January 19, 2015, http://www.nytimes .com/2015/01/20/world/middleeast/us-support-for-syria-peace-plans -demonstrates-shift-in-priorities.html?_r=0; Tom Hill, "Has America Decided It Must Work with Assad to Defeat ISIL?," *Telegraph,* November 11, 2014, http://www.telegraph.co.uk/news/worldnews/islamic -state/11221158/Has-America-decided-it-must-work-with-Assad-to -defeat-Isil.html; and "Assad Getting U.S. 'Information" on Air Strikes," CBS News (February 10, 2015), http://www.cbsnews.com/news/syria -leader-bashar-assad-getting-information-us-military-airstrikes-against -isis/.

196. Stephen Zunes, "How the U.S. Contributed to Yemen's Crisis," *Common Dreams,* April 20, 2015, http://www.commondreams.org/views/2015/04 /20/how-us-contributed-yemens-crisis; and Michah Zenko, "Make No Mistake—The United States Is at War in Yemen," *Foreign Policy,* March 30, 2015, http://foreignpolicy.com/2015/03/30/make-no-mistake -the-united-states-is-at-war-in-yemen-saudi-arabia-iran/.

197. The line often attributed to Churchill is: "The United States can always be counted on to do the right thing, after having exhausted every other alternative." In fact there is no decisive evidence that he ever said it. See Scott Horsely, "A Churchill 'Quote' that U.S. Politicians Will Never Surrender," NPR (October 28, 2013), http://www.npr.org/sections /itsallpolitics/2013/10/28/241295755/a-churchill-quote-that-u-s-politicians -will-never-surrender.

198. John Locke, "The Second Treatise: An Essay Concerning the True Original, Extent, and End of Civil Government," §6, in Locke, *Two Treatises of Government and a Letter Concerning Toleration,* ed. Ian Shapiro (Yale University Press, 2003), 102.

199. Indeed, he affirmed a robust commitment to human equality that was born of his unequivocal conviction that we are all equal before God. See my "John Locke's Democratic Theory," in *Real World of Democratic Theory,* 41–51.

200. U.S. democracy has also been compromised since the 9/11 attacks by the erosion of civil liberties in the PATRIOT Act legislation passed in 2001 and reauthorized in 2005 and 2006 as well as the increases in surveillance exposed through the Wikileaks scandals. See Owen Fiss, *A War Like No Other: The Constitution in a Time of Terror* (The New Press, 2015). I have focused on the torture question as most salient to the external perceptions, particularly of adversaries.

7. Politics against Domination

1. See Michael Walzer, *Spheres of Justice: A Defense of Pluralism and Equality* (Basic Books, 1982), 3–30; Ian Shapiro, "On Non-domination," *University of Toronto Law Journal* 62 (2012): 293–306; and Shapiro, "Against Impartiality," *Journal of Politics* 78, no. 2 (April 2016).

2. John Locke, "The Second Treatise: An Essay Concerning the True Original, Extent, and End of Civil Government," §96, p. 142, in Locke, *Two Treatises of Government and A Letter Concerning Toleration,* ed. Ian Shapiro (Yale University Press, 2003).

3. Jean-Jacques Rousseau, *The Social Contract,* in Rousseau, *The Social Contract and Other Later Political Writings,* ed. Victor Gourevitch (Cambridge University Press, 1997), 60.

4. "It has been said that democracy is the worst system of government, except for the others that have been tried from time to time." Winston Churchill, House of Commons, November 11, 1947, in *Churchill by Himself: The Definitive Collection of Quotations,* ed. Richard Langforth (Public Affairs Press, 2008), 974.

5. Samuel P. Huntington, *The Third Wave: Democratization in the Late 20th Century* (University of Oklahoma Press, 1993), 131–137.

6. See Nicholas Miller, "Pluralism and Social Choice," *American Political Science Review* 77, no. 3 (September 1983): 734–747.

7. See G. Bingham Powell Jr. and Georg Vanberg, "Election Laws, Disproportionality and Median Correspondence: Implications for Two Visions of Democracy," *British Journal of Political Science* 30, no. 3 (2000): 383–411.

8. See Kathleen Bawn and Frances Rosenbluth, "Short and Long Coalitions," *American Journal of Political Science* 50, no. 2 (April 2006): 251–265; and Torsten Persson, Gerard Roland, and Guido Tabellini, "Electoral Rules and Government Spending in Parliamentary Democracies," *Quarterly Journal of Political Science* 20, no. 2 (2007): 155–188.

9. This can be mitigated to some extent by a rule permitting only "constructive" votes of no confidence. In Germany, for instance, no-confidence motions can carry only if there is a declared alternative coalition waiting in the wings to take over. But this does nothing to foster coherent opposition politics, short of bringing down the government.

10. The U.S. Republicans learned this the hard way in 2005, when they deployed the same strategies to build support for privatizing Social Security that had worked well in repealing the estate tax four years earlier—all to no avail. A huge political advertising campaign and major barnstorming efforts by congressional Republicans and a newly reelected President Bush had no effect on public opinion. Nor did the allied efforts of conservative pundits, think tanks, and lobbyists for financial institutions that stood to benefit from privatization. It all came to naught because the median voter was intensely and immovably attached to the existing public system. See Mayling Birney, Ian Shapiro, and Michael Graetz, "The Political Uses of Public Opinion: Lesson from the Estate Tax Repeal," in *Divide and Deal: The Politics of Distribution in Democracies,* ed. Ian Shapiro, Peter Swenson, and Daniela Donno (NYU Press, 2008), 298–340; and Michael Graetz and Ian Shapiro, *Death by a Thousand Cuts: The Fight over Taxing Inherited Wealth* (Princeton University Press, 2005), 50–98, 118–130.

11. This suggests that we should be skeptical of proposals, like John McCormick's, to revive something like Machiavelli's Tribune of the Plebs, a group of fifty citizens who would be randomly selected from the population, excluding economic and political elites, and would be empowered to veto one piece of legislation a year, call one referendum a year, and impeach one official from each branch of government per year. McCormick, *Machiavellian Democracy* (Cambridge University Press, 2011), 178–188. It takes a pretty large leap of faith to believe that such an entity would not be manipulated via media campaigns demonizing immigrants or particular religious and ethnic groups, or that they would not protect corrupt populist leaders. Perhaps a Tribune of the Plebs would have gone after Silvio Berlusconi, but it might just as easily have gone after those who were trying

to hold him accountable for his abuses of office. See "Poll Shows Approval Rises for Berlusconi, Forza Italia," *Gazetta del Sud* online, November 20, 2013, http://www.gazzettadelsud.it/news/english/70871/Poll-shows -approval-rises-for-Berlusconi—Forza-Italia.html.

12. Philip Pettit, *Republicanism: A Theory of Freedom and Government* (Oxford University Press, 1997), 195.

13. Vanessa Williamson, Theda Skocpol, and John Coggin, "The Tea Party and the Remaking of Republican Conservatism," *Perspectives on Politics 9*, no. 1 (March 2011): 25–43.

14. Alasdair Roberts, "Why the Occupy Movement Failed," *Public Administration Review 72*, no. 5 (September/October 2012): 754–762.

15. Pettit, *Republicanism*, 171–240.

16. Ibid., 186.

17. Pettit's institutional recommendations conflict with one another in various ways that need not detain us here. For discussion, see Shapiro, "On Non-domination," 321–332.

18. See Anna Jarstad, "Power-Sharing: Former Enemies in Joint Government," in Anna Jarstad and Timothy Sisk, *From War to Democracy: Dilemmas of Peacebuilding* (Cambridge University Press, 2008), 105–133.

19. See Melissa Schwartzberg, *Democracy and Legal Change* (Cambridge University Press, 2009).

20. See Anne-Marie Slaughter, "International Relations: Principal Theories," in *Max Planck Encyclopedia of International Public Law,* ed. R. Wolfrum (Oxford University Press, 2011), http://ukcatalogue.oup.com/product /9780199231690.do.

21. See Michael Doyle, *The Question of Intervention: John Stuart Mill and the Responsibility to Protect* (Yale University Press, 2015), 33–34, 113–119, 123, 143–144; and Mark Mazower, *Governing the World: History of an Idea, 1815 to the Present* (Penguin, 2013), 396–420. It is ironic that the main cheerleading for the ICC emanates from the global north, and scarcely surprising that Africans in particular have grown increasingly impatient with its almost exclusive preoccupation with prosecuting Africans. See Kenneth Roth, "Africans Attack the International Criminal Court," *New York Review of Books,* February 6, 2014, http://www.nybooks.com/articles /archives/2014/feb/06/africa-attacks-international-criminal-court/. When Jacob Zuma's government refused to enforce an arrest warrant against Omar al-Bashir in June 2015, even ignoring a South African court order requiring his detention, there was little international fallout. Andrew England, "South Africa's Moral Beacon Dimmed by Defiance of ICC," *Financial Times,* June 16, 2015, http://www.ft.com/intl/cms/s/0/725d8eb0 -142d-11e5-abda-00144feabdc0.html#axzz3dzO3sKuy.

22. See Stephen Cohen, *Failed Crusade: America and the Tragedy of Post-Communist Russia* (W. W. Norton, 2001), 202–205; Mary Sarotte, *1989:*

The Struggle to Create Post Cold-War Europe (Princeton University Press, 2009), 204–214; and Dimitry Simes, "Losing Russia: The Costs of Renewed Confrontation," *Foreign Affairs* 86, no. 6 (November/December 2007), https://www.foreignaffairs.com/articles/russia-fsu/2007-11-01/losing-russia.

23. Hardin defines *K* as the size of any subgroup that "just barely stands to benefit from providing the good, even without cooperation from other members of the whole group." See Russell Hardin, *Collective Action* (Johns Hopkins University Press, 1982), 41.

24. Ian Shapiro, *Containment: Rebuilding a Strategy against Global Terror* (Princeton University Press, 2007), 119–133.

25. See Andrew Haldane and Vasileios Madouros, "The Dog and the Frisbee," paper presented at the Federal Reserve Bank of Kansas City's 366th economic policy symposium, "The Changing Policy Landscape," Jackson Hole, Wyoming, August 31, 2012, http://www.bis.org/review/r120905a.pdf.

26. Jean-Jacques Rousseau, *Of the Social Contract,* bk. 3, chap. 12, in Rousseau, *Social Contract,* 111.

27. John Rawls, *The Law of Peoples* (Harvard University Press, 1999), 6.

28. "Men make their own history, but they do not make it as they please; they do not make it under self-selected circumstances, but under circumstances existing already, given and transmitted from the past." Karl Marx, *The Eighteenth Brumaire of Louis Napoleon* (International, 1963 [1852]), 19.

29. See Louis Althusser, *For Marx* (London: Verso, 1979). See also Nicos Poulantzas, *Classes in Contemporary Capitalism* (London: Verso, 1979); and G. A. Cohen, *Karl Marx's Theory of History: A Defense* (Princeton University Press, 1978).

30. Anthony Giddens, *The Constitution of Society* (Cambridge University Press, 1984).

31. There is some debate on the economic front, where Obama might arguably be faulted for allowing financial reform to be captured by banking interests. See Ron Suskind, *Confidence Men: Wall Street, Washington, and the Education of a President* (Harper, 2011), 161–220. But few would maintain that he had much freedom with respect to the failing wars he inherited in Afghanistan and Iraq.

32. This was certainly the view of Samantha Power and Hillary Clinton as reported by, respectively, Robert Gates in *Duty: Memoirs of a Secretary of War* (W. H. Allen, 2014), 511–512, and Dan Bilefsky and Mark Landler in "As UN Backs Military Action in Libya, U.S. Role Is Unclear," *New York Times,* March 17, 2011, http://www.nytimes.com/2011/03/18/world/africa/18nations.html?pagewanted=all&_r=0.

INDEX